# History of Julius Cæsar Vol.- I

*by*

Napoleon III,

Emperor of the French

# History of Julius Cæsar
## Vol.- I
### by Napoleon III, Emperor of the French

ISBN: 978-93-60463-42-7

**Published by**

# DOUBLE 9 BOOKS

2/13-B, Ansari Road
Daryaganj, New Delhi – 110002
info@double9books.com
www.double9books.com
Tel. 011-40042856

# ABOUT THE AUTHOR

Charles-Louis Napoleon Bonaparte, better known as Napoleon III (20 April 1808 - 9 January 1873) was the first president of France from 1848 to 1852. He was also the last ruler of France as Emperor of the French from 1852 until he was removed from power in his absence on September 4, 1870.Napoleon III used to be called Louis Napoleon Bonaparte before he became king. He was born in Paris. His parents were King Louis Bonaparte of Holland and Hortense de Beauharnais. Napoleon II was a cousin of Napoleon I and was Louis Napoleon's uncle on his dad's side. There was only one president of the French Second Republic, and that was Louis Napoleon. He was chosen in 1848. It was against the law for him to be re-elected, so he took power by force in 1851. Later, he declared himself Emperor of France and started the Second Empire. He ruled until the French Army lost and Prussia and its allies captured him at the Battle of Sedan in 1870. Charles-Louis Napoleon Bonaparte was born in Paris on the night of April 19-20, 1808. He became Louis Napoleon and then Napoleon III. Louis Bonaparte was his father. Napoleon Bonaparte made Louis king of Holland from 1806 to 1810. However, Louis died in 1810.

# CONTENTS

# PREFACE

HISTORIC truth ought to be no less sacred than religion. If the precepts of faith raise our soul above the interests of this world, the lessons of history, in their turn, inspire us with the love of the beautiful and the just, and the hatred of whatever presents an obstacle to the progress of humanity. These lessons, to be profitable, require certain conditions. It is necessary that the facts be produced with a rigorous exactness, that the changes political or social be analysed philosophically, that the exciting interest of the details of the lives of public men should not divert attention from the political part they played, or cause us to forget their providential mission.

Too often the writer represents the different phases of history as spontaneous events, without seeking in preceding facts their true origin and their natural deduction; like the painter who, in re-producing the characteristics of Nature, only seizes their picturesque effect, without being able, in his picture, to give their scientific demonstration. The historian ought to be more than a painter; he ought, like the geologist, who explains the phenomena of the globe, to unfold the secret of the transformation of societies.

But, in writing history, by what means are we to arrive at truth? By following the rules of logic. Let us first take for granted that a great effect is always due to a great cause, never to a small one; in other words, an accident, insignificant in appearance, never leads to important results without a pre-existing cause, which has permitted this slight accident to produce a great effect. The spark only lights up a vast conflagration when it falls upon combustible matters previously collected. Montesquieu thus confirms this idea: "It is not fortune," he says, "which rules the world.... There are general causes, whether moral or physical, which act in every monarchy, raising, maintaining, or overthrowing it; all accidents are subject to these causes, and if the fortune of a battle—that is to say, a particular cause—has ruined a state, there was a general cause which made it necessary that that state should perish through a single battle: in a word, the principal cause drags with it all the particular accidents."[1]

If during nearly a thousand years the Romans always came triumphant out of the severest trials and greatest perils, it is because there existed a general cause which made them always superior to their enemies, and which did not permit partial defeats and misfortunes to entail the fall of the empire. If the Romans, after giving an example to the world of a people constituting itself and growing great by liberty, seemed, after Cæsar, to throw themselves blindly into slavery, it is because there existed a general reason which by fatality prevented the Republic from returning to the purity of its ancient institutions; it is because the new wants and interests of a society in labour required other means to satisfy them. Just as logic demonstrates that the reason of important events is imperious, in like manner we must recognise in the long duration of an institution the proof of its goodness, and in the incontestable influence of a man upon his age the proof of his genius.

The task, then, consists in seeking the vital element which constituted the strength of the institution, as the predominant idea which caused man to act. In following this rule, we shall avoid the errors of those historians who gather facts transmitted by preceding ages, without properly arranging them according to their philosophical importance; thus glorifying that which merits blame, and leaving in the shade that which calls for the light. It is not a minute analysis of the Roman organisation which will enable us to understand the duration of so great an empire, but the profound examination of the spirit of its institutions; no more is it the detailed recital of the most trivial actions of a superior man which will reveal the secret of his ascendency, but the attentive investigation of the elevated motives of his conduct.

When extraordinary facts attest an eminent genius, what is more contrary to good sense than to ascribe to him all the passions and sentiments of mediocrity? What more erroneous than not to recognise the pre-eminence of those privileged beings who appear in history from time to time like luminous beacons, dissipating the darkness of their epoch, and throwing light into the future? To deny this pre-eminence would, indeed, be to insult humanity, by believing it capable of submitting, long and voluntarily, to a domination which did not rest on true greatness and incontestable utility. Let us be logical, and we shall be just.

Too many historians find it easier to lower men of genius, than, with a generous inspiration, to raise them to their due height, by penetrating their vast designs. Thus, as regards Cæsar, instead of showing us Rome, torn to pieces by civil wars and corrupted by riches, trampling under foot her ancient institutions, threatened by powerful peoples, such as Gauls, Germans, and Parthians, incapable of sustaining herself without a central power stronger, more stable, and more just; instead, I say, of tracing this faithful picture, Cæsar is represented, from an early age, as already aspiring to the supreme power. If he opposes Sylla, if he disagrees with Cicero, if he allies himself with Pompey, it is the result of that far-sighted astuteness which divined everything with a view to bring everything under subjection. If he throws himself into Gaul, it is to acquire riches by pillage[2] or soldiers devoted to his projects; if he crosses the sea to carry the Roman eagles into an unknown country, but the conquest of which will strengthen that of Gaul,[3] it is to seek there pearls which were believed to exist in the seas of Great Britain.[4] If, after having vanquished the formidable enemies of Italy on the other side of the Alps, he meditates an expedition against the Parthians, to avenge the defeat of Crassus, it is, as certain historians say, because activity was a part of his nature, and that his health was better when he was campaigning.[5] If he accepts from the Senate with thankfulness a crown of laurel, and wears it with pride, it is to conceal his bald head. If, lastly, he is assassinated by those whom he had loaded with benefits, it is because he sought to make himself king; as though he were to his contemporaries, as well as for posterity, the greatest of all kings. Since Suetonius and Plutarch, such are the paltry interpretations which it has pleased people to give to the noblest actions. But by what sign are we to recognise a man's greatness? By the empire of his ideas, when his principles and his system triumph in spite of his death or defeat. Is it not, in fact, the peculiarity of genius to survive destruction, and to extend its empire over future generations? Cæsar disappeared, and his influence predominates still more than during his life. Cicero, his adversary, is compelled to exclaim: "All the acts of Cæsar, his writings, his words, his promises, his thoughts, have more force since his death, than if he were still alive."[6] For ages it was enough to tell the world that such was the will of Cæsar, for the world to obey it.

The preceding remarks sufficiently explain the aim I have in view in writing this history. This aim is to prove that, when Providence raises up such men as Cæsar, Charlemagne, and Napoleon, it is to trace out to peoples the path they ought to follow; to stamp with the seal of their genius a new era; and to accomplish in a few years the labour of many centuries. Happy the peoples who comprehend and follow them! woe to those who misunderstand and combat them! They do as the Jews did, they crucify their Messiah; they are blind and culpable: blind, for they do not see the impotence of their efforts to suspend the definitive triumph of good; culpable, for they only retard progress, by impeding its prompt and fruitful application.

In fact, neither the murder of Cæsar, nor the captivity of St. Helena, have been able to destroy irrevocably two popular causes overthrown by a league which disguised itself under the mask of liberty. Brutus, by slaying

Cæsar, plunged Rome into the horrors of civil war; he did not prevent the reign of Augustus, but he rendered possible those of Nero and Caligula. The ostracism of Napoleon by confederated Europe has been no more successful in preventing the Empire from being resuscitated; and, nevertheless, how far are we from the great questions solved, the passions calmed, and the legitimate satisfactions given to peoples by the first Empire!

Thus every day since 1815 has verified the prophecy of the captive of St. Helena:

"How many struggles, how much blood, how many years will it not require to realise the good which I intended to do for mankind!"[7]

Palace of the Tuileries, March 20th, 1862.

Napoleon.

I

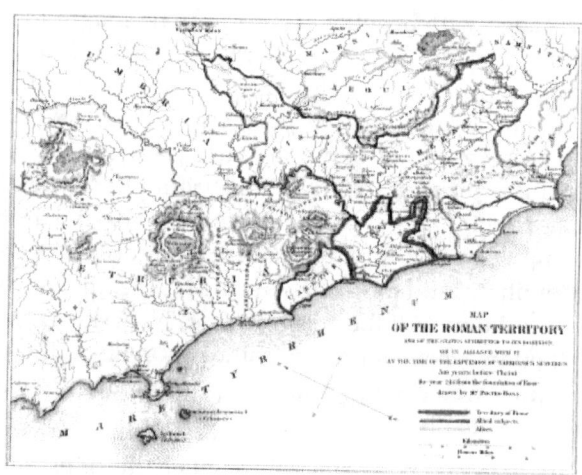

# BOOK I
# ROMAN HISTORY BEFORE CÆSAR

## CHAPTER I
## ROME UNDER THE KINGS

The Kings found the Roman Institutions.

I. "In the birth of societies," says Montesquieu, "it is the chiefs of the republics who form the institution, and in the sequel it is the institution which forms the chiefs of the republics." And he adds, "One of the causes of the prosperity of Rome was the fact that its kings were all great men. We find nowhere else in history an uninterrupted series of such statesmen and such military commanders."[8]

The story, more or less fabulous, of the foundation of Rome does not come within the limits of our design; and with no intention of clearing up whatever degree of fiction these earliest ages of history may contain, we purpose only to remind our readers that the kings laid the foundations of those institutions to which Rome owed her greatness, and so many extraordinary men who astonished the world by their virtues and exploits.

The kingly power lasted a hundred and forty-four years, and at its fall Rome had become the most powerful state in Latium. The town was of vast extent, for, even at that epoch, the seven hills were nearly all inclosed within a wall protected internally and externally by a consecrated space called the Pomœrium.[9]

This line of inclosure remained long the same, although the increase of the population had led to the establishment of immense suburbs, which finally inclosed the Pomœrium itself.[10]

The Roman territory properly so called was circumscribed, but that of the subjects and allies of Rome was already rather considerable. Some colonies had been founded. The kings, by a skilful policy, had succeeded in drawing into their dependence a great number of neighbouring states, and, when Tarquinius Superbus assembled the Hernici, the Latins, and the

Volsci, for a ceremony destined to seal his alliance with them, forty-seven different petty states took part in the inauguration of the temple of Jupiter Latialis.[11]

The foundation of Ostia, by Ancus Martius, at the mouth of the Tiber, shows that already the political and commercial importance of facilitating communication with the sea was understood; while the treaty of commerce concluded with Carthage at the time of the fall of the kingly power, the details of which are preserved by Polybius, indicates more extensive foreign relations than we might have supposed.[12]

Social Organisation.

II. The Roman social body, which originated probably in ancient transformations of society, consisted, from the earliest ages, of a certain number of aggregations, called gentes, formed of the families of the conquerors, and bearing some resemblance to the clans of Scotland or to the Arabian tribes. The heads of families (patresfamilias) and their members (patricii) were united among themselves, not only by kindred, but also by political and religious ties. Hence arose an hereditary nobility having for distinctive marks family names, special costume,[13] and waxen images of their ancestors (jus imaginum).

The plebeians, perhaps a race who had been conquered at an earlier period, were, in regard to the dominant race, in a situation similar to that of the Anglo-Saxons in regard to the Normans in the eleventh century of our era, after the invasion of England. They were generally agriculturists, excluded originally from all military and civil office.[14]

The patrician families had gathered round them, under the name of clients, either foreigners, or a great portion of the plebeians. Dionysius of Halicarnassus even pretends that Romulus had required that each of these last should choose himself a patron.[15] The clients cultivated the fields and formed part of the family.[16] The relation of patronage had created such reciprocal obligations as amounted almost to the ties of kindred. For the patrons, they consisted in giving assistance to their clients in affairs public and private; and for the latter, in aiding constantly the patrons with their person and purse, and in preserving towards them an inviolable fidelity: they could not cite each other reciprocally in law, or bear witness one against the other, and it would have been a scandal to see them take different sides in a political question. It was a state of things which had some analogy to feudalism; the great protected the little, and the little paid for protection by rents and services; yet there was this essential difference, that the clients were not serfs, but free men.

Slavery had long formed one of the constituent parts of society. The slaves, taken among foreigners and captives,[17] and associated in all the domestic labours of the family, often received their liberty as a recompense for their conduct. They were then named freedmen, and were received among the clients of the patron, without sharing in all the rights of a citizen. [18]

The gens thus consisted of the reunion of patrician families having a common ancestor; around it was grouped a great number of clients, freedmen, and slaves. To give an idea of the importance of the gentes in the first ages of Rome, it is only necessary to remind the reader that towards the year 251, a certain Attus Clausus, afterwards called Appius Claudius, a Sabine of the town of Regillum, distinguished, according to Dionysius of Halicarnassus, no less for the splendour of his birth than for his great wealth, took refuge among the Romans with his kinsmen, his friends, and his clients, with all their families, to the number of five thousand men capable of bearing arms.[19] When, in 275, the three hundred Fabii, forming the gens Fabia, offered alone to fight the Veians, they were followed by four thousand clients.[20] The high class often reckoned, by means of its numerous adherents, on carrying measures by itself. In 286, the plebeians having refused to take part in the consular comitia, the patricians, followed by their clients, elected the consuls;[21] and in 296, a Claudius declared with pride that the nobility had no need of the plebeians to carry on war against the Volsci.[22] The families of ancient origin long formed the state by themselves. To them exclusively the name of populus applied,[23] as that of plebs was given to the plebeians.[24] Indeed, although in the sequel the word populus took a more extensive signification, Cicero says that it is to be understood as applying, not to the universality of the inhabitants, but to a reunion of men associated by a community of rights and interests.[25]

Political Organisation.

III. In a country where war was the principal occupation, the political organisation must naturally depend on the military organisation. A single chief had the superior direction, an assembly of men pre-eminent in importance and age formed the council, while the political rights belonged only to those who supported the fatigues of war.

The king, elected generally by the assembly of the gentes,[26] commanded the army. Sovereign pontiff, legislator, and judge in all sacred matters, he dispensed justice[27] in all criminal affairs which concerned the Republic. He had for insignia a crown of gold and a purple robe, and for escort twenty-four lictors,[28] some carrying axes surrounded with rods, others merely rods.[29] At the death of the king, a magistrate, called interrex, was appointed by the Senate to exercise the royal authority during the five days which intervened before the nomination of his successor. This office continued, with the same title, under the Consular Republic, when the absence of the consuls prevented the holding of the comitia.

The Senate, composed of the richest and most illustrious of the patricians, to the number at first of a hundred, of two hundred after the union with the Sabines, and of three hundred after the admission of the gentes minores under Tarquin, was the council of the ancients, taking under its jurisdiction the interests of the town, in which were then concentrated all the interests of the State.

The patricians occupied all offices, supported alone the burden of war, and consequently had alone the right of voting in the assemblies.

The gentes were themselves divided into three tribes. Each, commanded by a tribune,[30] was obliged, under Romulus, to furnish a thousand soldiers (indeed, miles comes from mille) and a hundred horsemen (celeres). The tribe was divided into ten curiæ; at the head of each curia was a curion. The three tribes, furnishing three thousand foot soldiers and three hundred horsemen, formed at first the legion. Their number was soon doubled by the adjunction of new cities.[31]

The curia, into which a certain number of gentes entered, was then the basis of the political and military organisation, and hence originated the name of Quirites to signify the Roman people.

The members of the curia were constituted into religious associations, having each its assemblies and solemn festivals which established bonds of affiliation between them. When their assemblies had a political aim, the votes were taken by head;[32] they decided the question of peace or war; they nominated the magistrates of the town; and they confirmed or abrogated the laws.[33]

The appeal to the people,[34] which might annul the judgments of the magistrates, was nothing more than the appeal to the curia; and it was by having recourse to it, after having been condemned by the decemvirs, that the survivor of the three Horatii was saved.

The policy of the kings consisted in blending together the different races and breaking down the barriers which separated the different classes. To effect the first of these objects, they divided the lower class of the people into corporations,[35] and augmented the number of the tribes and changed their constitution;[36] but to effect the second, they introduced, to the great discontent of the higher class, plebeians among the patricians,[37] and raised the freedmen to the rank of citizens.[38] In this manner, each curia became considerably increased in numbers; but, as the votes were taken by head, the poor patricians were numerically stronger than the rich.

Servius Tullius, though he preserved the curiæ, deprived them of their military organisation, that is, he no longer made it the basis of his system of recruiting. He instituted the centuries, with the double aim of giving as a principle the right of suffrage to all the citizens, and of creating an army which was more national, inasmuch as he introduced the plebeians into it; his design was indeed to throw on the richest citizens the burden of war,[39] which was just, each equipping and maintaining himself at his own cost. The citizens were no longer classified by castes, but according to their fortunes. Patricians and plebeians were placed in the same rank if their income was equal. The influence of the rich predominated, without doubt, but only in proportion to the sacrifices required of them.

Servius Tullius ordered a general report of the population to be made, in which every one was obliged to declare his age, his fortune, the name of his tribe and that of his father, and the number of his children and of his slaves. This operation was called census.[40] The report was inscribed on tables,[41] and, once terminated, all the citizens were called together in arms in the Campus Martius. This review was called the closing of the lustrum, because it was accompanied with sacrifices and purifications named lustrations. The term lustrum was applied to the interval of five years between two censuses.[42]

· The citizens were divided into six classes,[43] and into a hundred and ninety-three centuries, according to the fortune of each, beginning with the richest and ending with the poorest. The first class comprised ninety-eight centuries, eighteen of which were knights; the second and fourth, twenty-two; the third, twenty; the fifth, thirty; and the sixth, although the most numerous, forming only one.[44] The first class contained a smaller number of citizens, yet, having a greater number of centuries, it was obliged to pay more than half the tax, and furnish more legionaries than any other class.

The votes continued to be taken by head, as in the curiæ, but the majority of the votes in each century counted only for one suffrage. Now, as the first class had ninety-eight centuries, while the others, taken together, had only ninety-five, it is clear that the votes of the first class were enough to carry the majority. The eighteen centuries of knights first gave their votes, and then the eighty centuries of the first class: if they were not agreed, appeal was made to the vote of the second class, and so on in succession; but, says Livy, it hardly ever happened that they were obliged to descend to the last.[45] Though, according to its original signification, the century should represent a hundred men, it already contained a considerably greater number. Each century was divided into the active part, including all the men from eighteen to forty-six years of age, and the sedentary part, charged with the guard of the town, composed of men from forty-six to sixty years old.[46]

With regard to those of the sixth class, omitted altogether by many authors, they were exempt from all military service, or, at any rate, they were enrolled only in case of extreme danger.[47] The centuries of knights, who formed the cavalry, recruited among the richest citizens, tended to introduce a separate order among the nobility,[48] which shows the importance of the chief called to their command. In fact, the chief of the celeres was, after the king, the first magistrate of the city, as, at a later period, under the Republic, the magister equitum became the lieutenant of the dictator.

The first census of Servius Tullius gave a force of eighty thousand men in a condition to bear arms,[49] which is equivalent to two hundred and ninety thousand persons of the two sexes, to whom may be added, from conjectures, which, however, are rather vague, fifteen thousand artisans, merchants, or indigent people, deprived of all rights of citizenship, and fifteen thousand slaves.[50]

The comitia by centuries were charged with the election of the magistrates, but the comitia by curiæ, being the primitive form of the patrician assembly, continued to decree on the most important religious and military affairs, and remained in possession of all which had not been formally given to the centuries. Solon effected, about the same epoch, in Athens, a similar revolution, so that, at the same time, the two most famous towns of the ancient world no longer took birth as the basis of the right of suffrage, but fortune.

Servius Tullius promulgated a great number of laws favourable to the people; he established the principle that the property only of the debtor, and not his person, should be responsible for his debt. He also authorised the plebeians to become the patrons of their freedmen, which allowed the richest of the former to create for themselves a clientèle resembling that of the patricians.[51]

Religion.

IV. Religion, regulated in great part by Numa, was at Rome an instrument of civilisation, but, above all, of government. By bringing into the acts of public or private life the intervention of the Divinity, everything was impressed with a character of sanctity. Thus the inclosure of the town with its services,[52] the boundaries of estates, the transactions between citizens, engagements, and even the important facts of history entered in the sacred books, were placed under the safeguard of the gods.[53] In the interior of the house, the gods Lares protected the family; on the field of battle, the emblem placed on the standard was the protecting god of the legion.[54] The national sentiment and belief that Rome would become one day the mistress of Italy was maintained by oracles or prodigies;[55] but if, on the one hand, religion, with its very imperfections, contributed to soften manners and to elevate minds,[56] on the other it wonderfully facilitated the working of the institutions, and preserved the influence of the higher classes.

Religion also accustomed the people of Latium to the Roman supremacy; for Servius Tullius, in persuading them to contribute to the building of the Temple of Diana,[57] made them, says Livy, acknowledge Rome for their capital, a claim they had so often resisted by force of arms.

The supposed intervention of the Deity gave the power, in a multitude of cases, of reversing any troublesome decision. Thus, by interpreting the flight of birds,[58] the manner in which the sacred chickens ate, the entrails of victims, the direction taken by lightning, they annulled the elections, or eluded or retarded the deliberations either of the comitia or of the Senate. No one could enter upon office, even the king could not mount his throne, if the gods had not manifested their approval by what were reputed certain signs of their will. There were auspicious and inauspicious days; in the latter it was not permitted either to judges to hold their audience, or to the people to assemble.[59] Finally, it might be said with Camillus, that the town was founded on the faith of auspices and auguries.[60]

The priests did not form an order apart, but all citizens had the power to enrol themselves in particular colleges. At the head of the sacerdotal hierarchy were the pontiffs, five in number,[61] of whom the king was the chief.[62] They decided all questions which concerned the liturgy and religious worship, watched over the sacrifices and ceremonies that they should be performed in accordance with the traditional rites,[63] acted as inspectors over the other minister of religion, fixed the calendar,[64] and were responsible for their actions neither to the Senate nor to the people.[65]

After the pontiffs, the first place belonged to the curions, charged in each curia with the religious functions, and who had at their head a grand curion; then came the flamens, the augurs,[66] the vestals charged with the maintenance of the sacred fire; the twelve Salian priests,[67] keepers of the sacred bucklers, named ancilia; and lastly, the feciales, heralds at arms, to the number of twenty, whose charge it was to draw up treaties and secure their execution, to declare war, and to watch over the observance of all international relations.[68]

There were also religious fraternities (sodalitates), instituted for the purpose of rendering a special worship to certain divinities. Such was the college of the fratres Arvales, whose prayers and processions called down the favour of Heaven upon the harvest; such also was the association having for its mission to celebrate the festival of the Lupercalia, founded in honour of the god Lupercus, the protector of cattle and destroyer of wolves. The gods Lares, tutelar genii of towns or families, had also their festival instituted by Tullus Hostilius, and celebrated at certain epochs, during which the slaves were entirely exempt from labour.[69]

The kings erected a great number of temples for the purpose of deifying, some, glory,[70] others, the virtues,[71] others, utility,[72] and others, gratitude to the gods.[73]

The Romans loved to represent everything by external signs: thus Numa, to impress better the verity of a state of peace or war, raised a temple to Janus, which was kept open during war and closed in time of peace; and, strange to say, this temple was only closed three times in seven hundred years.[74]

Results obtained by Royalty.

V. The facts which precede are sufficient to convince us that the Roman Republic[75] had already acquired under the kings a strong organisation.[76] Its spirit of conquest overflowed beyond its narrow limits. The small states of Latium which surrounded it possessed, perhaps, men as enlightened and citizens equally courageous, but there certainly did not exist among them, to the same degree as at Rome, the genius of war, the love of country, faith in high destinies, the conviction of an incontestible superiority, powerful motives of activity, instilled into them perseveringly by great men during two hundred and forty-four years.

Roman society was founded upon respect for family, for religion, and for property; the government, upon election; the policy, upon conquest. At the head of the State is a powerful aristocracy, greedy of glory, but, like all aristocracies, impatient of kingly power, and disdainful towards the multitude. The kings strive to create a people side by side with the privileged caste, and introduce plebeians into the Senate, freedmen among the citizens, and the mass of citizens into the ranks of the soldiery.

Family is strongly constituted; the father reigns in it absolute master, sole judge[77] over his children, his wife, and his slaves, and that during all their lives: yet the wife's position is not degraded as among the barbarians; she enjoys a community of goods with her husband; mistress of her house, she has the right of acquiring property, and shares equally with her brothers the paternal inheritance.[78]

The basis of taxation is the basis of recruiting and of political rights; there are no soldiers but citizens; there are no citizens without property. The richer a man is, the more he has of power and dignities; but he has more charges to support, more duties to fulfil. In fighting, as well as in voting, the Romans are divided into classes according to their fortunes, and in the comitia, as on the field of battle the richest are in the first ranks.

Initiated in the apparent practice of liberty, the people is held in check by superstition and respect for the high classes. By appealing to the intervention of the Divinity in every action of life, the most vulgar things become idealised, and men are taught that above their material interests there is a Providence which directs their actions. The sentiment of right and justice enters into their conscience, the oath is a sacred thing, and virtue, that highest expression of duty, becomes the general rule of public and private life.[79] Law exercises its entire empire, and, by the institution of the feciales, international questions are discussed with a view to what is just, before seeking a solution by force of arms. The policy of the State consists in drawing by all means possible the peoples around under the dependence of Rome; and, when their resistance renders it necessary to conquer them,[80] they are, in different degrees, immediately associated with the common fortune, and maintained in obedience by colonies—advanced posts of future dominion.[81]

The arts, though as yet rude, find their way in with the Etruscan rites, and come to soften manners, and lend their aid to religion; everywhere temples arise, circuses are constructed,[82] great works of public utility are erected, and Rome, by its institutions, paves the way for its pre-eminence.

Almost all the magistrates are appointed by election; once chosen, they possess an extensive power, and put in motion resolutely those two powerful levers of human actions, punishment and reward. To all citizens, for cowardice before the enemy or for an infraction of discipline,[83] the rod or the axe of the lictor; to all, for noble actions, crowns of honour;[84] to the generals, the ovation, the triumph,[85] the best of the spoils;[86] to the great men, apotheosis. To honour the dead, and for personal relaxation after their sanguinary struggles, the citizens crowd to the games of the circus, where the hierarchy gives his rank to each individual.[87]

Thus Rome, having reached the third century of her existence, finds her constitution formed by the kings with all the germs of grandeur which will develop themselves in the sequel. Man has created her institutions: we shall see now how the institutions are going to form the men.

# CHAPTER II
# ESTABLISHMENT OF THE CONSULAR
# REPUBLIC (From 244 to 416)

Advantage of the Republic.

I. THE kings are expelled from Rome. They disappear because their mission is accomplished. There exists, one would say, in moral as well as physical order, a supreme law which assigns to institutions, as to certain beings, a fated limit, marked by the term of their utility. Until this providential term has arrived, no opposition prevails; conspiracies, revolts, everything fails against the irresistible force which maintains what people seek to overthrow; but if, on the contrary, a state of things immovable in appearance ceases to be useful to the progress of humanity, then neither the empire of traditions, nor courage, nor the memory of a glorious past, can retard by a day the fall which has been decided by destiny.

Civilisation appears to have been transported from Greece into Italy to create there an immense focus from which it might spread itself over the whole world. From that moment the genius of force and imagination must necessarily preside over the first times of Rome. This is what happened under the kings, and, so long as their task was not accomplished, it triumphed over all obstacles. In vain the senators attempted to obtain a share in the power by each exercising it for five days;[88] in vain men's passions rebelled against the authority of a single chief: all was useless, and even the murder of the kings only added strength to royalty. But the moment once arrived when kings cease to be indispensable, the simplest accident hurls them down. A man outrages a woman, the throne gives way, and, in falling, it divides itself into two: the consuls succeed to all the prerogatives of the kings.[89] Nothing is changed in the Republic, except that instead of one chief, elective for life, there will be henceforward two chiefs, elected for a year. This transformation is evidently the work of the aristocracy; the senators will possess the government, and, by these annual elections, each hopes to take in his turn his share in the sovereign power. Such is the narrow calculation of man and his mean motive of action. Let us see what superior impulse he obeyed without knowing it.

That corner of land, situated on the bank of the Tiber, and predestined to hold the empire of the world, enclosed within itself, as we see, fruitful germs which demanded a rapid expansion. This could only be effected by the absolute independence of the most enlightened class, seizing for its own profit all the prerogatives of royalty. The aristocratic government has this advantage over monarchy, that it is more immutable in its duration, more constant in its designs, more faithful to traditions, and that it can dare everything, because where a great number share the responsibility, no one is individually responsible. Rome, with its narrow limits, had no longer need of the concentration of authority in a single hand, but it was in need of a new order of things, which should give to the great free access to the supreme power, and should second, by the allurement of honours, the development of the faculties of each. The grand object was to create a race of men of choice, who, succeeding each other with the same principles and the same virtues, should perpetuate, from generation to generation, the system most calculated to assure the greatness of their country. The fall of the kingly power was thus an event favourable to the development of Rome.

The patricians monopolised during a long time the civil, military, and religious employments, and, these employments being for the most part annual, there was in the Senate hardly a member who had not filled them; so that this assembly was composed of men formed to the combats of the Forum as well as to those of the field of battle, schooled in the difficulties of the administration, and indeed worthy, by an experience laboriously acquired, to preside over the destinies of the Republic.

They were not classed, as men are in our modern society, in envious and rival specialities; the warrior was not seen there despising the civilian, the lawyer or orator standing apart from the man of action, or the priest isolating himself from all the others. In order to raise himself to State dignities, and merit the suffrages of his fellow-citizens, the patrician was constrained, from his youngest age, to undergo the most varied trials. He was required to possess dexterity of body, eloquence, aptness for military exercises, the knowledge of civil and religious laws, the talent of commanding an army or directing a fleet, of administrating the town or commanding a province; and the obligation of these different apprenticeships not only gave a full flight to all capacities, but it united, in the eyes of the people, upon the magistrate invested with different dignities, the consideration attached to each of them. During a long time, he who was honoured with the confidence of his fellow-citizens, besides nobility of birth, enjoyed the triple prestige given by the function of judge, priest, and warrior.

An independence almost absolute in the exercise of command contributed further to the development of the faculties. At the present day, our constitutional habits have raised distrust towards power into a principle; at Rome, trust was the principle. In our modern societies, the depositary of any authority whatever is always under the restraint of powerful bonds; he obeys a precise law, a minutely detailed rule, a superior. The Roman, on the contrary, abandoned to his own sole responsibility, felt himself free from all shackles; he commanded as master within the sphere of his attributes. The counterpoise of this independence was the short duration of his office, and the right, given to every man, of accusing each magistrate at the end of it.

The preponderance of the high class, then, rested upon a legitimate superiority, and this class, besides, knew how to work to its advantage the popular passions. They desired liberty only for themselves, but they knew how to make the image glitter in the eyes of the multitude, and the name of the people was always associated with the decrees of the Senate. Proud of having contributed to the overthrow of the power of one individual, they took care to cherish among the masses the imaginary fear of the return of kingly power. In their hands the hate of tyrants will become a weapon to be dreaded by all who shall seek to raise themselves above their fellows, either by threatening their privileges, or by acquiring too much popularity by their acts of benevolence. Thus, under the pretext, renewed incessantly, of aspiring to kingly power, fell the consul Spurius Cassius, in 269, because he had presented the first agrarian law; Spurius Melius, in 315, because he excited the jealousy of the patricians by distributing wheat to the people during a famine;[90] in 369, Manlius, the saviour of Rome, because he had expended his fortune in relieving insolvent debtors.[91] Thus will fall victims to the same accusation the reformer Tiberius Sempronius Gracchus, and lastly, at a later period, the great Cæsar himself.

But if the pretended fear of the return of the ancient *régime* was a powerful means of government in the hands of the patricians, the real fear of seeing their privileges attacked by the plebeians restrained them within the bounds of moderation and justice.

In fact, if the numerous class, excluded from all office, had not interfered by their clamours to set limits to the privileges of the nobility, and thus compelled it to render itself worthy of power by its virtues, and re-invigorated it, in some sort, by the infusion of new blood, corruption and arbitrary spirit would, some ages earlier, have dragged it to its ruin. A caste which is not renewed by foreign elements is condemned to disappear; and absolute power, whether it belongs to one man or to a class of individuals, finishes always by being equally dangerous to him who exercises it. This concurrence of the plebeians excited in the Republic a fortunate emulation which produced great men, for, as Machiavelli says:[92] "The fear of losing gives birth in men's hearts to the same passions as the desire of acquiring." Although the aristocracy had long defended with obstinacy its privileges, it made opportunely useful concessions. Skilful in repairing incessantly its defeats, it took again, under another form, what it had been constrained to abandon, losing often some of its attributes, but preserving its prestige always untouched.

Thus, the characteristic fact of the Roman institutions was to form men apt for all functions. As long as on a narrow theatre the ruling class had the wisdom to limit its ambition to promoting the veritable interests of their country, as the seduction of riches and unbounded power did not come to exalt it beyond measure, the aristocratic system maintained itself with all its advantages, and overruled the instability of institutions. It alone, indeed, was capable of supporting long, without succumbing, a régime in which the direction of the State and the command of the armies passed annually into different hands, and depended upon elections the element of which is ever fickle. Besides, the laws gave rise to antagonisms more calculated to cause anarchy than to consolidate true liberty. Let us examine, in these last relations, the constitution of the Republic.

Institutions of the Republic.

II. The two consuls were originally generals, judges, and administrators; equal in powers, they were often in disagreement, either in the Forum,[93] or on the field of battle.[94] Their dissensions were repeated many times until the consulate of Cæsar and Bibulus; and they were liable to become the more dangerous as the decision of one consul was annulled by the opposition of his colleague. On the other hand, the short duration of their magistracy constrained them either to hurry a battle in order to rob their successor of the glory,[95] or to interrupt a campaign in order to proceed to Rome to hold the comitia. The defeats of the Trebia and Cannæ, with that of Servilius Cæpio by the Cimbri,[96] were fatal examples of the want of unity in the direction of war.

In order to lessen the evil effects of a simultaneous exercise of their prerogatives, the consuls agreed to take in campaign the command alternately day by day, and at Rome each to have the fasces during a month; but this innovation had also vexatious consequences.[97] It was even thought necessary, nine years after the fall of the kings, to have recourse to the dictatorship; and this absolute authority, limited to six months, that is, to the longest duration of a campaign, only remedied temporarily, and under extraordinary circumstances, the want of power concentrated in a single individual.

This dualism and instability of the supreme authority were not, therefore, an element of strength; the unity and fixity of direction necessary among a people always at war had disappeared; but the evil would have been more serious if the conformity of interests and views of individuals belonging to the same caste had not been there to lessen it. The man was worth more than the institutions which had formed him.

The creation of tribunes of the people, whose part became subsequently so important, was, in 260, a new cause of discord; the plebeians, who composed the greater part of the army, claimed to have their military chiefs for magistrates;[98] the authority of the tribunes was at first limited: we may convince ourselves of this by the following terms of the law which established the office:[99]—

"Nobody shall constrain a tribune of the people, like a man of the commonalty, to do anything against his will; it shall not be permitted either to strike him, or to cause him to be maltreated by another, or to slay him or cause him to be slain."[100]

We may judge by this the degree of inferiority to which the plebeians were reduced. The veto of the tribunes could nevertheless put a stop to the proposal of a law, prevent the decisions of the consuls and Senate, arrest the levies of troops, prorogue the convocation of the comitia, and hinder the election of magistrates.[101] From the year 297, their number was raised to ten, that is, two for each of the five classes specially subject to the recruitment;[102] but the plebeians profited little by this measure; the more the number of tribunes was augmented, the easier it became for the aristocracy to find among them an instrument for its designs. Gradually their influence increased; in 298, they laid claim to the right of convoking the Senate, and yet it was still a long time before they formed part of that body.[103]

As to the comitia, the people had there only a feeble influence. In the assemblies by centuries, the vote of the first classes, composed of the richest citizens, as we have seen, prevailed over all the others; in the comitia by curiæ, the patricians were absolute masters; and when, towards the end of the third century, the plebeians obtained the comitia by tribes,[104] this concession did not add sensibly to their prerogatives. It was confined to the power of assembling in the public places where, divided according to tribes, they placed their votes in urns for the election of their tribunes and ediles, previously elected by the centuries;[105] their decisions concerned themselves only, and entailed no obligations on the patricians; so that the same town then offered the spectacle of two cities each having its own magistrates and laws.[106] At first the patricians would not form part of the assembly by tribes, but they soon saw the advantage of it, and, towards 305, entered it with their clients.[107]

Transformation of the Aristocracy.

III. This political organisation, the reflex of a society composed of so many different elements, could hardly have constituted a durable order of things, if the ascendency of a privileged class had not controlled the causes of dissensions. This ascendency itself would soon have diminished if concessions, forced or voluntary, had not gradually lowered the barriers between the two orders.

In fact, the arbitrary conduct of the consuls, who were, perhaps, originally nominated by the Senate alone,[108] excited sharp recriminations: "the consular authority," cried the plebeians, "was, in reality, almost as heavy as that of the kings. Instead of one master they had two, invested with absolute and unlimited power, without rule or bridle, who turned against the people all the threats of the laws, and all their punishments."[109] Although after the year 283 the patricians and plebeians were subjected to the same judges,[110] the want of fixed laws left the goods and lives of the citizens delivered to the will either of the consuls or of the tribunes. It became, therefore, indispensable to establish the legislation on a solid basis, and in 303 ten magistrates called decemvirs were chosen, invested with the double power, consular and tribunitian, which gave them the right of convoking equally the assemblies by centuries and by tribes. They were charged with the compilation of a code of laws afterwards known as the Laws of the Twelve Tables, which, engraved on brass, became the foundation of the Roman public law. Yet they persisted in making illegal the union contracted between persons of the two orders, and left the debtor at the mercy of the creditor, contrary to the decision of Servius Tullius.

The decemvirs abused their power, and, on their fall, the claims of the plebeians increased; the tribuneship, abolished during three years, was re-established; it was decided that an appeal to the people from the decision of any magistrate should be permitted, and that the laws made in the assemblies by tribes, as well as in the assemblies by centuries, should be obligatory on all.[111] There were thus, then, three sorts of comitia; the comitia by curiæ, which, conferring the imperium on the magistrates elected by the centuries, sanctioned in some sort the election of the consuls;[112] the comitia by centuries, over which the consuls presided; and the comitia by tribes, over which the tribunes presided; the first named the consuls, the second the plebeian magistrates, and both, composed of nearly the same citizens, had equally the power of approving or rejecting the laws; but in the former, the richest men and the nobility had all the influence, because they formed the majority of the centuries and voted first; while in the latter, on the contrary, the voters were confounded with that of the tribe to which they belonged. "If," says an ancient author, "the suffrages are taken by gentes (ex generibus hominum), the comitia are by curiæ; if according to age and census, they are by centuries; finally, if the vote be given according to territorial circumscription (regionibus), they are by tribes."[113] In spite of these concessions, antagonism in matters of law reigned always between the powers, the assemblies, and the different classes of society.

The plebeians laid claim to all the offices of state, and especially to the consulship, refusing to enrol themselves until their demands had been satisfied; and they went so far in their claims that they insisted upon the plebeian origin of the kings. "Shall we, then," cried the tribune Canuleius, addressing himself to the people, "have consuls who resemble the decemvirs, the vilest of mortals, all patricians, rather than the best of our kings, all new men!" that is, men without ancestors.[114]

The Senate resisted, because it had no intention of conferring upon plebeians the right which formed an attribute of the consuls, for the convocation of the comitia, of taking the great auspices, a privilege altogether of a religious character, the exclusive apanage of the nobility.[115]

In order to obviate this difficulty, the Senate, after suppressing the legal obstacles in the way of marriages between the two orders, agreed in 309 to the creation of six military tribunes invested with the consular power; but, which was an essential point, it was the interrex who convoked the comitia and took the auspices.[116] During seventy-seven years the military tribunes were elected alternately with the consuls, and the consulship was only re-established permanently in 387, when it was opened to the plebeians. This was the result of one of the laws of Licinius Stolo. This tribune succeeded in obtaining the adoption of several measures which appeared to open a new era which would put an end to disputes. Still the patricians held with such tenacity to the privilege of alone taking the auspices, that in 398, in the absence of the patrician consul, an interrex was appointed charged with presiding over the comitia, in order not to leave this care to the dictator, and the other consul, who were both plebeians.[117]

But in permitting the popular class to arrive at the consulship, care had been taken to withdraw from that dignity a great part of its attributes, in order to confer them upon patrician magistrates. Thus they had successively taken away from the consuls, by the creation of two questors, in 307, the administration of the military chest;[118] by the creation of the censors, in 311, the right of drawing up the list of the census, the assessment of the revenue of the State, and of watching over public morals; by the creation of the prætors, in 387, the sovereign jurisdiction in civil affairs, under the pretext that the nobility alone possessed the knowledge of the law of the Quirites; and lastly, by the creation of the curule ediles, the presidency of the games, the superintendence of buildings, the police and the provisioning of the town, the maintenance of the public roads, and the inspection of the markets.

The intention of the aristocracy had been to limit the compulsory concessions; but after the adoption of the Licinian laws, it was no longer possible to prevent the principle of the admission of plebeians to all the magistracies. In 386 they had arrived at the important charge of master of the knights (magister equitum) who was in a manner the lieutenant of the dictator (magister populi);[119] in 387 access to the religious functions had been laid open to them;[120] in 345 they obtained the questorship; in 398, the dictatorship itself; in 403, the censorship; and lastly, in 417, the prætorship.

In 391, the people arrogated the right of appointing a part of the legionary tribunes, previously chosen by the consuls.[121]

In 415, the law of Q. Publilius Philo took from the Senate the power of refusing the *auctoritas* to the laws voted by the comitia, and obliged it to declare in advance if the proposed law were in conformity with public and religious law. Further, the obligation imposed by this law of having always one censor taken from among the plebeians, opened the doors of the Senate to the richest of them, since it was the business of the censor to fix the rank of the citizens, and pronounce on the admission or exclusion of the senators. The Publilian law thus tended to raise the aristocracy of the two orders to the same rank, and to create the nobility (*nobilitas*), composed of all the families rendered illustrious by the offices they had filled.

Elements of Dissolution.

IV. At the beginning of the fifth century of Rome, the bringing nearer together of the two orders had given a greater consistence to society; but, just as we have seen under the kingly rule, the principles begin to show themselves which were one day to make the greatness of Rome, so now we see the first appearance of dangers which will be renewed unceasingly. Electoral corruption, the law of perduellio, slavery, the increase of the poor class, the agrarian laws, and the question of debts, will come, under different circumstances, to threaten the existence of the Republic. Let us summarily state that these questions, so grave in the sequel, were raised at an early date.

Electoral Corruption.—Fraud found its way into the elections as soon as the number of electors increased and rendered it necessary to collect more suffrages to obtain public charges; as early as 396, indeed, a law on solicitation, proposed by the tribune of the people, C. Pœtelius, bears witness to the existence of electoral corruption.

Law of High-treason.—As early as 305 and 369, the application of the law of perduellio, or design against the Republic, furnished to arbitrary power an arm of which, at a later period, under the emperors, so deplorable a use was made under the name of the law of high-treason.[122]

Slavery.—Slavery presented serious dangers for society, for, on the one hand, it tended, by the lower price of manual labour, to substitute itself for the labour of free men; while, on the other, discontented with their lot, the slaves were always ready to shake off the yoke and become the auxiliaries of all who were ambitious. In 253, 294, and 336, partial insurrections announced the condition already to be feared of a class disinherited of all the advantages, though intimately bound up with all the wants, of ordinary life.[123] The number of slaves increased rapidly. They replaced the free men torn by the continual wars from the cultivation of the land. At a later period, when these latter returned to their homes, the Senate was obliged to support them by sending as far as Sicily to seek wheat to deliver to them either gratis or at a reduced price.[124]

Agrarian Laws.—As to the Agrarian laws and the question of debts, they soon became an incessant cause of agitation.

The kings, with the conquered lands, had formed a domain of the State (ager publicus), one of its principal resources,[125] and generously distributed part of it to the poor citizens.[126] Generally, they took from the conquered peoples two-thirds of their land.[127] Of these two-thirds, "the cultivated part," says Appian, "was always adjudged to the new colonists, either as a gratuitous grant, or by sale, or by lease paying rent. As to the uncultivated part, which, as a consequence of war, was almost always the most considerable, it was not the custom to distribute it, but the enjoyment of it was left to any one willing to clear and cultivate it, with a reservation to the State of the tenth part of the harvest and a fifth part of the fruits. A similar tax was levied upon those who bred cattle, large or small (in order to prevent the pasture land from increasing in extent to the detriment of the arable land). This was done in view of the increase of the Italic population, which was judged at Rome the most laborious, and to have allies of their own race. But the measure produced a result contrary to that which was expected from it. The rich appropriated to themselves the greatest part of the undistributed lands, and reckoning that the long duration of their occupation would permit nobody to expel them, they bought when they found a seller, or took by force from their neighbouring lesser proprietors their modest heritages, and thus formed vast domains, instead of the mere fields which they had themselves cultivated before."[128]

The kings had always sought to put a curb on these usurpations,[129] and perhaps it was a similar attempt which cost Servius Tullius his life. But after the fall of the kingly power, the patricians, having become more powerful, determined to preserve the lands which they had unjustly seized. [130]

And it must be acknowledged, as they supported the greatest share of the burthen of war and taxation, they had a better claim than the others to the conquered lands; they thought, moreover, that the colonies were sufficient to support an agricultural population, and they acted rather as State farmers than as proprietors of the soil. According to the public law, indeed, the ager publicus was inalienable, and we read in an ancient author:—"Lawyers deny that the soil which has once begun to belong to the Roman people, can ever, by usage or possession, become the property of anybody else in the world."[131]

In spite of this principle, it would have been wisdom to give, to the poor citizens who had fought, a part of the spoils of the vanquished; for the demands were incessant, and after 268, renewed almost yearly by the tribunes or by the consuls themselves. In 275, a patrician, Fabius Cæso, taking the initiative in a partition of lands recently conquered, exclaimed: "Is it not just that the territories taken from the enemy should become the property of those who have paid for it with their sweat and with their blood?"[132] The Senate was as inflexible for this proposition as for those which were brought forward by Q. Considius and T. Genucius in 278, by Cn. Genucius in 280, and by the tribunes of the people, with the support of the consuls Valerius and Æmilius, in 284.[133]

Yet, after fifty years of struggles since the expulsion of the Tarquins, the tribune Icilius, in 298, obtained the partition of the lands of Mount Aventine, by indemnifying those who had usurped a certain portion of them.[134] The application of the law Icilia to other parts of the ager publicus[135] was vainly solicited in 298 and the following years; but in 330, a new tax was imposed upon the possessors of the lands for the pay of the troops. The perseverance of the tribunes was unwearied, and, during the thirty-six years following, six different propositions were unsuccessful, even that relating to the territory of the Bolani, newly taken from the enemy.[136] In 361 only, a senatus consultus granted to each father of a family and to each free man seven acres of the territory which had just been conquered from the Veii.[137] In 371, after a resistance of five years, the Senate, in order to secure the concurrence of the people in the war against the Volsci, agreed to the partition of the territory of the Pomptinum (the Pontine Marshes), taken from that people by Camillus, and already given up to the encroachments of the aristocracy.[138] But these partial concessions were not enough to satisfy the plebeians or to repair past injustices; in the Licinian law the claims of the people, which had been resisted during a hundred and thirty-six years, triumphed;[139] it did not entirely deprive the nobles of the enjoyment of the lands unjustly usurped, but it limited the possession of them to five hundred jugera. When this repartition was made, the land which remained was to be distributed among the poor. The proprietors were obliged to maintain on their lands a certain number of free men, in order to augment the class from which the legions were recruited; lastly, the number of cattle on each domain was fixed, in order to restrain the culture of the meadows, in general the most lucrative, and augment that of the arable lands, which relieved Italy from the necessity of having recourse to foreign corn.

This law of Licinius Stolo secured happy results; it restrained the encroachments of the rich and great, but only proceeded with moderation in its retrospective effects; it put a stop to the alarming extension of the private domains at the expense of the public domain, to the absorption of the good of the many by the few, to the depopulation of Italy, and consequently to the diminution of the strength of the armies.[140]

The numerous condemnations for trespasses against the law Licinia prove that it was carried into execution, and for the space of two hundred years it contributed, with the establishment of new colonies,[141] to maintain this class of agriculturists—the principal sinews of the State. We see indeed that, from this moment, the Senate itself took the initiative of new distributions of land to the people.[142]

Debts.—The question of debts and the diminution of the rate of interest had long been the subject of strong prejudices and of passionate debates.

As the citizens made war at their own expense, the less rich, while they were under arms, could not take care of their fields or farms, but borrowed money to provide for their wants and for those of their families. The debt had, in this case, a noble origin, the service of their country.[143] Public opinion must, therefore, be favourable to the debtors and hostile to those who, speculating on the pecuniary difficulties of the defenders of the State, extorted heavy interest for the money they lent. The patricians also took advantage of their position and their knowledge of legal forms to exact heavy sums from the plebeians whose causes they defended.[144]

The kings, listening to the demands of the citizens who were overwhelmed with debts, often showed their readiness to help them;[145] but, after their expulsion, the rich classes, more independent, became more untractable, and men, ruined on account of their military service, were sold publicly, as slaves,[146] by their creditors. Thus, when war was imminent, the poor often refused to serve,[147] crying out, "What use will it be to us to conquer the enemies without, if our creditors put us in bonds for the debts we have contracted? What advantage shall we have in strengthening the empire of Rome, if we cannot preserve our personal liberty?"[148] Yet the patricians, who contributed more than the others to the costs of the war, demanded of their debtors, not without reason, the payment of the money they had advanced; and hence arose perpetual dissensions.[149]

In 305, the laws of the Twelve Tables decided that the rate of interest should be reduced to ten per cent. a year; but a law of Licinius Stolo alone resolved, in an equitable manner, this grave question. It enacted that the interests previously paid should be deducted from the principal, and that the principal should be repaid by equal portions during an interval of three years. This measure was advantageous to all, for, in the state of insolvency in which the debtors were involved, the creditors could not obtain the interest of their money, and even risked the loss of the principal; the new law guaranteed the debts; the debtors in their turn, having become landed proprietors, found the means of freeing themselves by means of the lands they had received and the delay which had been given them. The agreement established in 387 was of slight duration, and in the midst of disagreements more or less violent, things were carried so far, in 412, that the entire abolition of debts and the prohibition to exact any interest were decreed mere revolutionary and transitory measures.

Résumé.

V. This rapid sketch of the evils already perceptible which tormented Roman society leads us to this reflection: it is the lot of all governments, whatever be their form, to contain within themselves germs of life, which make their strength, and germs of dissolution, which must some day lead to their ruin; and accordingly, as the Republic was in progress or in decline, the first or the second became developed and dominant in turn; that is, so long as the aristocracy preserved its virtues and its patriotism, the elements of prosperity predominated; but no sooner did it begin to degenerate, than the causes of disturbance gained the upper hand, and shook the edifice which had been erected so laboriously.

If the fall of the kingly power, in giving more vitality and independence to the aristocracy, rendered the constitution of the State more solid and durable, the democracy had at first no reason for congratulation. Two hundred years passed away before the plebeians could obtain, not equality of political rights, but even a share in the ager publicus and an act of lenity in favour of debtors, overwhelmed with liabilities through incessant wars. About the same length of time was required by the Republic to re-conquer the supremacy over the neighbouring peoples which she had exercised under the last kings,[150] so many years a country requires to recover from the shocks and enfeebling influence of even the most legitimate revolutions.

Yet Roman society had been vigorously enough constituted to resist at the same time external attacks and internal troubles. Neither the invasions of Porsenna, nor those of the Gauls, nor the conspiracies of the neighbouring peoples, were able to compromise its existence. Already eminent men, such as Valerius Publicola, A. Postumius, Coriolanus, Spurius Cassius, Cincinnatus, and Camillus, had distinguished themselves as legislators and warriors, and Rome could put on foot ten legions, or forty-five thousand men. At home, important advantages had been obtained, and notable concessions had been made to effect a reconciliation between the two orders; written laws had been adopted, and the attributes of the different magistracies had been better defined, but the constitution of society remained the same. The facility granted to the plebeians of arriving at all the State employments only increased the strength of the aristocracy, which recovered its vigour of youth without modifying itself, diminished the number of its adversaries, and increased that of its adherents. The rich and important plebeian families soon began to mingle with the ancient patrician families, to share their ideas, their interests, and even their prejudices; and a learned German historian remarks with justice that after the abolition of the kingly power there was, perhaps, a greater number of plebeians in the Senate, but that personal merit, without birth and fortune, experienced greater difficulty than ever in reaching preferment.[151]

It is not indeed sufficient, for the application of the state of society, to study thoroughly its laws, but we must also take into consideration the influence exercised by the manners of the people. The laws proclaimed equality and liberty, but the manners left the honours and preponderance to the upper class. The admission to place was no longer forbidden to the plebeians, but the election almost always kept them from it. During fifty-nine years, two hundred and sixty-four military tribunes replaced the consuls, and of this number only eighteen were plebeians; although these latter might be candidates for the consulship, the choice fell generally upon patricians.[152] Marriage between the two orders had been long placed on a footing of equality, and yet, in 456, the prejudices of caste were far from being destroyed, as we learn from the history of the patrician Virginia, married to the plebeian Volumnius, whom the matrons drove away from the temple of Pudicitia patricia.[153]

The laws protected liberty, but they were rarely executed, as is shown by the continual renewal of the same regulations. Thus it had been decided in 305 that the plebiscita should have the force of law, yet in spite of that it was found necessary to re-enact the same regulation by the laws Hortensia, in 466, and Mænia, in 468. This last sanctioned also anew the law Publilia of 415. It was the same with the law of Valerius Publicola (of the year 246), which authorised an appeal to the people from the judgments of the magistrates. It appears to have been restored to vigour by Valerius and Horatius in 305, and again by Valerius Corvus in 454. And, on this occasion, the great Roman historian exclaims, "I can only explain this frequent renewal of the same law by supposing that the power of some of the great ones always succeeded in triumphing over the liberty of the people."[154] The right of admission to the Senate was acknowledged in principle, yet no one could enter it without having obtained a decree of the censor, or exercised a curule magistracy— favours almost always reserved to the aristocracy. The law which required a plebeian among the censors remained almost always in abeyance, and, to become censor, it was generally necessary to have been consul.

All offices ought to be annual, and yet the tribunes, as well as the consuls, obtained their re-election several times at short intervals—as in the instance of Licinius Stolo, re-elected tribune during nine consecutive years; of Sulpicius Peticus, five times consul (from 390 to 403); of Popilius Lænas and Marcius Rutilus, both four times, the first from 395 to 406, the second from 397 to 412. The law of 412 came in vain to require an interval of ten years before becoming again a candidate for the same magistracy. Several personages were none the less re-elected before the time required, such as Valerius Corvus, six times consul (from 406 to 455), and consecutively during the last three years; and Papirius Cursor, five times (from 421 to 441).

The lives of the citizens were protected by the laws, but public opinion remained powerless at the assassination of those who had incurred the hatred of the Senate; and, in spite of the law of the consul Valerius Publicola, the violent death of the tribune Genucius, or of the rich plebeian Spurius Melius, was a subject of applause.

The comitia were free, but the Senate had at its disposal either the veto of the tribunes or the religious scruples of the people. A consul could prevent the meeting of these assemblies, or cut short all their deliberations, either by declaring that he was observing the sky, or that a clap of thunder or some other celestial manifestation had occurred;[155] and it depended upon the declaration of the augurs to annul the elections. Moreover, the people in reality were satisfied with naming the persons on whom they wished to confer the magisterial offices, for, to enter upon their functions, the consuls and the prætors had to submit their powers to the sanction of the curiæ (lex curiata de imperio).[156] It was thus in the power of the nobility to reverse the elections which displeased them, a fact which Cicero explains in the following terms, while presenting this measure in a light favourable to the people: "Your ancestors required the suffrages twice for all magistracies, for, when a curiate law was proposed in favour of the patrician magistrates, they voted in reality a second time for the same persons, so that the people, if they repented of their choice, had the power of abandoning it."[157]

The dictatorship was also a lever left in the hands of the nobility to overthrow oppositions and influence the comitia. The dictator was never elected, but appointed by a consul.[158] In the space of only twenty-six years, from 390 to 416, there were eighteen dictators.

The Senate remained, therefore, all powerful in spite of the victory of the plebeians, for, independently of the means placed at its disposal, it was in its power to elude the plebiscita, the execution of which was entrusted to it. If the influence of a predominant class sobered the use of political liberty, the laws presented a still greater curb on individual liberty. Thus, not only all the members of the family were subjected to the absolute authority of the head, but each citizen was obliged further to obey a multitude of rigorous obligations.[159] The censor watched over the purity of marriages, the education of children, the treatment of slaves and clients, and the cultivation of the lands.[160] "The Romans did not believe," says Plutarch, "that each individual ought to be allowed the liberty to marry, to have children, to choose his walk in life, to give festivities, or even to follow his desires and tastes, without undergoing a previous inspection and judgment."[161]

The condition of Rome then bore a great resemblance to that of England before its electoral reform. For several centuries, the English Constitution was vaunted as the palladium of liberty, although then, as at Rome, birth and fortune were the unique source of honours and power. In both countries the aristocracy, master of the elections by solicitation, money, or rotten boroughs, caused, as the patricians at Rome, the members of the nobility to be elected to parliament, and no one was citizen in either of the two countries without the possession of wealth. Nevertheless, if the people, in England, had no part in the direction of affairs, they boasted justly, before 1789, a liberty which shone brightly in the middle of the silentious atmosphere of the Continental states. The disinterested observer does not examine if the scene where grave political questions are discussed is more or less vast, or if the actors are more or less numerous: he is only struck by the grandeur of the spectacle. Thus, far be from us the intention of blaming the nobility, any more in Rome than in England, for having preserved its preponderance by all the means which laws and habits placed at its disposal. The power was destined to remain with the patricians as long as they showed themselves worthy of it; and, it cannot but be acknowledged, without their perseverance in the same policy, without that elevation of views, without that severe and inflexible virtue, the distinguishing character of the aristocracy, the work of Roman civilisation would not have been accomplished.

At the beginning of the fifth century, the Republic, consolidated, is going to gather the fruit of the many efforts it has sustained. More united henceforward, in the interior, the Romans will turn all their energy towards the conquest of Italy, but it will require nearly a century to realise it. Always stimulated by their institutions, always restrained by an intelligent aristocracy, they will furnish the astonishing example of a people preserving, in the name of liberty and in the midst of agitation, the immobility of a system which will render them masters of the world.

# CHAPTER III
# CONQUEST OF ITALY (From 416 to 488)

Description of Italy.

I. ANCIENT Italy did not comprise all the territory which has for its natural limits the Alps and the sea. What is called the continental part, or the great plain traversed by the Po, which extends between the Alps, the Apennines, and the Adriatic, was separated from it. This plain, and part of the mountains on the coasts of the Mediterranean, formed Liguria, Cisalpine Gaul, and Venetia. The peninsula, or Italy proper, was bounded, on the north, by the Rubicon, and, probably, by the lower course of the Arno;[162] on the west, by the Mediterranean; on the east, by the Adriatic; on the south, by the Ionian Sea. (See the Maps, No. 1 and No. 2.)

II

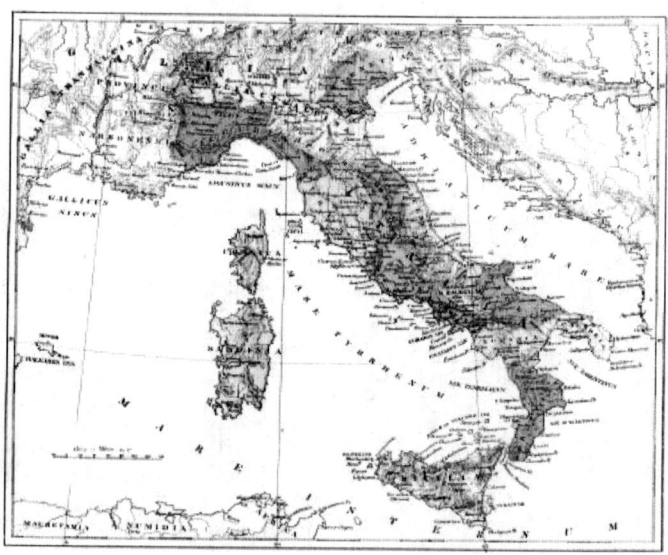

The Apennines traverse Italy in its whole length. They begin where the Alps end, near Savona, and their chain proceeds, continually rising in elevation, as far as the centre of the peninsula. Mount Velino is their culminating point, and from thence the Apennines continue decreasing in height, until they reach the extremity of the kingdom of Naples. In the northern region they approach the Adriatic; but, in the centre, they cut the peninsula into two parts nearly equal; then, at Mount Caruso (Vultur), near the source of the Bradano (Bradanus), they separate into two branches, one of which penetrates into Calabria, the other into the Terra di Bari as far as Otranto.

The two slopes of the Apennines give birth to various streams which flow some into the Adriatic and others into the Mediterranean. On the eastern side the principal are—the Rubicon, the Pisaurus (*Foglia*), the Metaurus (*Metauro*), the Æsis (*Esino*), the Truentus (*Tronto*), the Aternus (*Pescara*), the Sangrus (*Sangro*), the Trinius (*Trigno*), the Frento (*Fortore*), and the Aufidus (*Ofanto*), which follow generally a direction perpendicular to the chain of mountains. On the western side, the Arnus (*Arno*), the Ombrus (*Ombrone*), the Tiber, the Amasenus (*Amaseno*), the Liris (*Garigliano*), the Vulturnus (*Volturno*), and the Silarus (*Silaro* or *Sile*), run parallel to the Apennines; but towards their mouths they take a direction nearly perpendicular to the coast. The Bradanus (*Bradano*), the Casuentus (*Basiento*), and the Aciris (*Agri*), flow into the Gulf of Tarentum.

We may admit into ancient Italy the following great divisions and subdivisions:—

To the north, the Senones, a people of Gallic origin, occupying the shores of the Adriatic Sea, from the Rubicon to the neighbourhood of Ancona; Umbria, situated between the Senones and the course of the Tiber; Etruria, between the Tiber and the Mediterranean Sea.

In the centre the territory of Picenum, between Ancona and Hadria, in the Abruzzo Ulteriore; Latium, in the part between the Apennines and the Mediterranean, from the Tiber to the Liris; to the south of Latium, the Volsci, and the Aurunci, the *débris* of the ancient Ausones, retired between the Liris and the Amasenus, and bordering upon another people of the same race, the Sidicines, established between the Liris and the Vulturnus; the country of the Sabines, between Picenum and Latium; to the east of Latium, in the mountains, the Æqui; the Hernici, backed by the populations of Sabellian stock, namely, the Marsi, the Peligni, the Vestini, the Marrucini, and the Frentani, distributed in the valleys through which run the rivers received by the Adriatic from the extremity of Picenum to the River Fortore.

The territory of Samnium, answering to the great part of the Abruzzi and the province of Molisa, advanced towards the west as far as the upper arm of the Vulturnus, on the north to the banks of the Fortore, and to the south to Mount Vultur. Beyond the Vulturnus extended Campania (*Terra di Lavoro and part of the principality of Salerno*), from Sinuessa to the Gulf of Pæstum.

Southern Italy, or Magna Græcia, comprised on the Adriatic: first, Apulia (the Capitanata and Terra di Bari) and Messapia (Terra di Otranto); this last terminated in the Iapygian Promontory, and its central part was occupied by the Salentini and divers other Messapian populations, while there existed on the seaboard a great number of Greek colonies; secondly, Lucania, which answered nearly to the modern province of Basilicata, and was washed by the waters of the Gulf of Tarentum; thirdly, Bruttium (now the Calabrias), forming the most advanced point of Italy, and terminating in the Promontory of Hercules.

Dispositions of the People of Italy in regard to Rome.

II. In 416, Rome had finally subdued the Latins, and possessed part of Campania. Her supremacy extended from the present territory of Viterbo to the Gulf of Naples, from Antium (*Porto di Anzo*) to Sora.

The frontiers of the Republic were difficult to defend, her limits ill determined, and her neighbours the most warlike people of the peninsula.

To the north only, the mountains of Viterbo, covered with a thick forest (*silva Ciminia*), formed a rampart against Etruria. The southern part of this country had been long half Roman; the Latin colonies of Sutrium (*Sutri*) and Nepete (*Nepi*) served as posts of observation. But the Etruscans, animated for ages with hostile feeling towards Rome, attempted continually to recover the lost territory. The Gaulish Senones, who, in 364, had taken and burnt Rome, and often renewed their invasions, had come again to try their fortune. In spite of their defeats in 404 and 405, they were always ready to join the Umbrians and Etruscans in attacking the Republic.

The Sabines, though entertaining from time immemorial tolerably amicable relations with the Romans, offered but a doubtful alliance. Picenum, a fertile and populous country, was peaceful, and the greater part of the mountain tribes of Sabellic race, in spite of their bravery and energy, inspired as yet no fear. Nearer Rome, the Æqui and the Hernici had been reduced to inaction; but the Senate kept in mind their hostilities and nourished projects of vengeance.

On the southern coast, among the Greek towns devoted to commerce, Tarentum passed for the most powerful; but these colonies, already in decline, were obliged to have recourse to mercenary troops, to resist the native inhabitants. They disputed with the Samnites and the Romans the preponderance over the people of Magna Græcia. The Samnites, indeed, a manly and independent race, aimed at seizing the whole of Southern Italy; their cities formed a confederacy, redoubtable on account of its close union in time of war. The mountain tribes gave themselves up to brigandage, and it is worthy of attention that recent events show that in our days manners have not much changed in that country. The Samnites had amassed considerable riches; their arms displayed excessive extravagance, and, if we believe Cæsar,[163] they served as models for those of the Romans.

A jealous rivalry had long prevailed between the Romans and the Samnites. The moment these two peoples found themselves in presence of each other, it was evident that they would be at war; the struggle was long and terrible, and, during the fifth century, it was round Samnium that they disputed the empire of Italy. The position of the Samnites was very advantageous. Entrenched in their mountains, they could, at their will, either descend into the valley of the Liris, thence reach the country of the Aurunci, always ready to revolt, and cut off the communications of Rome with Campania; or follow the course of the upper Liris into the country of the Marsi, raise these latter, and hold out the hand to the Etruscans, turning Rome; or, lastly, penetrate into Campania by the valley of the Vulturnus, and fall upon the Sidicini, whose territory they coveted.

In the midst of so many hostile peoples, for a little state to succeed in raising itself above the others, and in subjugating them, it must have possessed peculiar elements of superiority. The peoples who surrounded Rome, warlike and proud of their independence, had neither the same unity, nor the same incentives to action, nor the same powerful aristocratic organisation, nor the same blind confidence in their destinies. They displayed more selfishness than ambition. When they fought, it was much more to increase their riches by pillage than to augment the number of their subjects. Rome triumphed, because alone, in prospect of a future, she made war not to destroy, but to conserve, and, after the material conquest, always set herself to accomplish the moral conquest of the vanquished.

During four hundred years her institutions had formed a race animated with the love of country and with the sentiment of duty; but, in their turn, the men, incessantly re-tempered in intestine struggles, had successively introduced manners and traditions stronger even than the institutions themselves. During three centuries, in fact, Rome presented, in spite of the annual renewal of powers, such a perseverance in the same policy, such a practice of the same virtues, that it might have been supposed that the government had but a single head, a single thought, and one might have believed that all its generals were great warriors, all its senators experienced statesmen, and all its citizens valiant soldiers.

The geographical position of Rome contributed no less to the rapid increase of its power. Situated in the middle of the only great fertile plain of Latium, on the banks of the only important river of Central Italy, which united it with the sea, it could be at the same time agricultural and maritime, conditions then indispensable for the capital of a new empire. The rich countries which bordered the coasts of the Mediterranean were sure to fall easily under her dominion; and as for the countries which surrounded her, it was possible to become mistress of them by occupying gradually the openings from all the valleys. The town of the seven hills, favoured by her natural situation as well as by her political constitution, carried thus in herself the germs of her future greatness.

Treatment of the Vanquished Peoples.

III. From the commencement of the fifth century Rome prepares with energy to subject and assimilate to herself the peoples who dwelt from the Rubicon to the Strait of Messina. Nothing will prevent her from surmounting all obstacles, neither the coalition of her neighbours conspiring against her, nor the new incursions of the Gauls, nor the invasion of Pyrrhus. She will know how to raise herself from her partial defeats, and establish the unity of Italy, not by subduing at once all these peoples to the same laws and the same rule, but by causing them to enter, by little and little and in different degrees, into the great Roman family. "Of one city she makes her ally; on another she confers the honour of living under the Quiritary law, to this one with the right of suffrage, to that with the permission to retain its own government. Municipia of different degrees, maritime colonies, Latin colonies, Roman colonies, prefectures, allied towns, free towns, all isolated by the difference of their condition, all united by their equal dependence on the Senate, they will form, as it were, a vast network which will entangle the Italian peoples, until the day when, without new struggles, they will awake subjects of Rome."[164]

Let us examine the conditions of these various categories:

The right of city, in its plenitude (jus civitatis optimo jure), comprised the political privileges peculiar to the Romans, and assured for civil life certain advantages, of which the concession might be made separately and by degrees. First came the commercium, that is, the right of possessing and transmitting according to the Roman law; next the connubium, or the right of contracting marriage with the advantages established by Roman legislation. [165] The commercium and connubium united formed the Quiritary law (jus quiritium).

There were three sorts of municipia:[166] first, the municipia of which the inhabitants, inscribed in the tribes, exercised all the rights and were subjected to all the obligations of the Roman citizens; secondly, the municipia sine suffragio, the inhabitants of which enjoyed in totality or in part the Quiritary law, and might obtain the complete right of Roman citizens on certain conditions;[167] it is what constituted the jus Latii; these first two categories preserved their autonomy and their magistrates; third, the towns which had lost all independence in exchange for the civil laws of Rome, but without enjoyment, for the inhabitants, of the most important political rights; it was the law of the Cærites, because Cære was the first town which had been thus treated.[168]

Below the municipia, which had their own magistrates, came, in this social hierarchy, the prefectures,[169] so called because a prefect was sent there every year to administer justice.

The dediticii were still worse treated. Delivered by victory to the discretion of the Senate, they had been obliged to surrender their arms and give hostages, to throw down their walls or receive a garrison within them, to pay a tax, and to furnish a determinate contingent. With the exclusion of these last, the towns which had not obtained for their inhabitants the complete rights of Roman citizens belonged to the class of allies (fœderati socii). Their condition differed according to the nature of their engagements. Simple treaties of friendship,[170] or of commerce,[171] or of offensive alliance, or offensive and defensive,[172] concluded on the footing of equality, were called fœdera æqua. On the contrary, when one of the contracting parties (and it was never the Romans) submitted to onerous obligations from which the other was exempted, these treaties were called fœdera non æqua. They consisted almost always in the cession of a part of the territory of the vanquished, and in the obligation to undertake no war of their own. A certain independence, it is true, was left to them; they received the right of exchange and free establishment in the capital, but they were bound to the interests of Rome by an alliance offensive and defensive. The only clause establishing the preponderance of Rome was conceived in these terms: Majestatem populi Romani comiter conservanto;[173] that is, "They shall loyally acknowledge the supremacy of the Roman people." It is a remarkable circumstance that, dating from the reign of Augustus, the freedmen were divided in categories similar to those which existed for the inhabitants of Italy.[174]

As to the colonies, they were established for the purpose of preserving the possessions acquired, of securing the new frontiers, and of guarding the important passes; and even for the sake of getting rid of the turbulent class. [175] They were of two sorts: the Roman colonies and the Latin colonies. The former differed little from the municipia of the first degree, the others from the municipia of the second degree. The first were formed of Roman citizens, taken with their families from the classes subjected to military service, and even, in their origin, solely among the patricians. The coloni preserved the privileges attached to the title of citizen,[176] and were bound by the same obligations, and the interior administration of the colony was an image of that of Rome.[177]

The Latin colonies differed from the others in having been founded by the confederacy of the Latins on different points of Latium. Emanating from a league of independent cities, they were not, like the Roman colonies, tied by close bonds to the metropolis.[178] But the confederacy once dissolved, these colonies were placed in the rank of allied towns (socii Latini). The act (formula) which instituted them was a sort of treaty guaranteeing their franchise.[179]

Peopled at first by Latins, it was not long before these colonies received Roman citizens who were induced by their poverty to exchange their title and rights for the advantages assured to the colonists. These did not figure on the lists of the censors. The formula fixed simply the tribute to pay and the number of soldiers to furnish. What the colony lost in privileges it gained in independence.[180]

The isolation of the Latin colonies, placed in the middle of the enemy's territory, obliged them to remain faithful to Rome, and to keep watch on the neighbouring peoples. Their military importance was at least equal to that of the Roman colonies; they merited as well as these latter the name of propugnacula imperii and of specula,[181] that is, bulwarks and watch-towers of the conquest. In a political point of view they rendered services of a similar kind. If the Roman colonies announced to the conquered people the majesty of the Roman name, their Latin sisters gave an ever-increasing extension to the nomen Latinum,[182] that is, to the language, manners, and whole civilisation of that race of which Rome was but the first representative. The Latin colonies were ordinarily founded to economise the colonies of Roman citizens, which were charged principally with the defence of the coasts and the maintenance of commercial relations with foreign people.

In making the privileges of the Roman citizen an advantage which every one was happy and proud to acquire, the Senate held out a bait to all ambitions; and this general desire, not to destroy the privilege, but to gain a place among the privileged, is a characteristic trait of the manners of antiquity. In the city not less than in the State, the insurgents or discontented did not seek, as in our modern societies, to overthrow, but to attain to. So every one, according to his position, aspired to a legitimate object: the plebeians to enter into the aristocracy, not to destroy it; the Italic peoples, to have a part in the sovereignty of Rome, not to contest it; the Roman provinces to be declared allies and friends of Rome, and not to recover their independence.

The peoples could judge, according to their conduct, what lot was reserved for them. The paltry interests of city were replaced by an effectual protection, and by new rights often more precious, in the eyes of the vanquished, than independence itself. This explains the facility with which the Roman domination was established. In fact, that only is destroyed entirely which may be replaced advantageously.

A rapid glance at the wars which effected the conquest of Italy will show how the Senate made application of the principles stated above; how it was skilful in profiting by the divisions of its adversaries, in collecting its whole strength to overwhelm one of them; after the victory in making it an ally; in using the aims and resources of that ally to subjugate another people; in crushing the confederacies which united the vanquished against it; in attaching them to Rome by new bonds; in establishing military posts on all the points of strategic importance; and, lastly, in spreading everywhere the Latin race by distributing to Roman citizens a part of the lands taken from the enemy.

But, before entering upon the recital of events, we must cast a glance upon the years which immediately preceded the pacification of Latium.

Submission of Latium after the first Samnite War.

IV. During a hundred and sixty-seven years, Rome had been satisfied with struggling against her neighbours to re-conquer a supremacy lost since the fall of her kings. She held herself almost always on the defensive; but, with the fifth century, she took the offensive, and inaugurated the system of conquests continued to the moment when she herself succumbed.

In 411, she had, in concert with the Latins, combated the Samnites for the first time, and commenced against that redoubtable people a struggle which lasted seventy-two years, and which brought twenty-four triumphs to the Roman generals.[183] Proud of having contributed to the two great victories of Mount Gaurus and Suessula, the Latins, with an exaggerated belief in their own strength and a pretension to equality with Rome, went so far as to require that one of the two consuls, and half of the senators, should be chosen from their nation. War was immediately declared. The Senate was willing enough to have allies and subjects, but it could not suffer equals; it accepted without scruple the services of those who had just been enemies, and the Romans, united with the Samnites, the Hernici, and the Sabellian peoples, were seen in the fields of the Veseris and Trifanum, fighting against the Latins and Volsci. Latium once reduced, it remained to determine the lot of the vanquished. Livy reports a speech of Camillus which explains clearly the policy recommended by that great citizen. "Will you," he exclaims, addressing the members of the assembly, "use the utmost rigour of the rights of victory? You are masters to destroy all Latium, and to make a vast desert of it, after having often drawn from it powerful succours. Will you, on the contrary, after the example of your fathers, augment the resources of Rome?

Admit the vanquished among the number of your citizens; it is a fruitful means of increasing at the same time your power and your glory."[184] This last counsel prevailed.

The first step was to break the bonds which made of the Latin people a sort of confederacy. All political communalty, all war on their own account, all rights of commercium and connubium, between the different cities, were taken from them.[185]

The towns nearest Rome received the rights of city and suffrage.[186] Others received the title of allies and the privilege of preserving their own institutions, but they lost a part of their territory.[187] As to the Latin colonies founded before in the old country of the Volsci, they formed the nucleus of the Latin allies (socii nominis Latini). Velitræ, alone, having already revolted several times, was treated with great rigour; Antium was compelled to surrender its ships, and become a maritime colony.

These severe, but equitable measures, had pacified Latium; applied to the rest of Italy, and even to foreign countries, they will facilitate everywhere the progress of Roman domination.

The momentary alliance with the Samnites had permitted Rome to reduce the Latins; nevertheless the Senate, without hesitation, turned against the former again as soon as the moment appeared convenient. It concluded, in 422, a treaty with the Gauls and Alexander Molossus, who, having landed near Pæstum, attacked the Lucanians and the Samnites. This King of Epirus, the uncle of Alexander the Great, had been called into Italy by the Tarentines; but his premature death disappointed the hopes to which his co-operation had given rise, and the Samnites recommenced their incursions on the lands of their neighbours. The intervention of Rome put a stop to the war. All the forces of the Republic were employed in reducing the revolt of the Volscian towns of Fundi and Privernum.[188] In 425, Anxur (Terracina) was declared a Roman colony, and, in 426, Fregellæ (Ceprano?), a Latin colony.

The establishment of these fortresses, and of those of Cales and Antium, secured the communications with Campania; the Liris and the Vulturnus became in that direction the principal lines of defence of the Romans. The cities situated on the shores of that magnificent gulf called *Crater* by the ancients, and in our days the *Gulf of Naples*, perceived then the dangers which threatened them. They turned their eyes towards the population of the interior, who were no less alarmed for their independence.

Second Samnite War.

V. The fertile countries which bordered the western shore of the peninsula were destined to excite the covetousness of the Romans and the

Samnites, and become the prey of the conqueror. "Campania, indeed," says Florus,[189] "is the finest country of Italy, and even of the whole world. There is nothing milder than its climate. Spring flourishes there twice every year. There can be nothing more fertile than its soil. It is called the garden of Ceres and Bacchus. There is not a more hospitable sea than that which bathes its shores." In 427, the two peoples disputed the possession of it, as they had done in 411. The inhabitants of Palæopolis having attacked the Roman colonists of the ager Campanus, the consuls marched against that place, which soon received succour from the Samnites and the inhabitants of Nola, while Rome formed an alliance with the Apulians and the Lucanians. The siege dragged on, and the necessity of continuing the campaign beyond the ordinary limit led to the prolongation of the command of Publilius Philo with the title of proconsul, which appeared for the first time in the military annals. The Samnites were soon driven from Campania; the Palæopolitans submitted; their town was demolished; but they formed close to it a new establishment, at Naples (Neapolis), where a new treaty guaranteed them an almost absolute independence, on the condition of furnishing a certain number of vessels to Rome. After that, nearly all the Greek towns, reduced one after another, obtained the same favourable conditions, and formed the class of the socii navales.[190]

Yet the war was protracted in the mountains of the Apennine. Tarentum united with the Samnites, the only people who were still to be feared,[191] and the Lucanians abandoned the alliance of the Romans; but, in 429, the two most celebrated captains of the time, Q. Fabius Rullianus and Papirius Cursor, penetrated into the country of Samnium, and compelled the enemy to pay an indemnity for the war and accept a year's truce.

At this epoch, an unforeseen event, which changed the destinies of the world, came to demonstrate the difference between the rapid creation of a man of genius and the patient work of an intelligent aristocracy. Alexander the Great, after having shone like a meteor, and brought into subjection the most powerful kingdoms of Asia, died at Babylon. His fruitful and decisive influence, which carried the civilization of Greece into the East, survived him, but at his death, the empire he founded became in a few years dismembered (431); the Roman aristocracy, on the contrary, perpetuating itself from age to age, pursued more slowly, but without interruption, the system which, binding again the peoples about a common centre, was destined by little and little to secure her domination over Italy first, and then over the universe.

The defection of a part of the Apulians, in 431, encouraged the Samnites to take arms again; defeated in the following years, they asked for the restoration of friendly relations, but the haughty refusal of Rome led, in 433, to the famous defeat of the Furcæ Caudinæ. The generosity of the Samnite general, Pontus Herennius, who granted their lives to so many thousands of prisoners on condition of restoring to force the old treaties, had no effect upon the Senate. Four legions had passed under the yoke—a circumstance in which the Senate only saw a new affront to revenge. The treaty of Caudium was not ratified, and subterfuges little excusable, although approved at a later period by Cicero,[192] gave to the refusal an appearance of justice.

Meanwhile the Senate exerted itself vigorously to repair this check, and soon Publilius Philo defeated the enemies in Samnium, and, in Apulia, Papirius, in his turn, caused seven thousand Samnites to pass under the yoke. The vanquished solicited peace, but in vain; they only obtained a truce for two years (436), and it had hardly expired, when, penetrating into the country of the Volsci, as far as the neighbourhood of Terracina, and taking a position at Lautulæ, they defeated a Roman army raised hastily and commanded by Q. Fabius (439). Capua deserted, and Nola, Nuceria, the Aurunci, and the Volsci of the Liris took part openly with the Samnites. The spirit of rebellion spread as far as Præneste. Rome was in danger. The Senate required its utmost energy to restrain populations whose fidelity was always doubtful. Fortune seconded its efforts, and the allies, who had proved traitors, received a cruel chastisement, explained by the terror they had inspired. In 440,[193] not far from Caudium, a numerous army encountered the Samnites, who lost 30,000 men, and were driven back into the Apennine territory. The Roman legions proceeded to encamp before their capital, Bovianum, and there took up their winter quarters.

The year following (441), Rome, less occupied in fighting, profited by this circumstance to seize upon advantageous positions, establishing in Campania and Apulia colonies which surrounded the territory of Samnium. At the same epoch, Appius Claudius transformed into a regular causeway the road which has preserved his name.[194] The Romans turned their attention to the defence of the coasts and communication by sea; a colony was sent to the isle of Pontia,[195] opposite Tarracina, and the armament of a fleet was commenced, which was placed under the command of duumviri navales.[196] The war had lasted fifteen years, and, although Rome had only succeeded in driving back the Samnites into their own territory, she had conquered two provinces, Apulia and Campania.

Third Samnite war. Coalition of Samnites, Etruscans, Umbrians, and Hernici (443-449).

VI. A struggle so desperate had produced its effect even in Etruria, and the old league was formed again. Inured to war by their daily combats with the Gauls, and emboldened by the reports of the defeat of Lautulæ, the Etruscans believed that the moment had arrived for recovering their ancient territory to the south of the Ciminian forest; they were further encouraged by the attitude of the peoples of Central Italy, who were weary of the continual passing of legions. From 443 to 449, the armies of the Republic were obliged to face different enemies at the same time. In Etruria, Fabius Rullianus relieved Sutrium, a rampart of Rome on the north;[197] he passed through the Ciminian forest, and by the victories of Lake Vadimo (445)[198] and Perusia compelled all the Etruscan towns to ask for peace. At the same time, an army laid waste the country of the Samnites; and a Roman fleet, composed of vessels furnished by the maritime allies, took the offensive for the first time. Its attempt near Nuceria Alfaterna (Nocera, a town of Campania) was unfortunate.

War next breaks out again in Apulia, Samnium, and Etruria, where the aged Papirius Cursor, named dictator anew, gains a brilliant victory at Langula (445). The year following Fabius penetrates again into Samnium, and the other consul, Decius, maintains Etruria. Suddenly the Umbrians conceive the project of seizing Rome by surprise. The consuls are recalled for the defence of the town. Fabius meets the Etruscans at Mevania (on the confines of Etruria and Umbria), and, the year following, at Allifæ (447). Among the prisoners were some Æqui and Hernici. Their towns, feeling themselves thus compromised, declared open war against the Romans (448). The Samnites recovered courage; but the prompt reduction of the Hernici allowed the Senate to concentrate its forces. Two armies, penetrating into Samnium by way of Apulia and Campania, re-established the old frontiers. Bovianum was taken for the third time, and during six months the country was delivered up to devastation. In vain Tarentum tried to raise new quarrels for the Republic, and to force the Lucanians to embrace the cause of the Samnites. The successes of the Roman arms led to the conclusion of treaties of peace with all the peoples of Southern Italy, constrained thenceforward to acknowledge the majesty of the Roman people. The Æqui remained alone exposed to the wrath of Rome; the Senate did not forget that at Allifæ they had fought in the ranks of the enemy, and, once freed from its more serious embarrassments, it inflicted on this people a terrible chastisement: forty-one places were taken and burnt in fifty days. This period of six years thus terminated with the submission of the Hernici and Æqui.

Five years less agitated left Rome time to regulate the position of its new subjects, and to establish colonies and ways of communication.

The Hernici were treated in the same manner as the Latins, in 416, and deprived of commercium and connubium. Prefects and the law of the Cærites were imposed on Anagnia, Frusino, and other towns guilty of desertion. The cities which had remained faithful preserved their independence and the title of allies (448);[199] the Æqui lost a part of their territory and received the right of city without suffrage (450). The Samnites, sufficiently humiliated, obtained at last the renewal of their ancient conventions (450). [200] Fœdera non æqua were concluded with the Marsi, the Peligni, the Marrucini, the Frentani (450), the Vestini (452), and the Picentini (455).[201] Rome treated with Tarentum on a footing of equality, and engaged not to let her fleet pass the Lacinian Promontory to the south of the Gulf of Tarentum. [202]

Thus, on the one hand, the territories shared among the Roman citizens; on the other, the number of the municipia were considerably augmented. Further, the Republic had acquired new allies; she possessed at length the passages of the Apennines and commanded both seas.[203] A girdle of Latin fortresses protected Rome and broke the communications between the north and south of Italy; among the Marsi and the Æqui, there were Alba and Carseoli; Sora, towards the sources of the Liris; and Narnia, in Umbria. Military roads connected the colonies with the metropolis.

Fourth Samnite War. Second coalition of the Samnites, Etruscans, Umbrians, and Gauls (456-464).

VII. Peace could not last long: between Rome and the Samnites it was a duel to death. In 456, these latter had already sufficiently recovered from their disasters to attempt once more the fortune of arms.[204] Rome sends to the succour of the Lucanians, suddenly attacked, two consular armies. Vanquished at Tifernum by Fabius, at Maleventum by Decius, the Samnites witness the devastation of their whole country. Still they do not lose courage; their chief, Gellius Egnatius, conceives a plan which places Rome in great danger. He divides the Samnite army into three bodies: the first remains to defend the country; the second takes the offensive in Campania; the third, which he commands in person, throws itself into Etruria, and, increased by the junction of the Etruscans, the Gauls, and the Umbrians, soon forms a numerous army.[205] The storm roared on all sides, and, while the Roman generals were occupied some in Samnium and others in Campania, despatches arrived from Appius, placed at the head of the army of Etruria, announcing a terrible coalition formed in silence by the peoples of the north, who were concentrating all their forces in Umbria for the purpose of marching upon Rome.

The terror was extreme, but the energy of the Romans was equal to the danger. All able men, even to the freedmen, were enrolled, and ninety thousand soldiers were raised. Under these grave circumstances (458), Fabius and Decius were, once again, raised to the supreme magistracy, and gained, under the walls of Sentinum, a brilliant victory, long disputed. During the battle, Decius devoted himself, as his father had done before.

The coalition once dissolved, Fabius defeated another army which had issued from Perusia, and then came to receive the honour of a triumph in Rome. Etruria was subdued (460), and obtained a truce of forty years.[206]

The Samnites still maintained an obstinate struggle of mingled successes and reverses. In 461, after having taken an oath to conquer or die, thirty thousand of them were left on the field of battle of Aquilonia. A few months later, the celebrated Pontius, the hero of Furcæ Caudinæ, reappeared, at the end of twenty-nine years, at the head of his fellow-citizens, and inflicted upon the son of Fabius a check, which the latter soon retrieved with the assistance of his father.[207] Finally, in 464, two Roman armies recommenced, in Samnium, a war of extermination, which led for the fourth time to the renewal of the ancient treaties and the cession of a certain extent of territory. At the same epoch, an insurrection which broke out in the Sabine territory was put down by Curius Dentatus. Central Italy was conquered.

The peace with the Samnites lasted five years (464-469). Rome extended her frontiers, and fortified those of the peoples placed under her protectorate; and at the same time established new military forts.

The right of city without suffrage was accorded to the Sabines, and prefects were given to some of the towns of the valley of the Vulturnus (Venafrum and Allifæ).[208] A Latin colony, of twenty thousand men, was sent to Venusia to watch over Southern Italy.[209] It commanded at the same time Samnium, Apulia, and Lucania. If, owing to the treaty concluded with the Greek towns, the Roman supremacy extended over the south of the peninsula, to the north the Etruscans could not be reckoned as allies, since nothing more than truces had been concluded with them. In Umbria, the small tribe of the Sarsinates remained independent, and all the coast district from the Rubicon to the Æsis was in the power of the Senones; on their southern frontier the Roman colony of Sena Gallica (Sinigaglia) was founded; the coast of Picenum was watched by that of Castrum Novum and by the Latin fortress of Hatria (465).[210]

Third coalition of the Etruscans, Gauls, Lucanians, and Tarentines (469-474).

VIII. The power of Rome had increased considerably. The Samnites, who hitherto had played the first part, were no longer in a condition to plan further coalitions, and one people alone could hardly be rash enough to provoke the Republic. Yet the Lucanians, always hesitating, gave this time the signal for a general revolt.

The attack on Thurium, by the Lucanians and Bruttians, became the occasion of a new league, into which entered successively the Tarentines, the Samnites, the Etruscans, and even the Gauls. The north was soon in flames, and Etruria again became the battle-field. A Roman army, which had hastened to relieve Arretium, was put to rout by the Etruscans united with Gaulish mercenaries. The Senones, to whom these belonged, having massacred the Roman ambassadors sent to expostulate on their violation of the treaty with the Republic, the Senate sent against them two legions who drove them back beyond the Rubicon. The Gaulish tribe of the Boians, alarmed by the fate of the Senones, descended immediately into Umbria, and, rallying the Etruscans, prepared to march to renew the sack of Rome; but their march was arrested, and two successive victories, at Lake Vadimo, (471) and Populonia (472), enabled the Senate to conclude a convention which drove back the Boians into their old territory. Hostilities continued with the Etruscans during two years, after which their submission completed the conquest of Northern Italy.

Pyrrhus in Italy. Submission of Tarentum (474-488).

IX. Free to the north, the Romans turned their efforts against the south of Italy; war was declared against Tarentum, the people of which had attacked a Roman flotilla. While the consul Æmilius invested the town, the first troops of Pyrrhus, called in by the Tarentines, disembarked in the port (474).

This epoch marks a new phase in the destinies of Rome, who is going, for the first time, to measure herself with Greece. Hitherto the legions have never had to combat really regular armies, but they have become disciplined in war by incessant struggles in the mountains of Samnium and Etruria; henceforth they will have to face old soldiers disciplined in skilful tactics and commanded by an experienced warrior. The King of Epirus, after having already twice lost and recovered his kingdom, and invaded and abandoned Macedonia, dreamt of conquering the West. On the news of his arrival at the head of twenty-five thousand soldiers and twenty elephants,[211] the Romans enrolled all citizens capable of bearing arms, even the proletaries; but, admirable example of courage! they rejected the support of the Carthaginian fleet with this proud declaration: "The Republic only entertains wars which it can sustain with its own forces."[212] While fifty thousand men, under the orders of the consul Lævinus, march against the King of Epirus, to prevent his junction with the Samnites, another army enters Lucania. The consul Tiberius Coruncanius holds Etruria, again in agitation. Lastly, an army of reserve guards the capital.

Lævinus encountered the King of Epirus near Heraclea, a colony of Tarentum (474). Seven times in succession the legions charged the phalanx, which was on the point of giving way, when the elephants, animals unknown to the Romans, decided the victory in favour of the enemy. A single battle had delivered to Pyrrhus all the south of the Peninsula, where the Greek towns received him with enthusiasm.

But, though victor, he had sustained considerable losses, and learned at the same time the effeminacy of the Greeks of Italy, and the energy of a people of soldiers. He offered peace, and asked of the Senate liberty for the Samnites, the Lucanians, and especially for the Greek towns. Old Appius Claudius declared it impossible so long as Pyrrhus occupied Italian soil, and peace was refused. The king then resolved to march upon Rome through Campania, where his troops made great booty.

Lævinus, made prudent by his defeat, satisfied himself with watching the enemy's army, and succeeded in covering Capua; whence he followed Pyrrhus from place to place, looking out for a favourable opportunity. This prince, advancing by the Latin Way, had reached Præneste without obstacle,[213] when, surrounded by three Roman armies, he found himself under the necessity of falling back and retiring into Lucania. Next year, reckoning on finding new auxiliaries among the peoples of the east, he attacked Apulia; but the fidelity of the allies in Central Italy was not shaken. Victorious at Asculum (Ascoli di Satriano) (475), but without a decisive success, and encountering always the same resistance, he seized the first opportunity of quitting Italy to conquer Sicily (476-78). During this time, the Senate re-established the Roman domination in Southern Italy, and even seized upon some of the Greek towns, among the rest Locri and Heraclea. [214] Samnium, Lucania, and Bruttium were again given up to the power of the legions, and forced to surrender lands and renew treaties of alliance; on the coast, Tarentum and Rhegium alone remained independent. The Samnites still resisted, and the Roman army encamped in their country in 478 and 479. Meanwhile Pyrrhus returns to Italy, reckoning on arriving in time to deliver Samnium; but he is defeated at Beneventum by Curius Dentatus, and returns to his country. The invasion of Pyrrhus, cousin of Alexander the Great; and one of his successors, appears as one of the last efforts of Grecian civilisation expiring at the feet of the rising grandeur of Roman civilisation.

The war against the King of Epirus produced two remarkable results: it improved the Romans in military tactics, and introduced between the combatants those mutual regards of civilised nations which teach men to honour their adversaries, to spare the vanquished, and to lay aside wrath when the struggle is ended. The King of Epirus treated his Roman prisoners with great generosity. Cineas, sent to the Senate at Rome, and Fabricius, envoy to Pyrrhus, carried back from their mission a profound respect for those whom they had combated.

In the following years Rome took Tarentum (482),[215] finally pacified Samnium, and took possession of Rhegium (483-485). Since the battle of Mount Gaurus, seventy-two years had passed, and several generations had succeeded each other, without seeing the end of this long and sanguinary quarrel. The Samnites had been nearly exterminated, and yet the spirit of independence and liberty remained deeply rooted in their mountains. When, at the end of two centuries and a half, the war of the allies shall come, it is there still that the cause of equality of rights will find its strongest support.

The other peoples underwent quickly the laws of the conqueror. The inhabitants of Picenum, as a punishment for their revolt, were despoiled of a part of their territory, and a certain number among them received new lands in the south of Campania, near the Gulf of Salernum (Picentini)(486). In 487, the submission of the Salentines allowed the Romans to seize Brundusium, the most important port of the Adriatic.[216] The Sarsinates were reduced the years following.[217] Finally, Volsinium, a town of Etruria, was again numbered among the allies of the Republic. The Sabines received the right of suffrage. Italy, become henceforth Roman, extended from the Rubicon to the Straits of Messina.

Preponderance of Rome.

X. During this period, the conquest of the subjugated countries was ensured by the foundation of colonies. Rome became thus encircled by a girdle of fortresses commanding all the passages which led to Latium, and closing the roads to Campania, Samnium, Etruria, and Gaul.[218]

At the opening of the struggle which ended in the conquest of Italy, there were only twenty-seven tribes of Roman citizens; the creation of eight new tribes (the two last in 513) raised finally the number to thirty-five, of which twenty-one were reserved to the old Roman people and fourteen to the new citizens. Of these the Etruscans had four; the Latins, the Volsci, the Ausones, the Æqui, and the Sabines, each two; but, these tribes being at a considerable distance from the capital, the new citizens could hardly take part in the comitia, and the majority, with its influence, remained with those who dwelt at Rome.[219] After 513, no more tribes were created; those who received the rights of citizens were only placed in the previously existing tribes; so that the members of one individual tribe were scattered in the provinces, and the number of those inscribed went on increasing continually by individual additions, and by the tendency more and more apparent to raise the municipia of the second order to the rank of the first order. Thus, towards the middle of the sixth century, the towns of the Æqui, the Hernici, the Volsci, and a part of those of Campania, including the ancient Samnite cities of Venafrum and Allifæ, obtained the right of city with suffrage.

Rome, towards the end of the fifth century, thus ruled, though in different degrees, the peoples of Italy proper. The Italian State, if we may give it that name, was composed of a reigning class, the citizens; of a class protected, or held in guardianship, the allies; and of a third class, the subjects. Allies or subjects were all obliged to furnish military contingents. The maritime Greek towns furnished sailors to the fleet. Even the cities, which preserved their independence for their interior affairs, obeyed, so far as the military administration was concerned, special functionaries appointed by the metropolis.[220] The consuls had the right of raising in the countries bordering on the theatre of war all men capable of bearing arms. The equipment and pay of the troops remained at the charge of the cities; Rome provided for their maintenance during war. The auxiliary infantry was ordinarily equal in number to that of the Romans, the cavalry double or triple.

In exchange for this military assistance, the allies had a right to a part of the conquered territory, and, in return for an annual rent, to the usufruct of the domains of the State. These domains, considerable in the peninsula,[221] formed the sole source of income which the treasury derived from the allies, free in other respects from tribute. Four questors (quæstores classici) were established to watch over the execution of the orders of the Senate, the equipment of the fleet, and the collection of the farm-rents.

Rome reserved to herself exclusively the direction of the affairs of the exterior, and presided alone over the destinies of the Republic. The allies never interfered in the decisions of the Forum, and each town kept within the narrow limits of its communal administration. The Italian nationality was thus gradually constituted by means of this political centralisation, without which the different peoples would have mutually weakened each other by intestine wars, more ruinous than foreign wars, and Italy would not have been in a condition to resist the double pressure of the Gauls and the Carthaginians.

The form adopted by Rome to rule Italy was the best possible, but only as a transition form. The object to be aimed at was, in fact, the complete assimilation of all the inhabitants of the peninsula, and this was evidently the aim of the wise policy of the Camilli and the Fabii. When we consider that the colonies of citizens presented the faithful image of Rome; that the Latin colonies had analogous institutions and laws; and that a great number of Roman citizens and Latin allies were dispersed, in the different countries of the peninsula, over the vast territories ceded as the consequence of war, we may judge how rapid must have been the diffusion of Roman manners and the Latin language.

If Rome, in later times, had not the wisdom to seize the favourable moment in which assimilation, already effected in people's minds, might have passed into the domain of facts, the reason of it was the abandonment of the principles of equity which had guided the Senate in the first ages of the Republic, and, above all, the corruption of the magnates, interested in maintaining the inferior condition of the allies. The right of city extended to all the peoples of Italy, time enough to be useful, would have given to the Republic a new force; but an obstinate refusal became the cause of the revolution commenced by the Gracchi, continued by Marius, extinguished for a moment by Sylla, and completed by Cæsar.

Strength of the Institutions.

XI. At the epoch with which we are occupied, the Republic is in all its splendour.

The institutions form remarkable men; the annual elections carry into power those who are most worthy, and recall them to it after a short interval. The sphere of action for the military chiefs does not extend beyond the natural frontiers of the peninsula, and their ambition, restrained in their duty by public opinion, does not exceed a legitimate object, the union of all Italy under one dominion. The members of the aristocracy seem to inherit the exploits as well as the virtues of their ancestors, and neither poverty nor obscurity of birth prevent merit from reaching it. Curius Dentatus, Fabricius, and Coruncanius, can show neither riches nor the images of their ancestors, and yet they attain to the highest dignities; in fact, the plebeian nobility walks on a footing of equality with the patrician. Both, in separating from the multitude, tend more and more to amalgamate together;[222] but they remain rivals in patriotism and disinterestedness.

In spite of the taste for riches introduced by the war of the Sabines,[223] the magistrates maintained their simplicity of manners, and protected the public domain against the encroachments of the rich by the rigorous execution of the law, which limited to five hundred acres the property which an individual was allowed to possess.[224]

The first citizens presented the most remarkable examples of integrity and self-denial. Marcus Valerius Corvus, after occupying twenty-one curule offices, returns to his fields without fortune, though not without glory (419). Fabius Rullianus, in the midst of his victories and triumphs, forgets his resentment towards Papirius Cursor, and names him dictator, sacrificing thus his private feelings to the interests of his country (429). Marcus Curius Dentatus keeps for himself no part of the rich spoils taken from the Sabines, and, after having vanquished Pyrrhus, resumes the simplicity of country life (479).[225] Fabricius rejects the money which the Samnites offer him for his generous behaviour towards them, and disdains the presents of Pyrrhus (476). Coruncanius furnishes an example of all the virtues.[226] Fabius Gurges, Fabius Pictor, and Ogulnius, pour into the treasury the magnificent gifts they had brought back from their embassy to Alexandria. [227] M. Rutilius Censorinus, struck with the danger of entrusting twice in succession the censorship in the same hands, refuses to be re-elected to that office (488).

The names of many others might be cited, who, then and in later ages, did honour to the Roman Republic; but let us add, that if the ruling class knew how to call to it all the men of eminence, it forgot not to recompense brilliantly those especially who favoured its interests: Fabius Rullianus, for instance, the victor in so many battles, received the name of "most great" (Maximus) only for having, at the time of his censorship, annulled in the comitia the influence of the poor class, composed of freedmen, whom he distributed among the urban tribes (454), where their votes were lost in the multitude of others.[228]

The popular party, on its own side, ceased not to demand new concessions, or to claim the revival of those which had fallen out of use. Thus, it obtained, in 428, the re-establishment of the law of Servius Tullius, which decided that the goods only of the debtor, and not his body, should be responsible for his debt.[229] In 450, Flavius, the son of a freedman, made public the calendar and the formulæ of proceedings, which deprived the patricians of the exclusive knowledge of civil and religious law.[230] But the lawyers found means of weakening the effects of the measure of Flavius by inventing new formulæ, which were almost unintelligible to the public. [231] The plebeians, in 454, were admitted into the college of the pontiffs, and into that of the augurs; the same year, it was found necessary to renew for the third time the law Valeria, de provocatione.

In 468, the people again withdrew to the Janiculum, demanding the remission of debts, and crying out against usury.[232] Concord was restored only when they had obtained, first, by the law Hortensia, that the plebiscita should be obligatory on all; and next, by the law Marcia, that the orders obtained through Publilius Philo in 415 should be restored to vigour. These orders, as we have seen above, obliged the Senate to declare in advance whether or not the laws presented to the comitia were contrary to public and religious law.[233]

The ambition of Rome seemed to be without bounds; yet all her wars had for reason or pretext the defence of the weak and the protection of her allies. Indeed, the cause of the wars against the Samnites was sometimes the defence of the inhabitants of Capua, sometimes that of the inhabitants of

Palæopolis, sometimes that of the Lucanians. The war against Pyrrhus had its origin in the assistance claimed by the inhabitants of Thurium; and the support claimed by the Mamertines will soon lead to the first Punic war.

The Senate, we have seen, put in practice the principles which found empires and the virtues to which war gives birth. Thus, for all the citizens, equality of rights; in face of danger to their country, equality of duties and even suspension of liberty. To the most worthy, honours and the command. No magisterial charge for him who has not served in the ranks of the army. The example is furnished by the most illustrious and richest families: at the battle of Lake Regillus (258), the principal senators were mingled in the ranks of the legions;[234] at the combat near the Cremera, the three hundred and six Fabii, who all, according to Titus Livius, were capable of filling the highest offices, perished fighting. Later, at Cannæ, eighty senators, who had enrolled themselves as mere soldiers, fell on the field of battle.[235] The triumph is accorded for victories which enlarged the territory, but not for those which only recovered lost ground. No triumph in civil wars:[236] in such case, success, be what it may, is always a subject for public mourning. The consuls or proconsuls seek to be useful to their country without false susceptibility; to-day in the first rank, to-morrow in the second, they serve with the same devotion under the orders of him whom they commanded the previous day. Servilius, consul in 281, becomes, the year following, the lieutenant of Valerius. Fabius, after so many triumphs, consents to be only lieutenant to his son. At a later period, Flamininus, who had vanquished the King of Macedonia, descends again through patriotism, after the victory of Cynoscephalæ, to the grade of tribune of the soldiers;[237] the great Scipio himself, after the defeat of Hannibal, serves as lieutenant under his brother in the war against Antiochus.

To sacrifice everything to patriotism is the first duty. By devoting themselves to the gods of Hades, like Curtius and the two Decii, people believed they bought, at the price of their lives, the safety of the others or victory.[238] Discipline is enforced even to cruelty: Manlius Torquatus, after the example of Postumius Tubertus, punishes with death the disobedience of his son, though he had gained a victory. The soldiers who have fled are decimated; those who abandon their ranks or the field of battle are devoted, some to execution, others to dishonour; and those who have allowed themselves to be made prisoners by the enemy are disdained as unworthy of the price of freedom.[239]

Surrounded by warlike neighbours, Rome must either triumph or cease to exist; hence her superiority in the art of war, for, as Montesquieu says, in transient wars most of the examples are lost; peace brings other ideas, and its faults and even its virtues are forgotten; hence that contempt of treason and that disdain for the advantages it promises: Camillus sends home to their parents the children of the first families of Falerii, delivered up to him by their schoolmaster; the Senate rejects with indignation the offer of the physician of Pyrrhus, who proposes to poison that prince;—hence that religious observance of oaths and that respect for engagements which have been contracted: the Roman prisoners to whom Pyrrhus had given permission to repair to Rome for the festival of Saturn, all return to him faithful to their word; and Regulus leaves the most memorable example of faithfulness to his oath!—hence that skilful and inflexible policy which refuses peace after a defeat, or a treaty with the enemy so long as he is on the soil of their country; which makes use of war to divert people from domestic troubles;[240] gains the vanquished by benefits if they submit, and admits them by degrees into the great Roman family; and, if they resist, strikes them without pity and reduces them to slavery;[241]—hence that anxious provision for multiplying upon the conquered territories the race of agriculturists and soldiers;—hence, lastly, the improving spectacle of a town which becomes a people, and of a people which embraces the world.

# CHAPTER IV
# PROSPERITY OF THE BASIN OF THE
# MEDITERRANEAN BEFORE THE PUNIC WARS

Commerce of the Mediterranean.

I. ROME had required two hundred and forty-four years to form her constitution under the kings, a hundred and seventy-two to establish and consolidate the consular Republic, seventy-two to complete the conquest of Italy, and now it will cost her nearly a century and a half to obtain the domination of the world—that is, of Northern Africa, Spain, the south of Gaul, Illyria, Epirus, Greece, Macedonia, Asia Minor, Syria, and Egypt. Before undertaking the recital of these conquests, let us halt an instant to consider the condition of the basin of the Mediterranean at this period, of that sea round which were successively unfolded all the great dramas of ancient history. In this examination we shall see, not without a feeling of regret, vast countries where formerly produce, monuments, riches, numerous armies and fleets—all, indeed, revealed an advanced state of civilisation—now deserts or in a state of barbarism.

The Mediterranean had seen grow and prosper in turn on its coasts Sidon, and Tyre, and then Greece.

III

Sidon, already a flourishing city before the time of Homer, is soon eclipsed by the supremacy of Tyre; then Greece comes to carry on, in competition with her, the commerce of the interior sea; an age of pacific greatness and fruitful rivalries. To the Phœnicians chiefly, the South, the East, Africa, Asia beyond Mount Taurus, the Erythrean Sea (the Red Sea and the Persian Gulf), the ocean, and the distant voyages. To the Greeks, all the northern coasts, which they covered with their thousand settlements. Phœnicia devotes herself to adventurous enterprises and lucrative speculations. Greece, artistic before becoming a trader, propagates by her colonies her mind and her ideas.

This fortunate emulation soon disappears before the creation of two new colonies sprung from their bosom. The splendour of Carthage replaces that of Tyre. Alexandria is substituted for Greece. Thus a Western or Spanish Phœnicia shares the commerce of the world with an Eastern and Egyptian Greece, the fruit of the intellectual conquests of Alexander.

Northern Africa.

II. Rich in the spoils of twenty different peoples, Carthage was the proud capital of a vast empire. Its ports, hollowed out by the hand of man, were capable of containing a great number of ships.[242] Her citadel, Byrsa, was two miles in circuit. On the land side the town was defended by a triple enclosure twenty-five stadia in length, thirty cubits high, and supported by towers of four storeys, capable of giving shelter to 4,000 horse, 300 elephants, and 20,000 foot soldiers;[243] it enclosed an immense population, since, in the last years of its resistance, after a struggle of a century, it still counted 700,000 inhabitants.[244] Its monuments were worthy of its greatness: among its remarkable buildings was the temple of the god Aschmoun, assimilated by the Greeks to Æsculapius;[245] that of the sun, covered with plates of gold valued at a thousand talents;[246] and the mantle or peplum, destined for the image of their great goddess, which cost a hundred and twenty.[247] The empire of Carthage extended from the frontiers of Cyrenaica (the country of Barca, in the regency of Tripoli) into Spain; she was the metropolis of all the north of Africa, and, in Libya alone, possessed three hundred towns.[248] Nearly all the isles of the Mediterranean, to the west and south of Italy, had received her factories. Carthage had imposed her sovereignty upon all the ancient Phœnician establishments in this part of the world, and had levied upon them an annual contingent of soldiers and tribute. In the interior of Africa, she sent caravans to seek elephants, ivory, gold, and black slaves, which she afterwards exported[249] to the trading places on the Mediterranean. In Sicily, she gathered oil and wine; in the isle of Elba, she mined for iron; from Malta, she drew valuable tissues; from Corsica, wax and honey; from Sardinia, corn, metals, and slaves; from the Baleares, mules and fruits; from Spain, gold, silver, and lead; from Mauritania, the hides of animals; she sent as far as the extremity of Britain, to the Cassiterides (the Scilly Islands), ships to purchase tin.[250] Within her walls industry flourished greatly, and tissues of great celebrity were fabricated.[251]

No market of the ancient world could be compared with that of Carthage, to which men of all nations crowded. Greeks, Gauls, Ligurians, Spaniards, Libyans, came in multitudes to serve under her standard;[252] the Numidians lent her a redoubtable cavalry.[253] Her fleet was formidable; it amounted at this epoch to five hundred vessels. Carthage possessed a considerable arsenal;[254] we may appreciate its importance from the fact, that, after her conquest by Scipio, she delivered to him two hundred thousand suits of armour, and three thousand machines of war.[255] So many troops and stores imply immense revenues. Even after the battle of Zama, Polybius could still call her the richest town in the world. Yet she had already paid heavy contributions to the Romans.[256] An excellent system of agriculture contributed no less than her commerce to her prosperity. A great number of agricultural colonies[257] had been established, which, in the time of Agathocles, amounted to more than two hundred. They were ruined by the war (440 of Rome).[258] Byzacena (the southern part of the regency of Tunis) was the granary of Carthage.[259]

This province, surnamed Emporia, as being the trading country par excellence, vaunted by the geographer Scylax[260] as the most magnificent and fertile part of Libya. It had, in the time of Strabo, numerous towns, so many magazines of the merchandise of the interior of Africa. Polybius[261] speaks of its horses, oxen, sheep, and goats, as forming innumerable herds, such as he had never seen elsewhere. The small town of Leptis alone paid to the Carthaginians the enormous contribution of a talent a day (5,821 francs [£232 16s.]).[262]

This fertility of Africa explains the importance of the towns on the coast of the Syrtes, an importance, it is true, revealed by later testimonies, because they date from the decline of Carthage, but which must apply still more forcibly to the flourishing condition which preceded it. In 537, the vast port of the isle Cercina (Kirkeni, in the regency of Tunis, opposite Sfax) had paid ten talents to Servilius.[263] More to the west, Hippo Regius (Bona) was still a considerable maritime town in the time of Jugurtha.[264] Tingis (Tangiers), in Mauritania, which boasted of a very ancient origin, carried on a great trade with Bætica. Three African peoples in these countries lay under the influence and often the sovereignty of Carthage: the Massylian Numidians, who afterwards had Cirta (Constantine) for their capital; the

Massæsylian Numidians, who occupied the provinces of Algiers and Oran; and the Mauri, or Moors, spread over Morocco. These nomadic peoples maintained rich droves of cattle, and grew great quantities of corn.

Hanno, a Carthaginian sea-captain, sent, towards 245, to explore the extreme parts of the African coast beyond the Straits of Gades, had founded a great number of settlements, no traces of which remained in the time of Pliny.[265] These colonies introduced commerce among the Mauritanian and Numidian tribes, the peoples of Morocco, and perhaps even those of Senegal. But it was not only in Africa that the possessions of the Carthaginians extended; they embraced Spain, Sicily, and Sardinia.

Spain.

III. Iberia or Spain, with its six great rivers, navigable to the ancients, its long chains of mountains, its dense woods, and the fertile valleys of Bætica (*Andalusia*), appears to have nourished a population numerous, warlike, rich by its mines, its harvests, and its commerce. The centre of the peninsula was occupied by the Iberian and Celtiberian races; on the coasts, the Carthaginians and the Greeks had settlements; through contact with the Phœnician merchants, the populations of the coast districts attained a certain degree of civilisation, and from the mixture of the natives with the foreign colonists sprang a mongrel population, which, while it preserved the Iberic character, had adopted the mercantile habits of the Phœnicians and Carthaginians.

Once established in Spain, the Carthaginians and Greeks turned to useful purpose the timber which covered the mountains. Gades (Cadiz), a sort of factory founded at the extremity of Bætica by the Carthaginians, became one of their principal maritime arsenals. It was there that the ships were fitted out which ventured on the ocean in search of the products of Armorica, or Britain, and even of the Canaries. Although Gades had lost some of its importance by the foundation of Carthagena (New Carthage), in 526, it had still, in the time of Strabo, so numerous a population that it was in this respect inferior only to Rome. The tables of the census showed five hundred citizens of the equestrian order, a number equalled by none of the Italian cities, except Patavium (Padua).[266] To Gades, celebrated for its temple of Hercules, flowed the riches of all Spain. The sheep and horses of Bætica rivalled in renown those of the Asturias. Corduba (Cordova), Hispalis (Seville), where, at a later period, the Romans founded colonies, were already great places of commerce, and had ports for the vessels which ascended the Bætis (Guadalquivir).[267]

Spain was rich in precious metals; gold, silver, iron, were there the object of industrial activity.[268] At Osca (Huesca), they worked mines of silver; at Sisapo (Almaden), silver and mercury.[269] At Cotinæ, copper was found along with gold. Among the Oretani, at Castulo (Cazlona, on the Guadalimar), the silver mines, in the time of Polybius, gave employment to 40,000 persons, and produced daily 25,000 drachmas.[270] In thirty-two years, the Roman generals carried home from the peninsula considerable sums.[271] The abundance of metals in Spain explains how so great a number of vessels of gold and silver was found among many of the chiefs or petty kings of the Iberian nations. Polybius compares one of them, for his luxury, with the king of the fabulous Phæaces.[272]

To the north, and in the centre of the peninsula, agriculture and the breeding of cattle were the principal sources of wealth. It was there that were made the says (vests of flannel or goats' hair), which were exported in great numbers to Italy.[273] In the Tarraconese, the cultivation of flax was very productive; the inhabitants had been the first to weave those fine cloths called carbasa, which were objects greatly prized as far as Greece. [274] Leather, honey, and salt were brought by cargoes to the principal ports along the coast; at Emporiæ (Ampurias), a settlement of the Phocæans in Catalonia; at Saguntum,[275] founded by Greeks from the island of Zacynthus; at Tarraco (Tarragona), one of the most ancient of the Phœnician settlements in Spain; and at Malaca (Malaga), whence were exported all sorts of salt fish.[276] Lusitania, neglected by the Phœnician or Carthaginian ships, was less favoured. Yet we see, by the passage of Polybius[277] which enumerates the mercantile exports of this province with their prices, that its agricultural products were very abundant.[278]

The prosperity of Spain appears also from the vast amount of its population. According to some authors, Tiberius Gracchus took from the Celtiberians three hundred oppida. In Turdetania (part of Andalusia), according to Strabo, there were counted no less than two hundred towns. [279] Appian, the historian of the Spanish wars, points out the multitude of petty tribes which the Romans had to reduce,[280] and during the campaign of Cn. Scipio, more than a hundred and twenty submitted.[281]

Thus the Iberian peninsula was at that time reckoned among the most populous and richest regions of Europe.

Southern Gaul.

IV. The part of Gaul which is bathed by the Mediterranean offers a spectacle no less satisfactory. Numerous migrations, arriving from the East, had pushed back the population of the Seine and the Loire towards the mouths of the Rhône, and already, in the middle of the fourth century before our era, the Gauls found themselves straitened in their frontiers. More civilised than the Iberians, but not less energetic, they combined gentle and hospitable manners with great activity, which was further developed by their contact with the Greek colonies spread from the maritime Alps to the Pyrenees. The cultivation of the fields and the breeding of cattle furnished their principal wealth, and their industry found support in the products of the soil and in its herds. Their manufacture consisted of says, not less in repute than those of the Celtiberians, and exported in great quantities to Italy. Good sailors, the Gauls transported by water, on the Seine, the Rhine, the Saône, the Rhône, and Loire, the merchandise and timber which, even from the coasts of the Channel, were accumulated in the Phocæan trading places on the Mediterranean.[282] Agde (Agatha), Antibes (Antipolis), Nice (Nicæa), the isles of Hyères (Stœchades), Monaco (Portus Herculis Monœcei), were so many naval stations which maintained relations with Spain and Italy.[283]

Marseilles possessed but a very circumscribed territory, but its influence reached far into the interior of Gaul. It is to this town we owe the acclimatisation of the vine and the olive. Thousands of oxen came every year to feed on the thyme in the neighbourhood of Marseilles.[284] The Massilian merchants traversed Gaul in all directions to sell their wines and the produce of their manufactures.[285] Without rising to the rank of a great maritime power, still the small Phocæan republic possessed sufficient resources to make itself respected by Carthage; it formed an early alliance with the Romans. Massilian houses had, as early as the fifth century of Rome, established at Syracuse, as they did subsequently at Alexandria, factories which show a great commercial activity.[286]

Liguria, Cisalpine Gaul, Venetia, and Illyria.

V. Alone in the Tyrrhene Sea, the Ligures had not yet risen out of that almost savage life which the Iberians, sprung from the same stock, had originally led. If some towns on the Ligurian coast, and especially Genoa (Genua), carried on a maritime commerce, they supported themselves by piracy[287] rather than by regular traffic.[288]

On the contrary, Cisalpine Gaul, properly so called, supported, as early as the time of Polybius, a numerous population. We may form some idea of it from the losses this province sustained during a period of twenty-seven years, from 554 to 582; Livy gives a total of 257,400 men killed, taken, or transported.[289] The Gaulish tribes settled in the Cisalpine, though preserving their original manners, had, through their contact with the Etruscans, arrived at a certain degree of civilisation. The number of towns in this country was not very considerable, but it contained a great abundance of villages.[290] Addicted to agriculture like the other Gauls, the Cisalpines bred in their forests droves of swine in such numbers, that they would have been sufficient, in the time of Strabo, to provision all Rome.[291] The coins of pure gold, which in recent times have been found in Cisalpine Gaul, especially between the Po and the Adda, and which were struck by the Boii and some of the Ligurian populations, furnish evidence of the abundance of that metal, which was collected in the form of gold sand in the waters of the rivers.[292] Moreover, certain towns of Etruscan origin, such as Mantua (Mantua) and Padua (Patavium), preserved vestiges of the prosperity they had reached at the time when the peoples of Tuscany extended their dominion beyond the Po. At once a maritime town and a place of commerce, Padua, at a remote epoch, possessed a vast territory, and could raise an army of 120,000 men.[293] The transport of goods was facilitated by means of canals crossing Venetia, partly dug by the Etruscans. Such were those especially which united Ravenna with Altinum (Altino), which became at a later period the grand store-house of the Cisalpine territory.[294]

The commercial relations entertained by Venetia with Germany, Illyria, and Rhætia, go back far beyond the Roman epoch, and, at a remote antiquity, it was Venetia which received the amber from the shores of the Baltic.[295] All the traffic which was afterwards concentrated at Aquileia, founded by the Romans after the submission of the Veneti, had then for its centre the towns of Venetia; and the numerous colonies established by the Romans in this part of the peninsula are proofs of its immense resources. Moreover, the Veneti, occupied in cultivating their lands and breeding horses, had peaceful manners which facilitated commercial relations, and contrasted with the piratical habits of the populations spread over the north and north-eastern coasts of the Adriatic.

The Istrians, the Liburni, and the Illyrians were the nations most formidable, both by their corsairs and by their armies; their light and rapid barques covered the Adriatic, and troubled the navigation between Italy and Greece. In the year 524, the Illyrians sent to sea a hundred lembi,[296] while their land army counted hardly more than 5,000 men.[297] Illyria was poor, and offered few resources to the Romans, notwithstanding the fertility of its soil. Agriculture was neglected, even in the time of Strabo. Istria contained a population much more considerable, in proportion to its extent. [298] Yet she had, no more than Dalmatia and the rest of Illyria, attained, at the epoch of which we are speaking, that high degree of prosperity which she acquired afterwards by the foundation of Tergeste (Trieste) and Pola. The Roman conquest delivered the Adriatic from the pirates who infested it,[299] and then only, the ports of Dyrrhachium and Apollonia obtained a veritable importance.

Epirus.

VI. Epirus, a country of pastures and shepherds, intersected by picturesque mountains, was a sort of Helvetia. Ambracia (now Arta), which Pyrrhus had chosen for his residence, had become a very fine town, and possessed two theatres. The palace of the king (Pyrrheum) formed a veritable museum for it furnished for the triumph of M. Fulvius Nobilior, in 565, two hundred and eighty-five statues in bronze, two hundred and thirty in marble,[300] and paintings by Zeuxis, mentioned in Pliny.[301] The town paid also, on this occasion, five hundred talents (2,900,000 francs, [£116,000]), and offered the consul a crown of gold weighing a hundred and fifty thousand talents (nearly 4,000 kilogrammes).[302] It appears that before the war of Paulus Æmilius, this country contained a rather numerous population, and counted seventy towns, most of them situated in the country of the Molossi.[303]. After the battle of Pydna, the Roman general made so considerable a booty, that, without reckoning the treasury's share, each foot-soldier received 200 denarii (about 200 francs [£8]), and each horse-soldier 400; in addition to which the sale of slaves arose to the enormous number of 150,000.

Greece.

VII. At the beginning of the first Punic War, Greece proper was divided into four principal powers: Macedonia, Ætolia, Achaia, and Sparta. All the continental part, which extends northward of the Gulf of Corinth as far as the mountains of Pindus, was under the dependence of Philip; the western part belonged to the Ætolians. The Peloponnesus was shared between the Achæans, the tyrant of Sparta, and independent towns. Greece had been declining during about a century, and seen her warlike spirit weaken and her population diminish; and yet Plutarch, comprising under this name the peoples of the Hellenic race, pretends that their country furnished King Philip with the money, food, and provisions of his army.[304] The Greek navy had almost disappeared. The Achæan league, which comprised Argolis, Corinth, Sicyon, and the maritime cities of Achæa, had few ships. On land the Hellenic forces were less insignificant. The Ætolian league possessed an army of 10,000 men, and, in the war against Philip, pretended to have contributed more than the Romans to the victory of Cynoscephalæ. Greece was still rich in objects of art of all descriptions. When, in 535, the King of Macedonia captured the town of Thermæ, in Ætolia, he found in it more than two thousand statues.[305]

Athens, in spite of the loss of her maritime supremacy, preserved the remains of a civilization which had already attained the highest degree of splendour,[306] and those incomparable buildings of the age of Pericles, the mere name of which reminds us of all that the arts have produced in greatest perfection. Among the most remarkable were the Acropolis, with its Parthenon and its Propylæa, masterpieces of Phidias, the statue of Minerva in gold and ivory, and another in bronze, the casque and spear of which were seen afar off at sea.[307] The arsenal of the Piræus, built by the architect Philo, was, according to Plutarch, an admirable work.[308]

Sparta, although greatly fallen, was distinguished by its monuments and by its manufactures; the famous portico of the Persians,[309] built after the Median wars—the columns of which, in white marble, represented the illustrious persons among the vanquished—was the principal ornament of the market. Iron, obtained in abundance from Mount Taygetus, was marvellously worked at Sparta, which was celebrated for the manufacture of arms and agricultural instruments.[310] The coasts of Laconia abounded in shells, from which was obtained the purple, most valued after that of Phœnicia.[311] The port of Gytheum, very populous, and very active in 559, still possessed great arsenals.[312]

In the centre of the peninsula, Arcadia, although its population was composed of shepherds, had the same love for the arts as the rest of Greece. It possessed two celebrated temples: that of Minerva at Tegæa, built by the architect Scopas,[313] in which were united the three orders of architecture, and that of Apollo, at Phigalea,[314] situated at an elevation of 3,000 feet above the level of the sea, and the remains of which still excite the wonder of travellers.

Elis, protected by its neutrality, was devoted to the arts of peace. There agriculture flourished; its fisheries were productive; it had manufactories of tissues of byssus which rivalled the muslins of Cos, and were sold for their weight in gold.[315] The town of Elis possessed the finest gymnasium in Greece; people came to it to prepare themselves (sometimes a year in advance) for competition in the Olympic games.[316]

Olympia was the holy city, celebrated for its sanctuary and its consecrated garden, where stood, among a multitude of masterpieces of art, one of the wonders of the world, the statue of Jupiter, the work of Phidias,[317] the majesty of which was such, that Paulus Æmilius, when he first saw it, believed he was in the presence of the divinity himself.

Argos, the country of several celebrated artists, possessed temples, fountains, a gymnasium, and a theatre; and its public place had served for a field of battle to the armies of Pyrrhus and Antigonus. It remained, until the subjugation by the Romans, one of the finest cities of Greece. Within its territory were the superb temple of Juno, the ancient sanctuary of the Argives, with the statue of the goddess in gold and silver—the work of Polycletus, and the vale of Nemæa, where one of the four national festivals of Greece was celebrated.[318] Argolis also possessed Epidaurus, with its hot springs; its temple of Æsculapius, enriched with the offerings of those who came to be cured of their diseases;[319] and its theatre, one of the largest in the country.[320]

Corinth, admirably situated upon the narrow isthmus which separates the Ægean Sea from the gulf which has preserved its name,[321] with its dye-houses, its celebrated manufactories of carpets and of bronze, bore witness also to the ancient prosperity of the Hellenic race. Its population must have been considerable, since there were reckoned in it 460,000 slaves;[322] marble palaces rose on all sides, adorned with statues and valuable vases. Corinth had the reputation of being the most voluptuous of towns. Among its numerous temples, that of Venus had in its service more than a thousand courtezans.[323] In the sale of the booty made by Mummius, a painting by Aristides, representing Bacchus, was sold for 600,000 sestertii.[324] There was seen in the triumph of Metellus surnamed Macedonicus, a group, the work of Lysippus, representing Alexander the Great, twenty-five horsemen, and nine foot-soldiers slain at the battle of the Granicus; this group, taken at Corinth, came from Dium in Macedonia.[325]

Other towns of Greece were no less rich in works of art.[326] The Romans carried away from the little town of Eretria, at the time of the Macedonian war, a great number of paintings and precious statues.[327] We know, from the traveller Pausanias, how prodigious was the quantity of offerings brought from the most diverse countries into the sanctuary of Delphi. This town, which, by its reputation for sanctity and its solemn games, the Pythian, was the rival of Olympia, gathered in its temple during ages immense treasures; and when it was plundered by the Phocæans, they found in it gold and silver enough to coin ten thousand talents of money (about 58 millions of francs [£2,320,000]). The ancient opulence of the Greeks had, nevertheless, passed into their colonies; and, from the extremity of the Black Sea to Cyrene, numerous establishments arose remarkable for their sumptuousness.

Macedonia.

VIII. Macedonia drew to herself, since the time of Alexander, the riches and resources of Asia. Dominant over a great part of Greece and Thrace, occupying Thessaly, and extending her sovereignty over Epirus, this kingdom concentrated in herself the vital strength of those cities formerly˙ independent, which, two centuries before, were her rivals in power and courage. Under an economical administration, the public revenues rising from the royal domains,[328] from the silver mines in Mount Pangeum, and from the taxes, were sufficient for the wants of the country.[329] In 527, Antigonus sent to Rhodes considerable succours, which furnish the measure of the resources of Macedonia.[330]

Towards the year 563 of Rome, Philip had, by wise measures, raised again the importance of Macedonia. He collected in his arsenals materials for equipping three armies and provisions for ten years. Under Perseus, Macedonia was no less flourishing. That prince gave Cotys, for a service of six months with 1,000 cavalry, the large sum of 200 talents.[331] At the battle of Pydna, which completed his ruin, nearly 20,000 men remained on the field, and 11,000 were made prisoners.[332] In richness of equipment, the Macedonian troops far surpassed other armies. The Leucaspidan phalanx was dressed in scarlet, and carried gilt armour; the Chalcaspidan phalanx had shields of the finest brass.[333] The prodigious splendour of the court of Perseus and that of his favourites reveal still more the degree of opulence at which Macedonia had arrived. All exhibited in their dresses and in their feasts a pomp equal to that of kings.[334] Among the booty made by Paulus Æmilius were paintings, statues, rich tapestries, vases of gold, silver, bronze, and ivory, which were so many masterpieces.[335] His triumph was unequalled by any other.[336]

Valerius of Antium estimates at more than 120 millions of sestertii (about 30 millions of francs [£1,200,000]) the gold and silver exhibited on this occasion.[337] Macedonia, as we see, had absorbed the ancient riches of Greece. Thrace, long barbarous, began also to rise out of the condition of inferiority in which it had so long languished. Numerous Greek colonies, founded on the shores of the Pontus Euxinus, introduced there civilisation and prosperity; and among these colonies, Byzantium, though often harassed by the neighbouring barbarians, had already an importance and prosperity which presaged its future destinies.[338] Foreigners, resorting to it from all parts, had introduced a degree of licentiousness which became proverbial. [339] Its commerce was, above all, nourished by the ships of Athens, which went there to fetch the wheat of Tauris and the fish of the Euxine.[340] When Athens, in her decline, became a prey to anarchy, Byzantium, where arts and letters flourished, served as a refuge to her exiles.

Asia Minor.

IX. Asia Minor comprised a great number of provinces, of which several became, after the dismemberment of the empire of Alexander, independent states. Of these, the principal formed into four groups, composing so many kingdoms, namely, Pontus, Bithynia, Cappadocia, and Pergamus. We must except from them some Greek cities on the coast, which kept their autonomy or were placed under the sovereignty of Rhodes. Their extent and limits varied often until the time of the Roman conquest, and several of them passed from one domination to another. All these kingdoms participated in different degrees in the prosperity of Macedonia.

"Asia," says Cicero, "is so rich and fertile, that the fecundity of its plains, the variety of its products, the extent of its pastures, the multiplicity of the objects of commerce exported from it, give it an incontestible superiority over all other countries of the earth.[341]"

The wealth of Asia Minor appears from the amount of impositions paid by it to the different Roman generals. Without speaking of the spoils carried away by Scipio, in his campaign against Antiochus, and by Manlius Volso in 565, Sylla, and afterwards Lucullus and Pompey, each drew from this country about 20,000 talents,[342] besides an equal sum distributed by them to their soldiers: which gives the enormous total of nearly seven hundred millions of francs [or twenty-eight millions sterling], received in a period of twenty-five years.

Kingdom of Pontus.

X. The most northern of the four groups named above formed a great part of the kingdom of Pontus. This province, the ancient Cappadocia Pontica, formerly a Persian satrapy, reduced to subjection by Alexander and his successor, recovered itself after the battle of Ipsus (453). Mithridates III. enlarged his territory by adding to it Paphlagonia, and afterwards Sinope and Galatia. Pontus soon extended from Colchis on the north-east to Lesser Armenia on the south-east, and had Bithynia for its boundary on the west. Thus, touching upon the Caucasus, and master of the Pontus Euxinus, this kingdom, composed of divers peoples, presented, under varied climates, a variety of different productions. It received wines and oils from the Ægean Sea, and wheat from the Bosphorus; it exported salt fish in great quantity,[343] dolphin oil,[344] and, as produce of the interior, the wools of the Gadilonitis,[345] the fleeces of Ancyra, the horses of Armenia, Media, and Paphlagonia,[346] the iron of the Chalybes, a population of miners to the south of Trapezus, already celebrated in the time of Homer, and mentioned by Xenophon.[347] There also were found mines of silver, abandoned in the time of Strabo,[348] but which have been re-opened in modern times. Important ports on the Black Sea facilitated the exportation of these products. It was at Sinope that Lucullus found a part of the treasures which he displayed at his triumph, and which gives us a lofty idea of the kingdom of Mithridates.[349] An object of admiration at Sinope was the statue of Autolycus, one of the protecting heroes of the town, the work of the statuary Sthenis.[350]

Trapezus (Trebizonde), which before the time of Mithridates the Great preserved a sort of autonomy under the kings of Pontus, had an extensive commerce; which was the case also with another Greek colony, Amisus (Samsoun),[351] regarded in the time of Lucullus as one of the most flourishing and richest towns in the country.[352] In the interior, Amasia, which became afterwards one of the great fortresses of Asia Minor, and the metropolis of Pontus, had already probably, at the time of the Punic wars, a certain renown. Cabira, called afterwards Sebaste, and then Neocæsarea, the central point of the resistance of Mithridates the Great to Lucullus, owed its ancient celebrity to its magnificent Temple of the Moon. From the country of Cabira, there was, according to the statement of Lucullus,[353] only the distance of a few days' march into Armenia, a country the riches of which may be estimated by the treasures gathered by Tigranes.[354]

We can hence understand how Mithridates the Great was able, two centuries later, to oppose the Romans with considerable armies and fleets. He possessed in the Black Sea 400 ships,[355] and his army amounted to 250,000 men and 40,000 horse.[356] He received, it is true, succours from Armenia and Scythia, from the Palus Mæotis, and even from Thrace.

Bithynia.

XI. Bithynia, a province of Asia Minor, comprised between the Propontis, the Sangarius, and Paphlagonia, formed a kingdom, which, at the beginning of the sixth century of Rome, was adjacent to Pontus, and comprised several parts of the provinces contiguous to Mysia and Phrygia. In it were found several towns, the commerce of which rivalled that of the maritime towns of Pontus, and especially Nicæa and Nicomedia. This last, founded in 475 by Nicomedes I., took a rapid extension.[357] Heraclea Pontica, a Milesian colony situated between the Sangarius and the Parthenius, preserved its extensive commerce, and an independence which Mithridates the Great himself could not entirely destroy; it possessed a vast port, safe and skilfully disposed, which sheltered a numerous fleet.[358] The power of the Bithynians was not insignificant, since they sent into the field, in the war of Nicomedes against Mithridates, 56,000 men.[359] If the traffic was considerable on the coasts of Bithynia, thanks to the Greek colonies, the interior was not less prosperous by its agriculture, and Bithynia was still, in the time of Strabo, renowned for its herds.[360]

One of the provinces of Bithynia fell into the hands of the Gauls (A.U.C. 478). Three peoples of Celtic origin shared it, and exercised in it a sort of feudal dominion. It was called Galatia from the name of the conquerors. Its places of commerce were: Ancyra, the point of arrival of the caravans coming from Asia, and Pessinus, one of the chief seats of the old Phrygian worship, where pilgrims repaired in great number to adore Cybele.[361] The population of Galatia was certainly rather considerable, since in the famous campaign of Cneius Manlius Volso,[362] in 565, the Galatians lost 40,000 men. The two tribes united of the Tectosagi and Trocmi raised at that period, in spite of many defeats, an army of 50,000 foot and 10,000 horse. [363]

Cappadocia.

XII. To the east of Galatia, Cappadocia comprised between the Halys and Armenia, distant from the sea, and crossed by numerous chains of mountains, formed a kingdom which escaped the conquests of Alexander, and which, a few years after his death, opposed Perdiccas with an army of 30,000 footmen and 15,000 horsemen.[364] In the time of Strabo, wheat and cattle formed the riches of this country.[365] In 566, King Ariarathes paid 600 talents for the alliance of the Romans.[366] Mazaca (afterwards Cæsarea), capital of Cappadocia, a town of an entirely Asiatic origin, had been, from a very early period, renowned for its pastures.[367]

Kingdom of Pergamus.

XIII. The western part of Asia Minor is better known. It had seen, after the battle of Ipsus, the formation of the kingdom of Pergamus, which, thanks to the interested liberality of the Romans towards Eumenes II., increased continually until the moment when it fell under their sovereignty. To this kingdom belonged Mysia, the two Phrygias, Lycaonia, and Lydia. This last province, crossed by the Pactolus, had for its capital Ephesus, the metropolis of the Ionian confederation, at the same time the mart of the commerce of Asia Minor and one of the localities where the fine arts were cultivated with most distinction. This town had two ports: one penetrated into the heart of the town, while the other formed a basin in the very middle of the public market.[368] The theatre of Ephesus, the largest ever built, was 660 feet in diameter, and was capable of holding 60,000 spectators. The most celebrated artists, Scopas, Praxiteles, etc., worked at Ephesus upon the great Temple of Diana. This monument, the building of which lasted two hundred and twenty years, was surrounded by 128 columns, each 60 feet high, presented by so many kings. Pergamus, the capital of the kingdom, passed for one of the finest cities in Asia, longe clarissimum Asiæ Pergamum, says Pliny;[369] the port of Elæa contained maritime arsenals, and could arm numerous vessels.[370] The acropolis of Pergamus, an inaccessible citadel, defended by two torrents, was the residence of the Attalides; these princes, zealous protectors of the sciences and arts, had founded in their capital a library of 200,000 volumes.[371] Pergamus carried on a vast traffic; its cereals were exported in great quantities to most places in Greece.[372] Cyzicus, situated on an island of the Propontis, with two closed ports forming a station for about two hundred ships,[373] rivalled the richest cities of Asia. Like Adramyttium, it carried on a great commerce in perfumery,[374] it worked the inexhaustible marble-quarries of the island of Proconnesus,[375] and its commercial relations were so extensive that its gold coins were current in all the Asiatic factories.[376] The town of Abydos possessed gold mines.[377] The wheat of Assus was reputed the best in the world, and was reserved for the table of the kings of Persia.[378]

We may estimate the population and resources of this part of Asia from the armies and fleets which the kings had at their command at the time of the conquest of Greece by the Romans. In 555, Attalus II., and, ten years later, Eumenes II., sent them numerous galleys of five ranks of oars.[379] The land forces of the kings of Pergamus were much less considerable.[380] Their direct authority did not extend over a great territory, yet they had many tributary towns; hence their great wealth and small army. The Romans drew from this country, now nearly barren and unpeopled, immense contributions both in gold and wheat.[381] The magnificence of the triumph of Manlius and the reflections of Livy, compared with the testimony of Herodotus, reveal all the splendour of the kingdom of Pergamus. It was after the war against Antiochus and the expedition of Manlius that extravagance began to display itself at Rome.[382] Soldiers and generals enriched themselves prodigiously in Asia.[383]

The ancient colonies of Ionia and Æolis, such as Clazomenæ, Colophon, and many others, which were dependent for the most part on the kingdom of Pergamus, were fallen from their ancient grandeur. Smyrna, rebuilt by Alexander, was still an object of admiration for the beauty of its monuments. The exportation of wines, as celebrated on the coast of Ionia as in the neighbouring islands, formed alone an important support of the commerce of the ports of the Ægean Sea.

The treasures of the temple of Samothrace were so considerable, that we are induced to mention here a circumstance relating to this little island, though distant from Asia, and near the coast of Thrace: Sylla's soldiers took in the sanctuary the Cabiri, an ornament of the value of 1,000 talents (5,820,000 francs [£232,800]).[384]

Caria, Lycia, and Cilicia.

XIV. On the southern coast of Asia Minor, some towns still sustained the rank they had attained one or two centuries before. The capital of Caria was Halicarnassus, a very strong town, defended by two citadels,[385] and celebrated for one of the finest works of Greek art, the Mausoleum. In spite of the extraordinary fertility of the country, the Carians were accustomed, like the people of Crete, to engage as mercenaries in the Greek armies.[386] On their territory stood the Ionian town of Miletus, with its four ports. [387] The Milesians alone had civilised the shores of the Black Sea by the foundation of about eighty colonies.[388]

In turn independent, or placed under foreign dominion, Lycia, a province comprised between Caria and Cilicia, possessed some rich commercial towns. One especially, renowned for its ancient oracle of Apollo, no less celebrated than that of Delphi, was remarkable for its spacious port;[389] this was Patara, which was large enough to contain the whole fleet of Antiochus, burnt by Fabius in 565.[390] Xanthus, the largest town of the province, to which place ships ascended, only lost its importance after having been pillaged by Brutus.[391] Its riches had at an earlier period drawn upon it the same fate from the Persians.[392] Under the Roman dominion, Lycia beheld its population decline gradually; and of the seventy towns which it had possessed, no more than thirty-six remained in the eighth century of Rome.[393]

More to the east, the coasts of Cilicia were less favoured; subjugated in turn by the Macedonians, Egyptians, and Syrians, they had become receptacles of pirates, who were encouraged by the kings of Egypt in their hostility to the Seleucidæ.[394] From the heights of the mountains which cross a part of the province, robbers descended to plunder the fertile plains situated on the eastern side (Cilicia Campestris).[395] Still, the part watered by the Cydnus and the Pyramus was more prosperous, owing to the manufacture of coarse linen and to the export of saffron. There stood ancient Tarsus, formerly the residence of a satrap, the commerce of which had sprung up along with that of Tyre;[396] and Soli, on which Alexander levied an imposition of a hundred talents as a punishment for its fidelity to the Persians,[397] and which, by its maritime position, excited the envy of the Rhodians.[398] These towns and other ports entered, after the battle of Ipsus, into the great commercial movement of which the provinces of Syria became the seat.

Syria.

XV. By the foundation of the empire of the Seleucidæ, Greek civilisation was carried into the interior of Asia, where the immobility of Eastern society was succeeded by the activity of Western life. Greek letters and arts flourished from the Sea of Phœnicia to the banks of the Euphrates. Numerous towns were built in Syria and Assyria, with all the richness and elegance of the edifices of Greece;[399] some were almost in ruins in the time of Pliny.[400] Seleucia, founded by Seleucus Nicator, at the mouth of the Orontes, and which received, with five other towns built by the same monarch, the name of the head of the Græco-Syrian dynasty, became a greatly frequented port. Antioch, built on the same river, rivalled the finest towns of Egypt and Greece by the number of its edifices, the extent of its places, and the beauty of its temples and statues.[401] Its walls, built by the architect Xenæos, passed for a wonder, and in the Middle Ages their ruins excited the admiration of travellers.[402] Antioch consisted of four quarters, having each its own enclosure;[403] and the common enclosure which surrounded them all appears to have embraced an extent of six leagues in circumference. Not far from the town was the delightful abode of Daphne, where the wood, consecrated to Apollo and Diana, was an object of public veneration, and the place where sumptuous festivals were celebrated.[404] Apamea was renowned for its pastures. Seleucus had formed there a stud of 30,000 mares, 300 stallions, and 500 elephants.[405] The Temple of the Sun at Heliopolis (now Baalbek) was the most colossal work of architecture that had ever existed.[406]

The power of the empire of the Seleucidæ went on increasing until the time when the Romans seized upon it. Extending from the Mediterranean to the Oxus and Caucasus, this empire was composed of nearly all the provinces of the ancient kingdom of the Persians, and included peoples of different origins.[407] Media was fertile, and its capital, Ecbatana, which Polybius represents as excelling in riches and the incredible luxury of its palaces the other cities of Asia, had not yet been despoiled by Antiochus III.;[408] Babylonia, once the seat of a powerful empire, and Phœnicia, long the most commercial country in the world, made part of Syria, and touched upon the frontiers of the Parthians. Caravans, following a route which has remained the same during many centuries, placed Syria in communication with Arabia,[409] whence came ebony, ivory, perfumes, resins, and spices; the Syrian ports were the intermediate marts for the merchants who proceeded as far as India, where Seleucus I. went to conclude a treaty with Sandrocottus. The merchandise of this country ascended the Euphrates as far as Thapsacus, and thence it was exported to all the provinces.[410] Communications so distant and multiplied explain the prosperity of the empire of the Seleucidæ. Babylonia competed with Phrygia in embroidered tissues; purple and the tissues of Tyre, the glass, goldsmiths' work, and dyes of Sidon, were exported far. Commerce had penetrated to the extremities of Asia. Silk stuffs were sent from the frontiers of China to Caspiæ Portæ, and thence conveyed by caravans at once towards the Tyrian Sea, Mesopotamia, and Pontus.[411] Subsequently, the invasion of the Parthians, by intercepting the routes, prevented the Greeks from penetrating into the heart of Asia. Hence Seleucus Nicator formed the project of opening a way of direct communication between Greece and Bactriana, by constructing a canal from the Black Sea to the Caspian Sea.[412] Mines of precious metals were rather rare in Syria; but there was abundance of gold and silver, introduced by the Phœnicians, or imported from Arabia or Central Asia. We may judge of the abundance of money possessed by Seleucia, on the Tigris, by the amount of the contribution which was extorted from it by Antiochus III. (a thousand talents).[413] The sums which the Syrian monarchs engaged to pay to the Romans were immense.[414] The soil gave produce equal in importance with that of industry.[415] Susiana, one of the provinces of Persia which had fallen under the dominion of the Seleucidæ, had so great a reputation for its corn, that Egypt alone could compete with it.[416] Cœle-Syria was, like the north of Mesopotamia, in repute for its cattle.[417] Palestine furnished abundance of wheat, oil, and wine. The condition of Syria was still so prosperous in the seventh century of Rome, that the philosopher Posidonius represents its inhabitants as indulging in continual festivals, and dividing their time between the labours of the field, banquets, and the exercises of the gymnasium.[418] The festivals of Antiochus IV., in the town of Daphne,[419] give a notion of the extravagance displayed by the grandees of that country.

The military forces assembled at different epochs by the kings of Syria enable us to estimate the population of their empire. In 537, at the battle of Raphia, Antiochus had under his command 68,000 men;[420] in 564, at Magnesia, 62,000 infantry, and more than 12,000 horsemen.[421] These armies, it is true, comprised auxiliaries of different nations. The Jews of the district of Carmel alone could raise 40,000 men.[422]

The fleet was no less imposing. Phœnicia counted numerous ports and well-stored arsenals; such were Aradus (Ruad), Berytus (Beyrout), Tyre (Sour). This latter town raised itself gradually from its decline. It was the same with Sidon (Saïde), which Antiochus III., in his war with Ptolemy, did not venture to attack on account of its soldiers, its stores, and its population. [423] Moreover, the greater part of the Phœnician towns enjoyed, under the Seleucidæ, a certain autonomy favourable to their industry. In Syria, Seleucia, which Antiochus the Great recovered from the Egyptians, had become the first port in the kingdom on the Mediterranean.[424] Laodicea carried on an active commerce with Alexandria.[425] Masters of the coasts of Cilicia and Pamphylia, the kings of Syria obtained from them great quantities of timber for ship-building, which was floated down the rivers from the mountains. [426] Thus uniting their vessels with those of the Phœnicians, the Seleucidæ launched upon the Mediterranean considerable armies.[427]

Distant commerce also employed numerous merchant vessels; the Mediterranean, like the Euphrates, was furrowed by barques which brought or carried merchandise of every description. Vessels sailing on the Erythræan Sea were in communication, by means of canals, with the shores of the Mediterranean. The great trade of Phœnicia with Spain and the West had ceased, but the navigation of the Euphrates and the Tigris replaced it for the transport of products, whether foreign or fabricated in Syria itself, and sent into Asia Minor, Greece, or Egypt. The empire of the Seleucidæ offered the spectacle of the ancient civilisation and luxury of Nineveh and Babylon, transformed by the genius of Greece.

Egypt.

XVI. Egypt, which Herodotus calls a present from the Nile, did not equal in surface a quarter of the empire of the Seleucidæ, but it formed a power much more compact. Its civilisation reached back more than three thousand years. The sciences and arts already flourished there, when Asia Minor, Greece, and Italy were still in a state of barbarism. The fertility of the valley of the Nile had permitted a numerous population to develop itself there to such a point, that under Amasis II., contemporary with Servius Tullius, twenty thousand cities were reckoned in it.[428] The skilful administration of the first of the Lagides increased considerably the resources of the country. Under Ptolemy II., the annual revenues amounted to 14,800 talents (86,150,800 francs [£3,446,032]), and a million and a half of artabi[429] of wheat.[430] Besides the Egyptian revenues, the taxes levied in the foreign possessions reached the amount of about 10,000 talents a year. Cœle-Syria, Phœnicia, and Judea, with the province of Samaria, yielded annually to Ptolemy Euergetes 8,000 talents (46 millions and a half [£1,860,000]).[431] A single feast cost Philadelphia 2,240 talents (more than 13 millions [more than half a million sterling]).[432] The sums accumulated in the treasury amounted to the sum, perhaps exaggerated, of 740,000 talents (about 4 milliards 300 millions of francs [172 millions sterling]).[433] In 527, Ptolemy Euergetes was able, without diminishing his resources too much, to send to the Rhodians 3,300 talents of silver, a thousand talents of copper, and ten millions of measures of wheat.[434] The precious metals abounded in the empire of the Pharaohs, as is attested by the traces of mining operations now exhausted, and by the multitude of objects in gold contained in their tombs. Masters for some time of the Libanus, the kings of Egypt obtained from it timber for ship-building. These riches had accumulated especially at Alexandria, which became, after Carthage, towards the commencement of the seventh century of Rome, the first commercial city in the world.[435] It was fifteen miles in circumference, had three spacious and commodious ports, which allowed the largest ships to anchor along the quay.[436] There arrived the merchandises of India, Arabia, Ethiopia, and of the coast of Africa; some brought on the backs of camels, from Myos Hormos (to the north of Cosseïr), and then transported down the Nile; others came by canals from the bottom of the Gulf of Suez, or brought from the port of Berenice, on the Red Sea.[437] The occupation of this sea by the Egyptians had put a stop to the piracies of the Arabs,[438] and led to the establishment of numerous factories. India furnished spices, muslins, and dyes; Ethiopia, gold, ivory, and ebony; Arabia, perfumes.[439] All these products were exchanged against those which came from the Pontus Euxinus and the Western Sea. The native manufacture of printed and embroidered tissues, and that of glass, assumed under the Ptolemies a new development. The objects exhumed from the tombs of this period, the paintings with which they are decorated, the allusions contained in the hieroglyphic texts and

Greek papyrus, prove that the most varied descriptions of industry were exercised in the kingdom of the Pharaohs, and had attained a high degree of perfection. The excellence of the products and the delicacy of the work prove the intelligence of the workmen. Under Ptolemy II., the army was composed of 200,000 footmen, 40,000 cavalry, 300 elephants, and 200 chariots; the arsenals were capable of furnishing arms for 300,000 men. [440] The Egyptian fleet, properly so called, consisted of a hundred and twelve vessels of the first class (from five to thirty ranges of oars), and two hundred and twenty-four of the second class, together with light craft; the king had, besides these, more than four thousand ships in the ports placed in subjection to him.[441] It was especially after Alexander that the Egyptian navy became greatly extended.

Cyrenaica.

XVII. Separating Egypt from the possessions of Carthage, Cyrenaica (the regency of Tripoli), formerly colonised by the Greeks and independent, had fallen into the hands of the first of the Ptolemies. It possessed commercial and rich towns, and fertile plains; its cultivation extended even into the mountains;[442] wine, oil, dates, saffron and different plants, such as the silphium (laserpitium),[443] were the object of considerable traffic.[444] The horses of Cyrenaica, which had all the lightness of the Arabian horses, were objects of research even in Greece,[445] and the natives of Cyrene could make no more handsome present to Alexander than to send him three hundred of their coursers.[446] Nevertheless, political revolutions had already struck at the ancient prosperity of the country,[447] which previously formed, by its navigation, its commerce, and its arts, probably the finest of the colonies founded by the Greeks.

Cyprus.

XVIII. The numerous islands of the Mediterranean enjoyed equal prosperity. Cyprus, colonised by the Phœnicians, and subsequently by the Greeks, passing afterwards under the dominion of the Egyptians, had a population which preserved, from its native country, the love of commerce and distant voyages. Almost all its towns were situated on the sea-coast, and furnished with excellent ports. Ptolemy Soter maintained in it an army of 30,000 Egyptians.[448] No country was richer in timber. Its fertility passed for being superior to that of Egypt.[449] To its agricultural produce were added precious stones, mines of copper worked from an early period,[450] and so rich, that this metal took its name from the island itself (Cuprum). In Cyprus were seen numerous sanctuaries, and especially the temple of Venus at Paphos, which contained a hundred altars.[451]

Crete.

XIX. Crete, peopled by different races, had attained even in the heroic age a great celebrity; Homer sang its hundred cities; but during several centuries it had been on the decline. Without commerce, without a regular navy, without agriculture, it possessed little else than its fruits and woods, and the sterility which characterises it now had already commenced. Nevertheless, there is every reason to believe that at the time of the Roman conquest, the island was still well peopled.[452] Devoted to piracy,[453] and reduced to sell their services, the Cretans, celebrated as archers, fought as mercenaries in the armies of Syria, Macedonia, and Egypt.[454]

Rhodes.

XX. If Crete was in decline, Rhodes, on the contrary, was extending its commerce, which took gradually the place of that of the maritime towns of Ionia and Caria. Already inhabited, in the time of Homer, by a numerous population, and containing three important towns, Lindos, Ialysus, and Camirus,[455] the isle was, in the fifth century of Rome, the first maritime power after Carthage. The town of Rhodes, built during the war of the Peloponnesus (346), had, like the Punic city, two ports, one for merchant vessels, the other for ships of war. The right of anchorage produced a revenue of a million of drachmas a year.[456] The Rhodians had founded colonies on different points of the Mediterranean shore,[457] and entertained friendly relations with a great number of towns from which they received more than once succours and presents.[458] They possessed upon the neighbouring Asiatic continent tributary towns, such as Caunus and Stratonicea, which paid them 120 talents (700,000 francs [£28,000]). The navigation of the Bosphorus, of which they strove to maintain the passage free, soon belonged to them almost exclusively.[459] All the maritime commerce from the Nile to the Palus Mæotis thus fell into their hands. Laden with slaves, cattle, honey, wax, and salt meats,[460] their ships went to fetch on the coast of the Cimmerian Bosphorus (Sea of Azof) the wheat then very celebrated,[461] and to carry wines and oils to the northern coast of Asia Minor. By means of its fleets, though its land army was composed wholly of foreigners,[462] Rhodes several times made war with success. She contended with Athens, especially from 397 to 399; she resisted victoriously, in 450, Demetrius Poliorcetes, and owed her safety to the respect of this prince for a magnificent painting of Ialysus, the work of Protogenes.[463] During the campaigns of the Romans in Macedonia and Asia, she furnished them with considerable fleets.[464] Her naval force was maintained until the civil war which followed the death of Cæsar, but was then annihilated.

The celebrity of Rhodes was no less great in arts and letters than in commerce. After the reign of Alexander, it became the seat of a famous school of sculpture and painting, from which issued Protogenes and the authors of the Laocoon and the Farnese Bull. The town contained three thousand statues,[465] and a hundred and six colossi, among others the famous Statue of the Sun, one of the seven wonders of the world, a hundred and five feet high, the cost of which had been three thousand talents (17,400,000 francs [£696,000]).[466] The school of rhetoric at Rhodes was frequented by students who repaired thither from all parts of Greece, and Cæsar, as well as Cicero, went there to perfect themselves in the art of oratory.

The other islands of the Ægean Sea had nearly all lost their political importance, and their commercial life was absorbed by the new states of Asia Minor, Macedonia, and Rhodes. It was not so with the Archipelago of the Ionian Sea, the prosperity of which continued until the moment when it fell into the power of the Romans. Corcyra, which received into its port the Roman forces, owed to its fertility and favourable position an extensive commerce. The rival of Corinth since the fourth century, she became corrupted like Byzantium and Zacynthus (Zante), which Agatharchides, towards 640, represents as grown effeminate by excess of luxury.[467]

Sardinia.

XXI. The flourishing condition of Sardinia arose especially from the colonies which Carthage had planted in it. The population of this island rendered itself formidable to the Romans by its spirit of independence. [468] From 541[469] to 580, 130,000 men were slain, taken, or sold.[470] The number of these last was so considerable, that the expression Sardinians to sell (Sardi venales) became proverbial.[471] Sardinia, which now counts not more than 544,000 inhabitants, then possessed at least a million. Its quantity of corn, and numerous herds of cattle, made of this island the second granary of Carthage.[472] The avidity of the Romans soon exhausted it. Yet, in 552, the harvests were still so abundant, that there were merchants who were obliged to abandon the wheat to the sailors for the price of the freight.[473] The working of the mines and the trade in wool of a superior quality[474] occupied thousands of hands.

Corsica.

XXII. Corsica was much less populous. Diodorus Siculus gives it hardly more than 30,000 inhabitants,[475] and Strabo represents them as savages, and living in the mountains.[476] According to Pliny, however, it had thirty towns.[477] Resin, wax, honey,[478] exported from factories founded by the Etruscans and Phocæans on the coasts, were almost the only products of the island.

Sicily.

XXIII. Sicily, called by the ancients the favourite abode of Ceres, owed its name to the Sicani or Siculi, a race which had once peopled a part of Italy; Phœnician colonies, and afterwards Greek colonies, had established themselves in it. In 371, the Greeks occupied the eastern part, about two-thirds of the island; the Carthaginians, the western part. Sicily, on account of its prodigious fertility, was, as may be supposed, coveted by both peoples; it was soon the same in regard to the Romans, and, after the conquest, it became the granary of Italy.[479] The orations of Cicero against Verres show the prodigious quantities of wheat which it sent, and to what a great sum the tenths or taxes amounted, which procured immense profits to the farmers of the revenues.[480]

The towns which, under Roman rule, declined, were possessed of considerable importance at the time of which we are speaking. The first among them, Syracuse, the capital of Hiero's kingdom, contained 600,000 souls; it was composed of six quarters, comprised in a circumference of 180 stadia (36 kilometres); it furnished, when it was conquered, a booty equal to that of Carthage.[481] Other cities rivalled Syracuse in extent and power. Agrigentum, in the time of the first Punic war, contained 50,000 soldiers;[482] it was one of the principal garrisons in Sicily.[483] Panormus (Palermo), Drepana (Trapani), and Lilybæum (Marsala), possessed arsenals, docks for ship-building, and vast ports. The roadstead of Messina was capable of holding 600 vessels.[484] Sicily is still the richest country in ancient monuments; our admiration is excited by the ruins of twenty-one temples and of eleven theatres, among others that of Taormina, which contained 40,000 spectators.[485]

This concise description of the countries bordering on the Mediterranean, two or three hundred years before our era, shows sufficiently the state of prosperity of the different peoples who inhabited them. The remembrance of such greatness inspires a very natural wish, namely, that henceforth the jealousy of the great powers may no longer prevent the East from shaking off the dust of twenty centuries, and from being born again to life and civilisation!

# CHAPTER V
# PUNIC WARS AND WARS OF MACEDONIA
# AND ASIA (From 488 to 621)

Comparison between Rome and Carthage.

I. ROME, having extended her dominion to the southern extremity of Italy, found herself in face of a power which, by the force of circumstances, was to become her rival.

Carthage, situated on the part of the African coast nearest to Sicily, was only separated from it by the channel of Malta, which divides the great basin of the Mediterranean in two. She had, during more than two centuries, concluded, from time to time, treaties with Rome, and, with a want of foresight of the future, congratulated the Senate every time it had gained great advantages over the Etruscans or the Samnites.

The superiority of Carthage at the beginning of the Punic wars was evident; yet the constitution of the two cities might have led any one to foresee which in the end must be the master. A powerful aristocracy reigned in both; but at Rome the nobles, identified continually with the people, set an example of patriotism and of all civic virtues, while at Carthage the leading families, enriched by commerce, made effeminate by an unbridled luxury, formed a selfish and greedy caste, distinct from the rest of the citizens. At Rome, the sole motive of action was glory, the principal occupation war, and the first duty military service. At Carthage, everything was sacrificed to interest and commerce; and the defence of the fatherland was, as an insupportable burden, abandoned to mercenaries. Hence, after a defeat, at Carthage the army was recruited with difficulty; at Rome it immediately recruited itself, because the populace was subject to the recruitment. If the poverty of the treasury caused the pay of the troops to be delayed, the Carthaginian soldiers mutinied, and placed the State in danger; the Romans supported privations and suffering without a murmur, out of mere love for their country.

The Carthaginian religion made of the Divinity a jealous and malignant power, which required to be appeased by horrible sacrifices or honoured by shameful practices: hence manners depraved and cruel; at Rome, good sense or the interest of the government moderated the brutality of paganism, and maintained in religion the sentiments of morality.[486]

And, again, what a difference in their policies! Rome had subdued, by force of arms, it is true, the people who surrounded her, but she had, so to say, obtained pardon for her victories in offering to the vanquished a greater country and a share in the rights of the metropolis. Moreover, as the inhabitants of the peninsula were in general of one and the same race, she had found it easy to assimilate them to herself. Carthage, on the contrary, had remained a foreigner in the midst of the natives of Africa, from whom she was separated by origin, language, and manners. She had made her rule hateful to her subjects and to her tributaries by the mercantile spirit of her agents, and their habits of rapacity; hence frequent insurrections, repressed with unexampled cruelty. Her distrust of her subjects had engaged her to leave all the towns on her territory open, in order that none of them might become a centre of support to a revolt. Thus two hundred towns surrendered without resistance to Agathocles immediately he appeared in Africa. Rome, on the contrary, surrounded her colonies with ramparts, and the walls of Placentia, Spoletum, Casilinum, and Nola, contributed to arrest the invasion of Hannibal.

The town of Romulus was at that time in all the vigour of youth, while Carthage had reached that degree of corruption at which States are incapable of supporting either the abuses which enervate them, or the remedy by which they might be regenerated.

To Rome then belonged the future. On one hand, a people of soldiers, restrained by discipline, religion, and purity of manners, animated with the love of their country, surrounded by devoted allies; on the other, a people of merchants with dissolute manners, unruly mercenaries, and discontented subjects.

First Punic War (490-513).

II. These two powers, of equal ambition, but so opposite in spirit, could not long remain in presence without disputing the command of the rich basin of the Mediterranean. Sicily especially was destined to excite their covetousness. The possession of that island was then shared between Hiero, tyrant of Syracuse, the Carthaginians, and the Mamertines. These last, descended from the old adventurers, mercenaries of Agathocles, who came from Italy in 490 and settled at Messina, proceeded to make war upon the Syracusans. They first sought the assistance of the Carthaginians, and surrendered to them the acropolis of Messina as the price of their protection; but soon, disgusted with their too exacting allies, they sent to demand succour of Rome under the name of a common nationality, for most of them called themselves Italiots, and consequently allies of the Republic; some even were or pretended to be Romans.[487]

The Senate hesitated; but public opinion carried the day, and, in spite of the little interest inspired by the Mamertines, war was decided. A body of troops, sent without delay to Messina, expelled the Carthaginians. Soon after, a consular army crossed the Strait, defeated first the Syracusans and then the Carthaginians, and effected a military settlement in the island. Thus commenced the first Punic War.

Different circumstances favoured the Romans. The Carthaginians had made themselves objects of hatred to the Sicilian Greeks. The towns still independent, comparing the discipline of the legions with the excesses of all kinds which had marked the progress of the mercenaries of Agathocles, Pyrrhus, and the Carthaginian generals, received the consuls as liberators. Hiero, master of Syracuse, the principal town in Sicily, had no sooner experienced the power of the Roman armies than he foresaw the result of the struggle, and declared for the strongest. His alliance, maintained faithfully during fifty years, was of great utility to the Republic.[488] With his support, the Romans, at the end of the third year of the war, had obtained possession of Agrigentum and the greater part of the towns of the interior; but the fleets of the Carthaginians remained masters of the sea and of the fortresses on the coast.

The Romans were deficient in ships of war.[489] They could, no doubt, procure transport vessels, or, by their allies (socii navales), a few triremes,[490] but they had none of those ships with five ranks of oars, better calculated, by their weight and velocity, to sink the ships of the enemy. An incomparable energy supplied in a short time the insufficiency of the fleet: a hundred and twenty galleys were constructed after the model of a Carthaginian quinquireme which had been cast on the coast of Italy; and soldiers were exercised on land in the handling of the oar.[491] At the end of two months, the crews were embarked, and the Carthaginians were defeated at Mylæ (494), and three years after at Tyndaris (497). These two sea-fights deprived Carthage of the prestige of her maritime superiority.

Still the struggle continued on land without decisive results, when the two rivals embraced the same resolution of making a final effort for the mastery of the sea. Carthage fitted out three hundred and fifty decked vessels; Rome, three hundred and thirty of equal force. In 498 the two fleets met between Heraclea Minora and the Cape of Ecnomus, and, in a memorable combat, in which 300,000 men[492] contended, the victory remained with the Romans. The road to Africa was open, and M. Atilius Regulus, inspired, no doubt, by the example of Agathocles, formed the design of carrying the war thither. His first successes were so great, that Carthage, in her terror, and to avoid the siege with which she was threatened, was ready to renounce her possessions in Sicily. Regulus, relying too much on the feebleness of the resistance he had hitherto encountered, thought he could impose upon Carthage the hardest conditions; but despair restored to the Africans all their energy, and Xanthippus, a Greek adventurer, but good general, placed himself at the head of the troops, defeated the consul, and almost totally destroyed his army.

The Romans never desponded in their reverses; they carried the war again into Sicily, and recovered Panormus, the head-quarters of the Carthaginian army. For several years the fleets of the two countries ravaged, one the coast of Africa, the other the Italian shores; in the interior of Sicily the Romans had the advantage; on the coast, the Carthaginians. Twice the fleets of the Republic were destroyed by tempests or by the enemy, and these disasters led the Senate on two occasions to suspend all naval warfare. The struggle remained concentrated during six years in a corner of Sicily: the Romans occupied Panormus; the Carthaginians, Lilybæum and Drepana. It might have been prolonged indefinitely, if the Senate, in spite of the poverty of the treasury, had not succeeded, by means of voluntary gifts, in equipping another fleet of two hundred quinquiremes. Lutatius, who commanded it, dispersed the enemy's ships near the Ægates, and, master of the sea, threatened to starve the Carthaginians. They sued for peace at the very moment when a great warrior, Hamilcar, had just restored a prestige to their arms. The fact is, that the enormity of her expenses and sacrifices for the last twenty-four years had discouraged Carthage, while at Rome, patriotism, insensible to material losses, maintained the national energy without change. The Carthaginians, obliged to give up all their establishments in Sicily, paid an indemnity of 2,200 talents.[493] From that time the whole island, with the exception of the kingdom of Hiero, became tributary, and, for the first time, Rome had a subject province.

If, in spite of this definitive success, there were momentary checks, we must attribute them in great part to the continual changes in the plans of campaign, which varied annually with the generals. Several consuls, nevertheless, were wanting neither in skill nor perseverance, and the Senate, always grateful, gave them worthy recompense for their services. Some obtained the honours of the triumph; among others, Duilius, who gained the first naval battle, and Lutatius, whose victory decided peace. At Carthage, on the contrary, the best generals fell victims to envy and ingratitude. Xanthippus, who vanquished Regulus, was summarily removed through the jealousy of the nobles, whom he had saved;[494] and Hamilcar, calumniated by a rival faction, did not receive from his government the support necessary for the execution of his great designs.

During this contest of twenty-three years, the war often experienced the want of a skilful and stable direction; but the legions lost nothing of their ancient valour, and they were even seen one day proceeding to blows with the auxiliaries, who had disputed with them the possession of the most dangerous post. We may cite also the intrepidity of the tribune Calpurnius Flamma, who saved the legions shut up by Hamilcar in a defile. He covered the retreat with three hundred men, and, found alive under a heap of dead bodies, received from the consul a crown of leaves—a modest reward, but sufficient then to inspire heroism. All noble sentiments were raised to such a point as even to do justice to an enemy. The consul, L. Cornelius, gave magnificent funeral rites to Hanno, a Carthaginian general, who had died valiantly in fighting against him.[495]

During the first Punic war, the Carthaginians had often threatened the coasts of Italy, but never attempted a serious landing. They could find no allies among the peoples recently subdued; neither the Samnites, nor the Lucanians who had declared for Pyrrhus, nor the Greek towns in the south of the Peninsula, showed any inclination to revolt. The Cisalpine Gauls, lately so restless, and whom we shall soon see taking arms again, remained motionless. The disturbances which broke out at the close of the Punic war among the Salentini and Falisci were without importance, and appear to have had no connection with the great struggle between Rome and Carthage.[496]

This resistance to all attempts at insurrection proves that the government of the Republic was equitable, and that it had given satisfaction to the vanquished. No complaint was heard, even after great disasters; and yet the calamities of war bore cruelly upon the cultivators—incessantly obliged to quit their fields to fill up the voids made in the legions. At home, the Senate had in its favour a great prestige, and abroad it enjoyed a reputation of good faith which ensured sincere alliances.

The first Punic war exercised a remarkable influence on manners. Until then the Romans had not entertained continuous relations with the Greeks. The conquest of Sicily rendered these relations numerous and active, and whatever Hellenic civilisation contained, whether useful or pernicious, made itself felt.

The religious ideas of the two peoples were different, although Roman paganism had great affinity with the paganism of Greece. This had its philosophers, its sophists, and its freethinkers. At Rome, nothing of the sort; there, creeds were profound, simple, and sincere; and, moreover, from a very remote period, the government had made religion subordinate to politics, and had laboured to give it a direction advantageous to the State.

The Greeks of Sicily introduced into Rome two sects of philosophy, the germs of which became developed at a later period, and which had perhaps more relation with the instincts of the initiated than with those of the initiators. *Stoicism* fortified the practice of the civic virtues, but without modifying their ancient roughness; *Epicurism*, much more extensively spread, soon flung the nation into the search after material enjoyments. Both sects, by inspiring contempt for death, gave a terrible power to the people who adopted them.

The war had exhausted the finances of Carthage. The mercenaries, whom she could not pay, revolted in Africa and Sardinia at the same time. They were only vanquished by the genius of Hamilcar. In Sardinia, the excesses of the mutineers had caused an insurrection among the natives, who drove them out of the country. The Romans did not let this opportunity for intervention escape them; and, as before in the case of the Mamertines, the Senate, according to all appearance, assumed as a pretext that there were Italiots among the mercenaries in Sardinia. The island was taken, and the conquerors imposed a new contribution on Carthage for having captured some merchant vessels navigating in those latitudes—a scandalous abuse of power, which Polybius loudly condemns.[497] Reduced to impotency by the loss of their navy and the revolt of their army, the Carthaginians submitted to the conditions of the strongest. They had quitted Sicily without leaving any regrets; but it was not the same with Sardinia; there their government and dominion were popular, probably from the community of religion and the Phœnician origin of some of the towns.[498] For a long time afterwards, periodical rebellions testified to the affection of the Sardinians for their old masters. Towards the same epoch, the Romans took possession of Corsica, and, from 516 to 518, repulsed the Ligures and the Gaulish tribes, with whom they had been at peace for forty-five years.

War of Illyria (525).

III. While the Republic protected its northern frontiers against the Gauls and Ligures, and combated the influence of Carthage in Sardinia and Corsica, she undertook, against a small barbarous people, another expedition, less difficult, it is true, but which was destined to have immense consequences. The war of Illyria, in fact, was on the point of opening to the Romans the roads to Greece and Asia, subjected to the successors of Alexander, and where Greek civilisation was dominant. Now become a great maritime power, Rome had henceforward among her attributes the police of the seas. The inhabitants of the eastern coasts of the Adriatic, addicted to piracy, were destructive to commerce. Several times they had carried their depredations as far as Messenia, and defeated Greek squadrons sent to repress their ravages.[499] These pirates belonged to the Illyrian nation. The Greeks considered them as barbarians, which meant foreigners to the Hellenic race; it is probable, nevertheless, that they had a certain affinity with it. Inconvenient allies of the kings of Macedonia, they often took arms either for or against them; intrepid and fierce hordes, they were ready to sell their services and blood to any one who would pay them, resembling, in this respect, the Albanians of the present day, believed by some to be their descendants driven into the mountains by the invasions of the Slaves.[500]

The king of the Illyrians was a child, and his mother, Teuta, exercised the regency. This fact alone reveals manners absolutely foreign to Hellenic and Roman civilisation. A chieftain of Pharos (Lesina), named Demetrius, in the pay of Teuta, occupied as a fief the island of Corcyra Nigra (now Curzola), and exercised the functions of prime minister. The Romans had no difficulty in gaining him; moreover, the Illyrians furnished a legitimate cause of war by assassinating an ambassador of the Republic.[501] The Senate immediately dispatched an army and a fleet to reduce them (525). Demetrius surrendered his island, which served as a basis against Apollonia, Dyrrhachium, Nutria, and a great part of the coast. After a resistance of some months, the Illyrians submitted, entered into an engagement to renounce piracy, surrendered several ports, and agreed to choose Demetrius, the ally of the Romans, for the guardian of their king.[502]

By this expedition, the Republic gained great popularity throughout Greece; the Athenians and the Achaian league especially were lavish of thanks, and began from that time to consider the Romans as their protectors against their dangerous neighbours, the kings of Macedonia. As to the Illyrians, the lesson they had received was not sufficient to correct them of their piratical habits. Ten years later another expedition was sent to chastise the Istrians at the head of the Adriatic,[503] and soon afterwards the disobedience of Demetrius to the orders of the Senate brought war again upon Illyria. He was compelled to take refuge with Philip of Macedon, while the young king became the ally or subject of the Republic.[504] In the mean time a new war attracted the attention of the Romans.

Invasion of the Cisalpines (528).

IV. The idea of the Senate was evidently to push its domination towards the north of Italy, and thus to preserve it from the invasion of the Gauls. In 522, at the proposal of the tribune Flaminius, the Senones had been expelled from Picenum, and their lands, declared public domain, were distributed among the plebeians. This measure, a presage to the neighbouring Gaulish tribes of the lot reserved for them, excited among them great uneasiness, and they began to prepare for a formidable invasion. In 528, they called from the other side of the Alps a mass of barbarians of the warlike race of the Gesatæ.[505] The terror at Rome was great. The same interests animated the peoples of Italy, and the fear of a danger equally threatening for all began to inspire them with the same spirit.[506] They rushed to arms; an army of 150,000 infantry and 6,000 cavalry was sent into the field, and the census of men capable of bearing arms amounted to nearly 800,000. The enumeration of the contingents of each country[507] furnishes valuable information on the general population of Italy, which appears, at this period, to have been, without reckoning the slaves, about the same as at the present day, yet with this difference, that the men capable of bearing arms were then in a much greater proportion.[508] These documents also give rise to the remark that the Samnites, only forty years recovered from the disasters of their sanguinary struggles, could still furnish 77,000 men.

The Gauls penetrated to the centre of Tuscany, and at Fesulæ defeated a Roman army; but, intimidated by the unexpected arrival of the consul L. Æmilius coming from Rimini, they retired, when, meeting the other consul, Caius Atilius, who, returning from Sardinia, had landed at Pisa, they were enclosed between two armies, and were annihilated. In the following year, the Gaulish tribes, successively driven back to the other side of the Po, were defeated again on the banks of the Adda; the coalition of the Cisalpine peoples was dissolved, without leading to the complete submission of the country. The colonies of Cremona and Placentia contributed, nevertheless, to hold it in check.

While the north of Italy seemed sufficient to absorb the attention of the Romans, great events were passing in Spain.

Second Punic War (536-552).

V. Carthage, humiliated, had lost the empire of the sea, with Sicily and Sardinia. Rome, on the contrary, had strengthened herself by her conquests in the Mediterranean, in Illyria, and in the Cisalpine. Suddenly the scene changes: the dangers which threatened the African town disappear, Carthage rises from her abasement, and Rome, which had lately been able to count 800,000 men in condition to carry arms, will soon tremble for her own existence. A change so unforeseen is brought about by the mere appearance in the ranks of the Carthaginian army of a man of genius, Hannibal.

His father, Hamilcar, chief of the powerful faction of the Barcas, had saved Carthage by suppressing the insurrection of the mercenaries. Charged afterwards with the war in Spain, he had vanquished the most warlike peoples of that country, and formed in silence a formidable array. Having discovered early the merit of a young man named Hasdrubal, he took him into his favour with the intention of making him his successor. In taking him for his son-in-law, he entrusted to him the education of Hannibal, on whom rested his dearest hopes. Hamilcar having been slain in 526, Hasdrubal had taken his place at the head of the army.

The progress of the Carthaginians in Spain, and the state of their forces in that country, had alarmed the Senate, which, in 526, obliged the government of Carthage to subscribe to a new treaty, prohibiting the Punic army from passing the Ebro, and attacking the allies of the Republic.[509] This last article referred to the Saguntines, who had already had some disputes with the Carthaginians. The Romans affected not to consider them as aborigines, and founded their plea on a legend which represented this people as a colony from Ardea, contemporary with the Trojan war.[510] By a similar conduct Rome created allies in Spain to watch her old adversaries, and this time, as in the case of the Mamertines, she showed an interested sympathy in favour of a weak nation exposed to frequent collisions with the Carthaginians. Hasdrubal had received the order to carry into execution the new treaty; but he was assassinated by a Gaul, in 534, and the army, without waiting for orders from Carthage, chose by acclamation for its chief Hannibal, then twenty-nine years of age. In spite of the rival factions, this choice was ratified, and perhaps any hesitation on the part of the council in Carthage would only have led to the revolt of the troops. The party of the Barcas carried the question against the government, and confirmed the power of the young general. Adored by the soldiers, who saw in him their own pupil, Hannibal exercised over them an absolute authority, and believed that with their old band he could venture upon anything.

The Saguntines were at war with the Turbuletæ,[511] allies or subjects of Carthage. In contempt of the treaty of 256, Hannibal laid siege to Saguntum, and took it after a siege of several months. He pretended that, in attacking his own allies, the Saguntines had been the aggressors. The people of Saguntum hastened to implore the succour of Rome. The Senate confined itself to despatching commissioners, some to Hannibal, who gave them no attention, and others to Carthage, where they arrived only when Saguntum had ceased to exist. An immense booty, sent by the conqueror, had silenced the faction opposed to the Barcas, and the people, as well as the soldiers, elevated by success, breathed nothing but war. The Roman ambassadors, sent to require indemnities, and even to demand the head of Hannibal, were ill received, and returned declaring hostilities unavoidable.

Rome prepared for war with her usual firmness and energy. One of the consuls was ordered to pass into Sicily, and thence into Africa; the other to lead an army by sea to Spain, and expel the Carthaginians from that country. But, without waiting the issue of negotiations, Hannibal was in full march to transfer the war into Italy. Sometimes treating with the Celtiberian or Gaulish hordes to obtain a passage through their territory, sometimes intimidating them by his arms, he had reached the banks of the Rhone, when the consul charged with the conquest of Spain, P. Cornelius Scipio, landing at the eastern mouth of that river, learnt that Hannibal had already entered the Alps. He then leaves his army to his brother Cneius, returns promptly to Pisa, places himself at the head of the troops destined to fight the Boii, crosses the Po with them, hoping by this rapid movement to surprise the Carthaginian general at the moment when, fatigued and weakened, he entered the plains of Italy.

The two armies met on the banks of the Tessino (536). Scipio, defeated and wounded, fell back on the colony of Placentia. Rejoined in the neighbourhood of that town by his colleague Tib. Sempronius Longus, he again, on the Trebia, offered battle to the Carthaginians. A brilliant victory placed Hannibal in possession of a great part of Liguria and Cisalpine Gaul, the warlike hordes of which received him with enthusiasm and reinforced his army, reduced, after the passage of the mountains, to less than 30,000 men. Flattered by the reception of the Gauls, the Carthaginian general tried also to gain the Italiots, and, announcing himself as the liberator of oppressed peoples, he took care, after the victory, to set at liberty all the prisoners taken from the allies. He hoped that these liberated captives would become for him useful emissaries. In the spring of 537 he entered Etruria, crossed the marshes of the Val di Chiana, and, drawing the Roman army to the neighbourhood of the Lake Trasimenus, into an unfavourable locality, destroyed it almost totally.

The terror was great at Rome; yet the conqueror, after devastating Etruria, and attacking Spoletum in vain, crossed the Apennines, threw himself into Umbria and Picenum, and thence directed his march through Samnium towards the coast of Apulia. In fact, having reached the centre of Italy, deprived of all communication with the mother country, without the engines necessary for a siege, with no assured line of retreat, having behind him the army of Sempronius, what must Hannibal do?—Place the Apennines between himself and Rome, draw nearer to the populations more disposed in his favour, and then, by the conquest of the southern provinces, establish a solid basis of operation, in direct communication with Carthage. In spite of the victory of Trasimenus, his position was critical, for, except the Cisalpine Gauls, all the Italiot peoples remained faithful to Rome, and so far no one had come to increase his army.[512] Thus Hannibal remained several months between Casilinum and Arpi, where Fabius, by his skilful movements, would have succeeded in starving the Carthaginian army, if the term of his command had not expired. Moreover, the popular party, irritated at a system of temporising which it accused of cowardice, raised to the consulship, as the colleague of Æmilius Paulus, Varro, a man of no capacity. Obliged to remain in Apulia, to procure subsistence for his troops, Hannibal, being attacked imprudently, entirely defeated, near Cannæ, two consular armies composed of eight legions and of an equal number of allies, amounting to 87,000 men (538).[513] One of the consuls perished, the other escaped, followed only by a few horsemen. 40,000 Romans had been killed or taken, and Hannibal sent to Carthage a bushel of gold rings taken from the fingers of knights who lay on the field of battle.[514] From that moment part of Samnium, Apulia, Lucania, and Bruttium declared for the Carthaginians, while the Greek towns of the south of the peninsula remained favourable to the Romans.[515] About the same time, as an increase of ill fortune, L. Postumus, sent against the Gauls, was defeated, and his army cut to pieces.

The Romans always showed themselves admirable in adversity; and thus the Senate, by a skilful policy, went to meet the consul Varro, and thank him for not having despaired of the Republic; it would, however, no longer employ the troops which had retreated from the battle, but sent them into Sicily with a prohibition to return into Italy until the enemy had been driven out of it. They refused to ransom the prisoners in Hannibal's hands. The fatherland, they said, had no need of men who allowed themselves to be taken arms in hand.[516] This reply made people report at Rome that the man who possessed power was treated very differently from the humble citizen.[517]

The idea of asking for peace presented itself to nobody. Each rivalled the other in sacrifices and devotion. New legions were raised, and there were enrolled 8,000 slaves, who were restored to freedom after the first combat. [518] The treasury being empty, all the private fortunes were brought to its aid. The proprietors of slaves taken for the army, the farmers of the revenue charged with the furnishing of provisions, consented to be repaid only at the end of the war. Everybody, according to his means, maintained at his own expense freedmen to serve on the galleys. After the example of the Senate, widows and minors carried their gold and silver to the public treasury. It was forbidden for anybody to keep at home either jewels, plate, silver or copper money, above a certain value, and, by the law Oppia, even the toilette of the ladies was limited.[519] Lastly, the duration of family mourning for relatives slain before the enemy was restricted to thirty days. [520]

After the victory of Cannæ it would have been more easy for Hannibal to march straight upon Rome than after Trasimenus; yet, since so great a captain did not think this possible to attempt, it is not uninteresting to inquire into his motives. In the first place, his principal force was in Numidian cavalry, which would have been useless in a siege;[521] then, he had generally the inferiority in attacking fortresses. Thus, after Trebia, he could not reduce Placentia;[522] after Trasimenus, he failed before Spoletum; three times he marched upon Naples, without venturing to attack it; later still, he was obliged to abandon the sieges of Nola, Cumæ, and Casilinum.[523] What, then, could be more natural than his hesitation to attack Rome, defended by a numerous population, accustomed to the use of arms?

The most striking proof of the genius of Hannibal is the fact of his having remained sixteen years in Italy, left almost to his own forces, reduced to the necessity of recruiting his army solely among his new allies, and of subsisting at their expense, ill seconded by the Senate of his own country, having always to face at least two consular armies, and, lastly, shut up in the peninsula by the Roman fleets, which guarded its coasts to intercept reinforcements from Carthage. His constant thought, therefore, was to make himself master of some important points of the coast in order to open a communication with Africa. After Cannæ, he occupies Capua, seeks to gain the sea by Naples,[524] Cumæ, Puteoli; unable to effect these objects, he seizes upon Arpi and Salapia, on the eastern coast, where he hopes to meet the ambassadors of the King of Macedonia. He next makes Bruttium his base of operation, and his attempts are directed against the maritime places, now against Brundusium and Tarentum, now against Locri and Rhegium.

All the defeats sustained by the generals of the Republic had been caused, first, by the superiority of the Numidian cavalry, and the inferiority of the hastily levied Latin soldiers,[525] opposed to old veteran troops; and, next, by excessive rashness in face of an able captain, who drew his adversaries to the position which he had chosen. Nevertheless, Hannibal, considerably weakened by his victories, exclaimed, after Cannæ, as Pyrrhus had done after Heraclea, that such another success would be his ruin. [526] Q. Fabius Maximus, recalled to power (539), continued a system of methodical war; while Marcellus, his colleague, bolder,[527] assumed the offensive, and arrested the progress of the enemy, by obliging him to shut himself up in a trapezium, formed on the north by Capua and Arpi, on the south by Rhegium and Tarentum. In 543 the war was entirely concentrated round two places; the citadel of Tarentum, blockaded by the Carthaginians, and Capua, besieged by the two consuls. These had surrounded themselves with lines of countervallation against the place, and of circumvallation against the attacks from without. Hannibal, having failed in his attempt to force these latter, marched upon Rome, in the hope of causing the siege of Capua to be raised, and by separating the two consular armies, defeating them one after the other in the plain country. Having arrived under the walls of the capital, and foreseeing too many difficulties in the way of making himself master of so large a town, he abandoned his plan of attack, and fell back to the environs of Rhegium. His abode there was prolonged during several years, with alternations of reverse and success, in the south of Italy, the populations of which were favourable to him; avoiding engagements, keeping near the sea, and not going beyond the southern extremity of the territory of Samnium.

In 547, a great army, which had left Spain under the command of one of his brothers, Hasdrubal, had crossed the Alps, and was advancing to unite with him, marching along the coast of the Adriatic. Two consular armies were charged with the war against the Carthaginians: one, under the command of the consul M. Livius Salinator, in Umbria; the other, having at its head the consul C. Claudius Nero, held Hannibal in check in Lucania, and had even obtained an advantage over him at Grumentum. Hannibal had advanced as far as Canusium, when the consul Claudius Nero, informed of the numerical superiority of the army of succour, leaves his camp under the guard of Q. Cassius, his lieutenant, conceals his departure, effects his junction with his colleague, and defeats, near the Metaurus, Hasdrubal, who perished in the battle with all his army.[528] From that moment Hannibal foresees the fate of Carthage; he abandons Apulia, and even Lucania, and retires into the only country which had remained faithful, Bruttium. He remains shut up there five years more, in continual expectation of reinforcements,[529] and only quits Italy when his country, threatened by the Roman legions, already on the African soil, calls him home to her defence.

In this war the marine of the two nations performed an important part. The Romans strained every nerve to remain masters of the sea; their fleets, stationed at Ostia, Brundusium, and Lilybæum, kept incessantly the most active watch upon the coasts of Italy; they even made cruises to the neighbourhood of Carthage and as far as Greece.[530] The difficulty of the direct communications induced the Carthaginians to send their troops by way of Spain and the Alps, where their armies recruited on the road, rather than dispatch them to the southern coast of Italy. Hannibal received but feeble reinforcements;[531] Livy mentions two only: the first of 4,000 Numidians and 40 elephants; and the second, brought by Bomilcar to the coast of the Ionian Gulf, near Locri.[532] All the other convoys appear to have been intercepted, and one of the most considerable, laden with stores and troops, was destroyed on the coast of Sicily.[533]

We cannot but admire the constancy of the Romans in face of enemies who threatened them on all sides. During the same period they repressed the Cisalpine Gauls and the Etruscans, combated the King of Macedonia, the ally of Hannibal, sustained a fierce war in Spain, and resisted in Sicily the attacks of the Syracusans, who, after the death of Hiero, had declared against the Republic. It took three years to reduce Syracuse, defended by Archimedes. Rome kept on foot, as long as the Second Punic war lasted, from sixteen to twenty-four legions,[534] recruited only in the town and in Latium.[535] These twenty-three legions represented an effective force of about 100,000 men, a number which will not appear exaggerated if we compare it with the census of 534, which gave 270,213 men, and only comprised persons in a condition to bear arms.

In the thirteenth year of the war the chances seemed in favour of the Republic. P. Cornelius Scipio, the son of the consul defeated at Trebia, had just expelled the Carthaginians from Spain. The people, recognising his genius, had conferred upon him, six years before, the powers of proconsul, though he was only twenty-four years of age. On his return to Rome, Scipio, elected consul (549), passed into Sicily, and from thence to Africa, where, after a campaign of two years, he defeated Hannibal in the plains of Zama, and compelled the rival of Rome to sue for peace (552). The Senate accorded to the conqueror the greatest honour which a Republic can confer upon one of her citizens—she left it to him to dictate terms to the vanquished. Carthage was compelled to give up her ships and her elephants, to pay 10,000 talents (58,000,000 francs [£2,320,000]), and, finally, to enter into the humiliating engagement not to make war in future without the authorisation of Rome.

Results of the Second Punic War.

VI. The second Punic war ended in the submission of Carthage and Spain, but it was at the price of painful sacrifices. During this struggle of sixteen years, a great number of the most distinguished citizens had perished; at Cannæ alone two thousand seven hundred knights, two questors, twenty-one tribunes of the soldiers, and many old consuls, prætors, and ediles were slain; and so many senators had fallen, that it was necessary to name a hundred and seventy-seven new ones, taken from among those who had occupied the magistracies.[536] But such hard trials had tempered anew the national character.[537] The Republic felt her strength and her resources unfold themselves; she rejoiced in her victories with a just pride, without yet experiencing the intoxication of a too great fortune, and new bonds were formed between the different peoples of Italy. War against a foreign invasion, in fact, has always the immense advantage of putting an end to internal dissensions, and unites the citizens against the common enemy. The greater part of the allies gave unequivocal proofs of their devotion. The Republic owed its safety, after the defeat of Cannæ, to the assistance of eighteen colonies, which furnished men and money.[538] The fear of Hannibal had fortunately given strength to concord, both in Rome and in

Italy: no more quarrels between the two orders,[539] no more divisions between the governing and the governed. Sometimes the Senate refers to the people the most serious questions; sometimes the people, full of trust in the Senate, submits beforehand to its decision.[540]

It was especially during the struggle against Hannibal that the inconvenience of the duality and of the annual change of the consular powers became evident;[541] but this never-ceasing cause of weakness was, as we have seen before, compensated by the spirit of patriotism. Here is a striking example: while Fabius was pro-dictator, Minucius, chief of the cavalry, was, contrary to the usual custom, invested with the same powers. Hurried on by his temper, he compromised the army, which was saved by Fabius. He acknowledged his error, submitted willingly to the orders of his colleague, and thus restored, by his own voluntary act, the unity of the command.[542] As to the continual change of the military chiefs, the force of circumstances rendered it necessary to break through this custom. The two Scipios remained seven years at the head of the army of Spain; Scipio Africanus succeeded them for almost as long a period. The Senate and the people had decided that, during the war of Italy, the powers of the proconsuls and prætors might be prorogued, and that the same consuls might be re-elected as often as might be thought fit.[543] And subsequently, in the campaign against Philip, the tribunes pointed out in the following terms the disadvantage of such frequent changes: "During the four years that the war of Macedonia lasted, Sulpicius had passed the greater part of his consulship in seeking Philip and his army; Villius had overtaken the enemy, but had been recalled before giving battle; Quinctius, retained the greater part of the year at Rome by religious cares, would have pushed the war with sufficient vigour to have entirely terminated it, if he could have arrived at his destination before the season was so far advanced. He had hardly entered his winter quarters, when he made preparations for recommencing the campaign with the spring, with a view of finishing it successfully, provided no successor came to snatch victory from him."[544] These arguments prevailed, and the consul was prorogued in his command.

Thus continual wars tended to introduce the stability of military powers and the permanence of armies. The same legions had passed ten years in Spain; others had been nearly as long in Sicily; and though, at the expiration of their service, the old soldiers were dismissed, the legions remained always under arms. Hence arose the necessity of giving lands to the soldiers who had finished their time of service; and, in 552, there were assigned to Scipio's veterans, for each year of service in Africa and Spain, two acres of the lands confiscated from the Samnites and Apulians.[545]

It was the first time that Rome took foreign troops into her pay, sometimes Celtiberians, at others Cretans sent by Hiero of Syracuse,[546] in fact, mercenaries, and a body of discontented Gauls who had abandoned the Carthaginian army.[547]

Many of the inhabitants of the allied towns were drawn to Rome,[548] where, in spite of the sacrifices imposed by the wars, commerce and luxury increased. The spoils which Marcellus brought from Sicily, and especially from Syracuse, had given development to the taste for the arts, and this consul boasted of having been the first who caused his countrymen to appreciate and admire the masterpieces of Greece.[549] The games of the circus, in the middle of the sixth century, began to be more in favour. Junius and Decius Brutus had, in 490, exhibited for the first time the combats of gladiators, the number of which was soon increased to twenty-two pairs.[550] Towards this period, also (559), theatrical representations were first given by the ediles. [551] The spirit of speculation had taken possession of the high classes, as appears by the law forbidding the senators (law Claudia, 536) to maintain at sea ships of a tonnage of more than three hundred amphoræ; as the public wealth increased, the knights, composed of the class who paid most taxes, increased also, and tended to separate into two categories, some serving in the cavalry, and possessing the horse furnished by the State (equus publicus),[552] the others devoting themselves to commerce and financial operations. The knights had long been employed in civil commissions,[553] and were often called to the high magistracies; and therefore Perseus justly called them "the nursery of the Senate, and the young nobility out of which issued consuls and generals (imperatores)."[554] During the Punic wars they had rendered great services by making large advances for the provisioning of the armies;[555] and if some, as undertakers of transports, had enriched themselves at the expense of the State, the Senate hesitated in punishing their embezzlements, for fear of alienating this class, already powerful.[556] The territorial wealth was partly in the hands of the great proprietors; this appears from several facts, and, among others, from the hospitality given by a lady of Apulia to 10,000 Roman soldiers, who had escaped from the battle of Cannæ, whom she entertained at her own private cost on her own lands.[557]

Respect for the higher classes had been somewhat shaken, as we learn from the adoption of a measure of apparently little importance. Since the fall of the kingly power, there had been established in the public games no distinction between the spectators. Deference for authority rendered all classification superfluous, and "never would a plebeian," says Valerius Maximus,[558] "have ventured to place himself before a senator." But, towards 560, a law was passed for assigning to the members of the Senate reserved places. It is necessary, for the good order of society, to increase the severity of the laws as the feeling of the social hierarchy becomes weakened.

Circumstances had brought other changes; the tribuneship, without being abolished, had become an auxiliary of the aristocracy. The tribunes no longer exclusively represented the plebeian order; they were admitted into the Senate; they formed part of the government, and employed their authority in the interest of justice and the fatherland.[559] The three kinds of comitia still remained,[560] but some modifications had been introduced into them. The assembly of the curiæ[561] consisted now only of useless formalities. Their attributes, more limited every day, were reduced to the conferring of the imperium, and the deciding of certain questions about auspices and religion. The comitia by centuries, which in their origin were the assembly of the people in arms, voting in the Campus Martius, and nominating their military chiefs, retained the same privileges; only, the century had become a subdivision of the tribe. All the citizens inscribed in each of the thirty-five tribes were separated into five classes, according to their fortune; each class was divided into two centuries, the one of the young men (juniores) the other of the older men (seniores).

As to the comitia by tribes, in which each voted without distinction of rank or fortune, their legislative power continued to increase as that of the comitia by centuries diminished.

Thus the Roman institutions, while appearing to remain the same, were incessantly changing. The political assemblies, the laws of the Twelve Tables, the classes established by Servius Tullius, the yearly election to offices, the military services, the tribuneship, the edileship, all seemed to remain as in the past, and in reality all had changed through the force of circumstances. Nevertheless, this appearance of immobility in the midst of progressing society was one advantage of Roman manners. Religious observers of tradition and ancient customs, the Romans did not appear to destroy what they displaced; they applied ancient forms to new principles, and thus introduced innovations without disturbance, and without weakening the prestige of institutions consecrated by time.

The Macedonian War (554).

VII. During the second Punic war, Philip III., king of Macedonia, had attacked the Roman settlements in Illyria, invaded several provinces of Greece, and made an alliance with Hannibal. Obliged to check these dangerous aggressions, the Senate, from 540 to 548, maintained large forces on the coasts of Epirus and Macedonia; and, united with the Ætolian league, and with Attalus, king of Pergamus, had forced Philip to conclude peace. But in 553, after the victory of Zama, when this prince again attacked the free cities of Greece and Asia allied to Rome, war was declared against him. The Senate could not forget that at this last battle a Macedonian contingent was found among the Carthaginian troops, and that still there remained in Greece a large number of Roman citizens sold for slaves after the battle of Cannæ.[562] Thus from each war was born a new war, and every success was destined to force the Republic into the pursuit of others. Now the Adriatic was to be passed, first, to curb the power of the Macedonians, and then to call to liberty those famous towns, the cradles of civilisation. The destinies of Greece could not be a matter of indifference to the Romans, who had borrowed her laws, her science, her literature, and her arts.

Sulpicius, appointed to combat Philip, landed on the coast of Epirus, and penetrated into Macedonia, where he gained a succession of victories, while one of his lieutenants, sent to Greece with the fleet, caused the siege of Athens to be raised. During two years the war languished, but the Roman fleet, combined with that of Attalus and the Rhodians, remained master of the sea (555). T. Quinctius Flamininus, raised to the consulship while still young, justified, by his intelligence and energy, the confidence of his fellow-citizens. He detached the Achaians and Bœtians from their alliance with the King of Macedonia, and, with the aid of the Ætolians, gained the battle of Cynoscephalæ in Thessaly (557), where the legion routed the celebrated phalanx of Philip II. and Alexander the Great. Philip III., compelled to make peace, was fain to accept hard conditions; the first of which was the obligation to withdraw his garrisons from the towns of Greece and Asia, and the prohibition to make war without the permission of the Senate.

The recital of Livy, which speaks of the decree proclaiming liberty to Greece, deserves to be quoted. We see there what value the Senate then attached to moral influence, and to that true popularity which the glory of having freed a people gives:—

"The epoch of the celebration of the Isthmian games generally attracted a great concourse of spectators, either because of the natural taste of the Greeks for all sorts of games, or because of the situation of Corinth, which, seated on two seas, offered easy access to the curious. But on this occasion an immense multitude flocked thither from all parts, in expectation of the future fate of Greece in general, and of each people in particular: this was the only subject of thought and conversation. The Romans take their place, and the herald, according to custom, advances into the middle of the arena, whence the games are announced according to a solemn form. The trumpet sounds, silence is proclaimed, and the herald pronounces these words: 'The Roman Senate, and S.T. Quinctius, imperator, conquerors of Philip and the Macedonians, re-establish in the enjoyment of liberty, their laws, and privileges, the Corinthians, the Phocians, the Locrians, the island of Eubœa, the Magnetes, the Thessalians, the Perrhœbi, and the Achæans of Phthiotis.' These were the names of all the nations which had been under the dominion of Philip. At this proclamation, the assembly was overcome with excess of joy. Hardly anybody could believe what he heard. The Greeks looked at each other as if they were still in the illusions of a pleasant dream, to be dissipated on awakening, and, distrusting the evidence of their ears, they asked their neighbours if they were not deceived. The herald is recalled, each man burning, not only to hear, but to see the messenger of such good news; he reads the decree a second time. Then, no longer able to doubt their happiness, they uttered cries of joy, and bestowed on their liberator such loud and repeated applause as make it easy to see that, of all good, liberty is that which has most charm for the multitude. Then the games were celebrated, but hastily, and without attracting the looks or the attention of the spectators. One interest alone absorbed their souls, and took from them the feeling of every other pleasure.

"The games ended, the people rush towards the Roman general; everybody is anxious to greet him, to take his hand, to cast before him crowns of flowers and of ribbons, and the crowd was so great that he was almost suffocated. He was but thirty-three years of age, and the vigour of life, joined with the intoxication of a glory so dazzling, gave him strength to bear up against such a trial. The joy of the peoples was not confined to the enthusiasm of the moment: the impression was kept up long afterwards in their thoughts and speech. 'There was then,' they said, 'one nation upon earth, which, at its own cost, at the price of fatigues and perils, made war for the liberty of peoples even though removed from their frontiers and continent: this nation crossed the seas, in order that there should not be in the whole world one single unjust government, and that right, equity, and law should be everywhere dominant. The voice of a herald had been sufficient to restore freedom to all the cities of Greece and Asia. The idea alone of such a design supposed a rare greatness of soul; but to execute it needed as much courage as fortune.'"[563]

There was, however, a shadow on the picture. All Peloponnesus was not freed, and Flamininus, after having taken several of his possessions from Nabis, king of Sparta, had concluded peace with him, without continuing the siege of Lacedæmon, of which he dreaded the length. He feared also the arrival of a more dangerous enemy, Antiochus III., who had already reached Thrace, and threatened to go over into Greece with a considerable army. For this the allied Greeks, occupied only with their own interests, reproached the Roman consul with having concluded peace too hastily with Philip, whom, in their opinion, he could have annihilated.[564] But Flamininus replied that he was not commissioned to dethrone Philip, and that the existence of the kingdom of Macedonia was necessary as a barrier against the barbarians of Thrace, Illyria, and Gaul.[565] Meanwhile, accompanied even to their ships by the acclamations of the people, the Roman troops evacuated the cities restored to liberty (560), and Flamininus returned to a triumph at Rome, bringing with him that glorious protectorate of Greece, so long an object of envy to the successors of Alexander.

War against Antiochus (563).

VIII. The policy of the Senate had been to make Macedonia a rampart against the Thracians, and Greece herself a rampart against Macedonia. But, though the Romans had freed the Achæan league, they did not intend to create a formidable power or confederation. Then, as formerly, the Athenians, the Spartans, the Bœotians, the Ætolians, and, finally, the Achæans, each endeavoured to constitute an Hellenic league for their own advantage; and each aspiring to dominate over the others, turned alternately to those from whom it hoped the most efficient support at the time. In the Hellenic peninsula, properly so called, the Ætolians, to whose territory the Senate had promised to join Phocis and Locris, coveted the cities of Thessaly, which the Romans obstinately refused them.

Thus, although reinstated in the possession of their independence, neither the Ætolians, the Achæans, nor yet the Spartans, were satisfied: they all dreamt of aggrandisement. The Ætolians, more impatient, made, in 562, three simultaneous attempts against Thessaly, the island of Eubœa, and Peloponnesus. Having only succeeded in seizing Demetrias, they called Antiochus III. to Greece, that they might place him at the head of the hegemony, which they sought in vain to obtain from the Romans.

The better part of the immense heritage left by Alexander the Great had fallen to this prince. Already, some years before, Flamininus had given him notice that it belonged to the honour of the Republic not to abandon Greece, of which the Roman people had loudly proclaimed itself the liberator; and that after having delivered it from the yoke of Philip, the Senate now wished to free from the dominion of Antiochus all the Asian cities of Hellenic origin.[566] Hannibal, who had taken refuge with the King of Syria, encouraged him to resist, by engaging him to carry the struggle into Italy, as he himself had done. War was then declared by the Romans. To maintain the independence of Greece against an Asiatic prince was at once to fulfil treaties and undertake the defence of civilisation against barbarism. Thus, in proclaiming the most generous ideas, the Republic justified its ambition.

The services rendered by Rome were already forgotten.[567] Antiochus thus found numerous allies in Greece, secret or declared. He organised a formidable confederacy, into which entered the Ætolians, the Athamanes, the Elians, and the Bœotians, and, having landed at Chalcis, conquered Eubœa and Thessaly. The Romans opposed to him the King of Macedonia and the Achæans. Beaten at Thermopylæ, in 563, by the consul Acilius Glabrio, aided by Philip, the King of Syria withdrew to Asia, and the Ætolians, left to themselves, demanded peace, which was granted them in 563.

It was not enough to have compelled Antiochus to abandon Greece. L. Scipio, having his brother, the vanquisher of Carthage, for his lieutenant, went in 564 to seek him out in his own territory. Philip favoured the passage of the Roman army, which crossed Macedonia, Thrace, and the Hellespont without difficulty. The victories gained at Myonnesus by sea, and at Magnesia by land, terminated the campaign, and compelled Antiochus to yield up all his provinces on this side Mount Taurus, and pay 15,000 talents—a third more than the tax imposed on Carthage after the second Punic war. The Senate, far from reducing Asia then to a province, exacted only just and moderate conditions.[568] All the Greek towns of that country were declared free, and the Romans only occupied certain important points, and enriched their allies at the expense of Syria. The King of Pergamus and the Rhodian fleet had seconded the Roman army. Eumenes II., the successor of Attalus I., saw his kingdom increased; Rhodes obtained Lycia and Caria; Ariarathes, king of Cappadocia, who had given aid to Antiochus, paid two hundred talents.[569]

The War in the Cisalpine (558-579).

IX. The prompt submission of the East was a fortunate occurrence for the Republic, for near at home, enemies, always eager and watchful, might at any moment, supported or excited by their brethren on the other side of the Alps, attack her in the very centre of her empire.

Indeed, since the time of Hannibal, war had been perpetuated in the Cisalpine, the bellicose tribes of which, though often beaten, engaged continually in new insurrections. The settlement of the affairs of Macedonia left the Senate free to act with more vigour, and in 558 the defeat of the Ligures, of the Boii, of the Insubres, and of the Cenomani, damped the ardour of these barbarous peoples. The Ligures and the Boii, however, continued the strife; but the bloody battle of 561, fought near Modena, and, later, the ravages committed by L. Flamininus, brother of the conqueror of Cynoscephalæ, and Scipio Nasica, during the following years, obliged the Boii to treat. Compelled to yield the half of their territory, they retired towards the Danube in 564, and three years afterwards Cisalpine Gaul was formed into a Roman province.

As to the Ligures, they maintained a war of desperation to the end of the century. Their resistance was such that Rome was obliged to meet it with measures of excessive rigour; and in 574, more than 47,000 Ligures were transported into a part of Samnium which had been left almost without inhabitants since the war with Hannibal. In 581, lands beyond the Po were distributed to other Ligures.[570] Every year the frontiers receded more towards the north, and military roads,[571] the foundation of important colonies, secured the march of the armies—a system which had been interrupted during the second Punic war, but was afterwards adopted, and especially applied to the south of Italy and the Cisalpine.[572]

In achieving the submission of this last province, Rome had put an end to other less important wars. In 577 she reduced the Istrians; in 579, the Sardinians and the Corsicans; finally, from 569 to 573, she extended her conquests into Spain, where she met the same enemies as Carthage had encountered.

War against Persia (583).

X. For twenty-six years had peace been maintained with Philip, the Ætolians vanquished, the peoples of Asia subdued, and the greater part of Greece restored to liberty. Profiting by its co-operation with the Romans against Antiochus, the Achæan league had largely increased, and Philopœmen had brought into it Sparta, Messene, and the island of Zacynthus; but these countries, impatient of the Achæan rule, soon sought to free themselves from it. Thus was realised the prediction of Philip, who told the Thessalian envoys, after the battle of Cynoscephalæ, that the Romans would soon repent of having given liberty to peoples incapable of enjoying it, and whose dissensions and jealousies would always keep up a dangerous agitation.[573] In fact, Sparta and Messene rebelled, and sued for help from Rome. Philopœmen, after having cruelly punished the first of these cities, perished in his struggle with the second. Thessaly and Ætolia were torn by anarchy and civil war.

Whilst the Republic was occupied in restoring tranquillity to these countries, a new adversary came to imprudently attract its wrath. One would say that Fortune, while raising up so many enemies against Rome, took pleasure in delivering them, one after the other, into her hands. The old legend of Horatius killing the three Curiatii in succession was a lesson which the Senate had never forgotten.

Perseus, heir to his father's crown and enmities, had taken advantage of the peace to increase his army and his resources, to make allies, and to rouse up the kings and peoples of the East against Rome. Besides the warlike population of his own country, he had at his beck barbarous peoples like the Illyrians, the Thracians, and the Bastarnæ, dwelling not far from the Danube. Notwithstanding the treaty, which forbad Macedonia to make war without the consent of the Senate, Perseus had silently aggrandised himself on the side of Thrace; he had placed garrisons in the maritime cities of Oenoe and Maronia, excited the Dardanians[574] to war, brought under subjection the Dolopes, and advanced as far as Delphi.[575] He endeavored to draw the Achæans into an alliance, and skilfully obtained the good-will of the Greeks. Eumenes II., king of Pergamus, who, like his father Attalus I., feared the encroachments of Macedonia, denounced at Rome this infraction of the old treaties. The fear with which a powerful prince inspired him, and the gratitude which he owed to the Republic for the aggrandisement of his kingdom after the Asian war, obliged him to cultivate the friendship of the Roman people. In 582 he came to Rome, and, honourably received by the Senate, forgot nothing which might excite it against Perseus, whom he accused of ambitious designs hostile to the Republic. This denunciation raised violent enmities against Eumenes. On his way back to his kingdom, he was attacked by assassins, and dangerously wounded. Suspicion fell on the Macedonian monarch, not without show of reason, and was taken by the Republic as sufficient ground for declaring war on a prince whose power began to offend it.

Bold in planning, Perseus displayed cowardice when it was necessary to act. After having from the first haughtily rejected the Roman claims, he waited in Thessaly for their army, which, ill-commanded and ill-organised, was beaten by his lieutenants and repulsed into mountain gorges, where it might have been easily destroyed. He then offered peace to P. Licinius Crassus; but, notwithstanding his check, the consul replied, with all the firmness of the Roman character, that peace was only possible if Perseus would abandon his person and his kingdom to the discretion of the Senate. [576] Struck by so much assurance, the king recalled his troops, and suffered the enemy to effect his retreat undisturbed. The incapacity of the Roman generals, however, their violences, and the want of discipline among the soldiers, had alienated the Greeks, who naturally preferred a prince of their own race to a foreign captain; moreover, they did not see the Macedonians get the better of the Romans without a certain satisfaction. In their eyes, it was the Hellenic civilisation overthrowing the presumption of the Western barbarians.

The campaigns of 584 and 585 were not more fortunate for the Roman arms. A consul had the rash idea of invading Macedonia by the passes of Callipeuce, where his army would have been annihilated if the king had had the courage to defend himself. At the approach of the legions he took to flight, and the Romans escaped from their perilous position without loss.

[577] At length, the people, feeling the necessity of having an eminent man at the head of the army, nominated Paulus Æmilius consul, who had given many proofs of his military talents in the Cisalpine. Already the greater part of the Gallo-græci were in treaty with Perseus. The Illyrians and the people of the Danube offered to second him. The Rhodians, and the King of Pergamus himself, persuaded that Fortune was going to declare herself for the King of Macedonia, made him offers of alliance; he chaffered with them with the most inexplicable levity. In the mean time, the Roman army, ably conducted, advanced by forced marches. One single combat terminated the war; and the battle of Pydna, in 586, once more proved the superiority of the Roman legion over the phalanx. This, however, did not yield ingloriously; and, though abandoned by their king, who fled, the Macedonian hoplites died at their post.

When they heard of this defeat, Eumenes and the Rhodians hastened to wipe out the remembrance of their ever having doubted the fortune of Rome[578] by the swiftness of their repentance. At the same time, L. Anicius conquered Illyria and seized the person of Gentius. Macedonia was divided into four states called free, that is to say, presided over by magistrates chosen by themselves, but under the protectorate of the Republic. By the law imposed on these new provinces, all marriages, and all exchange of immovable property, were interdicted between the citizens of different states,[579] and the imports reduced one-half. As we see, the Republic applied the system practised in 416 to dissolve the Latin confederacy, and later, in 449, that of the Hernici. Illyria was also divided into three parts. The towns which had first yielded were exempt from all tribute, and the taxes of the others reduced to half.[580]

It is not uninteresting to recall to mind how Livy appreciates the institutions which Macedonia and Illyria received at this epoch. "It was decreed," he says, "that liberty should be given to the Macedonians and Illyrians, to prove to the whole universe that, in carrying their arms so far, the object of the Romans was to deliver the enslaved peoples, not to enslave the free peoples; to guarantee to these last their independence, to the nations subject to kings a milder and more just government; and to convince them that, in the wars which might break out between the Republic and their sovereigns, the result would be the liberty of the peoples: Rome reserving to herself only the honour of victory."[581]

Greece, and above all Epirus, sacked by Paulus Æmilius, underwent the penalty of defection. As to the Achæan league, the fidelity of which had appeared doubtful, nearly a thousand of the principal citizens, guilty or suspected of having favoured the Macedonians, were sent as hostages to Rome.[582]

Modification of Roman policy.

XI. In carrying her victorious arms through almost all the borders of the Mediterranean, the Republic had hitherto obeyed either legitimate needs or generous inspirations. Care for her future greatness, for her existence even, made it absolute on her to dispute the empire of the sea with Carthage. Hence the wars, of which Sicily, Sardinia, Spain, Italy, and Africa, by turns, became the theatre. It was also her duty to combat the warlike peoples of the Cisalpine, that she might ensure the safety of her frontiers. As to the expeditions of Macedonia and Asia, Rome had been drawn into them by the conduct of foreign kings, their violation of treaties, their guilty plottings, and their attacks on her allies.

To conquer thus became to her an obligation, under pain of seeing fall to ruin the edifice which she had built up at the price of so many sacrifices; and, what is remarkable, she showed herself after victory magnificent towards her allies, clement to the vanquished, and moderate in her pretensions. Leaving to the kings all the glory of the throne, and to the nations their laws and liberties, she had reduced to Roman provinces only a part of Spain, Sicily, Sardinia, and Cisalpine Gaul. In Sicily she preserved the most intimate alliance with Hiero, tyrant of Syracuse, for fifty years. The constant support of this prince must have shown the Senate how much such alliances were preferable to direct dominion. In Spain she augmented the territory of all the chiefs who consented to become her allies. After the battle of Cynoscephalæ, as after that of Magnesia, she maintained on their thrones Philip and Antiochus, and imposed on this last only the same conditions as those offered before the victory. If, after the battle of Pydna, she overthrew Perseus, it was because he had openly violated his engagements; but she gave equitable laws to Macedonia. Justice then ruled her conduct, even towards her oldest rival; for when Masinissa asked the help of the Senate in his quarrels with Carthage, he received for answer that, even in his favour, justice could not be sacrificed.[583]

In Egypt her protection preserved the crown on the head of Ptolemy Philometor and of his sister Cleopatra.[584] Finally, when all the kings came after the victory of Pydna to offer their congratulations to the Roman people, and to implore their protection, the Senate regulated their demands with extreme justice. Eumenes, himself an object of suspicion, sent his brother Attalus to Rome; and he, willing to profit by the favourable impression he had made, thought to ask for him a part of the kingdom of Pergamus. He was recommended to give up the design. The Senate restored his son to Cotys, king of Thrace, without ransom, saying that the Roman people did not make a traffic of their benefits.[585] Finally, in the disputes between Prusias, king of Bithynia, and the Gallo-græcians, it declared that justice alone could dictate its decision.[586]

How, then, did so much nobleness of views, so much magnanimity in success, so much prudence in conduct seem to be belied, dating from that period of twenty-two years which divides the war against Persia from the third Punic war? Because too much success dazzles nations as well as kings. When the Romans began to think that nothing could resist them in the future because nothing had resisted them in the past, they believed that all was permitted them. They no longer made war to protect their allies, defend their frontiers, or destroy coalitions, but to crush the weak, and use nations for their own profit. We must also acknowledge that the inconstancy of the peoples, faithful in appearance, but always plotting some defection, and the hatred of the kings, concealing their resentment under a show of abasement, concurred to render the Republic more suspicious and more exacting, and caused it to count from henceforth rather on its subjects than on its allies. Vainly did the Senate seek to follow the grand traditions of the past; it was no longer strong enough to curb individual ambitions; and the same institutions which formerly brought forth the virtues, now only protected the vices of aggrandised Rome. The generals dared no longer to obey; thus, the consul Cn. Manlius attacks the Gallo-græcians in Asia without the orders of the Senate;[587] A. Manlius takes on himself to make an expedition into Istria;[588] the consul C. Cassius abandons the Cisalpine, his province, and attempts of his own accord to penetrate into Macedonia by Illyria;[589] the prætor Furius, on his own authority, disarms one of the peoples of Cisalpine Gaul, the Cenomani, at peace with Rome;[590] Popilius Lænas attacks the Statiellates without cause, and sells ten thousand of them; others also oppress the peoples of Spain.[591] All these things doubtless incur the blame of the Senate; the consuls and prætors are disavowed, even accused, but their disobedience none the less remain unpunished, and the accusations without result. In 599, it is true, L. Lentulus, consul in the preceding year, underwent condemnation for exaction, but that did not prevent him from being raised again to the chief honours.[592]

As long as the object was only to form men destined for a modest part on a narrow theatre, nothing was better than the annual election of the consuls and prætors, by which, in a certain space of time, a great number of the principal citizens of both the patrician and plebeian nobility participated in the highest offices. Powers thus exercised under the eyes of their fellow-citizens, rather for honour than interest, obliged them to be worthy of their trust; but when, leading their legions into the most remote countries, the generals, far from all control, and invested with absolute power, enriched themselves by the spoils of the vanquished, dignities were sought merely to furnish them with wealth during their short continuance. The frequent re-election of the magistrates, in multiplying the contests of candidates, multiplied the ambitious, who scrupled at nothing to attain their object. Thus Montesquieu justly observes, that "good laws which have made a small republic great, become a burden to it when it has increased, because their natural effect was to create a grand people, and not to govern it."[593]

The remedy for this overflowing of unruly passions would have been, on the one hand, to moderate the desire for conquest; on the other, to diminish the number of aspirants to power, by giving them a longer term of duration. But then, the people alone, guided by its instincts, felt the need of remedying this defect in the institution, by retaining in authority those who had their confidence. Thus, they wished to appoint Scipio Africanus perpetual dictator;[594] while pretended reformers, such as Portius Cato, enslaved to old customs, and in a spirit of exaggerated rigorism, made laws to interdict the same man from aspiring twice to the consulship, and to advance the age at which it was lawful to try for this high office.

All these measures were contrary to the object at which they aimed. In maintaining annual elections, the way was left free to vulgar covetousness; in excluding youth from high functions, they repressed the impulses of those choice natures which early reveal themselves, and the exceptional elevation of which had so often saved Rome from the greatest disasters. Have we not seen, for example, in 406, Marcus Valerius Corvus, raised to the consulate at twenty-three years of age, gain the battle of Mount Gaurus against the Samnites; Scipio Africanus, nominated proconsul at twenty-four, conquer Spain and humiliate Carthage; the consul Quinctius Flamininus, at thirty, carry off from Philip the victory of Cynoscephalæ? Finally, Scipio Æmilianus, who is to destroy Carthage, will be elected consul, even before the age fixed by the law of Cato.

No doubt, Cato the Censor, honest and incorruptible, had the laudable design of arresting the decline of morals. But, instead of attacking the cause, he only attacked the effect; instead of strengthening authority, he tended to weaken it; instead of leaving the nations a certain independence, he urged the Senate to bring them all under its absolute dominion; instead of adopting what came from Greece with an enlightened discernment, he indiscriminately condemned all that was of foreign origin.[595] There was in Cato's austerity more ostentation than real virtue. Thus, during his censorship, he expelled Manlius from the Senate for having kissed his wife before his daughter in open daylight; he took pleasure in regulating the toilette and extravagance of the Roman ladies; and, by an exaggerated disinterestedness, he sold his horse when he quitted Spain, to save the Republic the cost of transport.[596]

But the Senate contained men less absolute, and wiser appreciators of the needs of the age; they desired to repress abuses, to carry out a policy of moderation, to curb the spirit of conquest, and to accept from Greece all that she had of good. Scipio Nasica and Scipio Æmilianus figured among the most important.[597] One did not reject whatever might soften manners and increase human knowledge; the other cultivated the new muses, and was even said to have assisted Terence.

The irresistible inclination of the people towards all that elevates the soul and ennobles existence was not to be arrested. Greece had brought to Italy her literature, her arts, her science, her eloquence; and when, in 597, there came to Rome three celebrated philosophers—Carneades the Academician, Diogenes the Stoic, and Critolaus the Peripatetic—as ambassadors from Athens, they produced an immense sensation. The young men flocked in crowds to see and hear them; the Senate itself approved this homage paid to men whose talent must polish, by the culture of letters, minds still rude and unformed.[598] Cato alone, inexorable, pretended that these arts would soon corrupt the Roman youth, and destroy its taste for arms; and he caused these philosophers to be dismissed.

Sent to Africa as arbiter to appease the struggle between Masinissa and Carthage, he only embittered it. Jealous at seeing this ancient rival still great and prosperous, he did not cease pronouncing against her that famous decree of death: Delenda est Carthago. Scipio Nasica, on the contrary, opposed the destruction of Carthage, which he considered too weak to do injury, yet strong enough to keep up a salutary fear, which might prevent the people from casting themselves into all those excesses which are the inevitable consequences of the unbounded increase of empires.[599] Unhappily, the opinion of Cato triumphed.

As one of our first writers says, it must be "that truth is a divine thing, since the errors of good men are as fatal to humanity as vice, which is the error of the wicked."

Cato, by persecuting with his accusations the principal citizens, and, among others, Scipio Africanus, taught the Romans to doubt virtue.[600] By exaggeration in his attacks, and by delivering his judgments with passion, he caused his justice to be suspected.[601] By condemning the vices from which he himself was not exempt, he deprived his remonstrances of all moral force. [602] When he scourged the people as accuser and judge, without seeking to raise them by education and laws, he resembled, says a learned German, that Persian king who whipped the sea with rods to make the tempest cease.[603] His influence, though powerless to arrest the movement of one civilisation taking the place of another, failed not to produce a fatal effect on the policy of that period.[604] The Senate, renouncing the moderation and justice which hitherto had stamped all its deeds, adopted in their stead a crafty and arrogant line of action, and a system of extermination.

Towards the beginning of the seventh century, everything disappears before the Roman power. The independence of peoples, kingdoms, and republics ceases to exist. Carthage is destroyed, Greece gives up her arms, Macedonia loses her liberty, that of Spain perishes at Numantia, and shortly afterwards Pergamus undergoes the same fate.

Third Punic War (605-608).

XII. Notwithstanding her abasement, Carthage still existed, the eternal object of hatred and distrust. She was accused of connivance with the Macedonians, ever impatient of their yoke; and to her was imputed the resistance of the Celtiberian hordes. In 603, Masinissa and the Carthaginians engaged in a new struggle. As, according to their treaties, these last could not make war without authorisation, the Senate deliberated on the course it was to take. Cato desired war immediately. Scipio Nasica, on the contrary, obtained the appointment of a new embassy, which succeeded in persuading Masinissa to evacuate the territory in dispute; on its part, the Senate of Carthage consented to submit to the wisdom of the ambassadors, when the populace at Carthage, excited by those men who in troublous times speculate on the passions of the mob, breaks out in insurrection, insults the Roman envoys, and expels the chief citizens.[605] A fatal insurrection; for in moments of external crisis all popular movements ruin a nation,[606] as all political change is fatal in the presence of a foreigner invading the soil of the fatherland. However, the Roman Senate judged it best to temporise, because of the war in Spain, where Scipio Æmilianus then served in the capacity of tribune. Ordered to Africa (603), to obtain from Masinissa elephants for the war against the Celtiberians, he witnessed a sanguinary defeat of the Carthaginian army. This event decided the question of Roman intervention; the Senate, in fact, had no intention of leaving the entire sovereignty of Africa to the Numidian king, whose possessions already extended from the ocean to Cyrene.[607]

In vain did Carthage send ambassadors to Rome to explain her conduct. They obtained no satisfaction. Utica yielded to the Romans (604), and the two consuls, L. Marcius Censorinus, and M. Manlius Nepos, arrived there at the head of 80,000 men in 605. Carthage sues for peace; they impose the condition that she shall give up her arms; she delivers them up, with 2,000 engines of war. But soon exactions increase; the inhabitants are commanded to quit their city and retire ten miles inland. Exasperated by so much severity, the Carthaginians recover their energy; they forge new weapons, raise the populace, fling into the campaign Hasdrubal, who has soon collected 70,000 men in his camp at Nepheris, and gives the consuls reason to fear the success of their enterprise.[608]

The Roman army met with a resistance it was far from expecting. Endangered by Manlius, it was saved by the tribune, Scipio Æmilianus, on whom all eyes were turned. On his return to Rome, he was in 607 elected consul at the age of thirty-six years, and charged with the direction of the war, which henceforth took a new aspect. Carthage is soon inclosed by works of prodigious labour; on land, trenches surround the place and protect the besiegers; by sea, a colossal bar interrupts all communication, and gives up the city to famine; but the Carthaginians build a second fleet in their inner port, and excavate a new communication with the sea. During the winter Scipio goes and forces the camp at Nepheris, and on the return of spring makes himself master of the first enclosure; finally, after a siege which lasted for three years, with heroic efforts on both sides, the town and its citadel Byrsa are carried, and entirely razed to the ground. Hasdrubal surrendered, with fifty thousand inhabitants, the remains of an immense population; but on a fragment of the wall which had escaped the fire, the wife of the last Carthaginian chief, dressed in her most gorgeous robes, was seen to curse her husband, who had not had the courage to die; then, after having slain her two children, she flung herself into the flames. A mournful image of a nation which achieves her own ruin, but which does not fall ingloriously.

When the vessel laden with magnificent spoils, and adorned with laurels, entered the Tiber, bearer of the grand news, all the citizens rushed out into the streets embracing and congratulating each other on so joyful a victory. Now only did Rome feel herself free from all fear, and the mistress of the world. Nevertheless, the destruction of Carthage was a crime which Caius Gracchus, Julius Cæsar, and Augustus sought to repair.

Greece, Macedonia, Numantia, and Pergamus reduced to Provinces.

XIII. The same year saw the destruction of the Greek autonomy. Since the war with Persia, the preponderance of Roman influence had maintained order in Achaia; but on the return of the hostages, in 603, coincident with the troubles of Macedonia, party enmities were re-awakened. Dissensions soon broke out between the Achæan league and the cities of the Peloponnesus, which it coveted, and the resistance of which it did not hesitate to punish by destruction and pillage.

Sparta soon rebelled, and Peloponnesus was all in flames. The Romans made vain efforts to allay this general disturbance. The envoys of the Senate carried a decree to Corinth, which detached from the league Sparta, Argos,

Orchomenus, and Arcadia. On hearing this, the Achæans massacred the Lacedæmonians then at Corinth, and loaded the Roman commissioners with insults.[609] Before using severity, the Roman Senate resolved to make one appeal to conciliation; but the words of the new envoys were not listened to.

The Achæan league, united with Eubœa and Bœotia, then dared to declare war against Rome, which they knew to be occupied in Spain and Africa. The league was soon vanquished at Scarphia, in Locris, by Metellus, and at Leucopetra, near Corinth, by Mummius. The towns of the Achæan league were treated rigorously; Corinth was sacked; and Greece, under the name of Achaia, remained in subjection to the Romans (608).[610]

However, Mummius, as Polybius himself avows,[611] showed as much moderation as disinterestedness after the victory. He preserved in their places the statues of Philopœmen, kept none of the trophies taken in Greece for himself, and remained so poor that the Senate conferred a dowry upon his daughter from the public treasury.

About the same time the severity of the Senate had not spared Macedonia. During the last Punic war, a Greek adventurer, Andriscus, pretending to be the son of Perseus, had stirred up the country to rebellion, with an army of Thracians. Driven out of Thessaly by Scipio Nasica, he returned there, slew the prætor Juventius Thalna, and formed an alliance with the Carthaginians. Beaten by Metellus, he was sent to Rome loaded with chains. Some years later, a second impostor having also endeavoured to seize the succession of Perseus, the Senate reduced Macedonia to a Roman province (612). It was the same with Illyria after the submission of the Ardæi (618). Never had so many triumphs been seen. Scipio Æmilianus had triumphed over Africa, Metellus over Macedonia, Mummius over Achaia, and Fulvius Flaccus over Illyria.

Delivered henceforth from its troubles in the east and south, the Senate turned its attention towards Spain. This country had never entirely yielded: its strength hardly restored, it took up arms again. After the pacification which Scipio Africanus and Sempronius Gracchus successively induced, new insurrections broke forth; the Lusitanians, yielding to the instigations of Carthage, had revolted in 601, and had gained some advantages over Mummius and his successor Galba (603). But this last, by an act of infamous treachery, massacred thirty thousand prisoners. Prosecuted for this act at Rome by Cato, he was acquitted. Subsequently, another consul showed no less perfidy: Licinius Lucullus, having entered the town of Cauca, which had surrendered, slew twenty thousand of its inhabitants, and sold the rest. [612]

So much cruelty excited the indignation of the peoples of Northern Spain, and, as always happens, the national feeling brought forth a hero. Viriathus, who had escaped the massacre of the Lusitanians, and from a shepherd had become a general, began a war of partisans, and, for five years, having vanquished the Roman generals, ended by rousing the Celtiberians. Whilst these occupied Metellus the Macedonian, Fabius, left alone against Viriathus, was hemmed into a defile by him, and constrained to accept peace. The murder of Viriathus left the issue of the war no longer doubtful. This death was too advantageous to the Romans not to be imputed to Cæpio, successor to his brother Fabius. But when the murderers came to demand the wages of their crime, they were told that the Romans had never approved of the massacre of a general by his soldiers.[613] The Lusitanians, however, submitted, and the legions penetrated to the ocean.

The war, ended in the west, became concentrated round Numantia,[614] where, in the course of five years, several consuls were defeated. When, in 616, Mancinus, surrounded by the enemy on all sides, was reduced to save his army by a shameful capitulation, like that of the Furculæ Caudinæ, the Senate refused to ratify the treaty, and gave up the consul loaded with chains. The same fate was reserved for Tiberius Gracchus, his questor, who had guaranteed the treaty; but, through the favour of the people, he remained at Rome. The Numantines still resisted for a long time with rare energy. The conqueror of Carthage himself had to go to direct the siege, which required immense works; and yet the town was taken only by famine (621). Spain was overcome, but her spirit of independence survived for a great number of years.

Although the fall of the kingdom of Pergamus was posterior to the events we have just related, we will speak of it here because it is the continuation of the system of reducing all peoples to subjection. Attalus III., a monster of cruelty and folly, had, when dying, bequeathed his kingdom to the Roman people, who sent troops to take possession of it; but a natural son of Eumenes, Aristonicus, raised the inhabitants, and defeated the consul Licinius Crassus, soon avenged by one of his successors. Aristonicus was taken, and the kingdom, pacified, passed by the name of Asia under Roman domination (625).

Summary.

XIV. The more the Republic extended its empire, the more the number of the high functions increased, and the more important they became. The consuls, the proconsuls, and the prætors, governed not only foreign countries, but Italy itself. In fact, Appian tells us that the proconsuls exercised their authority in certain countries of the peninsula.[615]

The Roman provinces were nine in number:—1. Cisalpine Gaul. 2. Farther Spain. 3. Nearer Spain. 4. Sardinia and Corsica. 5. Sicily. 6. Northern Africa. 7. Illyria. 8. Macedonia and Achaia. 9. Asia. The people appointed yearly two consuls and seven prætors to go and govern these distant countries; but generally these high offices were attainable only by those who had been questors or ediles. Now, the edileship required a large fortune; for the ediles were obliged to spend great sums in fêtes and public works to please the people. The rich alone could aspire to this first dignity; consequently, it was only the members of the aristocracy who had a chance of arriving at the elevated position, where, for one or two years, they were absolute masters of the destinies of vast kingdoms. Thus, the nobility sought to keep these high offices closed against new men. From 535 to 621—eighty-six years—nine families alone obtained eighty-three consulships. Still later, twelve members of the family Metellus gained various dignities in less than twelve years (630-642.)[616] Nabis, tyrant of Sparta, was right then, when, addressing the consul Quinctius Flamininus, he said, "With you, it is regard for the pay which determines enlistments into the cavalry and infantry. Power is for a small number; dependence is the lot of the multitude. Our lawgiver (Lycurgus), on the contrary, did not wish to put all the power into the hands of certain citizens, whose assembling together you call the Senate, nor to give a legal pre-eminence to one or two orders."[617]

It is curious to see a tyrant of Greece give lessons in democracy to a Roman. In reality, notwithstanding the changes introduced into the comitia, the bearing of which is difficult to explain, the nobility preserved its preponderance, and the habit of addressing the people only after having taken the sense of the Senate, was still persisted in.[618] The Roman government, always aristocratic, became more oppressive in proportion as the State increased in extent, and it lost in influence what the people of Italy gained in intelligence and in legitimate aspirations towards a better future.

Besides, ever since the beginning of the Republic, it had harboured in its breast two opposite parties, the one seeking to extend, the other to restrict, the rights of the people. When the first came into power, all the liberal laws of the past were restored to force; when the second came in, these laws were evaded. Thus we see now the law Valeria, which consecrates appeal to the people, thrice revived; now the law interdicting the re-election of the consuls before an interval of ten years, promulgated by Genucius in 412,[619] and immediately abandoned, renewed in 603, and subsequently restored by Sylla; now the law which threw the freedmen into the urban tribes, in order to annul their vote, revived at three different epochs;[620] now the measures against solicitation, against exactions, against usury, continually put into force; and finally, the right of election to the sacerdotal office by turn, refused or granted to the people.[621] By the Portian laws of 557 and 559, it was forbidden to strike with rods, or put to death, a Roman citizen, before the people had pronounced upon his doom. And yet Scipio Æmilianus, to evade this law, caused his auxiliaries to be beaten with sticks and his soldiers with vine-stalks.[622] At the beginning of the seventh century, the principle of secret voting was admitted in all elections; in 615, in the elections of the magistrates; in 617, for the decision of the people in judicial condemnations; in 623, in the votes on proposals for laws. Finally, by the institution of permanent tribunals (quæstiones perpetuæ), established from 605, it was sought to remedy the spoliation of the provinces; but these institutions, successively adopted or abandoned, could not heal the ills of society. The manly virtues of an intelligent aristocracy had until then maintained the Republic in a state of concord and greatness; its vices were soon to shake it to its foundations.

We have just related the principal events of a period of one hundred and thirty-three years, during which Rome displayed an energy which no nation has ever equalled. On all sides, and almost at the same time, she has passed her natural limits. In the north, she has subdued the Cisalpine Gauls and crossed the Alps; in the west and south, she has conquered the great islands of the Mediterranean and the greater part of Spain. Carthage, her powerful rival, has ceased to exist. To the east, the coasts of the Adriatic are colonised; the Illyrians, the Istrians, the Dalmatians, are subjected; the kingdom of Macedonia has become a tributary province; and the legions have penetrated even to the Danube.[623] Farther than this exist only unknown lands, the country of barbarians, too weak yet to cause alarm. Continental Greece, her isles, Asia Minor up to Mount Taurus, all this country, the cradle of civilisation, has entered into the Roman empire. The rest of Asia receives her laws and obeys her influence. Egypt, the most powerful of the kingdoms which made part of the heritage of Alexander, is under her tutelage. The Jews implore her alliance. The Mediterranean has become a Roman lake. The Republic vainly seeks an adversary worthy of her arms. But if from without no serious danger seems to threaten her, within exist great interests not satisfied, and peoples discontented.

# CHAPTER VI
# THE GRACCHI, MARIUS, AND SYLLA (621-676)

State of the Republic.

I. THE age of disinterestedness and stoic virtues was passed; it had lasted nearly four hundred years, and during that period, the antagonism created by divergency of opinions and interests had never led to sanguinary conflicts. The patriotism of the aristocracy and the good sense of the people had prevented this fatal extremity; but, dating from the first years of the seventh century, everything had changed, and at every proposal of reform, or desire of power, nothing was seen but sedition, civil wars, massacres, and proscriptions.

"The Republic," says Sallust, "owed its greatness to the wise policy of a small number of good citizens,"[624] and we may add that its decline began the day on which their successors ceased to be worthy of those who had gone before them. In fact, most of those who, after the Gracchi, acted a great part, were so selfish and cruel that it is difficult to decide, in the midst of their excesses, which was the representative of the best cause.

As long as Carthage existed, like a man who is on his guard before a dangerous rival, Rome showed an anxiety to maintain the purity and wisdom of her ancient principles; but Carthage fallen, Greece subjugated, the kings of Asia vanquished, the Republic, no longer held by any salutary check, abandoned herself to the excesses of unlimited power.[625]

Sallust draws the following picture of the state of society: "When, freed from the fear of Carthage, the Romans had leisure to give themselves up to their dissensions, then there sprang up on all sides troubles, seditions, and at last civil wars. A small number of powerful men, whose favour most of the citizens sought by base means, exercised a veritable despotism under the imposing name, sometimes of the Senate, at other times of the People. The title of good and bad citizen was no longer the reward of what he did for or against his country, for all were equally corrupt; but the more any one was rich, and in a condition to do evil with impunity, provided he supported the present order of things, the more he passed for a man of worth. From this moment, the ancient manners no longer became corrupted gradually as before; but the depravation spread with the rapidity of a torrent, and youth was to such a degree infected by the poison of luxury and avarice, that there came a generation of people of which it was just to say, that they could neither have patrimony nor suffer others to have it."[626]

The aggrandisement of the empire, frequent contact with strangers, the introduction of new principles in philosophy and religion, the immense riches brought into Italy by war and commerce, had all concurred in causing a profound deterioration of the national character. There had taken place an exchange of populations, ideas, and customs. On the one hand, the Romans, whether soldiers, traders, or farmers of the revenues, in spreading themselves abroad in crowds all over the world,[627] had felt their cupidity increase amid the pomp and luxury of the East; on the other, the foreigners, and especially the Greeks, flowing into Italy, had brought, along with their perfection in the arts, contempt for the ancient institutions. The Romans had undergone an influence which may be compared with that which was exercised over the French of the fifteenth and sixteenth centuries by Italy, then, it is true, superior in intelligence, but perverted in morals. The seduction of vice is irresistible when it presents itself under the form of elegance, wit, and knowledge. As in all epochs of transition, the moral ties were loosened, and the taste for luxury and the unbridled love of money had taken possession of all classes.

Two characteristic facts, distant from one another by one hundred and sixty-nine years, bear witness to the difference of morals at the two periods. Cineas, sent by Pyrrhus to Rome, with rich presents, to obtain peace, finds nobody open to corruption (474). Struck with the majesty and patriotism of the senators, he compares the Senate to an assembly of kings. Jugurtha, on the contrary, coming to Rome (643) to plead his cause, finds his resources quickly exhausted in buying everybody's conscience, and, full of contempt for that great city, exclaims in leaving it: "Venal town, which would soon perish if it could find a purchaser!"[628]

Society, indeed, was placed, by noteworthy changes, in new conditions: for the populace of the towns had increased, while the agricultural population had diminished; agriculture had become profoundly modified; the great landed properties had absorbed the little; the number of proletaries and freedmen had increased, and the slaves had taken the place of free labour. The military service was no longer considered by the nobles as the first honour and the first duty. Religion, that fundamental basis of the Republic, had lost its prestige. And, lastly, the allies were weary of contributing to the greatness of the empire, without participating in the rights of Roman citizens.[629] There were, as we have seen, two peoples, quite distinct: the people of the allies and subjects, and the people of Rome. The allies were always in a state of inferiority; their contingents, more considerable than those of the metropolis, received only half the pay of the latter, and were subjected to bodily chastisement from which the soldiers of the legions were exempted. Even in the triumphs, their cohorts, by way of humiliation, followed, in the last rank and in silence, the chariot of the victor. It was natural then that, penetrated with the feelings of their own dignity and the services they had rendered, they should aspire to be treated as equals. The Roman people, properly so named, occupying a limited territory, from Cære to Cumæ, preserved all the pride of a privileged class. It was composed of from about three to four hundred thousand citizens,[630] divided into thirty five tribes, of which four only belonged to the town, and the others to the country. In these last, it is true, had been inscribed the inhabitants of the colonies and of several towns of Italy, but the great majority of the Italiotes were deprived of political rights, and at the very gates of Rome there still remained disinherited cities, such as Tibur, Præneste, Signia, and Norba. [631]

The richest citizens, in sharing among them the public domain, composed of about two-thirds of the totality of the conquered territory, had finished by getting nearly the whole into their own hands, either by purchase from the small proprietors, or by forcibly expelling them; and this occurred even beyond the frontiers of Italy.[632] At a later time, when the Republic, mistress of the basin of the Mediterranean, received, either under the name of contribution, or by exchange, an immense quantity of corn from the most fertile countries, the cultivation of wheat was neglected in Italy, and the fields were converted into pastures and sumptuous parks. Meadows, indeed, which required fewer hands, would naturally be preferred by the great proprietors. Not only did the vast domains, latifundia, appertain to a small number, but the knights had monopolised all the elements of riches of the country. Many had retired from the ranks of the cavalry to become farmers-general (publicani), bankers, and, almost alone, merchants. Formed, over the whole face of the empire, into financial companies, they worked the provinces, and formed a veritable money aristocracy, whose importance was continually increasing, and which, in the political struggles, made the balance incline to the side where it threw its influence.

Thus, not only was the wealth of the country in the hands of the patrician and plebeian nobility, but the free men diminished incessantly in numbers in the rural districts. If we believe Plutarch,[633] there were no longer in Etruria, in 620, any but foreigners for tillers of the soil and herdsmen, and everywhere slaves had multiplied to such a degree, that, in Sicily alone, 200,000 took part in the revolt of 619.[634] In 650, the King of Bithynia declared himself unable to furnish a military contingent, because all the young adults had been carried away for slaves by Roman collectors. [635] In the great market of Delos, 10,000 slaves were sold and embarked in one day for Italy.[636]

The excessive number of slaves was then a danger to society and a cause of weakness to the State;[637] and there was the same inconvenience in regard to the freedmen. Citizens since the time of Servius Tullius, but without right of suffrage; free in fact, but remaining generally attached to their old masters; physicians, artists, grammarians, they were incapable, they and their children, of becoming senators, or of forming part of the college of pontiffs, or of marrying a free woman, or of serving in the legions, unless in case of extreme danger. Sometimes admitted into the Roman communalty, sometimes rejected; veritable mulattoes of ancient times, they participated in two natures, and bore always the stigma of their origin.[638] Confined to the urban tribes, they had, with the proletaries, augmented that part of the population of Rome for which the conqueror of Carthage and Numantia often showed a veritable disdain: "Silence!" he shouted one day, "you whom Italy does not acknowledge for her children;" and as the noise still continued, he proceeded, "Those whom I caused to be brought here in chains will not frighten me because to-day their bonds have been broken."[639] When the people of the town assembled in the Forum without the presence of the rural tribes, which were more independent, they were open to all seductions, and to the most powerful of these—the money of the candidates and the distributions of wheat at a reduced price. They were also influenced by the mob of those deprived of political rights, when, crowding the public place, as at the English hustings, they sought, by their cries and gestures, to act on the minds of the citizens.

On another hand, proud of the deeds of their ancestors, the principal families, in possession of the soil and of the power, desired to preserve this double advantage without being obliged to show themselves worthy of it; they seemed to disdain the severe education which had made them capable of filling all offices,[640] so that it might be said that there existed then at Rome an aristocracy without nobility, and a democracy without people.

There were, then, injustices to redress, exigencies to satisfy, and abuses to repress; for neither the sumptuary laws, nor those against solicitation, nor the measures against the freedmen, were sufficient to cure the diseases of society. It was necessary, as in the time of Licinius Stolo (378), to have recourse to energetic measures—to give more stability to power, confer the right of city on the peoples of Italy, diminish the number of slaves, revise the titles to landed property, distribute to the people the lands illegally acquired, and thus give a new existence to the agricultural class.

All the men of eminence saw the evil and sought the remedy. Caius Lælius, among others, the friend of Scipio Æmilianus, and probably at his instigation, entertained the thought of proposing salutary reforms, but was prevented by the fear of raising troubles.[641]

Tiberius Gracchus (621).

II. Tiberius Sempronius Gracchus alone dared to take a courageous initiative. Illustrious by birth, remarkable for his physical advantages as well as eloquence,[642] he was son of the Gracchus who was twice consul, and of Cornelia, the daughter of Scipio Africanus.[643] At the age of eighteen, Tiberius had been present, under the orders of his brother-in-law, Scipio Æmilianus, at the ruin of Carthage, and was the first to mount to the assault.[644] Questor of the Consul Mancinus in Spain, he had contributed to the treaty of Numantia. Animated with the love of virtue,[645] far from being dazzled by the splendour of the moment, he foresaw the dangers of the future, and wished to prevent them while there was still time. At the moment of his elevation to the tribuneship, in 621, he took up again, with the approval of men of eminence and philosophers of most distinction the project which had been entertained by Scipio Æmilianus[646] to distribute the public domain among the poor.[647] The people themselves demanded the concession with great outcries, and the walls of Rome were daily covered with inscriptions calling for it.[648]

Tiberius, in a speech to the people, pointed out eloquently all the germs of destruction in the Roman power, and traced the picture of the deplorable condition of the citizens spread over the territory of Italy without an asylum in which to repose their bodies enfeebled by war, after they had shed their blood for their country. He cited revolting examples of the arbitrary conduct of certain magistrates, who had caused innocent men to be put to death on the most futile pretexts.[649]

He then spoke with contempt of the slaves, of that restless, uncertain class, invading the rural districts, useless for the recruitment of the armies, dangerous to society, as the last insurrection in Sicily clearly proved. He ended by proposing a law, which was simply a reproduction of that of Licinius Stolo, that had fallen into disuse. Its object was to withdraw from the nobility a portion of the lands of the domain which they had unjustly seized. No landholder should retain more than five hundred jugera for himself and two hundred and fifty for each of his sons. These lands should belong to them for ever; the part confiscated should be divided into lots of thirty jugera and farmed hereditarily, either to Roman citizens, or to Italiote auxiliaries, on condition of a small rent to the treasury, and with an express prohibition to alienate. The proprietors were to be indemnified for the part of their lands which they so lost. This project, which all the old writers judged to be just and moderate, raised a tempest among the aristocracy. The Senate rejected it, and, when the people were on the point of adopting it, the tribune Octavius, gained over by the rich citizens,[650] opposed to it his inflexible veto. Suddenly interrupted in his designs, Tiberius embraced the resolution, as bold as it was contrary to the laws, of obtaining a vote of the tribes to depose the tribune. These having pronounced accordingly, the new law was published, and three triumvirs appointed for carrying it into execution: they were, Tiberius, his brother Caius, and his father-in-law Appius Claudius. Upon another proposition, he obtained a decision that the money left by the King of Pergamus to the Roman people should be employed for the expenses of establishing those who were to receive the lands.[651]

The agrarian law had only passed by the assistance of the votes of the country tribes.[652] Nevertheless, the popular party, in its enthusiasm, carried Tiberius home in triumph, calling him not only the benefactor of one city, but the father of all the peoples of Italy.

The possessors of the great domains, struck in their dearest interests, were far from sharing in this joy. Not satisfied with having attempted to carry off the urns at the time the law was voted, they plotted the assassination of Tiberius.[653] In fact, as Machiavelli says: "Men value riches even more than honours, and the obstinacy of the Roman aristocracy in defending its possessions constrained the people to have recourse to extremities."[654]

The chiefs of the opposition, great landholders, such as the tribune Octavius and Scipio Nasica, attacked in every possible way the author of the law which despoiled them, and one day the senator Pompeius went so far as to say that the King of Pergamus had sent Tiberius a robe of purple and the diadem, signs of the tribune's future royalty.[655] The latter, in self-defence, had recourse to proposals inspired rather by the desire of a vain popularity than the general interest. The struggle became daily more and more embittered, and his friends persuaded him to secure his re-election as tribune, in order that the inviolability of his office might afford a refuge against the attacks of his enemies. The people was convoked; but the most substantial support of Tiberius failed him: the country people, retained by the harvest, did not obey the call.[656]

Tiberius only sought a reform, and, unknowingly, he had commenced a revolution. But to accomplish this he did not possess all the necessary qualities. A singular mixture of gentleness and audacity, he unchained the tempest, but dared not launch the thunderbolt. Surrounded by his adherents, he walked to the comitia with more appearance of resignation than assurance. The tribes, assembled in the Capitol, were beginning to give their votes, when the senator Fulvius Flaccus came to warn Tiberius that, in the meeting of the Senate, the rich, surrounded by their slaves, had resolved on his destruction. This information produced a considerable agitation round the tribune, and those at a distance demanding the cause of the tumult, Tiberius raised his hand to his head to explain by signs the danger which threatened him.[657] Then his enemies hurried to the Senate, and, giving their own interpretation to his gesture, denounced him as aiming at the kingly power. The Senate, preceded by the sovereign pontiff, Scipio Nasica, repaired to the Capitol. The mob of Tiberius was dispersed, and he himself was slain, with three hundred of his friends, near the gate of the sacred inclosure. All his partisans were hunted out, and underwent the same fate, and among others Diophanes the rhetorician.

The man had succumbed, but the cause remained standing, and public opinion forced the Senate to discontinue its opposition to the execution of the agrarian law, to substitute for Tiberius, as commissioner for the partition of lands, Publius Crassus, an ally of the Gracchi; the people commiserated the fate of the victims and cursed the murderers. Scipio Nasica gained nothing by his triumph; to withdraw him from the general resentment he was sent to Asia, where he died miserably.

The execution of the law encountered, nevertheless, many obstacles. The limits of the *ager publicus* had never been well defined; few title-deeds existed, and those which could be produced were often unintelligible. The value of this property, too, had changed prodigiously. It was necessary to indemnify those who had cleared uncultivated grounds or made improvements. Most of the lots contained religious buildings and sepulchres. According to the antique notions, it was a sacrilege to give them any other destination. The possessors of the *ager publicus*, supported by the Senate and the equestrian order, made the most of all these difficulties. The Italiotes showed no less ardour in protesting against the partition of the lands, knowing well that it would be less favourable to them than to the Romans.

The struggles which had preceded had so excited men's passions, that each party, as the opportunity occurred, presented laws the most opposite to each other. At one time, on the motion of the tribune Junius Pennus, it is a question of expelling all foreigners from Rome (628), in order to deprive the party of the people of auxiliaries; at another, on that of M. Fulvius, the right of city is claimed in favour of the Italiotes (629). This demand leads to disturbances: it is rejected, and the Senate, to rid itself of Fulvius, sends him against the Salluvii, who were threatening Massilia. But already the allies themselves, impatient at seeing their rights incessantly despised, were attempting to secure them by force, and the Latin colony of Fregellæ revolts first; but it is soon destroyed utterly by the prætor M. Opimius (629). The rigour of this act of repression was calculated to intimidate the other towns; but there are questions which must be resolved, and cannot be put down. The cause which has been vanquished ten years is on the point of finding in the brother of Tiberius Gracchus a new champion.

Caius Gracchus (631).

III. Caius Gracchus, indeed, nourished in his heart, as a sacred deposit, the ideas of his brother and the desire to revenge him. After serving in twelve campaigns, he returned to Rome to solicit the tribuneship. On his arrival, the nobles trembled, and, to combat his ascendency, they accused him of being concerned in the insurrection of Fregellæ; but his name brought him numerous sympathies. On the day of his election, a vast crowd of citizens arrived in Rome from all parts of Italy, and so great was the confluence that the Campus Martius could not hold them; and many gave their votes even from the roofs.[658] Invested with the tribunitian power, Gracchus made use of it to submit to the sanction of the people several laws; some directed merely against the enemies of his brother;[659] others, of great political meaning, which require more particular notice.

First, the importance of the tribunes was increased by the faculty of being re-elected indefinitely,[660] which tended to give a character of permanence to functions which were already so preponderant. Next, the law frumentaria, by turn carried into effect and abandoned,[661] gained him adherents by his granting without distinction, to all the poor citizens, the monthly distribution of a certain quantity of wheat; and for this purpose vast public granaries were constructed.[662] The shortening of the time of service of the soldiers,[663] the prohibition to enrol them under seventeen years of age, and the payment by the treasury of their equipment, which was previously deducted from their pay, gained him the favour of the army. The establishment of new tolls (portoria) augmented the resources of the State; new colonies were founded,[664] not only in Italy, but in the possessions out of the peninsula.[665] The agrarian law, which was connected with the establishment of these colonies, was confirmed, probably with the view of restoring to the commissioners charged with its execution their judicial powers, which had fallen into disuse.[666] Long and wide roads, starting from Rome, placed the metropolis in easy communication with the different countries of Italy.[667]

Down to this time, the appointments to the provinces had taken place after the consular elections, which allowed the Senate to distribute the great commands nearly according to its own convenience; it was now arranged, in order to defeat the calculations of ambition and cupidity, that the Senate should assign, before the election of the consuls, the provinces which they should administrate.[668] To elevate the title of Roman citizen, the dispositions of the law Porcia were put in force again, and it was forbidden not only to pronounce capital punishment[669] on a Roman citizen, except in case of high treason (perduellio), but even for this offence to apply it without the ratification of the people. It was equivalent to repealing the law of provocation, the principle of which had been inscribed in the laws of the Twelve Tables.

C. Gracchus attempted still more in the cause of equality. He proposed to confer the right of city on the allies who enjoyed the Latin law, and even to extend this benefit to all the inhabitants of Italy.[670] He wished that in the comitia all classes should be admitted without distinction to draw lots for the century called præogativa, or which had precedency in voting;[671] this "prerogative" had in fact a great influence, because the suffrage of the first voters was regarded as a divine presage; but these propositions were rejected. Desirous of diminishing the power of the Senate, Gracchus resolved to oppose to it the knights, whose importance he increased by new attributes. He caused a law to be passed which authorised the censor to let to farm, in Asia, the lands taken from the inhabitants of the conquered towns.[672] The knights then took in farm the rents and tithes of those countries, of which the soil belonged of right to the Roman people;[673] the old proprietors were reduced to the condition of simple tenants. Finally, Caius gave the knights a share in the judiciary powers, exercised exclusively by the Senate, the venality of which had excited public contempt.[674] Three hundred knights were joined with three hundred senators, and the cognisance of all actions at law thus devolved upon six hundred judges. [675] These measures gained for him the good-will of an order which, hostile hitherto to the popular party, had contributed to the failure of the projects of Tiberius Gracchus.

The tribune's success was immense; his popularity became so great that the people surrendered to him the right of naming the three hundred knights among whom the judges were to be chosen, and his simple recommendation was enough to secure the election of Fannius, one of his partisans, to the consulship. Desiring further to show his spirit of justice towards the provinces, he sent back to Spain the wheat arbitrarily carried away from the inhabitants by the proprætor Fabius. The tribunes had thus, at that epoch, a veritable omnipotence: they had charge of the great works; disposed of the public revenues; dictated, so to say, the election of the consuls; controlled the acts of the governors of provinces; proposed the laws, and saw to their execution.

These measures taken together, from the circumstance that they were favourable to a great number of interests, calmed for some time the ardour of the opposition, and reduced it to silence. Even the Senate became reconciled in appearance with Caius Gracchus; but under the surface the feeling of hatred still existed, and another tribune was raised up against him, Livius Drusus, whose mission was to propose measures destined to restore to the Senate the affection of the people. C. Gracchus had designed that the allies enjoying Latin rights should be admitted to the right of city. Drusus caused it to be declared that, like the Roman citizens, they should no longer be subject to be beaten with rods. According to the law of the Gracchi, the lands distributed to the poor citizens were burdened with a small rent for the profit of the public treasury; Drusus freed them from it.[676] In rivalry to the agrarian law, he obtained the creation of twelve colonies of three thousand citizens each. Lastly, it was thought necessary to remove Caius Gracchus himself out of the way, by appointing him to lead to Carthage, to raise it from its ruins, the colony of six thousand individuals, taken from all parts of Italy,[677] of which he had obtained the establishment.

During his absence, things took an entirely new turn. If, on the one hand, the measures of Drusus had satisfied a part of the people, on the other, Fulvius, the friend of Caius, a man of excessive zeal, compromised his cause by dangerous exaggerations. Opimius, the bitter enemy of the Gracchi, offered himself for the consulship. Informed of these different intrigues, Caius returned suddenly to Rome to solicit a third renewal of the tribuneship. He failed, while Opimius, elected consul, with the prospect of combating a party so redoubtable to the nobles, caused all citizens who were not Romans to be banished from the town, and, under a religious pretext, attempted to obtain the revocation of the decree relating to the colony of Carthage. When the day of deliberation arrived, two parties occupied the Capitol at an early hour.

The Senate, in consideration of the gravity of the circumstances and in the interest of the public safety, invested the consul with extraordinary powers, declaring that it was necessary to exterminate tyrants—a treacherous qualification always employed against the defenders of the people, and, in order to make more sure of triumph, they had recourse to foreign troops. The Consul Opimius, at the head of a body of Cretan archers, easily put to the rout a tumultuous assembly. Caius took flight, and, finding himself pursued, slew himself. Fulvius underwent a similar fate. The head of the tribune was carried in triumph. Three thousand men were thrown into prison and strangled. The agrarian laws and the emancipation of Italy ceased, for some time, to torment the Senate.

Such was the fate of the Gracchi, two men who had at heart to reform the laws of their country, and who fell victims to selfish interests and prejudices still too powerful. "They perished," says Appian,[678] "because they employed violence in the execution of an excellent measure."[679] In fact, in a State where legal forms had been respected for four hundred years, it was necessary either to observe them faithfully, or to have an army at command.

Yet the work of the Gracchi did not die with them. Several of their laws continued long to subsist. The agrarian law was executed in part, inasmuch as, at a subsequent period, the nobles bought back the portions of lands which had been taken from them,[680] and its effects were only destroyed at the end of fifteen years. Implicated in the acts of corruption imputed to Jugurtha, of which we shall soon have to speak, the Consul Opimius had the same fate as Scipio Nasica, and a no less miserable end. It is curious to see two men, each vanquisher of a sedition, terminate their lives in a foreign land, exposed to the hatred and contempt of their fellow-citizens. Yet the reason is natural: they combated with arms ideas which arms could not destroy. When, in the midst of general prosperity, dangerous Utopias spring up, without root in the country, the slightest employment of force extinguishes them; but, on the contrary, when society, deeply tormented by real and imperious needs, requires reform, the success of the most violent repression is but momentaneous: the ideas repressed appear again incessantly, and, like the fabled hydra, for one head struck off a hundred others grow up in its place.

War of Jugurtha (637).

IV. An arrogant oligarchy had triumphed in Rome over the popular party: will it have at least the energy to raise again the honour of the Roman name abroad? Such will not be the case: events, of which Africa is on the point of becoming the theatre, will show the baseness of these men who sought to govern the world by repudiating the virtues of their ancestors.

Jugurtha, natural son of Mastanabal, king of Numidia, by a concubine, had distinguished himself in the Roman legions at the siege of Numantia. Reckoning on the favour he enjoyed at Rome, he had resolved to seize the inheritance of Micipsa, to the prejudice of the two legitimate children, Hiempsal and Adherbal. The first was murdered by his orders, and, in spite of this crime, Jugurtha had succeeded in corrupting the Roman commissioners charged with the task of dividing the kingdom between him and Adherbal, and in obtaining from them the larger part. But soon master of the whole country by force of arms, he put Adherbal to death also. The Senate sent against Jugurtha the consul Bestia Calpurnius, who, soon bribed as the commissioners had been, concluded a disgraceful peace. So many infamous deeds could not remain in the shade. The consul, on his return, was attacked by C. Memmius, who, in forcing Jugurtha to come to Rome to give an account of himself, seized the occasion of reminding his hearers of the grievances of the people and of the scandalous conduct of the nobles, in the following words:—

"After the assassination of Tiberius Gracchus, who, according to the nobles, aspired to the kingly power, the Roman people saw itself exposed to their vigorous persecutions. Similarly, after the murder of Caius Gracchus and Marcus Fulvius, how many people of your order have they not caused to be imprisoned? At either of these epochs it was not the law, but their caprice alone, which put an end to the massacres. Moreover, I acknowledge that to restore to the people their rights, is to aspire to the kingly power; and we must regard as legitimate all vengeance obtained by the blood of the citizens.... In these last years you groaned in secret to see the public treasure wasted, the kings and free people made the tributaries of a few nobles—of those who alone are in possession of splendid dignities and great riches. Nevertheless, it is too little for them to be able with impunity to commit such crimes; they have finished by delivering to the enemies of the State your laws, the dignity of your empire, and all that is sacred in the eyes of gods and men.... But who are they, then, those who have invaded the Republic? Villains covered with blood, devoured by a monstrous cupidity, the most criminal, and at the same time the most arrogant, of men. For them, good faith, honour, religion, and virtue, are, like vice, objects of traffic. Some have put to death tribunes of the people; others have commenced unjust proceedings against you; most of them have shed your blood; and these excesses are their safeguard: the further they have gone in the course of their crimes, the more they feel themselves in safety.... Ah! could you count upon a sincere reconciliation with them? They seek to rule over you, you seek to be free; it is their will to oppress you, you resist oppression; lastly, they treat your allies as enemies, your enemies as allies."[681]

He then reminded his audience of all Jugurtha's crimes. The latter rose to justify himself; but the tribune C. Bæbius, with whom he was in league, ordered the king to keep silence. The Numidian was on the point of gathering the fruit of such an accumulation of corruptions, when, having caused a dangerous rival, Massiva, the grandson of Masinissa, to be assassinated at Rome, he became the object of public reprobation, and was compelled to return to Africa. War then re-commences; the consul Albinus lets it drag on in length. Recalled to Rome to hold the comitia, he entrusts the command to his brother, the proprætor Aulus, whose army, soon seduced by Jugurtha, lets itself be surrounded, and is under the necessity of making a dishonourable capitulation. The indignation at Rome is at its height. On the proposal of a tribune, an inquiry is opened against all the presumed accomplices in the misdeeds of Jugurtha; they were punished, and, as often happens under such circumstances, the vengeance of the people passed the limits of justice. At last, after warm debates, an honourable man is chosen, Metellus, belonging to the faction of the nobles, and he is charged with the war in Africa. Public opinion, by forcing the Senate to punish corruption, had triumphed over bad passions; and "it was the first time," says Sallust, "that the people put a bridle on the tyrannical pride of the nobility."[682]

Marius (647).

V. The Gracchi had made themselves, so to say, the civil champions of the popular cause: Marius became its stern soldier. Born of an obscure family, bred in camps, having arrived by his courage at high grades, he had the roughness and the ambition of the class which feels itself oppressed. A great captain, but a partisan in spirit, naturally inclined to good and to justice, he became, towards the end of his life, through love of power, cruel and inexorable.[683]

After having distinguished himself at the siege of Numantia, he was elected tribune of the people, and displayed in that office a great impartiality. [684] It was the first step of his fortune. Having become the lieutenant of Metellus, in the war against Jugurtha he sought to supplant his general; and, at a later period, succeeded in allying himself to an illustrious family by marrying Julia, paternal aunt of the great Cæsar. Guided by his instinct or intelligence, he had learnt that beneath the official people there existed a people of proletaries and of allies which demanded a consideration in the State.

Having reached the consulship through his high military reputation, backed by intrigues, he was charged with the war of Numidia, and, before his departure, expressed with energy, in an address to the people, the rancours and principles of the democratic party of that time.

"You have charged me," he said, "with the war against Jugurtha; the nobility is irritated at your choice: but why do you not change your decree, by going to seek for this expedition a man among that crowd of nobles, of old lineage, who counts many ancestors, but not a single campaign?... It is true that he would have to take among the people an adviser who could teach him his business. With these proud patricians compare Marius, a new man. What they have heard related by others, what they have read of, I have seen in part, I have in part done.... They reproach me with the obscurity of my birth and fortune; I reproach them with their cowardice and personal infamy. Nature, our common mother, has made all men equal, and the bravest is the most noble.... If they think they are justified in despising me, let them also despise their ancestors, ennobled like me by their personal merits.... And is it not more worthy to be oneself the author of his name than to degrade that which has been transmitted to you?

"I cannot, to justify your confidence, make a display of images, nor boast of the triumphs or consulships of my ancestors; but I can produce, if necessary, javelins, a standard, the trappings of war, twenty other military gifts, besides the scars which furrow my breast. These are my images, these my nobility, not left by inheritance, but won for myself by great personal labours and perils."[685]

After this oration, in which is revealed the legitimate ardour of those who, in all aristocratic countries, demand equality, Marius, contrary to the ancient system, enrolled more proletaries than citizens. The veterans also crowded under his standards. He conducted the war of Africa with skill; but he was robbed of part of his glory by his questor, P. Cornelius Sylla. This man, called soon afterwards to play so great a part, sprung from an illustrious patrician family, ambitious, ardent, full of boldness and confidence in himself, recoiled before no obstacle. The successes, which cost so many efforts to Marius, seemed to come of themselves to Sylla. Marius defeated the Numidian prince, but, by an adventurous act of boldness, Sylla received his submission, and ended the war. From that time began, between the proconsul and his young questor, a rivalry which, in time, was changed into violent hatred. They became, one, the champion of the democracy; the other, the hope of the oligarchic faction. So the Senate extolled beyond measure Metellus and Sylla, in order that the people should not consider Marius as the first of the generals.[686] The gravity of events soon baffled this manœuvre.

While Marius was concluding the war with Jugurtha, a great danger threatened Italy. Since 641, an immense migration of barbarians had moved through Illyria into Cisalpine Gaul, and had defeated, at Noreia (in Carniola) the consul Papirius Carbo. They were the Cimbri, and all their peculiarities, manners, language, habits of pillage, and adventures, attested their relationship to the Gauls.[687] In their passage through Rhætia into the country of the Helvetii, they dragged with them different peoples, and during some years devastated Gaul; returned in 645 to the neighbourhood of the Roman province, they demanded of the Republic lands to settle in. The consular army sent to meet them was defeated, and they invaded the province itself. The Tigurini (647), a people of Helvetia, issuing from their mountains, slew the consul L. Cassius, and made his army pass under the yoke. It was only a prelude to greater disasters. A third invasion of the Cimbri, followed by two new defeats in 649, on the banks of the Rhine, excites the keenest apprehensions, and points to Marius as the only man capable of saving Italy; the nobles, moreover, in presence of this great danger, sought no longer to seize the power.[688] Marius was, contrary to the law, named a second time consul, in 650, and charged with the war in Gaul.

This great captain laboured during several years to restore military discipline, practise his troops, and familiarise them with their new enemies, whose aspect filled them with terror. Marius, considered indispensable, was re-elected from year to year; from 650 to 654, he was five times elected consul, and beat the Cimbri, united with the Ambrones and Teutones, near Aquæ Sextiæ (Aix), re-passed into Italy, and exterminated, near Vercellæ, the Cimbri who had escaped from the last battle and those whom the Celtiberians had driven back from Spain. These immense butcheries, these massacres of whole peoples, removed for some time the barbarians from the frontiers of the Republic.

Consul for the sixth time (654), the saviour of Rome and Italy, by a generous deference, would not triumph without his colleague Catulus,[689] and did not hesitate to exceed his powers in granting to two auxiliary cohorts of Cameria, who had distinguished themselves, the rights of city. [690] But his glory was obscured by culpable intrigues. Associated with the most turbulent chiefs of the democratic party, he excited them to revolt, and sacrificed them as soon as he saw that they could not succeed. When governments repulse the legitimate wishes of the people and true ideas, then factious men seize on them as a powerful arm to serve their passions and personal interests; the Senate having rejected all the proposals of reform, those who sought to raise disorders found in them a pretext and support in their perverse projects. L. Appuleius Saturninus, one of Marius's creatures, and Glaucia, a fellow of loose manners, were guilty of incredible violences. The first revived the agrarian laws of the Gracchi, and went beyond them in proposing the partition of the lands taken from the Cimbri; a measure which he sought to impose by terror and murder. In the troubles which broke out at the election of the consuls for 655, the urban tribes came to blows with the country tribes. In the midst of the tumult, Saturninus, followed by a troop of desperadoes, made himself master of the Capitol, and fortified himself in it. Charged, in his quality of consul, with the repression of sedition, Marius first favoured it by an intentional inaction; then, seeing all good citizens run to arms, and the factious without support, even deserted by the urban plebeians, he placed himself at the head of some troops, and occupied the avenues to the Capitol. From the first moment of the attack, the rebels threw down their arms and demanded quarter. Marius left them to be massacred by the people, as though he had wished that the secret of the sedition might die with them.

The question of Italian emancipation was not foreign to the revolt of Saturninus. It is certain that the claims of the Italiotes, rejected after the death of C. Gracchus, and then adjourned at the approach of the Cimbri, who threatened all the peninsula with one common catastrophe, were renewed with more earnestness than ever after the defeat of the barbarians. The earnestness of the allies to come to the succour of Italy, the courage which they had shown in the battle-fields of Aquæ Sextiæ and Vercellæ, gave them new claims to become Romans. Yet, if some prudent politicians believed that the time was arrived for yielding to the wishes of the Italiotes, a numerous and powerful party revolted at the idea of such a concession. The more the privileges of the citizens became extended, the more the Roman pride resisted the thought of having sharers in them. M. Livius Drusus (663), tribune of the people, son of the Drusus already mentioned, having under his command in Rome an immense body of clients, the acknowledged patron of all the Italiote cities, dared to attempt this salutary reform, and had nearly carried it by force of party. He was not ignorant that there was already in existence a formidable confederacy of the peoples of the south and east of Italy, and that more than once their chiefs had meditated a general insurrection. Drusus, trusting in their projects, had had the art to restrain them and to obtain from them the promise of a blind obedience. The success of the tribune seemed certain. The people were gained over by distributions of wheat and concessions of lands; the Senate, intimidated, appeared to have become powerless, when, a few days before the vote of the tribes, Drusus was assassinated. All Italy accused the senators of this crime, and war became inevitable.

The obstinate refusal of the Romans to share with the Italiotes all their political rights, had been long a cause of political agitation. More than two hundred years before, the war of the Latins and the revolt of the inhabitants of Campania, after the battle of Cannæ, had no other motives. About the same time (536), Spurius Carvilius proposed to admit into the Senate two senators taken from each people in Latium. "The assembly," says Livy,[691] "burst into a murmur of indignation, and Manlius, raising his voice over the others, declared that there existed still a descendant of that consul who once, in the Capitol, threatened to kill with his own hand the first Latin he should see in the curia;" a striking proof of this secular resistance of the Roman aristocracy to everything which might threaten its supremacy. But, after this epoch, the ideas of equality had assumed a power which it was impossible to mistake.

Wars of the Allies (663).

VI. This civil war, which was called the War of Allies,[692] showed once more the impotence of material force against the legitimate aspirations of peoples, and it covered the country with blood and ruins. Three hundred thousand citizens, the choice of the nation, perished on the field of battle. [693] Rome had the superiority, it is true, and yet it was the cause of the vanquished which triumphed, since, after the war, the only object of which was the assertion of the rights of citizenship, these rights were granted to most of the peoples of Italy. Sylla subsequently restricted them, and we may be convinced, by examining the different censuses, that the entire emancipation was only accomplished under Cæsar.[694]

The revolt burst out fortuitously before the day fixed. It was provoked by the violence of a Roman magistrate, who was massacred by the inhabitants of Asculum; but all was ready for an insurrection, which was not long before it became general. The allies had a secret government, chiefs appointed, and an army organised. At the head of the peoples confederated against Rome were distinguished the Marsi and the Samnites; the first excited rather by a feeling of national pride than by the memory of injuries to be revenged; the second, on the contrary, by the hatred which they had vowed against the Romans during long struggles for their independence—struggles renewed on the invasion of Hannibal. Both shared the honour of the supreme command. It appears, moreover, that the system of government adopted by the confederation was a copy of the Roman institutions. To substitute Italy for Rome, and to replace the denomination of a single town by that of a great people, was the avowed aim of the new league. A Senate was named, or rather a Diet, in which each city had its representatives; they elected two consuls, Q. Pompædius Silo, a Marsian, and C. Papius Mutilus, a Samnite. For their capital, they chose Corfinium, the name of which was changed to that of Italia, or Vitelia, which, in the Oscan language, spoken by a part of the peoples of Southern Italy, had the same signification.[695]

The allies were wanting neither in skilful generals nor in brave and experienced soldiers; in the two camps, the same arms, the same discipline. The war, commenced at the end of the year 663, was pursued on both sides with the utmost animosity. It extended through Central Italy, from the north to the south, from Firmum (*Fermo*) to Grumentum, in Lucania, and from east to west from Cannæ to the Liris. The battles were sanguinary, and often indecisive, and, on both sides, the losses were so considerable, that it soon became necessary to enrol the freedmen, and even the slaves.

The allies obtained at first brilliant successes. Marius had the glory of arresting their progress, although he had only troops demoralised by reverses. Fortune, this time again, served Sylla better; conqueror wherever he appeared, he sullied his exploits by horrible cruelties to the Samnites, whom he seemed to have undertaken to destroy rather than to subdue. The Senate displayed more humanity, or more policy, in granting spontaneously the right of Roman city to all the allies who remained faithful to the Republic, and in promising it to all those who should lay down their arms. It treated in the same manner the Cisalpine Gauls; as to their neighbours on the left bank of the Po, it conferred upon them the right of Latium. This wise measure divided the confederates;[696] the greater part submitted. The Samnites, almost alone, continued to fight in their mountains with the fury of despair. The emancipation of Italy was accompanied, nevertheless, with a restrictive measure which was designed to preserve to the Romans the preponderance in the comitia. To the thirty-five old tribes, eight new ones were added, in which all the Italiotes were inscribed; and, as the votes were reckoned by tribes, and not by head, it is evident that the influence of the new citizens must have been nearly null.[697]

Etruria had taken no part in the Social War. The nobility was devoted to Rome, and the people lived in a condition approximating to bondage. The law Julia, which gave to the Italiotes the right of Roman city, and which took its name from its author, the consul L. Julius Cæsar, produced among the Etruscans a complete revolution. It was welcomed with enthusiasm.

While Italy was in flames, Mithridates VI., king of Pontus, determined to take advantage of the weakness of the Republic to aggrandise himself. In 664, he invaded Bithynia and Cappadocia, and expelled the kings, allies of Rome. At the same time he entered into communication with the Samnites, to whom he promised subsidies and soldiers. Such was the hatred then inspired by the Romans in foreign countries, that an order of Mithridates was sufficient to raise the province of Asia, where, in one day, eighty thousand Romans were massacred.[698] At this time the Social War was already approaching its end. With the exception of Samnium, all Italy was subdued, and the Senate could turn its attention to the distant provinces.

Sylla (666).

VII. Sylla, appointed consul in recompénse for his services, was charged with the task of chastising Mithridates. While he was preparing for this mission, the tribune of the people, P. Sulpicius, had formed a powerful party. A remarkable man, though without scruples, he had the qualities and the defects of most of those who played a part in these epochs of dissension.[699] Escorted by six hundred Roman knights, whom he called the Anti-Senate,[700] he sold publicly the right of citizen to freedmen and foreigners, and received the price on tables raised in the middle of the public place.[701] He caused a plebiscitum to be passed to put an end to the subterfuge of the law Julia, which, by an illusory re-partition, cheated the Italiotes of the very rights which it seemed to accord to them; and instead of maintaining them in the eight new tribes, he caused them to be inscribed in the thirty-five old ones. The measure was not adopted without warm discussions; but Sulpicius was supported by all the new citizens, together with the democratic faction and Marius. A riot carried the vote and Sylla, threatened with death, was obliged to take refuge in the house of Marius, and hastily quit Rome. Master of the town, Sulpicius showed the influences he obeyed, by causing to be given to the aged Marius the province of Asia, and the command of the expedition against Mithridates. But Sylla had his army in Campania, and was determined to support his own claims. While the faction of Marius, in the town, indulged in acts of violence against the contrary faction, the soldiers of Sylla were irritated at seeing the legions of his rival likely to snatch from them the rich booty which Asia promised; and they swore to avenge their chief. Sylla placed himself at their head, and marched from Nola upon Rome, with his colleague, Pompeius Rufus, who had just joined him. The greater part of the superior officers dared not follow him, so great was still the prestige of the eternal city.[702] In vain deputations are addressed to him; he marches onwards, and penetrates into the streets of Rome. Assailed by the inhabitants, and attacked by Marius and Sulpicius, he triumphs only by dint of boldness and energy. It was the first time that a general, entering Rome as a conqueror, had seized the power by force of arms.

Sylla restored order, prevented pillage, convoked the assembly of the people, justified his conduct, and, wishing to secure for his party the preponderance in the public deliberations, he recalled to force the old custom of requiring the previous assent of the Senate before the presentation of a law. The comitia by centuries were substituted for the comitia by tribes, to which was left only the election of the inferior magistrates.[703] Sylla caused Sulpicius to be put to death, and abrogated his decrees; and he set a price on the head of Marius, forgetting that he had himself, a short time before, found a refuge in the house of his rival. He proscribed the chiefs of the democratic faction, but most of them had fled before he entered Rome. Marius and his son had reached Africa through a thousand dangers. This revolution appears not to have been sanguinary, and, with the exception of Sulpicius, the historians of the time mention no considerable person as having been put to death. The terror inspired at first by Sylla lasted no long time. Reprobation of his acts was shown both in the Senate and among the people, who seized every opportunity to mark their discontent. Sylla was to resume the command of the army of Asia, and that of the army of Italy had fallen to Pompeius. The massacre of this latter by his own soldiers made the future dictator feel how insecure was his power; he sought to put a stop to the opposition to which he was exposed by accepting as a candidate at the consular comitia L. Cornelius Cinna, a known partisan of Marius, taking care, however, to exact from him a solemn oath of fidelity. But Cinna, once elected, held none of his engagements, and the other consul, Cn. Octavius, had neither the authority nor the energy necessary to balance the influence of his colleague.

Sylla, after presiding at the consular comitia, went in all haste to Capua to take the command of his troops, whom he led into Greece against the lieutenants of Mithridates. Cinna determined to execute the law of Sulpicius, which assimilated the new citizens to the old ones;[704] he demanded at the same time the return of the exiles, and made an appeal to the slaves. Immediately the Senate, and even the tribunes of the people, pronounced against him. He was declared deposed from the consulate. "A merited disgrace," says Paterculus, "but a dangerous precedent."[705] Driven from Rome, he hurried to Nola to demand an asylum of the Samnites, who were still in arms. Thence he went to sound the temper of the Roman army employed to observe Samnium, and, once assured of the dispositions of the soldiers in his favour, he penetrated into their camp, demanding protection against his enemies. His speeches and promises seduced the legions: they chose Cinna for their chief by acclamation, and followed him without hesitating. Meanwhile two lieutenants of Marius, Q. Sertorius and Cn. Papirius Carbo, both exiled by Sylla, proceeded to levy troops in the north of Italy; and the aged Marius landed in Etruria, where his presence was immediately followed by an insurrection. The Etruscan peasants accused the Senate as the cause of all their sufferings; and the enemy of the nobles and the rich appeared to them as an avenger sent by the gods. In ranging themselves under his banner, they believed that they were on the way with him to the pillage of the eternal city.

War was on the point of re-commencing, and this time Romans and Italiotes marched united against Rome. From the north, Marius, Sertorius, and Carbo were advancing with considerable forces. Cinna, master of Campania, was penetrating into Latium, while a Samnite army invaded it on the other side. To these five armies the Senate could oppose but one; that of Cn. Pompeius Strabo, an able general, but an intriguing politician, who hoped to raise himself under favour of the disorder. Quitting his cantonments in Apulia, he had arrived, by forced marches, under the walls of Rome, seeking either to sell his services to the Senate or to effect a conciliation with Marius. He soon saw that the insurgents were strong enough to do without him. His soldiers, raised in the Picenum and in the country of the Marsi, refused to fight for the Senate against their old confederates, and would have abandoned their general but for the courage and presence of mind of his son, a youth of twenty years of age, the same who subsequently was the great Pompey. One day the legionaries, snatching their ensigns, threatened to desert in mass: young Pompey laid himself across the gateway of the camp, and challenged them to pass over his body.[706] Death delivered Pompeius Strabo from the shame of being present at an inevitable catastrophe. According to some authors, he sank under the attacks of an epidemic disease; according to others, he was struck by lightning in the very midst of his camp. Deprived of its chief, his army passed over to the enemy; the Senate was without defenders, and the populace rose against it: Rome opened her gates to Cinna and Marius.

The conquerors were without pity in putting to death, often with refinements in cruelty unknown to the Romans, the partisans of the aristocratic faction who had fallen into their hands. During several days, the slaves, whom Cinna had restored to liberty, gave themselves up to every excess. Sertorius, the only one of the chiefs of the democratic party who had some feelings of justice, made an example of these wretches, and massacred nearly four thousand of them.[707]

Marius and Cinna had proclaimed, as they advanced upon Rome in arms, that their aim was to assure to the Italiotes the entire enjoyment of the rights of Roman city; they declared themselves both consuls for the year 668. Their power was too considerable to be contested, for the new citizens furnished them with a contingent of thirty legions, or about 150,000 men.[708] Marius died suddenly thirteen days after entering upon office, and the democratic party lost in him the only man who still preserved his prestige. A fact which arose out of his funeral, paints the manners of the epoch, and the character of the revolution which had just been effected. An extraordinary sacrifice was wanted for his tomb: the pontiff Q. Mucius Scævola, one of the most respectable old men of the nobility, was chosen as the victim. Conducted in pomp before the funeral pile of the conqueror of the Cimbri, he was struck by the sacrificer, who, with an inexperienced hand, plunged the knife into his throat without killing him. Restored to life, Scævola was cited in judgment, by a tribune of the people, for not having received the blow fairly.[709]

While Rome and all Italy were plunged in this fearful anarchy, Sylla drove out of Greece the generals of Mithridates VI., and gained two great battles at Chæronea (668) and Orchomenus (669). He was still in Bœotia, when Valerius Flaccus, sent by Cinna to replace him, landed in Greece, penetrated into Thessaly, and thence passed into Asia. Sylla followed him thither immediately, in haste to conclude with the King of Pontus an arrangement which would enable him to lead his army back into Italy. Circumstances were favourable. Mithridates had need to repair his losses, and he found himself in presence of a new enemy, the lieutenant of Valerius Flaccus, the fierce Flavius Fimbria, who, having by the murder of his general become head of the army of Asia, had seized upon Pergamus. Mithridates subscribed to the conditions imposed by Sylla; he restored all the provinces of which he had taken possession, and gave plate and money. Sylla then advanced into Lydia against Fimbria; but the latter, at the approach of the victor of Chæronea, could not restrain his soldiers. His whole army disbanded and passed over to Sylla. Threatened by his rival, the murderer of Flaccus was driven to slay himself. Nothing now stood in the way of Sylla's projects on Italy, and he prepared to make his enemies at Rome pay dearly for their temporary triumph. At the moment of setting sail, he wrote to the Senate to announce the conclusion of the war in Asia, and his own speedy return. Three years, he said, had been sufficient to enable him to re-unite with the Roman empire Greece, Macedonia, Ionia, and Asia, and to shut up Mithridates within the limits of his old possessions; he was the first Roman who received an embassy from the King of the Parthians.[710] He complained of the violence exercised against his friends and his wife, who had fled with a crowd of fugitives to seek an asylum in his camp.[711] He added, without vain threats, his intention to restore order by force of arms; but he promised not to repeal the great measure of the emancipation of Italy, and ended by declaring that the good citizens, new as well as old, had nothing to fear from him.

This letter, which the Senate ventured to receive, redoubled the fury of the men who had succeeded Marius. Blood flowed again. Cinna, who caused himself to be re-elected consul for the fourth time, and Cn. Papirius Carbo, his colleague, collecting in haste numerous troops, but ill disciplined, prepared to do their best to make head against the storm which was approaching. Persuaded that Sylla would proceed along the Adriatic to invade Italy from the north, Cinna had collected at Ancona a considerable army, with the design of surprising him in the midst of his march, and attacking him either in Epirus or Illyria. But his soldiers, Italiotes in great part, encouraged by the promises of Sylla, and, moreover, full of contempt for their own general, said openly that they would not pass the sea. Cinna attempted to make an example of some of the mutineers. A revolt broke out, and he was massacred. To avoid a similar lot, Carbo, who came to take the command, hastened to promise the rebels that they should not quit Italy.

Sylla landed at Brundusium, in 671, at the head of an army of forty thousand men, composed of five legions, six thousand cavalry, and contingents from Peloponnesus and Macedonia. The fleet numbered sixteen hundred vessels.[712] He followed the Appian Way, and reached Campania after a single battle, fought not far from Canusium.[713] He brought the gold of Mithridates and the plunder of the temples of Greece, means of seduction still more dangerous than his ability on the field of battle. Hardly arrived in Italy, he rallied round him the proscripts and all those who detested the inapt and cruel government of the successors of Marius. The remains of the great families decimated by them repaired to his camp as to a safe place of refuge. M. Licinius Crassus became one of his ablest lieutenants, and it was then that Cn. Pompeius, the son of Strabo, a general at twenty-three years of age, raised an army in the Picenum, beat three bodies of the enemies, and came to offer to Sylla his sword, already redoubtable.

It was the beginning of the year 672 when Sylla entered Latium; he completely defeated, near Signia, the legions of the younger Marius, whose name had raised him to the consulship. This battle rendered Sylla master of Rome; but to the north, in Cisalpine Gaul and Etruria, Carbo, in spite of frequent defeats, disputed the ground with obstinacy against Pompey and Sylla's other lieutenants. In the south, the Samnites had raised all their forces, and were preparing to succour Præneste, besieged by Sylla in person, and defended by young Marius. Pontius Telesinus, the general of the Samnites, finding it out of his power to raise the siege, conceived then the audacious and almost desperate idea of carrying his whole army to Rome, taking it by surprise, and sacking it. "Let us burn the wolves' den,"[714] he said to his soldiers: "so long as it exists, there will be no liberty in Italy."

By a rapid night-march, Telesinus deceived the vigilance of his adversary; but, exhausted with fatigue, on arriving at the foot of the ramparts of Rome, the Samnites were unable to give the assault, and Sylla had time to arrive with the choicest of his legions.

A sanguinary battle took place at the very gates of the town, on the day of the calends of November, 672, and it continued far into the night. The left wing of the Romans was beaten and took to flight, in spite of the efforts of Sylla to rally it; Telesinus perished in the fight, and Crassus, who commanded the right wing, gained a complete victory. At daylight, the Samnites who had escaped the slaughter laid down their arms and demanded quarter.[715]

More than a year still passed away before the complete pacification of Italy, and it was only obtained by employing the most violent and sanguinary measures. Sylla made this terrible declaration, that he would not pardon one of his enemies. At Præneste, all the senators who were the partisans of Marius had their throats cut, and the inhabitants were put to the sword. Those of Norba, surprised through treason, rather than surrender, buried themselves under the ruins of their city.

Sylla had scrupled at nothing in his way to power; the corruption of the armies,[716] the pillage of towns, the massacre of the inhabitants, and the extermination of his enemies; nor did he show any more scruples in maintaining himself in it. He inaugurated his return to the Senate by the slaughter, near the Temple of Bellona, of three thousand Samnites who had surrendered prisoners.[717] A considerable number of the inhabitants of Italy were deprived of the right of city which had been granted them after the war of the allies;[718] he invented a new punishment, that of proscription,[719] and, in Rome alone, he banished four thousand seven hundred citizens, among whom were ninety senators, fifteen consulars, and two thousand seven hundred knights.[720] His fury fell heaviest upon the Samnites, whose spirit of independence he feared, and he almost entirely annihilated that nation.[721] Although his triumph had been a reaction against the popular party, he treated as prisoners of war the children of the noblest and most respectable families, and, by a monstrous innovation, even the women suffered the same lot.[722] Lists of proscription, placarded on the Forum with the names of the intended victims, threw terror into families; to laugh or cry on looking at these was a crime.[723] M. Pletorius was slaughtered for having fainted at the sight of the punishment inflicted on the prætor, M. Marius;[724] to denounce the hiding-place of the proscripts, or put them to death, formed a title to recompenses paid from the public treasury, amounting in some cases to twelve thousand drachmas (about 11,640 francs [£460]) a head;[725] to assist them, to have had friendly or any other relations with the enemies of Sylla, was enough to subject the offender to capital punishment. From one end of Italy to the other, all those who had served under the orders of Marius, Carbo, or Norbanus, were massacred or banished, and their goods sold by auction. They were to be struck even in their posterity: the children and grandchildren of the proscripts were deprived of the right of inheritance and of being candidates for public offices.[726] All these acts of pitiless vengeance had been authorised by a law called Valeria, promulgated in 672, and which, in appointing Sylla dictator, conferred upon him unlimited powers. Yet, though Sylla kept the supreme power, he permitted the election of the consuls every year, an example which was subsequently followed by the emperors.

Calm re-established in Rome, a new constitution was promulgated, which restored the aristocracy to its ascendency. The dictator fell into the delusion of believing that a system founded by violence, upon selfish interests, could survive him. It is easier to change laws than to arrest the course of ideas.

The legislation of the Gracchi was abolished. The senators, by the law judiciaria, acquired again the exclusive privilege of the judiciary functions. The colony of Capua, a popular creation, was destroyed and restored to the domain. Sylla assumed to himself one of the first privileges of the censorship, which he had suppressed — the nomination of the members of the Senate.

He introduced into that assembly, decimated during the civil wars, three hundred knights. By the law on the priesthood, he removed from the votes of the people and restored to the college the choice of the pontiffs and of the sovereign pontiff. He limited the power of the tribunes, leaving them only the right of protection (auxilium),[727] and forbidding their access to the superior magistracies.[728] He flattered himself that he had thus removed the ambitious from a career henceforward profitless.

He admitted into Rome ten thousand new citizens (called Cornelians),[729] taken from among the slaves whose masters had been proscribed. Similar enfranchisements took place in the rest of Italy. He had almost exterminated two nations, the Etruscans and the Samnites; he re-peopled their deserted countries by distributing the estates of his adversaries among a considerable number of his soldiers, whom some authors raise to the prodigious number of forty-seven legions,[730] and created for his veterans twenty-three military colonies on the territory taken from the rebel towns.[731]

All these arbitrary measures were dictated by the spirit of reaction; but those which follow were inspired by the desire to re-establish order and the hierarchy.

The rules formerly adopted for the succession of the magistracies were restored.[732] No person could offer himself for the consulship without having previously held the office of prætor; or for the prætorship before he had held that of questor. Thirty years were fixed as the age necessary for the questorship, forty for the prætorship, and forty-three for the consulship. The law required an interval of two years between the exercise of two different magistracies, and often between the same magistracy, a rule so severely maintained, that, for having braved it in merely soliciting for the consulship,[733] Lucretius Ofella, one of Sylla's most devoted partisans, was put to death. The dictator withdrew from the freedmen the right of voting, from the knights the places of honour in the spectacles; he put a stop to the adjudications entrusted to the farmers-general and the distributions of wheat, and suppressed the corporations, which threatened a real danger to public tranquillity. Lastly, to put limits to extravagance, the sumptuary laws were promulgated.[734]

By the law de provinciis ordinandis, he sought to regulate the provinces and ameliorate their administration. The two consuls and the eight prætors were retained at Rome during their year of office by the administration of civil affairs. They took afterwards, in quality of proconsuls or proprætors, the command of one of the ten provinces, which they exercised during a year; after which a new curiate law became necessary to renew the imperium;

they preserved it until their return to Rome. Thirty days were allowed to them for quitting the province after the arrival of their successors.[735] The number of prætors, questors, pontiffs, and augurs was augmented. [736] Every year twenty questors were to be named, which would ensure the recruitment of the Senate, since this office gave entrance to it. Sylla multiplied the commissions of justice. He took measures for putting a stop to the murders which desolated Italy (lex de sicariis), and to protect the citizens against outrages (lex de injuriis). The lex magistratis completed, so to say, the preceding.[737] In the number of crimes of high treason, punished capitally, are the excesses of magistrates charged with the administration of the provinces; quitting their government without leave of the Senate; conducting an army beyond the limits of his province; undertaking a war unauthorised; treating with foreign chiefs: such were the principal acts denounced as crimes against the Republic. There was not one of them of which Sylla himself had not been guilty.

Sylla abdicated in 675, the only extraordinary act which remained for him to accomplish. He who had carried mourning into so many families returned into his own house alone, through a respectful and submissive crowd. Such was the ascendency of his old power, supported, moreover, by the ten thousand Cornelians present in Rome and devoted to his person,[738] that, though he had resumed his position of simple citizen, he was still allowed to act as absolute master, and even on the eve of his death, which occurred in 676, he made himself the executioner of pitiless justice, in daring to cause to be slaughtered before his eyes the prætor Granius, guilty of exaction.[739]

Unexampled magnificence was displayed at his funeral; his body was carried to the Campus Martius, where previously none but the kings had been inhumed.[740] He left Italy tamed, but not subdued; the great nobles in power, but without moral authority; his partisans enriched, but trembling for their riches; the numerous victims of tyranny held down, but growling under the oppression; lastly, Rome taught that henceforth she is without protection against the boldness of any fortunate soldier.[741]

Effects of Sylla's Dictatorship.

VII. The history of the last fifty years, and especially the dictatorship of Sylla, show beyond doubt that Italy demanded a master. Everywhere institutions gave way before the power of an individual, sustained not only by his own partisans, but also by the irresolute multitude, which, fatigued by the action and reaction of so many opposite parties, aspired to order and repose. If the conduct of Sylla had been moderated, what is called the Empire would probably have commenced with him; but his power was so cruel and so partial, that after his death, the abuses of liberty were forgotten in the memory of abuses of tyranny. The more the democratic spirit had expanded, the more the ancient institutions lost their prestige. In fact, as democracy, trusting and passionate, believes always that its interests are better represented by an individual than by a political body, it was incessantly disposed to deliver its future to the man who raised himself above others by his own merit. The Gracchi, Marius, and Sylla, had in turn disposed at will of the destinies of the Republic, and trampled under foot with impunity ancient institutions and ancient customs; but their reign was ephemeral,[742] for they only represented factions. Instead of embracing collectively the hopes and interests of all the peninsula of Italy, they favoured exclusively particular classes of society. Some sought before all to secure the prosperity of the proletaries of Rome, or the emancipation of the Italiotes, or the preponderance of the knights; others, the privileges of the aristocracy. They failed.

To establish a durable order of things there wanted a man who, raising himself above vulgar passions, should unite in himself the essential qualities and just ideas of each of his predecessors, avoiding their faults as well as their errors. To the greatness of soul and love of the people of certain tribunes, it was needful to join the military genius of great generals and the strong sentiments of the Dictator in favour of order and the hierarchy.

The man capable of so lofty a mission already existed; but perhaps, in spite of his name, he might have still remained long unknown, if the penetrating eye of Sylla had not discovered him in the midst of the crowd, and, by persecution, pointed him out to public attention. That man was Cæsar.

# BOOK II
# HISTORY OF JULIUS CÆSAR

## CHAPTER I
## (654-684)

First Years of Cæsar.

I. ABOUT the time when Marius, by his victories over the Cimbri and Teutones, saved Italy from a formidable invasion, was born at Rome the man who would one day, by again subduing the Gauls and Germans, retard for several centuries the irruption of the barbarians, give the knowledge of their rights to oppressed peoples, assure continuance to Roman civilisation, and bequeath his name to the future chiefs of nations, as a consecrated emblem of power.

Caius Julius Cæsar was born at Rome on the 4th of the ides of Quintilis (July 12), 654,[743] and the month Quintilis, called Julius [July] in honour of him, has borne for 1,900 years the name of the great man. He was the son of C. Julius Cæsar,[744] prætor, who died suddenly at Pisa about 670,[745] and of Aurelia, descended from an illustrious plebeian family.

By ancestry and alliances, Cæsar inherited that double prestige which is derived from ancient origin and recent renown.

On one side, he claimed to be descended from Anchises and Venus;[746] on the other, he was the nephew of the famous Marius who had married his aunt Julia. When the widow of this great captain died in 686, Cæsar pronounced her funeral oration, and thus traced out his own genealogy:— "My aunt Julia, on the maternal side, is of the issue of kings; on the paternal side, she descends from the immortal gods: for her mother was a Marcia,[747] and the family Marcius Rex are the descendants of Ancus Marcius. The Julia family, to which I belong, descends from Venus herself. Thus our house unites to the sacred character of kings, who are the most powerful among men, the venerated holiness of the gods, who hold kings themselves under their subjection."[748]

This proud glorification of his race attests the value which was set at Rome upon antiquity of origin; but Cæsar, sprung from that aristocracy which had produced so many illustrious men, and impatient to follow in their footsteps, showed, from early youth, that nobility obliges, instead of imitating those whose conduct would make one believe that nobility dispenses.

Aurelia, a woman of lofty character and severe morals,[749] helped above all in the development of his great abilities, by a wise and enlightened education, and prepared him to make himself worthy of the part which destiny had reserved for him.[750] This first education, given by a tender and virtuous mother, has ever as much influence over our future as the most precious natural qualities. Cæsar reaped the fruits of it. He also received lessons from M. Antonius Gnipho, the Gaul, a philosopher and master of eloquence, of a rare mind, of vast learning, and well versed in Greek and Latin letters, which he had cultivated at Alexandria.[751]

Greece was always the country of the arts and sciences, and the language of Demosthenes was familiar to every lettered Roman.[752] Thus Greek and Latin might be called the two languages of Italy, as they were, at a later period, by the Emperor Claudius.[753] Cæsar spoke both with the same facility; and, when falling beneath the dagger of Brutus, he pronounced in Greek the last words that issued from his lips.[754]

Though eager for pleasure, he neglected nothing, says Suetonius, by which to acquire those talents which lead to the highest honours. Now, according to Roman habits, the first offices were attainable only by the union of the most diverse merits. The patrician youth, still worthy of their ancestors, were not idle: they sought religious appointments, to give them power over consciences; administrative employments, to influence material interests; discussions and public discourses, to captivate minds by their eloquence; finally, military labours, to strike imaginations by the brilliancy of their glory. Emulous of distinction in all, Cæsar did not confine himself to the study of letters; he early composed works, among which are cited "The Praises of Hercules," a tragedy of "Œdipus," "A Collection of Choice Phrases,"[755] a book on "Divination."[756] It seems that these works were written in a style so pure and correct, that they gained for him the reputation of an eminent writer, gravis auctor linguæ Latinæ.[757] He was less happy in the art of poetry, if we may believe Tacitus.[758] However, there remain to us some verses addressed to the memory of Terence, which are not wanting in elegance.[759]

Education, then, had made Cæsar a distinguished man before he was a great man. He united to goodness of heart a high intelligence, to an invincible courage,[760] an enthralling eloquence,[761] a wonderful memory,[762] an unbounded generosity; finally, he possessed one very rare quality—calmness under anger.[763] "His affability," says Plutarch, "his politeness, his gracious address—qualities which he had to a degree beyond his age—gained him the affection of the people."[764]

Two anecdotes of later date must come in here. Plutarch relates that Cæsar, during his campaigns, one day, surprised by a violent storm, took shelter in a hut where was only one room, too small to contain many people. He hastened to offer it to Oppius, one of his officers, who was sick; and himself passed the night in the open air, saying to those who accompanied him, "We must leave to the great the places of honour, but yield to the sick those that are necessary to them." Another time, Valerius Leo, with whom he was dining at Milan, having set before him an ill-seasoned dish, the companions of Cæsar remonstrated, but he reproached them sharply for their want of consideration for his host, saying "that they were free not to eat of a dish they did not like, but that to complain of it aloud was a want of good breeding."[765]

These facts, of small importance in themselves, yet testify to Cæsar's goodness of heart, and to the delicacy of the well-bred man who is always observant of propriety.

To his natural qualities, developed by a brilliant education, were added physical advantages. His tall stature, his rounded and well-proportioned limbs, stamped his person with a grace that distinguished him from all others.[766] He had black eyes, a piercing look, a pale complexion, a straight and high nose. His mouth, small and regular, but with rather thick lips, gave a kindly expression to the lower part of his face, whilst his breadth of brow betokened the development of the intellectual faculties. His face was full, at least, in his youth; for in his busts, doubtless made towards the end of his life, his features are thinner, and bear traces of fatigue.[767] He had a sonorous and penetrating voice, a noble gesture, and an air of dignity reigned over all his person.[768] His constitution, at first delicate, became robust by a frugal regimen and the habit of exposing himself to the inclemency of the weather.[769] Accustomed from his youth to all bodily exercises, he was a bold horseman,[770] and bore privations and fatigues without difficulty.[771] Habitually temperate, his health was impaired neither by excess of labour nor by excess of pleasure. However, on two occasions—the first at Corduba, the second at Thapsus—he was seized with nervous attacks, wrongly mistaken for epilepsy.[772]

He paid special attention to his person, carefully shaved or plucked out his beard, and artistically brought his hair forward to the front of his head, which, in more advanced age, served to conceal his bald forehead. He was reproached with the affectation of scratching his head with one finger only, so that he should not disarrange his hair.[773] His toilette was refined; his toga was generally ornamented with a laticlavia, fringed down to the hands, and fastened by a girdle carelessly tied about his loins; a costume which distinguished the elegant and effeminate youths of the period. But Sylla was not deceived by these appearances of frivolity, and repeated that they must take care of this young man with the loose girdle.[774] He had a taste for pictures, statues, and jewels; and, in memory of his origin, always wore on his finger a ring, on which was engraved the figure of an armed Venus.[775]

In fine, we discover in Cæsar, both physically and morally, two natures rarely united in the same person. He joined an aristocratic delicacy of body to the muscular constitution of the warrior; the love of luxury and the arts to a passion for military life, in all its simplicity and rudeness: in a word, he allied the elegance of manner which seduces with the energy of character which commands.

Cæsar persecuted by Sylla (672).

II. Such was Cæsar at the age of eighteen, when Sylla seized the dictatorship.[776] Already he attracted all eyes at Rome by his name, his intellect, his affable manners, which pleased men, and, perhaps, women still more.

The influence of his uncle Marius caused him to be nominated priest of Jupiter (flamen dialis) at the age of fourteen.[777] At sixteen, betrothed, doubtless against his will, to Cossutia, the daughter of a rich knight, he broke his engagement,[778] after the death of his father, to draw still closer his alliance with the popular party by marrying, a year after, in 671, Cornelia, daughter of L. Cornelius Cinna, the ancient colleague of Marius, and the representative of his cause. From this marriage was born, the following year, Julia, who became, in after time, the wife of Pompey.[779]

Sylla saw with displeasure this young man, who already occupied men's thoughts, although, as yet, he had done nothing, linking himself more closely with those who were opposed to him. He wished to force him to divorce Cornelia, but he found him inflexible. When every one yielded to his will; when, by his orders, Piso separated from Annia, the widow of Cinna,[780] and Pompey ignominiously dismissed his wife, the daughter of Antistius, who died for his cause,[781] to marry Emilia, the daughter-in-law of the dictator, Cæsar maintained his independence at the price of his personal safety.

Become suspected, he was deprived of his priesthood,[782] and of his wife's dowry, and declared incapable of inheriting from his family. Obliged to conceal himself in the outskirts of Rome to escape persecution, he changed his place of retreat every night, though ill with fever; but, arrested by a band of assassins in the pay of Sylla, he gained the chief, Cornelius Phagita, by giving him two talents (about 12,000 francs),[783] and his life was preserved. Let us note here that, arrived at sovereign power, Cæsar met this same Phagita, and treated him with indulgence, without reminding him of the past.[784] Meanwhile, he still wandered about in the Sabine country. His courage, his constancy, his illustrious birth, his former quality of flamen, excited general interest. Soon important personages, such as Aurelius Cotta, his mother's brother, and Mamercus Lepidus, a connection of his family, interceded in his favour.[785] The vestals also, whose sole intervention put an end to all violence, did not spare their prayers.[786] Vanquished by so many solicitations, Sylla yielded at last, exclaiming, "Well! be it so, you will it; but know that he, whose pardon you demand, will one day ruin the party of the great for which we have fought together, for, trust me, there are several Mariuses in this young man."[787]

Sylla had judged truly: many Mariuses, in effect, had met together in Cæsar: Marius, the great captain, but with a larger military genius; Marius, the enemy of the oligarchy, but without hatred and without cruelty; Marius, in a word, no longer the man of a faction, but the man of his age.

Cæsar in Asia (673, 674).

III. Cæsar could not remain a cold spectator of the sanguinary reign of Sylla, and left for Asia, where he received the hospitality of Nicomedes, king of Bithynia. A short time afterwards he took part in the hostilities which continued against Mithridates. The young men of good family who wished to serve their military apprenticeship followed a general to the army. Admitted to his intimacy under the name of contubernales, they were attached to his person. It was in this capacity that Cæsar accompanied the prætor M. Minucius Thermus,[788] who sent him to Nicomedes to claim his co-operation in the siege of Mitylene, occupied by the troops of Mithridates. Cæsar succeeded in his mission, and on his return aided in the capture of the city. Having saved the life of a Roman soldier, he received from Thermus a civic crown.[789]

Shortly afterwards he returned to Bithynia, to defend the cause of one of his clients. His frequent presence at the court of Nicomedes served as the pretext for an accusation of shameful condescension. But Cæsar's relations with the Bithynians may be explained quite naturally by his feelings of gratitude for the hospitality he had received from them; it was the reason which made him always defend their interests, and at a later period become their patron, as may be gathered from the fragment of a speech preserved by Aulus Gellius.[790] The motives of his conduct were, nevertheless, so misconstrued, that insulting allusions are to be found in certain debates of the Senate, and even in the songs of the soldiers who followed his triumphal car.[791] But these sarcasms, which told rather of hatred than of truth, as Cicero himself says, magis odio firmata quam præsidio,[792] were only set afloat by his adversaries very much later, that is to say, at one of those moments of excitement when political parties shrink from no calumny[793] to mutually decry each other. Notwithstanding the relaxation of morals, nothing could have ruined the reputation of Cæsar more than this accusation, for such a crime was not only abhorred in the army,[794] but, committed with a foreigner, would have been the most degrading disregard of Roman dignity. Wherefore Cæsar, whose love for women ought to have shielded him from such a suspicion, repelled it with just indignation.[795]

After having made his first campaign at the siege of Mitylene, Cæsar served in the fleet of the proconsul P. Servilius (676), commissioned to make war on the Cilician pirates, who subsequently received the surname of Isauricus, because he had taken Isaura, their chief place of refuge,[796] and conquered part of Cilicia. However, he remained but a short time with Servilius, for, having been informed of the death of Sylla, he returned to Rome.[797]

Cæsar on his return to Rome (676).

IV. The Republic, divided into two parties, was on the eve of falling into civil war through the diversity of opinion between the two consuls, Lepidus and Catulus. They were ready to come to blows. The former, elevated to the consulship by the influence of Pompey, against the advice of Sylla, fomented an insurrection. "He lighted up," says Florus, "the fire of civil war at the very funeral pyre of the dictator."[798] He wished to abrogate the Cornelian laws, restore to the tribunes their power, to the proscribed their rights, to the allies their lands.[799] These designs against the system established by the dictator agreed with Cæsar's ideas, and endeavours were made, by seductive offers, to draw him into the intrigues which were then going on; but he kept aloof.[800]

The Senate succeeded in making the consuls swear that they would be reconciled, and thought to ensure peace by giving each a military command. Catulus received the government of Italy, and Lepidus that of Cisalpine Gaul. The latter, before going to his province, visited Etruria, where the partisans of Marius flocked to him. The Senate, informed of these doings, recalled him to Rome, towards the end of the year, to hold the comitia. [801] Lepidus, leaving Brutus the prætor encamped near Mutina (Modena), marched back to Rome at the head of his army. Beaten by Catulus and Pompey at the bridge of Milvius, he withdrew to the coast of Etruria, and, after a new defeat, fled to Sardinia, where he ended his career miserably. [802] Perpenna, his lieutenant, went, with the wreck of his army, to rejoin Sertorius in Spain.

Cæsar acted wisely in keeping out of these movements, for not only did the character of Lepidus inspire him with no confidence,[803] but he must have thought that the dictatorship of Sylla was too recent, that it had inspired too many fears, and created too many new interests, to admit of the reaction, still incomplete in men's minds, succeeding by arms. For the present, they must limit themselves to acting on public opinion, by branding with words the instruments of the past tyranny.

The most general way of entering on a political career was by instituting a prosecution against some high personage.[804] Its success mattered little; the real point was to be brought prominently forward by some remarkable speech, and offer a proof of patriotism.

Cornelius Dolabella, one of the friends of Sylla, who had had the honours of the consulate and triumph, and who, two years before, was governor of Macedonia, was now accused by Cæsar of excesses committed in his government (677). He was acquitted by the tribunal composed of the creatures of the dictator.[805] Public opinion did not praise Cæsar the less for having dared to attack a man who was supported and defended by orators such as Hortensius and L. Aurelius Cotta. Besides, he displayed so much eloquence, that this first speech gave him at once a veritable celebrity. [806] Encouraged by this success, Cæsar cited C. Antonius Hybrida before the prætor M. Lucullus for having, at the head of a body of cavalry, pillaged certain parts of Greece when Sylla was returning from Asia.[807] The accused was also acquitted, but the popularity of the accuser still increased. He also spoke, probably, in other causes now unknown. Tacitus speaks of a speech of Cæsar's in favour of a certain Decius the Samnite,[808] without doubt the same mentioned by Cicero, who, flying from the proscription of Sylla, was kindly received by Aulus Cluentius.[809] Thus Cæsar boldly offered himself as the defender of the oppressed Greeks or Samnites, who had suffered so much from the regime preceding. He gained especially the good-will of the former, whose opinions, highly influential at Rome, helped to make reputations.

These attacks were certainly a means of attracting public attention, but they also showed the courage of the man, since the partisans of Sylla were still all in power.

Cæsar goes to Rhodes (678-680).

V. Notwithstanding his celebrity as an orator, Cæsar resolved to keep out of the troubles which agitated Italy, and doubtless felt his presence in

Rome useless to his cause and irksome to himself. It is often advantageous to political men to disappear for a time from the scene; they thus avoid compromising themselves in daily struggles without aim, and their reputation, instead of losing, increases by absence. During the winter of 678 Cæsar again quitted Italy, for the purpose of going to Rhodes to complete his studies. This island, then the centre of intellectual lights, the dwelling-place of the most celebrated philosophers, was the school of all the well-born youth. Cicero himself had gone there for lessons some years before.

In his passage, Cæsar was taken by pirates near Pharmacusa, a small island in the archipelago of the Sporades, at the mouth of the Gulf of Jassius. [810] Notwithstanding the campaign of P. Servilius Isauricus, these pirates still infested the sea with numerous fleets. They demanded twenty talents (£2,329) for his ransom. He offered fifty (£11,640), which must naturally have given them a high notion of their prisoner, and insured him better treatment. He sent trusty agents, and among others Epicrates, one of his Milesian slaves, to raise this sum in the neighbouring towns.[811] Though the allied provinces and towns were in this case obliged to furnish the ransom, it was none the less curious, as a proof of their wealth, to see a young man of twenty-four, arrested in a little island of Asia Minor, instantly able to borrow so large a sum.

Left alone with a physician and two slaves[812] in the midst of these ferocious brigands, he held them in awe by his force of character, and passed nearly forty days on board without ever loosing either his sandals or his girdle, to avoid all suspicion of wishing to escape by swimming. [813] He seemed less a captive, says Plutarch, than a prince surrounded by his guards; now playing with them, now reciting poems to them, he made himself loved and feared, and laughingly told them that, once free, he would have them crucified.[814] Yet the remembrance of Rome recurred to his mind, and recalled the strifes and enmities he had left there. He was often heard to say, "What pleasure Crassus will have at knowing me in these straits!"[815]

As soon as he received his ransom from Miletus and the other towns, he paid it. Landed on the coast, he hastened to equip ships, impatient to revenge himself. The pirates, surprised at anchor in the harbour of the island, were almost all made prisoners, and their booty fell into his hands. He secured them in the prison at Pergamus, to deliver them up to Junius Silanus, the proconsul of Asia, whose duty it was to punish them. But, wishing to sell them and make a profit, Junius replied in an evasive manner. Cæsar returned to Pergamus, and had them crucified.[816]

He went afterwards to Rhodes, to attend the lessons of Apollonius Molo, the most illustrious of the masters of eloquence of that time, who had formerly been to Rome, in 672, as the Rhodian ambassador. About the same time one of his uncles, the proconsul M. Aurelius Cotta, was appointed governor of Bithynia, bequeathed by Nicomedes to the Roman people, and charged, with Lucullus, to oppose the new invasions of Mithridates. Cotta, beaten by land and sea near Chalcedon, was reduced to great straits, and Mithridates was advancing against Cyzicus, an allied town, which Lucullus afterwards relieved. On another side, Eumachius, a lieutenant of the King of Pontus, ravaged Phrygia, where he massacred all the Romans, and seized several of the southern provinces of Asia Minor. The rumours of war, the perils into which the allies were falling, took Cæsar from his studies. He went over into Asia, levied troops on his own authority, drove out from the province the king's governor, and kept in allegiance towns whose faith was doubtful or shaken.[817]

Cæsar Pontiff and Military Tribune (680-684).

VI. Whilst he was making war on the coasts of Asia, his friends at Rome did not forget him; and, seeing clearly the importance of Cæsar's being clothed with a sacred character, they nominated him pontiff, in the place of his uncle, L. Aurelius Cotta, consul in 680, who had died suddenly in Gaul the following year.[818]

This circumstance obliged him to return to Rome. The sea continued to swarm with pirates, who must necessarily owe him a grudge for the death of their comrades. The better to escape them, he crossed the Adriatic in a boat of four oars, accompanied only by two friends and ten slaves.[819] In the passage, thinking that he saw sails in the horizon, he seized his sword, resolved to sell his life dearly; but his fears were not justified, and he landed safe and sound in Italy.

Immediately on his return to Rome, he was elected military tribune, and succeeded by a large majority over his rival, C. Popilius.[820] This already elevated rank, since it gave him the command of about a thousand men, was the first step which the young nobility easily attained, either by election or by the choice of the generals.[821] Cæsar does not seem to have profited by his new position to take part in the important wars in which the Republic was then engaged. And yet the clang of arms echoed from all quarters.

In Spain Sertorius successfully continued the war begun in 674 against the lieutenants of Sylla, joined in 677 by Perpenna, at the head of thirty cohorts,[822] he had got together a formidable army, bravely maintained the standard of Marius, and given the name of Senate to an assemblage of 300 Romans. Vanquisher of Metellus for several years, Sertorius, gifted with a vast military genius, exercising great influence over the Celtiberians and Lusitanians, and master of the passes,[823] was dreaming of crossing the Alps. The Spaniards had already given him the name of a second Hannibal. But Pompey, sent in all haste to Spain, reinforced the army of Metellus, deprived Sertorius of all hope of penetrating into Italy, and even drove him far back from the Pyrenees. The united efforts of the two generals, however, did not effect the subjugation of Spain, which, since 680, had been entirely re-conquered by Sertorius. But soon after this, his lieutenants experiencing reverses, desertion began among his soldiers, and he himself lost his confidence. Yet he would have resisted for a long time still, had not Perpenna caused him to be assassinated by an infamous act of treachery. This murder did not profit its author. Though Perpenna succeeded Sertorius in the command of the troops, he found himself an object of their hatred and contempt. Soon defeated and taken prisoner by Pompey, he was put to death. Thus ended the war in Spain in 682.

In Asia, Lucullus successfully pursued the campaign against Mithridates, who courageously maintained the struggle, and had even been able to come to an understanding with Sertorius. Lucullus beat him in Cappadocia (683), and forced him to take refuge with Tigranes, his son-in-law, King of Armenia, who soon experienced a sanguinary defeat, and lost his capital, Tigranocerta.

In the East, the barbarians infested the frontiers of Macedonia, the pirates of Cilicia sailed from end to end of all the seas with impunity, and the Cretans flew to arms to defend their independence.

Italy was torn by the Servile War. This disinherited class had risen up anew, despite the bloody repression of the Sicilian insurrection from 620 to 623. It had acquired the knowledge of its strength chiefly from the circumstance that each party in the civil troubles had by turns granted its liberty to increase the number of its respective adherents. In 681, seventy gladiators, kept at Capua, revolted; their chief was Spartacus, formerly a soldier, made prisoner, then sold as a slave. In less than a year his band had so much increased that consular armies were needed to combat him, and, having gained a victory in Picenum, for a moment he had entertained the thought of marching upon Rome at the head of 40,000 men.[824] Nevertheless, forced to withdraw to the south of Italy, he contended against the Roman forces successfully for two years, when at last, in 683, Licinius Crassus, at the head of eight legions, conquered him in Apulia. Spartacus perished in the fight; the remainder of the army of slaves separated into four bodies, one of which, retiring towards Gaul, was easily dispersed by Pompey, who was returning from Spain. The 6,000 prisoners taken in the battle fought in Apulia were hanged all along the road from Capua to Rome.

Occasions for making himself perfect in the art of war were not wanting to Cæsar; but we can understand his inaction, for Sylla's partisans alone were at the heads of the armies; in Spain, Metellus and Pompey—the first the brother-in-law of the Dictator, the second formerly his best lieutenant; in Italy, Crassus, the enemy of Cæsar, equally devoted to the party of Sylla; in Asia, Lucullus, an old friend of the Dictator, who had dedicated his "Memoirs"[825] to him. Cæsar, then, found everywhere either a cause he would not defend, or a general under whom he would not serve. In Spain, however, Sertorius represented the party he would most willingly have embraced; but Cæsar had a horror of civil wars. Whilst faithful to his convictions, he seems, in the first years of his career, to have carefully avoided placing between him and his adversaries that eternal barrier which for ever separates the children of the same country, after blood has once been shed. He had it at heart to be able, in his exalted future, to appeal to a past pure from all violence, so that, instead of being the man of a party, he might rally round him all good citizens.

The Republic had triumphed everywhere, but she had yet to reckon with her conquering generals: she found herself in the presence of Crassus and Pompey, who, proud of their successes, advanced upon Rome at the head of their armies, to demand or seize the chief power. The Senate could be but little at ease as to the intentions of the latter, who, not long before, had sent an insolent letter from Spain, in which he menaced his country with the sword unless they sent him the supplies necessary to carry on the war against Sertorius.[826] The same ambition animated Pompey and Crassus: neither of the two would be the first to disband his army; each, indeed, brought his own to the gates of the city. Both were elected consuls, allowed a triumph, and forced by the augurs and public opinion to be reconciled together; and they held out their hands to each other, disbanded their troops, and for some time the Republic recovered an unexpected calm.[827]

# CHAPTER II
## (684-691)

State of the Republic (684).

I. WHEN Pompey and Crassus came to the consulship, Italy had been a prey to intestine convulsions for sixty-three years. But, notwithstanding the repose which society demanded, and which the reconciliation of the two rivals seemed to promise, many opposing passions and interests still seethed in her bosom.[828]

Sylla believed he had re-established the Republic on its ancient basis, but, instead, he had thrown everything into disorder. The property, the life even of each citizen, was at the mercy of the stronger; the people had lost the right of appeal, and their legitimate share in the elections; the poor, the distribution of wheat; the tribuneship, its secular privileges; and the influential order of the knights, their political and financial importance.

At Rome, no more guarantee for justice; in Italy, no more security for the rights of citizenship, so dearly acquired; in the provinces, no more consideration for subjects and allies. Sylla had restored their prerogatives to the upper class without being able to restore their former prestige; having made use of only corrupt elements, and appealed to only sordid passions, he left behind him a powerless oligarchy, and a thoroughly distracted people. The country was divided between those whom his tyranny had enriched and those whom it had despoiled; the one fearing to lose what they had just acquired, the other hoping to regain what they had lost.

The aristocracy, proud of their wealth and ancestry, absorbed in all the pleasures of luxury, kept the new men[829] out of the highest offices, and, by a long continuance of power, had come to look on the chief magistracies as their property. Cato, in a discourse to the Senate, exclaimed: — "Instead of the virtues of our ancestors we have luxury and avarice; the poverty of the State, and the opulence of individuals; we boast of our riches, we cherish idleness; no distinction is made between the good and the wicked; all rewards due to merit are the price of intrigue. Why then are we astonished at this, since each man, isolating himself from the rest, consults only his own interest? At home, the slaves of pleasure; here, of wealth or of favour."[830]

The elections had for a long time been the result of a shameless traffic, where every mean of success was allowable. Lucullus himself, to obtain the government of Asia, did not blush to have recourse to the good offices of a courtesan, the mistress of Cethegus.[831] The sale of consciences had so planted itself in public morals, that the several instruments of electoral corruption had functions and titles almost recognised. Those who bought votes were called divisores; the go-betweens were interpretes; and those with whom was deposited the purchase money[832] were sequestres. Numerous secret societies were formed for making a trade of the right of suffrage; they were divided into decuries, the several heads of which obeyed a supreme head, who treated with the candidates and sold the votes of the associates, either for money, or on the stipulation of certain advantages for himself or his friends. These societies carried most of the elections, and Cicero himself, who so often boasted of the unanimity with which he had been chosen consul, owed to them a great part of the suffrages he obtained.[833]

All the sentences of the tribunals composed of senators were dictated by a venality so flagrant, that Cicero brands it in these terms:—"I will demonstrate by positive proofs the guilty intrigues, the infamies which have sullied the judicial powers for the ten years that they have been entrusted to the Senate. The Roman people shall learn from me how the knightly order has administered justice for nearly fifty consecutive years, without the faintest suspicion resting on any of its members of having received money for a judgment delivered; how, since senators alone have composed our tribunals, since the people have been despoiled of the right which they had over each of us, Q. Calidius has been able to say, after his condemnation, that they could not honestly require less than 300,000 sestertii to condemn a prætor; how, when the senator P. Septimius was found guilty of embezzlement before the prætor Hortensius, the money he had received in his quality of judge was included in his fine; how C. Herennius and C. Popilius, both senators, having been convicted of the crime of peculation, and M. Atilius of the crime of high treason, it was proved that they had received money as the price of one of their sentences; how it was found that certain senators, when their names were taken from the urn held by C. Verres, then prætor urbanus, instantly went to vote against the accused, without having heard the suit; how, finally, we have seen a senator, judge in this same suit, receive money from the accused to distribute to the other judges, and money from the accuser to condemn the accused. Can I, then, sufficiently deplore this blot, this shame, this calamity which weighs on the whole order?"[834]

Notwithstanding the severity of the laws against the avidity of the generals and farmers of the revenues, notwithstanding the patronage of the great at Rome, the conquered peoples[835] were always a prey to the exactions of the magistrates, and Verres was a type of the most shameless immorality, which drew this exclamation from Cicero: "All the provinces groan; all free peoples lament; all the kingdoms cry out against our cupidity and our violence. There is not between the Ocean and ourselves a spot so remote or so little known that the injustice and tyranny of our fellow-citizens of these days have not penetrated to it."[836] The inhabitants of foreign countries were obliged to borrow, either to satisfy the immoderate demands of their governors and their retinue, or to pay the farmers of the public revenues. Now, capital being nowhere but at Rome, they could only procure it at an excessive rate of interest; and the nobles, giving themselves up to usury, held the provinces in their power.

The army itself had been demoralised by civil wars, and the chiefs no longer maintained discipline. "Flamininus, Aquilius, Paulus Æmilius," says Dio Cassius, "commanded men well disciplined, who had learnt to execute the orders of their generals in silence. The law was their rule; with a royal soul, simple in life, bounding their expenses within reasonable limits, they held it more shameful to flatter the soldiery than to fear the enemy. From the time of Sylla, on the contrary, the generals, raised to the first rank by violence and not by merit, forced to turn their arms against each other rather than against the enemy, were reduced to court popularity. Charged with the command, they squandered gold to procure enjoyments for an army, the fatigues of which they paid dearly; they rendered their country venal, without caring for it; and made themselves the slaves of the most depraved men, to bring under their authority those who were worth more than themselves. This is what drove Marius out of Rome, and led him back against Sylla; this is what made Cinna the murderer of Octavius, and Fimbria the murderer of Flaccus. Sylla was the principal cause of these evils, he who, to seduce the soldiers enrolled under other chiefs, and bring them under his own flag, scattered gold in handfuls among his army."[837]

Far were they from the times when the soldier, after a short campaign, laid down his arms to take up the plough again; since then, retained under his standards for long years, and returning in the train of a victorious general to vote in the Campus Martius, the citizen had disappeared; there remained the warrior, with the sole inspiration of the camp. At the end of the expeditions, the army was disbanded, and Italy thus found itself overrun with an immense number of veterans, united in colonies or dispersed over the territory, more inclined to follow a leader than to obey the law. The veterans of the ancient legions of Marius and Sylla were to be counted by hundreds of thousands.

A State, moreover, is often weakened by an exaggeration of the principle on which it rests; and as war was the chief occupation at Rome, all the institutions had originally a military character. The consuls, the first magistrates of the Republic, elected by centuries—that is to say, by the people voting under arms—commanded the troops. The army, composed of all there was most honourable in the nation, did not take an oath to the Republic, but to the chief who recruited it and led it against the enemy; this oath, religiously kept, rendered the generals the absolute masters of their soldiers, who, in their turn, decreed to them the title of *Imperator* after a victory: what more natural, then, even after the transformation of society, than that these soldiers should believe themselves the real people, and the generals elected by them the legitimate chiefs of the Republic? Every abuse has deep roots in the past, and we may find the original cause of the power of the prætorians under the emperors in the primitive organisation and functions of the centuries established by Servius Tullius.

Although the army had not as yet acquired this preponderance, it nevertheless weighed heavily on the decisions of the Forum. By the side of men habituated to the noble chances of the fight existed a true army of turbulence, kept at the expense of the State or of private persons, in the principal towns of Italy—above all, at Capua: these were the gladiators, ever ready to undertake anything for those who paid them, either in the electoral contests[838] or as soldiers in the times of civil war.[839]

Thus all was struck with decadence. Brute force bestowed power, and corruption the magistracies. The empire no longer belonged to the Senate, but to the commanders of the armies; the armies no longer belonged to the Republic, but to the chiefs who led them to victory. Numerous elements of dissolution afflicted society: the venality of the judges, the traffic in elections, the absolutism of the Senate, the tyranny of wealth, which oppressed the poor by usury, and braved the law with impunity.

Rome found herself divided into two thoroughly distinct parties; the one, seeing salvation only in the past, attached itself to abuses, in the fear that to displace one stone would be to shatter the whole edifice; the other wished to consolidate it by rendering the base larger and the summit less unsteady. The first party supported itself on the institutions of Sylla; the second had taken the name of Marius as the symbol of its hopes.

Great causes need an historical figure to personify their interests and tendencies. The man once adopted, his faults, his very crimes are forgotten, and his great deeds alone remembered. Thus, the vengeance and massacres of Marius had faded away from memory at Rome. Only his victories, which had preserved Italy from the invasions of the Cimbri and the Teutones, were recalled; his misfortunes were pitied, his hatred to the aristocracy vaunted. The preferences of public opinion were clearly manifested by the language of the orators, even those most favourable to the Senate. Thus Catulus and Cicero, speaking of Sylla or of Marius, the tyranny of both of whom had been substantially almost equally cruel, thought themselves obliged to glorify the one and to brand the other;[840] yet the legislation of Sylla was still in full vigour, his party omnipotent—that of Marius dispersed and powerless.[841]

The struggle, which was perseveringly continued for sixty-three years against the Senate, had never succeeded, because the defence of the people had never been placed in hands either sufficiently strong or sufficiently pure. To the Gracchi had been wanting an army; to Marius a power less disgraced by excesses; to the war of the allies a character less hostile to the national unity of which Rome was the representative. As to Spartacus, by rousing the slaves he went beyond his aim, and his success threatened the whole of society; he was annihilated. To triumph over a long accumulation of prejudices, the popular cause needed a chief of transcendent merit, and a concurrence of circumstances difficult to foresee. But then the genius of Cæsar was not yet revealed, and the vanquisher of Sertorius was the only one who dominated the situation by his antecedents and high achievements.

Consulship of Pompey and Crassus.

II. By a line of conduct quite opposite to that of Cæsar, Pompey had greatly risen during the civil wars. From the age of twenty-three he had received from Sylla the title Imperator, and the name of "Great;"[842] he passed for the first warrior of his time, and had distinguished himself in Italy, Sicily, and Africa against the partisans of Marius, whom he caused to be pitilessly massacred.[843] Fate had ever favoured him. In Spain, the death of Sertorius had made victory easy to him; on his return, the fortuitous defeat of the fugitive remains of the army of Spartacus allowed him to assume the honour of having put an end to that formidable insurrection; soon he will profit by the success already obtained by Lucullus against Mithridates. Thus a distinguished writer has justly said that Pompey always came in time to terminate, to his own glory, the wars which were just going to end to the glory of another.[844]

The vulgar, who hail good fortune as the equal of genius, surrounded then the conqueror of Spain with their homage, and he himself, of a poor and vain spirit, referred the favours of fortune to his own sole merit. Seeking power for ornament rather than service, he courted it not in the hope of making a cause or a principle triumphant, but to enjoy it peaceably by trimming between different parties. Thus, whilst to Cæsar power was a means, to him it was only the end. Honest, but vacillating, he was unconsciously the instrument of those who flattered him. His courteous manners, and the show of disinterestedness which disguised his ambition, removed all suspicions of his aspiring to the supreme power.[845] An able general in ordinary times, he was great only while events were not greater than he. Nevertheless, he then enjoyed the highest reputation at Rome. By his antecedents he was rather the representative of the party of the aristocracy; but the desire of conciliating public favour, and his own intelligence, made him comprehend the necessity of certain modifications in the laws: thus, before entering Rome to celebrate his triumph over the Celtiberians, he manifested the intention of re-establishing the prerogative of the tribunes, of putting an end to the devastation and oppression of the provinces, of restoring impartiality to justice, and respect to the judges.[846] He was then consul-elect; his promises excited the most lively enthusiasm; for it was the evil administration of the provinces, and the venality of the senators in their judicial functions, which more than all else made the people demand so ardently the re-establishment of the privileges of the tribuneship, notwithstanding the abuses which they had engendered.[847] Excesses in power always give birth to an immoderate desire for liberty.

In publishing the programme of his conduct, of his own free will, before entering Rome, Pompey did not yield to a fascination cleverly exerted over him by Cæsar, as several historians pretend; he obeyed a stronger impulse, that of public opinion. The nobles reproached him with having abandoned their cause,[848] but the popular party was satisfied, and Cæsar, seeing the new consul take his ideas and sentiments to heart, resolved to support him energetically.[849] Doubtless, he thought that with so many elements of corruption, so much contempt of the laws, so many jealous rivalries, and so much boundless ambition, the ascendency of him whom fortune had raised so high could alone, for the time, assist the destinies of the Republic. Was this a loyal co-operation? We believe so, but it did not exclude a noble rivalry, and Cæsar could not be afraid of smoothing for Pompey the platform on which they must one day meet. The man who understands his own worth has no perfidious jealousy against those who have preceded him in his career; rather, he goes to their aid, for then he has more glory in rejoining them. Where would be the emulation of the contest if one was alone in the power of attaining the end?

Pompey's colleague was M. Licinius Crassus. This remarkable man, as we have seen, had distinguished himself as a general, but his influence was owing rather to his wealth and his amiable and courteous disposition. Enriched under Sylla by purchasing the property of the proscribed, he possessed whole quarters of the city of Rome, rebuilt after several fires;

his fortune was more than forty millions of francs [a million and a half sterling],[850] and he pretended that to be rich, one must be able to maintain an army at his own expense.[851] Though his chief passion was the love of gold, avarice did not with him exclude liberality. He lent to all his friends without interest, and sometimes scattered his largesses with profusion. Versed in letters, gifted with a rare eloquence, he accepted eagerly all the causes which Pompey, Cæsar, and Cicero disdained to defend; by his eagerness to oblige all those who claimed his services, either to borrow, or to obtain some situation, he acquired a power which balanced that of Pompey. This last had accomplished greater deeds, but his airs of grandeur and dignity, his habit of avoiding crowds and sights, alienated the multitude from him; while Crassus, of easy access, always in the midst of the public and of business, had the advantage over him by his affable manners.[852] We do not find very defined principles in him, either in political or private life; he was neither a constant friend nor an irreconcilable enemy.[853] Fitter to serve as an instrument for the elevation of another, than to elevate himself to the front rank, he was very useful to Cæsar, who did his best to gain his confidence. "There existed then at Rome," says Plutarch, "three factions, the chiefs of which were Pompey, Cæsar, and Crassus; Cato, whose power did not equal his glory, was more admired than followed. The wise and moderate part of the citizens were for Pompey; energetic, speculative, and bold men attached themselves to the hopes of Cæsar; Crassus, who held the mean between these two factions, used both."[854]

During his first consulship, Crassus seems to have been only occupied with extravagant expenditure, and to have preserved a prudent neutrality. He made a grand sacrifice to Hercules, and consecrated to him the tenth part of his revenues; he gave the people an enormous feast, spread out on ten thousand tables, and bestowed corn for three months to every citizen.[855]

Pompey occupied himself in more serious matters, and, supported by Cæsar, favoured the adoption of several laws, all of which announced a reaction against the system of Sylla.

The effect of the first was to give the tribunes the right anew of presenting laws and appealing to the people; already, in 679, the power of obtaining other magistracies had been restored to them.

The second was connected with justice. Instead of leaving to the Senate alone the whole judicial power, the prætor Aurelius Cotta, Cæsar's uncle, proposed a law which would conciliate all interests, by making it legal to take the judges by thirds from the three classes: that is to say, from the Senate, the equestrian order, and the tribunes of the treasury, who were for the most part plebeians.[856]

But the measure which most helped to heal the wounds of the Republic was the amnesty proposed by the tribune Plotius in favour of all those who had taken part in the civil war. In this number was comprised the wreck of the army of Lepidus, which had remained in Spain after the defeat of Sertorius, and amongst which was to be found C. Cornelius Cinna, brother-in-law of Cæsar. This last, in speeches which have not come down to us, but which are quoted by different authors, spared nothing to assure among the people the success of the proposition.[857] "He insisted on the propriety of deciding promptly on this measure of reconciliation, and observed that there could not be a more opportune moment for its adoption."[858] It was adopted without difficulty. All seemed to favour a return to the old institutions. The censorship, interrupted for seventeen years, was re-established, and L. Gellius and C. Lentulus, the censors chosen, exercised their office with so much severity, that they expelled from the Senate sixty-four of its members, probably creatures of Sylla. In the number of those expelled figured Caius Antonius, previously accused by Cæsar, and Publius Lentulus Sura, consul in the year 683.

All these changes had been proposed or accepted by Pompey rather to please the multitude than to obey distinct convictions. And by them he lost his true supporters in the upper classes, without gaining, in the opposite party, the foremost place, already occupied by Cæsar. But Pompey, blind to real worth, imagined then that no one could surpass him in influence; always favoured by circumstances, he had been accustomed to see both the arrogance of Sylla and the majesty of the laws yield before him. Notwithstanding a first refusal by the Dictator, at twenty-six years of age he had obtained the honours of the triumph, without having fulfilled any of the legal conditions. Contrary to the laws, a second triumph had been accorded him, as also the consulship, though out of Rome, and without having followed the necessary order of hierarchy of the magistracies. Full of presumption through the examples of the past, full of confidence in the future through the adulation of the present, he thought he might wound the interests of the nobles without alienating them, and flatter the tastes and passions of the people without losing his dignity. Towards the end of his consulship, he, the chief magistrate of the Republic, he, who thought himself above all others, presented himself as a mere soldier at the annual review of the knights. The momentary effect was immense when the censors, seated on their tribunal, saw Pompey traversing the crowd, preceded by all the pomp of the consular power, and leading before them his horse, which he held by the bridle. The crowd, silent till then, burst out into transports of joy, overcome with admiration at the sight of so great a man glorifying himself for being a simple knight, and modestly submitting himself to the legal forms. But on the demand of the censors if he had made all the campaigns required by law, he answered, "Yes, I have made them all, never having had any other general than myself."[859] The ostentation of this reply shows that this step of Pompey's was a false modesty, the most insupportable form of pride, according to the expression of Marcus Aurelius.

Cæsar Questor (686).

III. Neither did Cæsar disdain ceremonial; but he sought to give it a significance which should make an impression upon the mind. The opportunity soon presented itself. Soon after he was nominated questor and admitted to the Senate, he lost his aunt Julia and his wife Cornelia, and hastened to make a veritable political manifestation of their funeral oration. [860] It was the custom at Rome to pronounce a eulogy on women only when they died at an advanced age. Cæsar obtained public approbation by departing from this usage in favour of his young wife; they saw in it, according to Plutarch,[861] a proof of sensibility and softness of manners; but they applauded not the family sentiment only, they glorified much more the inspiration of the politician who dared to make a panegyric on the husband of Julia, the celebrated Marius, whose image, in wax, carried by Cæsar's orders in the funeral procession, re-appeared for the first time since the proscription of Sylla.[862]

After having rendered these last honors to his wife, he accompanied, in the capacity of questor, the prætor Antistius Vetus, sent into Ulterior Spain. [863] The peninsula was then divided into two great provinces: Citerior Spain, since called Tarraconensis, and Ulterior Spain, comprising Bætica and Lusitania.[864] The positive limits, we may well believe, were not very exactly determined, but at this epoch the Saltus Castulonensis, which corresponds with the Sierras Nevada and Cazorla,[865] was considered as such between these two provinces. To the north, the limitation could not be made any more distinct, the Asturias not being thoroughly conquered. The capital of Ulterior Spain was Corduba (Cordova), where the prætor resided. [866]

The chief towns, doubtless connected by military roads, formed so many centres of general meeting, where assizes for the regulation of business were held. These meetings were called conventus civium Romanorum,[867] because the members who composed them were Roman citizens dwelling in the country. The prætor, or his delegate, presided over them once a year. [868] Each province in Spain had several of them. In the first century of our era, there were three for Lusitania and four for Bætica.[869]

Cæsar, the delegate of the prætor, visited these towns, presiding over the assemblies and administering justice. He was noted for his spirit of conciliation and equity,[870] and showed a lively solicitude for the interests of the Spaniards.[871] As the character of illustrious men is revealed in their smallest actions, it is not a matter of indifference to mention the gratitude which Cæsar always had for the good offices of Vetus. Plutarch informs us that a strict union reigned between them ever after, and Cæsar took care to name the son of Vetus questor when he himself was raised to the prætorship,[872] as sensible of friendship as he was later forgetful of injuries.

Yet the love of glory and the consciousness of his high faculties made him aspire to a more important part. He manifested his impatient desire for this one day when he went to visit the famous temple of Hercules at Gades, as Hannibal and Scipio had done before.[873] At the sight of the statue of Alexander, he deplored with a sigh that he had done nothing at the age when this great man had conquered the whole world.[874] In fact, Cæsar was then thirty-two years old, nearly the age at which Alexander died. Having obtained his recall to Rome, he stopped on his return in Gallia Transpadana (687).[875] The colonies founded in this country possessed the Latin law (jus Latii), which Pompeius Strabo had granted them, but they vainly demanded the rights of Roman city. The presence of Cæsar, already known for his friendly feelings towards the provinces, excited a lively emotion among the inhabitants, who saw in him the representative of their interests and their cause. The enthusiasm was such, that the Senate, terrified, thought itself obliged to retain for some time longer in Italy the legions destined for the army in Asia.[876]

The ascendency of Pompey still continued, though, since his consulship, he had remained without command, having undertaken, in 684, not to accept the government of any province at the expiration of his magistracy;[877] but his popularity began to disquiet the Senate, so much is it in the very essence of the aristocracy to distrust those who raise themselves, and extend their powers beyond itself. This was an additional motive for Cæsar to connect himself more closely with Pompey; whereupon he backed him with all his influence; and either to cement this alliance, or because of his inclination for a beautiful and graceful woman, shortly after his return he married Pompeia, the kinswoman of Pompey, and granddaughter of Sylla.[878] He was thus, at one and the same time, the arbiter of elegance, the hope of the democratic party, and the only public man whose opinions and conduct had never varied.

The Gabinian Law (687).

IV. The decadence of a political body is evident when the measures most useful to the glory of a country, instead of arising from its provident initiative, are inaugurated by obscure and often disreputable men, the faithful but dishonoured organs of public opinion. Thus the propositions made at this epoch, far from being inspired by the Senate, were put forward by uninfluential individuals, and carried by the violent attitude of the people. The first referred to the pirates, who, upheld and encouraged by Mithridates, had long infested the seas, and ravaged all the coasts; an energetic repression was indispensable. These bold adventurers, whose number the civil wars had greatly increased, had become a veritable power. Setting out from Cilicia, their common centre, they armed whole fleets, and found a refuge in important towns.[879] They had pillaged the much-frequented port of Caieta (Gaëta), dared to land at Ostia, and carry off the inhabitants to slavery; sunk in mid seas a Roman fleet under the orders of a consul, and made two prætors prisoners.[880] Not only strangers deputed to Rome, but the ambassadors of the Republic, had fallen into their hands, and had undergone the shame of being ransomed.[881] Finally, the pirates intercepted the imports of wheat indispensable for the feeding of the city. To remedy so humiliating a state of things, the tribune of the people, Aulus Gabinius, proposed to confide the war against the pirates to one sole general; to give him, for three years, extended powers, large forces, and to place three lieutenants under his orders.[882] The assembly of the people instantly accepted this proposition, notwithstanding the small esteem in which the character of its author was held; and the name of Pompey was in every mouth; but "the senators," says Dio Cassius, "would have preferred to suffer the greatest evils from the pirates, than to have invested Pompey with such a power;"[883] they were ready to put to death, in the curia itself, the tribune who was the author of the motion. Scarcely had the multitude heard of the opposition of the senators, when they flocked in crowds, invaded the place of meeting, and would have massacred them, had they not been protected from their fury.[884]

The projected law, submitted to the suffrages of the people, attacked by Catulus and Q. Hortensius, energetically supported by Cæsar, is then adopted; and they confer on Pompey, for three years, the proconsular authority over all the seas, over all the coasts, and for fifty miles into the interior; they grant him 6,000 talents (35 millions [£1,400,000]),[885] twenty-five lieutenants, and the power of taking such vessels and troops as he should judge necessary. The allies, foreigners, and the provinces, were called on to concur in this expedition. They equipped five hundred ships, they levied a hundred and twenty thousand infantry and five thousand horse. The Senate, in spite of itself, sanctioned the clauses of this law, the utility of which was so manifest that its publication alone was sufficient to lower the price of wheat all through Italy.[886]

Pompey adopted an able plan for putting an end to piracy. He divided the Mediterranean coasts from the Columns of Hercules to the Hellespont and the southern shores of the Black Sea into ten separate commands;[887]

at the head of each he placed one of his lieutenants. He himself, retaining the general surveillance, went to Cilicia with the rest of his forces. This vast plan protected all the shores, left the pirates no refuge, and enabled him to destroy their fleet and attack them in their dens at once. In three months Pompey re-established the safety of the seas, took a thousand castles or strongholds, destroyed three hundred towns, took eight hundred ships, and made twenty thousand prisoners, whom he transferred into the interior of Asia, where he employed them in building a city, which received the name of Pompeiopolis.[888]

The Manilian Law (688).

V. At these tidings, the enthusiasm for Pompey, then in the island of Crete, redoubled, and they talked of placing in his hands the fate of another war. Although Lucullus had obtained brilliant successes over Mithridates and Tigranes, his military position in Asia began to be compromised. He had experienced reverses; insubordination reigned among his soldiers; his severity excited their complaints; and the news of the arrival of the two proconsuls from Cilicia, Acilius Glabrio and Marcius Rex, sent to command a part of the provinces until then under his orders, had weakened respect for his authority.[889] These circumstances determined Manlius, tribune of the people, to propose that the government of the provinces trusted to Lucullus should be given to Pompey, joining to them Bithynia, and preserving to him the power which he already exercised over all the seas. "It was," says Plutarch, "to submit the whole Roman empire to one sole man, and to deprive Lucullus of the fruits of his victories."[890] Never, indeed, had such power been confided to any citizen, neither to the first Scipio to ruin Carthage, nor to the second to destroy Numantia. The people grew more and more accustomed to regard this concentration of power in one hand as the only means of salvation. The Senate, taxing these proposals with ingratitude, combated them with all its strength; Hortensius asserted that if all the authority was to be trusted to one man, no person was more worthy of it than Pompey, but that so much authority ought not to be centred in one person.[891] Catulus cried that they had done with liberty, and that, henceforth to enjoy this, they would be forced to retire to the woods and mountains.[892] Cicero, on the contrary, inaugurated his entrance into the Senate by a magnificent oration, which has been preserved to us; he showed that it was for the best interest of the Republic to give the conduct of this war to a captain whose noble deeds in the past, and whose moderation and integrity, vouched for the future. "So many other generals," he said at the close, "proceed on an expedition only with the hope of enriching themselves. Can those who think we ought not to grant all these powers to one man alone ignore this, and do we not see that what renders Pompey so great is not only his own virtues, but the vices of others?"[893] As to Cæsar, he seconded, with all his power, the efforts of Cicero[894] for the adoption of the law, which, supported by public feeling, and submitted to the suffrage of the tribes, was adopted unanimously.

Certainly, Lucullus had deserved well of his country, and it was cruel to deprive him of the glory of terminating a war which he had prosperously begun;[895] but the definitive success of the campaign demanded his substitution, and the instinct of the people did not deceive them. Often, in difficult cases, they see more clearly than an assembly preoccupied with the interests of castes or of persons, and events soon show that they are right.

Lucullus had announced at Rome the end of the war; yet Mithridates was far from being conquered. This fierce enemy of the Romans, who had continued the struggle twenty-four years, and whom evil fortune had never been able to discourage, would not treat, despite his sixty four years and recent reverses, save on conditions inadmissible by the Romans. The fame of Pompey then was not useless against such an adversary. His ascendency alone could bring back discipline into the army and intimidate the enemy. In fact, his presence was sufficient to re-establish order, and retain under their standards the old soldiers who had obtained their discharge, and wished to return to their homes;[896] they formed the flower of the army, and were known under the name of Valerians.[897] On the other hand, Tigranes, having learned the arrival of Pompey, abandoned the party of his father-in-law, declaring that this general was the only one to whom he would submit,[898] so much does the prestige of one man, says Dio Cassius, lord it over that of another.[899]

Manilius then demanded the re-establishment of the law of Caius Gracchus, by virtue of which the centuria prærogativa, instead of being drawn by lot from the first classes of the tribes, was taken indiscriminately from all the classes, which destroyed the distinctions of rank and fortune in the elections, and deprived the richer of their electoral privileges.[900]

We see that it was generally the tribunes of the people who, obeying the inspiration of greater men, took the initiative in the more popular measures. But the major part, without disinterestedness or moderation, often compromised those who had recourse to their services by their unruly ardour and subversive opinions. Manilius, in 688, suddenly re-opened a question which always created great agitation at Rome; this was the political emancipation of the freedmen. He obtained, by a surprise, the readoption of the law Sulpicia, which gave a vote to the freedmen by distributing them among the thirty-five tribes, and asserted that he had the consent of Crassus and Pompey. But the Senate revoked the law some time after its adoption, agreeing in this with the chiefs of the popular party, who did not think it was demanded by public opinion.[901]

Cæsar Curule Ædile (689).

VI. Whilst all the favours of fortune seemed to have accumulated on the idol of the moment, Cæsar, remaining at Rome, was chosen inspector (curator) of the Appian Way (687).[902] The maintenance of the highways brought much popularity to those who undertook the charge with disinterestedness; Cæsar gained all the more by his, as he contributed largely to the cost, and even compromised his own fortune thereby.

Two years afterwards (689), nominated curule ædile with Bibulus, he displayed a magnificence which excited the acclamations of the crowd, always greedy of sights. The place named Comitium, the Forum, the Basilicæ, the Capitol itself, were magnificently decorated. Temporary porticoes were erected, under which were exposed a crowd of precious objects.[903] These expenses were not unusual: since the triumph of the dictator Papirius Cursor, all the ædiles were accustomed to contribute to the embellishment of the Forum.[904] Cæsar celebrated with great pomp the Roman games, and the feast of Cybele, and gave the finest shows of wild beasts and gladiators ever yet beheld.[905] The number of the combatants amounted to three hundred and twenty couples, according to Plutarch, a contemptuous expression, which proves the small account made of the lives of these men. Cicero, writing to Atticus, speaks of them as we in our day should speak of racehorses;[906] and the grave Atticus himself had gladiators, as had most of the great people of his time. These bloody games, which seem so inhuman to us, still preserved the religious character which at first they so exclusively possessed; they were celebrated in honour of the dead;[907] Cæsar gave them as a sacrifice to his father's memory, and displayed in them an unwonted pomp.[908] The number of gladiators which he got together terrified the Senate, and for the future it was forbidden to exceed a given number. Bibulus, his colleague, it is true, bore half the expense; nevertheless, the public gave Cæsar all the credit of this sumptuous discharge of the duties of their office. Thus Bibulus said that he was like the temple of Castor and Pollux, which, dedicated to the two brothers, was never called anything but the temple of Castor.[909]

The nobles saw in the sumptuousness of these games only a vain ostentation, a frivolous desire to shine; they congratulated themselves on the prodigality of the ædile, and predicted in his near ruin a term to his influence; but Cæsar, while spending millions to amuse the multitude, did not make this fleeting enthusiasm the sole basis of his popularity; he established this on more solid grounds, by re-awakening in the people the memories of glory and liberty.

Not content with having helped in several healing measures, with having gained over Pompey to his opinions, and sought for the first time to revive the memory of Marius, he wished to sound public opinion by an astounding manifestation. At the moment when the splendour of his ædileship had produced the most favourable impression on the crowd, he secretly restored the trophies of Marius, formerly overturned by Sylla, and ordered them to be placed in the Capitol[910] during the night. The next day, when they saw these images shining with gold, chiselled with infinite art, and adorned with inscriptions which recalled the victories gained over Jugurtha, the Cimbri, and the Teutones, the nobles began to murmur, blaming Cæsar for having dared to revive seditious emblems and proscribed remembrances; but the partisans of Marius flocked in large numbers to the Capitol, making its sacred roof resound with their acclamations. Many shed tears on seeing the venerated features of their old general, and proclaimed Cæsar the worthy successor of that great captain.[911]

Uneasy at these demonstrations, the Senate assembled, and Lutatius Catulus, whose father had been one of the victims of Marius, accused Cæsar of wishing to overthrow the Republic, "no longer secretly, by undermining it, but openly, in attacking it by breach."[912] Cæsar repelled this attack, and his partisans, delighted at his success, vied with each other in saying "that he would carry it over all his rivals, and with the help of the people would take the first rank in the Republic."[913] Henceforth the popular party had a head.

The term of his ædileship having expired, Cæsar solicited the mission of transforming Egypt into a Roman province.[914] The matter in hand was the execution of the will of King Ptolemy Alexas, or Alexander,[915] who, following the example of other kings, had left his state to the Roman peoples. But the will was revoked as doubtful,[916] and it seems that the Senate shrank from taking possession of so rich a country, fearing, as did Augustus later, to make the proconsul who should govern it too powerful. [917] The mission of reducing Egypt to a Roman province was brilliant and fruitful. It would have given to those who might be charged with it extensive military power, and the disposal of large resources. Crassus also placed himself on the list, but after long debates the Senate put an end to all rival pretensions.[918]

About the same time when Crassus was endeavouring to get the inhabitants of Gallia Transpadana admitted to the rights of Roman citizens, the tribune of the people, Caius Papius, caused to be adopted a law for the expulsion of all foreigners from Rome.[919] For, in their pride, the Romans thus called those who were not Latins by origin.[920] This measure would specially affect the Transpadanes, who were devoted to Cæsar, because he had formerly promised to procure for them the title of citizen, which had been refused. It was feared that they would get into the comitia, for, since the emancipation of the Italiotes, it was difficult to distinguish among those who had the right of voting, since often even slaves fraudulently participated in the elections.[921]

Cæsar *judex quæstionis* (660).

VIII. Cæsar soon re-commenced the political struggle against the still living instruments of past oppression, in which he had engaged at the beginning of his career. He neglected no opportunity of calling down upon them the rigours of justice or the opprobrium of public opinion.

The long duration of the civil troubles had given birth to a class of malefactors called sicarii,[922] who committed all sorts of murders and robberies. In 674 Sylla had promulgated a severe edict against them, which, however, excepted the executors of his vengeance in the pay of the treasury. [923] These last were exposed to public animadversion; and though Cato had obtained the restitution of the sums allotted as the price of the heads of the proscribed,[924] no one had yet dared to bring them to justice.[925] Cæsar, notwithstanding the law of Sylla, undertook their prosecution.

Under his presidency, in his capacity as judex quæstionis, L. Luscius, who, by the dictator's order, had slain three of the proscribed, and L. Bellienus, uncle of Catiline and murderer of Lucretius Ofella, were prosecuted and condemned.[926] Catiline, accused, at the instigation of L. Lucceius, orator and historian, the friend of Cæsar, of having slain the celebrated M. Marius Gratidianus, was acquitted.[927]

Conspiracies against the Senate (690).

VIII. Whilst Cæsar endeavoured to react legally against the system of Sylla, another party, composed of the ambitious and discontented, ruined by debt, had long sought to arrive at power by plotting. Of this number had been, since 688, Cn. Piso, P. Sylla, P. Autronius, and Catiline. These men, with diverse antecedents and different qualities, were equally decried, yet they did not want for adherents among the lower class, whose passions they flattered, or among the upper class, to whose policy or enmity they were serviceable. P. Sylla and Autronius, after having been made consuls-elect in 688, had been effaced from the senatorial list for solicitation. Public report mixed up the names of Crassus and Cæsar with these secret manœuvres; but was it possible that these two men, in such opposite positions, and even divided between themselves, should enter into an understanding together for the sake of a vulgar plot; and was it not a new inconsistency of calumny to associate in the same conspiracy Cæsar because of his immense debts, and Crassus because of his immense riches?

Let us remark, besides, that each of the factions then in agitation necessarily sought to compromise, for the purpose of appropriating to itself, such a personage as Cæsar, notorious for his name, his generosity, and his courage.

A matter which has remained obscure, but which then made a great noise, shows the progress of the ideas of disorder. One of the conspirators, Cn. Piso, had taken part in the attempt to assassinate the Consuls Cotta and Torquatus; yet he obtained, through the influence of Crassus, the post of questor pro prætore into Citerior Spain; the Senate, either to get rid of him, or in the doubtful hope of finding in him some support against Pompey, whose power began to appear formidable, consented to grant him this province. But in 691, on his arrival in Spain, he was slain by his escort— some say by the secret emissaries of Pompey.[928] As to Catiline, he was not the man to bend under the weight of the misfortunes of his friends, or under his own losses; he employed new ardour in braving the perils of a conspiracy, and in pursuing the honours of the consulship. He was the most dangerous adversary the Senate had. Cæsar supported this candidature. In a spirit of opposition, he supported all that could hurt his enemies and favour a change of system. Besides, all parties were constrained to deal with those who enjoyed the popular favour. The nobles accepted as candidate C. Antonius Hybrida, a worthless man, capable only of selling himself and of treachery.[929] Cicero, in 690, had promised Catiline to defend him;[930] and a year before, the Consul Torquatus, one of the most esteemed chiefs of the Senate, pleaded for the same individual accused of embezzlement.[931]

the difficulty of constituting a New Party.

IX. We thus see that the misfortunes of the times obliged the most notable men to have dealings with those whose antecedents seemed to devote them to contempt.

In times of transition, when a choice must be made between a glorious past and an unknown future, the rock is, that bold and unscrupulous men alone thrust themselves forward; others, more timid, and the slaves of prejudices, remain in the shade, or offer some obstacle to the movement which hurries away society into new ways. It is always a great evil for a country, a prey to agitations, when the party of the honest, or that of the good, as Cicero calls them, do not embrace the new ideas, to direct by moderating them. Hence profound divisions. On the one side, unknown men often take possession of the good or bad passions of the crowd; on the other, honourable men, immovable or morose, oppose all progress, and by their obstinate resistance excite legitimate impatience and lamentable violence. The opposition of these last has the double inconvenience of leaving the way clear to those who are less worthy than themselves, and of throwing doubts into the minds of that floating mass, which judges parties much more by the honourableness of men than by the value of ideas.

What was then passing in Rome offers a striking example of this. Was it not reasonable, in fact, that men should hesitate to prefer a faction which had at its head such illustrious names as Hortensius, Catulus, Marcellus, Lucullus, and Cato, to that which had for its main-stays individuals like Gabinius, Manilius, Catiline, Vatinius, and Clodius? What more legitimate in the eyes of the descendants of the ancient families than this resistance to all change, and this disposition to consider all reform as Utopian and almost as sacrilege? What more logical for them than to admire Cato's firmness of soul, who, still young, allowed himself to be menaced with death rather than admit the possibility of becoming one day the defender of the cause of the allies claiming the rights of Roman citizens?[932] How not comprehend the sentiments of Catulus and Hortensius obstinately defending the privileges of the aristocracy, and manifesting their fears at this general inclination to concentrate all power in the hands of one individual?

And yet the cause maintained by these men was condemned to perish, as everything which has had its time. Notwithstanding their virtues, they were only an additional obstacle to the steady march of civilisation, because they wanted the qualities most essential for a time of revolution—an appreciation of the wants of the moment, and of the problems of the future. Instead of trying what they could save from the shipwreck of the ancient regime, just breaking to pieces against a fearful rock, the corruption of political morals, they refuse to admit that the institutions to which the Republic owed its grandeur could bring about its decay. Terrified at all innovation, they confounded in the same anathema the seditious enterprises of certain tribunes, and the just reclamations of the citizens. But their influence was so considerable, and ideas consecrated by time have so much empire over minds, that they would have yet hindered the triumph of the popular cause, if Cæsar, in putting himself at its head, had not given it a new glory and an irresistible force. A party, like an army, can only conquer with a chief worthy to command it; and all those who, since the Gracchi, had unfurled the standard of reform, had sullied it with blood, and compromised it by revolts. Cæsar raised and purified it. To constitute his party, it is true, he had recourse to agents but little estimated; the best architect can build only with the materials under his hand; but his constant endeavour was to associate to himself the most trustworthy men, and he spared no effort to gain by turns Pompey, Crassus, Cicero, Servilius Cæpio, Q. Fufius Calenus, Serv. Sulpicius, and many others.

In moments of transition, when the old system is at an end, and the new not yet established, the greatest difficulty consists, not in overcoming the obstacles which are in the way of the advent of a regime demanded by the country, but to establish the latter solidly, by establishing it upon the concurrence of honourable men penetrated with the new ideas, and steady in their principles.

# CHAPTER III
## (691-695)

Cicero and Antonius, Consuls (691).

I. IN the year 690, the candidates for the consulship were Cicero, C. Antonius Hybrida, L. Cassius Longinus, Q. Cornificius, C. Lucinius Sacerdos, P. Sulpicius Galba, and Catiline.[933] Informed of the plots so long in progress, the Senate determined to combat the conspiracies of the last by throwing all the votes they could dispose of upon Cicero, who was thus unanimously elected, and took possession of his office at the beginning of 691. This choice made up for the mediocrity of his colleague Antonius.

The illustrious orator, whose eloquence had such authority, was born at Arpinum, of obscure parents; he had served some time in the war of the allies;[934] afterwards, his orations acquired for him a great reputation, amongst others the defence of the young Roscius, whom the dictator would have despoiled of his paternal heritage. After the death of Sylla, he was appointed questor and sent to Sicily. In 684, he lashed with his implacable speech the atrocities of Verres; at last, in 688, he obtained the prætorship, and displayed in this capacity those sentiments of high probity and of justice which distinguished him throughout his whole career. But the esteem of his fellow-citizens would not have sufficed, in ordinary times, to have raised him to the first magistracy. "The dread of the conspiracy," says Sallust, "was the cause of his elevation. Under other circumstances, the pride of the nobility would have revolted against such a choice. The consulship would have been considered profaned, if, even with superior merit, a new man[935] had obtained it; but, on the approach of danger, envy and pride became silent."[936] The Roman aristocracy must have greatly lost its influence, when, at a critical moment, it allowed a new man to possess more authority over the people than one from its own ranks.

By birth, as well as by his instincts, Cicero belonged to the popular party; nevertheless, the irresolution of his mind, sensible to flattery, and his fear of innovations, led him to serve by turn the rancours of the great or those of the people.[937] Of upright heart, but pusillanimous, he only saw rightly when his self-esteem was not at stake or his interest in danger.

Elected consul, he ranged himself on the side of the Senate, and resisted all proposals advantageous to the multitude. Cæsar honoured his talent, but had little confidence in his character; hence he was averse to his candidature, and hostile during the whole of his consulship.

Agrarian Law of Rullus.

II. Scarcely had Cicero entered on his functions, when the tribune P. Servilius Rullus revived one of those projects which, for ages, have had the effect of exciting to the highest degree both the avidity of the proletaries and the anger of the Senate: it was an agrarian law.

It contained the following provisions: To sell, with certain exceptions,[938] the territories recently conquered, and some other domains but little productive to the State; devoting the proceeds to the purchase, by private contract, of lands in Italy which were to be divided among the indigent citizens; to cause to be nominated, according to the customary mode for the election of grand pontiff—that is, by seventeen tribes, drawn by lot from the thirty-five—ten commissioners or decemvirs, to whom should be left, for five years, the power, absolute and without control, of distributing or alienating the domains of the Republic and private properties wherever they liked. No one could be appointed who was not present in Rome, which excluded Pompey, and the authority of the decemvirs was to be sanctioned by a curiate law. To them alone was intrusted the right to decide what belonged to the State and what to individuals. The lands of the public domain which should not be alienated were to be charged with a considerable impost.[939] The decemvirs had also the power of compelling all the generals, Pompey excepted, to account for the booty and money received during war, but not yet deposited in the treasury, or employed upon some monument. They were allowed to found colonies anywhere they thought proper, particularly in the territory of Stella, and in the ager of Campania, where five thousand Roman citizens were to be established. In a word, the administration of the revenues and the resources of the State came almost wholly into their hands; they had, moreover, their lictors; they could take the omens, and choose amongst the knights two hundred persons to execute their decrees in the provinces, and these were without appeal.

This project offered inconveniences, but also great advantages. Rullus, certainly, was to blame for not designating all the places where he wished to establish colonies; for making two exemptions, one favourable, the other unfavourable to Pompey; for assigning to the decemvirs powers too extensive, tending to arbitrary acts and speculations: nevertheless, his project had an important political aim. The public domain, encroached upon by usurpations or by the colonies of Sylla, had almost disappeared.

The law was to re-constitute it by the sale of conquered territories. On the other side, the lands confiscated in great number by Sylla, and given or sold at a paltry price to his partisans, had suffered a general depreciation, for the ownership was liable to be contested, and they no longer found purchasers. The Republic, while desirous of relieving the poorer class, had thus an interest in raising the price of these lands and in securing the holders. The project of Rullus was, in fact, a veritable law of indemnity. There are injustices which, sanctioned by time, ought also to be sanctioned by law, in order to extinguish the causes of dissension, by restoring their security to existing things, and its value to property.

If the great orator had known how to raise himself above the questions of person and of party, he would, like Cæsar, have supported the proposal of the tribune, amending only what was too absolute or too vague in it; but, overreached by the faction of the great, and desiring to please the knights, whose interests the law injured, he attacked it with his usual eloquence, exaggerating its defects. It would only benefit, he said, a small number of persons. Whilst appearing to favour Pompey, it deprived him, on account of his absence, of the chance of being chosen decemvir. It allowed some individuals to dispose of kingdoms like Egypt, and of the immense territories of Asia. Capua would become the capital of Italy, and Rome, surrounded by a girdle of military colonies devoted to ten new tyrants, would lose its independence. To purchase the lands, instead of apportioning the ager publicus, was monstrous, and he could not admit that they would engage the people to abandon the capital to go and languish in the fields. Then, exposing the double personal interest of the author of the law, he reminded them that the father-in-law of Rullus was enriched with the spoils of proscripts, and that Rullus himself had reserved the right of being nominated decemvir.

Cicero, nevertheless, pointed out clearly the political bearing of the project, although censuring it, when he said; "The new law enriches those who occupied the domain lands, and withdraws them from public indignation. How many men are embarrassed by their vast possessions, and cannot support the odium attached to the largesses of Sylla! How many would sell them, and find no buyers! How many seek means, of whatever kind, to dispossess themselves of them!... And you, Romans, you are going to sell those revenues which your ancestors have acquired at the cost of so much sweat and blood, to augment the fortune and assure the tranquillity of the possessors of the goods confiscated by Sylla!"[940]

We see thus that Cicero seems to deny the necessity of allaying the inquietudes of the new and numerous acquirers of this kind of national property; and yet, when a short time afterwards another tribune proposed to relieve from civic degradation the sons of proscripts, he opposed him, not because this reparation appeared to him unjust, but for fear the rehabilitation in political rights should carry with it the reintegration into the properties, a measure, according to his views, subversive of all interests.[941] Thus, with a strange inconsistency, Cicero combated these two laws of conciliation; the one because it re-assured, the other because it disquieted the holders of the effects of the proscribed. Why must it be that, amongst men of superiority, but without convictions, talent only too often serves to sustain with the like facility the most opposite causes? The opinion of Cicero triumphed, nevertheless, thanks to his eloquence; and the project, despite the lively adhesion of the people, encountered in the Senate such a resistance, that it was abandoned without being referred to the comitia.

Cæsar advocated the agrarian law, because it raised the value of the soil, put an end to the disfavour attached to the national property, augmented the resources of the treasury, prevented the extravagance of the generals, delivered Rome from a turbulent and dangerous populace by wresting it from degradation and misery. He supported the rehabilitation of the children of proscripts, because that measure, profoundly reparative, put an end to one of the great iniquities of the past regime.

There are victories which enfeeble the conquerors more than the vanquished. Such was the success of Cicero. The rejection of the agrarian law, and of the claims of the sons of proscripts, augmented considerably the number of malcontents. A crowd of citizens, driven by privations and the denial of justice, went over to swell the ranks of the conspirators, who, in the shade, were preparing a revolution; and Cæsar, pained at seeing the Senate reject that sage and ancient policy which had saved Rome from so many agitations, resolved to undermine by every means its authority. For this purpose he engaged the tribune, T. Labienus, the same who was afterwards one of his best lieutenants, to get up a criminal accusation which was a direct attack upon the abuse of one of the prerogatives of the government.[942]

Trial of Rabirius (691).

III. For a long time, when internal or external troubles were apprehended, Rome was put, so to speak, in a state of siege, by the sacramental formula, according to which the consuls were enjoined to see that the Republic received no injury; then the power of the consuls was unlimited;[943] and often, in seditions, the Senate had profited by this omnipotence to rid itself of certain factious individuals without observing the forms of justice. The more frequent the agitations had become, the more they had used this extreme remedy. The tribunes always protested ineffectually against a measure which suspended all the established laws, legalised assassination, and made Rome a battle-field. Labienus tried anew to blunt in the hands of the Senate so formidable a weapon.

Thirty-seven years before, as will be remembered, Saturninus, the violent promoter of an agrarian law, had, by the aid of a riot, obtained possession of the Capitol; the country had been declared in danger. The tribune perished in the struggle, and the senator C. Rabirius boasted of having killed him. Despite this long interval of time, Labienus accused Rabirius under an old law of perduellio, which did not leave to the guilty, like the law of treason, the power of voluntary exile, but, by declaring him a public enemy, authorised against him cruel and ignominious punishments. [944] This procedure provoked considerable agitation; the Senate, which felt the blow struck at its privileges, was unwilling to put any one to trial for the execution of an act authorised by itself. The people and the tribunes, on the contrary, insisted that the accused should be brought before a tribunal. Every passion was at work. Labienus claimed to avenge one of his uncles, massacred with Saturninus; and he had the audacity to expose in the Campus Martius the portrait of the factious tribune, forgetting the case of Sextus Titius, condemned, on a former occasion, for the mere fact of having preserved in his house the likeness of Saturninus.[945] The affair was brought, according to ancient usage, before the decemvirs. Cæsar, and his cousin Lucius Cæsar, were designated by the prætor to perform the functions of judges. The very violence of the accusation, compared with the eloquence of his defenders, Hortensius and Cicero, overthrew the charge of perduellio. Nevertheless, Rabirius, condemned, appealed to the people; but the animosity against him was so great that the fatal sentence was about to be irrevocably pronounced, when the prætor, Metellus Celer, devised a stratagem to arrest the course of justice; he carried away the standard planted at the Janiculum.[946] This battered flag formerly announced an invasion of the country round Rome. Immediately all deliberation ceased, and the people rushed to arms. The Romans were great formalists; and, moreover, as this custom left to the magistrates the power of dissolving at their will the comitia, they had the most cogent motives for preserving it; the assembly soon separated, and the affair was not taken up again. Cæsar, nevertheless, had hoped to attain his object. He did not demand the head of Rabirius, whom, when he was subsequently dictator, he treated with favour; he only wished to show to the Senate the strength of the popular party, and to warn it that henceforth it would no more be permitted, as in the time of the Gracchi, to sacrifice its adversaries in the name of the public safety.

If, on the one hand, Cæsar let no opportunity escape of branding the former regime, on the other he was the earnest advocate of the provinces, which vainly looked for justice and protection from Rome. He had, for example, the same year accused of peculation C. Calpurnius Piso, consul in 687, and afterwards governor of Transpadane Gaul, and brought him to trial for having arbitrarily caused an inhabitant of that country to be executed. The accused was acquitted through the influence of Cicero; but Cæsar had shown to the Transpadanes that he was ever the representative of their interests and their vigilant patron.

Cæsar Grand Pontiff (691).

IV. He soon received a brilliant proof of the popularity he enjoyed. The dignity of sovereign pontiff, one of the most important in the Republic, was for life, and gave great influence to the individual clothed with it, for religion mingled itself in all the public and private acts of the Romans.

Metellus Pius, sovereign pontiff, dying in 691, the most illustrious citizens, such as P. Servilius Isauricus, and Q. Lutatius Catulus, prince of the Senate, put themselves at the head of the ranks of candidates to replace him. Cæsar also solicited the office, and, desirous of proving himself worthy of it, he published, at this time doubtless, a very extensive treatise on the augural law, and another on astronomy, designed to make known in Italy the discoveries of the Alexandrian school.[947]

Servilius Isauricus and Catulus, relying on their antecedents, and on the esteem in which they were held, believed themselves the more sure of election, because, since Sylla, the people had not interfered in the nomination of grand pontiff, the college solely making the election. Labienus, to facilitate Cæsar's access to this high dignity, obtained a plebiscitum restoring the nomination to the suffrages of the people. This manœuvre disconcerted the other competitors without discouraging them, and, as usual, they attempted to seduce the electors with money. All who held with the party of the nobles united against Cæsar, who combated solicitation by solicitation, and sustained the struggle by the aid of considerable loans; he knew how to interest in his success, according to Appian, both the poor that he had paid, and the rich from whom he borrowed.[948] Catulus, knowing Cæsar to be greatly in debt, and mistaking his character, offered him a large sum to desist. He answered him that he would borrow a much greater sum of him if he would support his candidature.[949]

At length the great day arrived which was to decide the future of Cæsar; when he started to present himself at the comitia, the most gloomy thoughts agitated his ardent mind, and calculating that if he should not succeed, his debts would constrain him perhaps to go into exile, he embraced his mother and said, "To-day thou wilt see me grand pontiff or a fugitive."[950] The most brilliant success crowned his efforts, and what added to his joy was his obtaining more votes in the tribes of his adversaries than they had in all the tribes put together.[951]

Such a victory made the Senate fear whether Cæsar, strong in his ascendency over the people, might not proceed to the greatest excesses; but his conduct remained the same.

Hitherto he had inhabited a very moderate house, in the quarter called Suburra; nominated sovereign pontiff, he was lodged in a public building in the Via Sacra.[952] This new position necessarily obliged him, indeed, to a sumptuous life, if we may judge by the luxuriousness displayed at the reception of a simple pontiff, at which he assisted as king of the sacrifices, and of which Macrobius has preserved to us the curious details.[953] Moreover, he built himself a superb villa on the Lake of Nemi, near Aricia.

Catiline's Conspiracy.

V. Catiline, who has already been spoken of, had twice failed in his designs upon the consulship; he solicited it again for the year 692, without abandoning his plans of conspiracy. The moment seemed favourable. Pompey being in Asia, Italy was bared of troops; Antonius, associated in the plot, shared the consulship with Cicero. Calm existed on the surface, whilst passions, half extinguished, and bruised interests, offered to the first man bold enough, numerous means of raising commotions.[954] The men whom Sylla had despoiled, as well as those he had enriched, but who had dissipated the fruits of their immense plunder, were equally discontented; so that the same idea of subversion formed a bond of union between the victims and the accomplices of the past oppression.

Addicted to excesses of every kind, Catiline dreamed, in the midst of his orgies, of the overthrow of the oligarchy; but we may doubt his desire to put all to fire and sword, as Cicero says, and as most historians have repeated after him. Of illustrious birth, questor in 677, he distinguished himself in Macedonia, in the army of Curio; he had been prætor in 686, and governor of Africa the year following. He was accused of having in his youth imbrued his hands in Sylla's murders, of having associated with the most infamous men, and of having been guilty of incest and other crimes; there would be no reason for exculpating him if we did not know how prodigal political parties in their triumph are of calumnies against the vanquished. Besides, we must acknowledge that the vices with which he was charged he shared in common with many personages of that epoch, among others with Antonius, the colleague of Cicero, who subsequently undertook his defence. Gifted with a high intelligence and a rare energy, Catiline could not have meditated a thing so insensate as massacre and burning. It would have been to seek to reign over ruins and tombs. The truth will present itself better in the following portrait, traced by Cicero seven years after the death of Catiline, when, returning to a calmer appreciation, the great orator painted in less sombre colours him whom he had so disfigured: — "This Catiline, you cannot have forgotten, I think had, if not the reality, at least the appearance of the greatest virtues. He associated with a crowd of perverse men, but he affected to be devoted to men of greatest estimation. If for him debauchery had powerful attractions, he applied himself with no less ardour to labour and affairs. The fire of passions devoured his heart, but he had also a taste for the labours of war. No, I do not believe there ever existed on this earth a man who offered so monstrous an assemblage of passions and qualities so varied, so contrary, and in continual antagonism with each other."[955]

The conspiracy, conducted by the adventurous spirit of its chief, had acquired considerable development. Senators, knights, young patricians, a great number of the notable citizens of the allied towns, partook in it. Cicero, informed of these designs, assembles the Senate in the Temple of Concord, and communicates to it the information he had received: he informs it that, on the 5th of the calends of November, a rising was to take place in Etruria; that on the morrow a riot would break out in Rome; that the lives of the consuls were threatened; that, lastly, everywhere stores of warlike arms and attempts to enlist the gladiators indicated the most alarming preparations. Catiline, questioned by the consul, exclaims, that the tyranny of some men, their avarice, their inhumanity, are the true causes of the uneasiness which torments the Republic; then, repelling with scorn the projects of revolt which they imputed to him, he concludes with this threatening figure of speech: "The Roman people is a robust body, but without head: I shall be that head."[956] He departed with these words, leaving the Senate undecided and trembling. The assembly, meanwhile, passed the usual decree, enjoining the consuls to watch that the Republic received no injury.

The election of consuls for the following year, till then deferred, took place on the 21st of October, 691, and Silanus having been nominated with Murena, Catiline was a third time rejected. He then dispatched to different parts of Italy his agents, and among others, C. Mallius into Etruria, Septimius to the Picenum, and C. Julius into Apulia, to organise the revolt. [957] At the mouth of the Tiber, a division of the fleet, previously employed against the pirates, was ready to second his projects.[958] At Rome even the assassination of Cicero was boldly attempted.

The Senate was convened again on the 8th of November. Catiline dared to attend, and take his seat in the midst of his colleagues. Cicero, in a speech which has become celebrated, apostrophised him in terms of the strongest indignation, and by a crushing denunciation forced him to retire.[959] Catiline, accompanied by three hundred of his adherents, left the capital next morning to join Mallius.[960] During the following days, alarming news arriving from all parts threw Rome into the utmost anxiety. Stupor reigned there. To the animation of fêtes and pleasures had, all of a sudden, succeeded a gloomy silence. Troops were raised; armed outposts were placed at various points; Q. Marcius Rex is dispatched to Fæsulæ (Fiesole); Q. Metellus Creticus into Apulia; Pomponius Rufus to Capua; Q. Metellus Celer into the Picenum; and, lastly, the consul, C. Antonius, led an army into Etruria. Cicero had detached the latter from the conspiracy by giving him the lucrative government of Macedonia.[961] He accepted in exchange that of Gaul, which he also subsequently renounced, not wishing, after his consulship, to quit the city and depart as proconsul. The principal conspirators, at the head of whom were the prætor Lentulus and Cethegus, remained at Rome. They continued energetically the preparations for the insurrection, and entered into communication with the envoys of the Allobroges. Cicero, secretly informed by his spies, among others by Curius, watched their doings, and, when he had indisputable proofs, caused them to be arrested, convoked the Senate, and exposed the plan of the conspiracy.

Lentulus was obliged to resign the prætorship. Out of nine conspirators convicted of the attempt against the Republic, five only failed to escape; they were confided to the custody of the magistrates appointed by the consul. Lentulus was delivered to his kinsman Lentulus Spinther; L. Statilius to Cæsar; Gabinius to Crassus; Cethegus to Cornificius; and Cæparius, who was taken in his flight, to the senator Cn. Terentius.[962] The Senate was on the point of proceeding against them in a manner in which all the forms of justice would have been violated. The criminal judgments were not within its competence, and neither the consul nor the assembly had the right to condemn a Roman citizen without the concurrence of the people. Be that as it may, the senators assembled for a last time on the 5th of December, to deliberate on the punishment of the conspirators; they were less numerous than on the preceding days. Many of them were unwilling to pass sentence of death against citizens belonging to the great patrician families. Some, however, were in favour of capital punishment, in spite of the law Portia. After others had spoken, Cæsar made the following speech, the bearing of which merits particular attention:—

"Conscript fathers, all who deliberate upon doubtful matters ought to be uninfluenced by hatred, affection, anger, or pity. When we are animated by these sentiments, it is hard to unravel the truth; and no one has ever been able to serve at once his passions and his interests. Free your reason of that which beclouds it, and you will be strong; if passion invade your mind and rules it, you will be without strength. It would be here the occasion, conscript fathers, to recall to mind how many kings and peoples, carried away by rage or pity, have taken fatal resolutions; but I prefer reminding you how our ancestors, unswayed by prejudice, performed good and just deeds. In our Macedonian war against King Perseus, the Republic of Rhodes, in its power and pride, although it owed its greatness to the support of the Roman people, proved disloyal and hostile to us; but when, on the termination of this war, the fate of the Rhodians was brought under deliberation, our ancestors left them unpunished in order that no one should ascribe the cause of the war to their riches rather than to their wrongs. So, also, in all the Punic wars, although the Carthaginians had often, both during peace and during the truces, committed perfidious atrocities, our fathers, in spite of the opportunity, never imitated them, because they thought more of their honour than of vengeance, however just.

"And you, conscript fathers, take care that the crime of P. Lentulus and his accomplices overcome not the sentiment of your dignity, and consult not your anger more than your reputation. Indeed, if there be a punishment adequate to their offences, I will approve the new measure; but if, on the contrary, the vastness of the crime exceeds all that can be imagined, we should adhere, I think, to that which has been provided by the laws.

"Most of those who have expressed their opinion before me have deplored in studied and magniloquent terms the misfortune of the Republic; they have recounted the horrors of war and the sufferings of the vanquished, the rapes of young girls and boys, infants torn from the arms of their parents, mothers delivered to the lusts of the vanquisher, the pillage of temples and houses, the carnage and burning everywhere; in short, arms, corpses, blood, and mourning. But, by the immortal gods, to what tend these speeches? To make you detest the conspiracy? What! will he whom a plot so great and so atrocious has not moved, be inflamed by a speech? No, not so; men never consider their personal injuries slight; many men resent them too keenly. But, conscript fathers, that which is permitted to some is not permitted to others. Those who live humbly in obscurity may err by passion, and few people know it; all is equal with them, fame and fortune; but those who, invested with high dignities, pass their life in an exalted sphere, do nothing of which every mortal is not informed. Thus, the higher the fortune the less the liberty; the less we ought to be partial, rancorous, and especially angry. What, in others, is named hastiness, in men of power is called pride and cruelty.

"I think then, conscript fathers, that all the tortures known can never equal the crimes of the conspirators; but, among most mortals, the last impressions are permanent, and the crimes of the greatest culprits are forgotten, to remember only the punishment, if it has been too severe.

"What D. Silanus, a man of constancy and courage, has said, has been inspired in him, I know, by his zeal for the Republic, and in so grave a matter he has been swayed neither by partiality nor hatred. I know too well the wisdom and moderation of that illustrious citizen. Nevertheless, his advice seems to me, I will not say cruel (for can one be cruel towards such men?), but contrary to the spirit of our government. Truly, Silanus, either fear or indignation would have forced you, consul-elect, to adopt a new kind of punishment. As to fear, it is superfluous to speak of it, when, thanks to the active foresight of our illustrious consul, so many guards are under arms. As to the punishment, we may be permitted to say the thing as it is: in affliction and misfortune death is the termination of our sufferings, and not a punishment; it takes away all the ills of humanity; beyond are neither cares nor joy. But, in the name of the immortal gods, why not add to your opinion, Silanus, that they shall be forthwith beaten with rods? Is it because the law Portia forbids it? But other laws also forbid the taking away the lives of condemned citizens, and prescribe exile. Is it because it is more cruel to be beaten with rods than to be put to death? But is there anything too rigorous, too cruel, against men convicted of so black a design? If, then, this penalty is too light, is it fitting to respect the law upon a less essential point, and break it in its most serious part? But, it may be said, who will blame your decree against the parricides of the Republic? Time, circumstances, and fortune, whose caprice governs the world. Whatever happens to them, they will have merited. But you, senators, consider the influence your decision may have upon other offenders. Abuses often grow from precedents good in principle; but when the power falls into the hands of men less enlightened or less honest, a just and reasonable precedent receives an application contrary to justice and reason.

"The Lacedæmonians imposed upon Athens vanquished a government of thirty rulers. These began by putting to death without judgment all those whose crimes marked them out to public hatred; the people rejoiced, and said it was well done. Afterwards, when the abuses of this power multiplied, good and bad alike were sacrificed at the instigation of caprice; the rest were in terror. Thus Athens, crushed under servitude, expiated cruelly her insensate joy. In our days, when Sylla, conqueror, caused to be butchered Damasippus and other men of that description, who had attained to dignities to the curse of the Republic, who did not praise such a deed? Those villains, those factious men, whose seditions had harassed the Republic, had, it was said, merited their death. But this was the signal for a great carnage. For if any one coveted the house or land of another, or only a vase or vestment, it was somehow contrived that he should be put in the number of the proscribed. Thus, those to whom the death of Damasippus had been a subject for joy, were soon themselves dragged to execution, and the massacres ceased not until Sylla had gorged all his followers with riches.

"It is true, I dread nothing of the sort, either from M. Tullius or from present circumstances; but, in a great state, there are so many different natures! Who knows if at another epoch, under another consul, master of an army, some imaginary plot may not be believed real? And if a consul, armed with this example and with a decree of the Senate, once draw the sword, who will stay his hand or limit vengeance?

"Our ancestors, conscript fathers, were never wanting in prudence or decision, and pride did not hinder them from adopting foreign customs provided they appeared good. From the Samnites they borrowed their arms, offensive and defensive; from the Etruscans, the greater part of the insignia of our magistrates; in short, all that, amongst their allies or their enemies, appeared useful to themselves, they appropriated with the utmost eagerness, preferring to imitate good examples than to be envious of them. At the same epoch, adopting a Grecian custom, they inflicted rods upon the citizens, and death upon criminals. Afterwards the Republic increased; and with the increase of citizens factions prevailed more, and the innocent were oppressed; they committed many excesses of this kind. Then the law Portia and many others were promulgated, which only sanctioned the punishment of exile against the condemned. This consideration, conscript fathers, is, in my opinion, the strongest for rejecting the proposed innovation. Certainly those men were superior to us in virtue and wisdom, who, with such feeble means, have raised so great an empire, whilst we preserve with difficulty an inheritance so gloriously acquired. Are we then to set free the guilty, and increase with them the army of Catiline? In no wise; but I vote that their goods be confiscated, themselves imprisoned in the municipia best furnished with armed force, to the end that no one may hereafter propose their restoration to the Senate or even to the people; that whoever shall act contrary to this measure be declared by the Senate an enemy of the State and of the public tranquillity."[963]

With this noble language, which reveals the statesman, compare the declamatory speeches of the orators who pleaded for the penalty of death: "I wish," cries Cicero, "to snatch from massacre your wives, your children, and the sainted priestesses of Vesta; from the most frightful outrages, your temples and sanctuaries; our fair country from the most horrible conflagration; Italy from devastation....[964] The conspirators seek to slaughter all, in order that no one may remain to weep for the Republic, and lament over the ruin of so great an empire."[965] And when he speaks of Catiline: "Is there in all Italy a poisoner, is there a gladiator, a brigand, an assassin, a parricide, a forger of wills, a suborner, a debauchee, a squanderer, an adulterer; is there a disreputable woman, a corrupter of youth, a man tarnished in character, a scoundrel, in short, who does not confess to having lived with Catiline in the greatest familiarity?"[966] Certainly, this is not the cool and impartial language which becomes a judge.

Cicero holds cheap the law and its principles; he must have, above all, arguments for his cause, and he goes to history to seek for facts which might authorise the putting to death of Roman citizens. He holds forth, as an example to follow, the murder of Tiberius Gracchus by Scipio Nasica, and that of Caius Gracchus by the consul Lucius Opimius;[967] forgetting that but lately, in a famous oration, he had called the two celebrated tribunes the most brilliant geniuses, the true friends of the people;[968] and that the murderers of the Gracchi, for having massacred inviolable personages, became a butt to the hatred and scorn of their fellow-citizens. Cicero himself will shortly pay with exile for his rigour towards the accomplices of Catiline.

Cæsar's speech had such an effect upon the assembly that many of the senators, amongst others the brother of Cicero, adopted his opinion. [969] Decimus Silanus, consul-elect, modified his own, and Cicero at last seemed ready to withdraw from his responsibility, when he said: "If you adopt the opinion of Cæsar, as he has always attached himself to the party which passes in the Republic as being that of the people, it is probable that a sentence of which he shall be the author and guarantee will expose me less to popular storms."[970] However, he persevered in his demand for the immediate execution of the accused. But Cato mainly decided the vacillating majority of the Senate by words the most calculated to influence his auditors. Far from seeking to touch the strings of the higher sentiments and of patriotism, he appeals to selfish interests and fear. "In the name of the immortal gods," cried he, "I adjure you, you, who have ever held your houses, your lands, your statues, your pictures, in greater regard than the Republic, if these goods, of whatever kind they be, you desire to preserve; if for your enjoyments you would economise a necessary leisure; rise at last from your lethargy, and take in hand the Republic;"[971] which means, in other terms: "If you wish to enjoy peaceably your riches, condemn the accused without hearing them." This is what the Senate did.

A singular incident happened, in the midst of these debates, to show to what point Cæsar had awakened people's suspicions. At the most animated moment of the discussion, a letter was brought to him. He read it with eagerness. Cato and other senators, supposing it to be a message from one of the conspirators, insisted upon its being read to the Senate. Cæsar handed the letter to Cato, who was seated near him. The latter saw it was a love-letter from his sister Servilia, and threw it back indignantly, crying out, "There! keep it, drunkard!"[972] a gratuitous insult, since he himself did justice to the temperance of Cæsar the day when he said that, of all the men who had overthrown the State, he was the only one who had done it fasting. [973] Cato expressed with still greater force the fears of his party when he said: "If, in the midst of such great and general alarms, Cæsar alone is without fear, it is for you as well as me an additional motive for fear."[974] Cato went further. After the condemnation of the accused to death, he tried to drive Cæsar to extremities by turning against them an opinion which the latter had expressed in their interest: he proposed to confiscate their goods. The debate became then warmer than ever. Cæsar declared that it was an indignity, after having rejected the humane part of his opinion, to adopt from it the rigorous spirit it contained, for the purpose of aggravating the lot of the condemned and adding to their punishment.[975] As his protestation met with no echo in the Senate, he adjured the tribunes to use their right of intercession, but they remained deaf to his appeal. The agitation was at its height, and to put an end to it, the consul, in haste to terminate a struggle the issue of which might become doubtful, agreed that the confiscation should not form a part of the Senatus-consultum.

Whilst the populace outside, excited by the friends of the conspirators, raised seditious clamours, the knights who formed the guard around the Temple of Concord, exasperated by the language of Cæsar and the length of the debates, broke in upon the assembly; they surrounded Cæsar, and with threatening words, despite his rank of pontiff and of prætor-elect, they drew their swords upon him, which M. Curio and Cicero generously turned aside.[976] Their protection enabled him to regain his home: he declared, however, that he would not appear again in the Senate until the new consuls could ensure order and liberty for the deliberations.

Cicero, without loss of time, went with the prætors to seek the condemned, and conducted them to the prison of the Capitol, where they were immediately executed. Then a restless crowd, ignorant of what was taking place, demanding what had become of the prisoners, Cicero replied with these simple words, "They have lived."[977]

We are easily convinced that Cæsar was not a conspirator; but this accusation is explained by the pusillanimity of some and the rancour of others. Who does not know that in times of crisis, feeble governments always tax sympathy for the accused with complicity, and are not sparing of calumny towards their adversaries? Q. Catulus and C. Piso were animated against him with so deep a hatred that they had importuned the consul to include him in the prosecutions directed against the accomplices of Catiline. Cicero resisted. The report of his participation in the plot was not the less spread, and had been accredited eagerly by the crowd of the envious. [978] Cæsar was not one of the conspirators; if he had been, his influence would have been sufficient to have acquitted them triumphantly.[979] He had too high an idea of himself; he enjoyed too great a consideration to think of arriving at power by an underground way and reprehensible means. However ambitious a man may be, he does not conspire when he can attain his end by lawful means. Cæsar was quite sure of being raised to the consulship, and his impatience never betrayed his ambition. Moreover, he had constantly shown a marked aversion to civil war; and why should he throw himself into a vulgar conspiracy with infamous individuals, he who refused his participation in the attempts of Lepidus when at the head of an army? If Cicero had believed Cæsar guilty, would he have hesitated to accuse him, seeing he scrupled not to compromise, by the aid of a false witness, so high a personage as Licinius Crassus?[980] How, on the eve of the condemnation, could he have trusted to Cæsar the custody of one of the conspirators? Would he have exculpated him in the sequel when the accusation was renewed? Lastly, if Cæsar, as will be seen afterwards, according to Plutarch, preferred being the first in a village in the Alps to being second in Rome, how could he have consented to be the second to Catiline?

The attitude of Cæsar in this matter presents nothing, then, which does not admit an easy explanation. Whilst blaming the conspiracy, he was unwilling that, to repress it, the eternal rules of justice should be set aside. He reminded men, blinded by passion and fear, that unnecessary rigour is always followed by fatal reactions. The examples drawn from history served him to prove that moderation is always the best adviser. It is clear also that, whilst despising most of the authors of the conspiracy, he was not without sympathy for a cause which approached his own by common instincts and enemies. In countries delivered up to party divisions, how many men are there not who desire the overthrow of the existing government, yet without the will to take part in a conspiracy? Such was the position of Cæsar.

On the contrary, the conduct of Cicero and of the Senate can hardly be justified. To violate the law was perhaps a necessity; but to misrepresent the sedition in order to make it odious, to have recourse to calumny to vilify the criminals, and to condemn them to death without allowing them a defence, was an evident proof of weakness. In fact, if the intentions of Catiline had not been disguised, the whole of Italy would have responded to his appeal, so weary were people of the humiliating yoke which weighed upon Rome; but they proclaimed him as one meditating conflagration, murder, and pillage. "Already," it was said, "the torches are lit, the assassins are at their posts, the conspirators drink human blood, and dispute over the shreds of a man they have butchered."[981] It was by these rumours dexterously spread, by these exaggerations which Cicero himself afterwards ridiculed,[982] that the disposition of the people, at first favourable to the insurrection, soon turned against it.[983]

That Catiline might have associated, like all promoters of revolutions, with men who had nothing to lose and everything to gain, cannot be disputed; but how can we believe that the majority of his accomplices was composed of criminals loaded with vices? By the confession of Cicero, many honourable individuals figured amongst the conspirators.[984] Inhabitants of colonies and municipia belonging to the first families in their country, allied themselves with Catiline. Many sons of senators, and amongst others Aulus Fulvius,[985] were arrested on their way to join the insurgents, and put to death by the order of their fathers. Nearly all the Roman youth, says Sallust, favoured at that time the designs of the bold conspirator, and, on the other hand, throughout the whole empire, the populace, eager for novelty, approved of his enterprise.[986]

That Catiline may have been a perverse and cruel man of the kind of Marius and Sylla, is probable; that he wished to arrive at power by violence, is certain; but that he had gained to his cause so many important individuals, that he had inspired their enthusiasm, that he had so profoundly agitated the peoples of Italy, without having proclaimed one great or generous idea, is not probable. Indeed, although attached to the party of Sylla by his antecedents, he knew that the only standard capable of rallying numerous partisans was that of Marius. Thus for a long time he preserved in his house, with a religious care, the silver eagle which had guided the legions of that illustrious captain.[987] His speeches confirm still further this view: in addressing himself to his accomplices, he laments seeing the destinies of the Republic in the hands of a faction who excluded the greatest number from all participation in honours and riches.[988] He wrote to Catulus, a person of the highest respect, with whom he was intimate, the following letter, deficient neither in simplicity nor in a certain grandeur, the calmness of which offers a striking contrast to the vehemence of Cicero:—

"L. Catiline to Q. Catulus, salutation,—Thy tried friendship, which has always been precious to me, gives me the assurance that in my misfortune thou wilt hear my prayer. I do not wish to justify the part I have taken. My conscience reproaches me with nothing, and I wish only to expose my motives, which truly thou wilt find lawful. Driven to extremity by the insults and injustices of my enemies, robbed of the recompense due to my services, finally hopeless of ever obtaining the dignity to which I am entitled, I have taken in hand, according to my custom, the common cause of all the unfortunate. I am represented as constrained by debts to this bold resolution: it is a calumny. My personal means are sufficient to acquit my engagements; and it is known that, thanks to the generosity of my wife and of her daughter, I have done honour to other engagements which were foreign to me. But I cannot see with composure unworthy men at the pinnacle of honours, whilst they drive me away from them with groundless accusations. In the extremity to which they have thus reduced me, I embrace the only part that remains to a man of heart to defend his political position. I should like to write more fully, but I hear they are setting on foot against me the last degree of violence. I commend to thee Orestilla, and confide her to thy faith. Protect her, I beseech thee, by the head of thy children. Adieu."

The same sentiments inspired the band of conspirators commanded by Mallius. They reveal themselves in these words: "We call gods and men to witness that it is not against our country that we have taken up arms, nor against the safety of our fellow-citizens. We, wretched paupers as we are, who, through the violence and cruelty of usurers, are without country, all condemned to scorn and indigence, are actuated by one only wish, to guarantee our personal security against wrong. We demand neither power nor wealth, those great and eternal causes of war and strife among mankind. We only desire freedom, a treasure that no man will surrender except with life itself. We implore you, senators, have pity on your wretched fellow-citizens."[989]

These quotations indicate with sufficient clearness the real character of the insurrection; and that the partisans of Catiline did not altogether deserve contempt is proved by their energy and resolution. The Senate having declared Catiline and Mallius enemies of their country, promised a free pardon and two hundred thousand sestertii[990] to all who would abandon the ranks of the insurgents; "but not one," says Sallust,[991] "of so vast an assemblage, was persuaded by the lure of the reward to betray the plot; not one deserted from the camp of Catiline, so deadly was the disease, which, like a pestilence, had infected the minds of most of the citizens." There is no doubt that Catiline, though without a conscience and without principles, had notwithstanding good feeling enough to maintain a cause that he wished to see ennobled, because, so far from offering freedom to the slaves, as Sylla, Marius, and Cinna had done, an example so full of charms for a conspirator,[992] he refused to make use of them, in despite of the advice of Lentulus, who addressed him in these pregnant words: "Outlawed from Rome, what purpose can a Catiline have in refusing the services of slaves?"[993] Finally, that among these insurgents, who are represented to us as a throng of robbers, ready to melt away without striking a blow,[994] there existed, notwithstanding, a burning faith and a genuine fanaticism, is proved by the heroism of their final struggle. The two armies met in the plain of Pistoja, on the 5th of January, 692: a terrible battle ensued, and though victory was hopeless, not one of Catiline's soldiers gave way. To a man they were slain, following the example of their leader, sword in hand; all were found lifeless, but with ranks unbroken, heaped round the eagle of Marius,[995] that glorious relic of the campaign against the Cimbri, that venerated standard of the cause of the people.

We must admit that Catiline was guilty of an attempt to overthrow the laws of his country by violence; but in doing so he was only following the examples of a Marius and a Sylla. His dreams were of a revolutionary despotism, of the ruin of the aristocratic party, and, according to Dio Cassius,[996] of a change in the constitution of the Republic, and of the subjugation of the allies. Yet would his success have been a misfortune: a permanent good can never be the production of hands that are not clean. [997]

Error of Cicero.

VI. Cicero believed that he had destroyed an entire party. He was wrong: he had only foiled a conspiracy, and disencumbered a grand cause of the rash men who were compromising it. The judicial murder of the conspirators gave them new life, and one day the tomb of Catiline was found covered with flowers.[998] Laws may be justly broken when society is hurrying on to its own ruin, and a desperate remedy is indispensable for its salvation; and again, when the government, supported by the mass of the people, becomes the organ of its interests and their hopes. But when, on the contrary, a nation is divided into factions, and the government represents only one of them, its duty, if it intends to foil a plot, is to bind itself to the most exact and scrupulous respect for the law; for at such a juncture every measure not sanctioned by the letter of the law appears to be due rather to a selfish feeling of interest than to a desire for the general weal; and the majority of the public, indifferent or hostile, is always disposed to pity the accused, whoever he may be, and to blame the severity with which he was put down.

Cicero was intoxicated with his success. His vanity made him ridiculous. [999] He thought himself as great as Pompey, and wrote to him with all the pride of a conqueror. But he received a chilling answer,[1000] and in a short time saw the accomplishment of Cæsar's prophetic words: "If even the greatest criminals are too severely dealt with, the heinousness of their offence is lost in the severity of their sentence."[1001]

Even before the battle of Pistoja, whilst the pursuit of the adherents of Catiline was still being prosecuted, public opinion was already hostile to him who had urged the measure, and Metellus Nepos, sent recently from Asia by Pompey, openly found fault with Cicero's conduct. When the latter, on quitting office, wished to address the people for the purpose of glorifying his consulship, Metellus, who had been elected tribune, silenced him with these words: "We will not hear the defence of the man who refused to hear the defence of accused persons," and ordered him to confine himself to the usual oath, that he had in no way contravened the laws. "I swear," answered Cicero, "that I have saved the Republic." However loudly this boastful exclamation might be applauded by Cato and the bystanders, who hail him with Father of his Country, their enthusiasm will have but a short duration.[1002]

Cæsar Prætor (692).

VII. Cæsar, prætor-elect of the city (urbanus) the preceding year, entered upon his office in the year 692. Bibulus, his former colleague in the edileship, and his declared opponent, was his colleague. The more his influence increased, the more he seems to have placed it at the service of Pompey, upon whom, since his departure, the hopes of the popular party rested. He had more share than all the others in causing extraordinary honours to be decreed to the conqueror of Mithridates,[1003] such as the privilege of attending the games of the circus in a robe of triumph and a crown of laurels, and of sitting in the theatre in the official dress of the magistrates, the prætexta.[1004] Still more, he used all his endeavours to reserve for Pompey one of those opportunities of gratifying personal vanity which the Romans prized so highly.

It was the custom for those who were charged with the restoration of any public monument to have their name engraved on it when the work was completed. Catulus had caused his to be inscribed on the Temple of Jupiter, burnt in the Capitol in 671, and of which he had been intrusted with the rebuilding by Sylla. This temple, however, had not been entirely completed. Cæsar appealed against this infraction of the law, accused Catulus of having appropriated a part of the money intended for the restoration, and proposed that the completion of the work should be confided to Pompey on his return, that his name should be placed thereon instead of that of Catulus, and that he should perform the ceremony of dedication.[1005] Cæsar thus not only gave a proof of deference to Pompey, but he sought to please the multitude by gaining a verdict against one of the most esteemed chiefs of the aristocratic party.

The news of this accusation caused a sensation in the Senate, and the eagerness with which the nobles hurried into the Forum to vote against the proposal was such, that on that day they omitted to go, according to custom, to congratulate the new consuls; a proof that in this case also it was entirely a question of party. Catulus pronounced his own defence, but without being able to gain the tribune; and the tumult increasing, Cæsar was obliged to give way to force. The affair went no farther.[1006]

The reaction of public opinion against the conduct of the Senate continued, and men did not hesitate to accuse it openly of having murdered the accomplices of Catiline. Metellus Nepos, supported by the friends of the conspirators, by the partisans of his patron, and by those of Cæsar, proposed a law for the recall of Pompey with his army, that he might, as he said, maintain order in the city, protect the citizens, and prevent their being put to death without a trial. The Senate, and notably Cato and Q. Minucius, offended already by the success of the army of Asia, offered a steady resistance to these proposals.

On the day when the tribes voted, scenes of the greatest turbulence took place. Cato seated himself between the prætor Cæsar and the tribune Metellus, to prevent their conversing together. Blows were given, swords were drawn,[1007] and each of the two factions was in turn driven from the Forum; until at last the senatorial party gained the day. Metellus, obliged to fly, declared that he was yielding to force, and that he was going to join Pompey, who would know well how to avenge them both. It was the first time that a tribune had been known to abandon Rome and take refuge in the camp of a general. The Senate deprived him of his office, and Cæsar of that of prætor.[1008] The latter paid no attention, kept his lictors, and continued the administration of justice; but, on being warned that it was intended to make use of compulsion against him, he voluntarily resigned his office, and shut himself up in his house.

Nevertheless, this outrage against the laws was not submitted to with indifference. Two days afterwards, a crowd assembled before Cæsar's house: the people with loud cries urged him to resume his office; while Cæsar, on his part, engaged them not to transgress the laws. The Senate, which had met on hearing of this riot, sent for him, thanked him for his respect for the laws, and reinstated him in his prætorship.

It was thus that Cæsar maintained himself within the pale of the law, and obliged the Senate to overstep it. This body, heretofore so firm, and yet so temperate, no longer shrank from extraordinary acts of authority; a tribune and a prætor were at the same time obliged to fly from their arbitrary proceedings. Ever since the days of the Gracchi, Rome had witnessed the same scenes of violence, sometimes on the part of the nobles, at others on the part of the people.

The justice which the fear of a popular movement had caused to be rendered to Cæsar had not discouraged the hatred of his enemies. They tried to renew against him the accusation of having been an accomplice in Catiline's conspiracy. At their instigation, Vettius, a man who had been formerly employed by Cicero as a spy to discover the plot, summoned him before the questor Novius Niger;[1009] and Curius, to the latter of whom a public reward had been decreed, accused him before the Senate. They both swore to his enrolment among the conspirators, pretending that they had received their information from the lips of Catiline himself. Cæsar had no difficulty in defending himself, and appealed to the testimony of Cicero, who at once declared his innocence. The court, however, sat for a long time; and the rumour of the charge having been spread abroad in the city, the crowd, uneasy as to what might be Cæsar's fate, assembled in great numbers to demand his release. So irritated they appeared, that to calm them, Cato conceived it necessary to propose to the Senate a decree ordering a distribution of wheat to the poor: a largess which cost the treasury more than 1,250 talents yearly (7,276,250 francs [£291,050]).[1010]

No time was lost in pronouncing the charge calumnious; Curius was deprived of his promised reward; and Vettius, on his way to prison, was all but torn to pieces before the rostra.[1011] The questor Nevius was in like manner arrested for having allowed a prætor, whose authority was superior to his own, to be accused before his tribunal.[1012]

Not satisfied with conciliating the good-will of the people, Cæsar won for himself the favour of the noblest dames of Rome; and, notwithstanding his notorious passion for women, we cannot help discovering a political aim in his choice of mistresses, since all held by different ties to men who were then playing, or were destined to play, an important part. He had had important relations with Tertulla, the wife of Crassus; with Mucia, wife of Pompey; with Lollia, wife of Aulus Gabinius, who was consul in 696; with Postumia, wife of Servius Sulpicius, who was raised to the consulship in 703, and persuaded to join Cæsar's party by her influence; but the woman he preferred was Servilia, sister of Cato and mother of Brutus, to whom, during his first consulship, he gave a pearl valued at six millions of sestertii (1,140,000 francs [£45,600]).[1013] This connection throws an air of improbability over the reports in circulation that Servilia favoured an intrigue between him and her daughter Tertia.[1014] Was it by the intermediation of Tertulla that Crassus was reconciled with Cæsar? or was that reconciliation due to the injustice of the Senate, and the jealousy of Crassus towards Pompey? Whatever was the cause that brought them together, Crassus seems to have made common cause with him in all the questions in which he was interested, subsequent to the consulship of Cicero.

Attempt of Clodius (692).

VIII. At this period a great scandal arose. A young and wealthy patrician, named Clodius, an ambitious and violent man, conceived a passion for Pompeia, Cæsar's wife; but the strict vigilance of Aurelia, her mother-in-law, made it difficult to find opportunities for meeting privately.[1015] Clodius, disguised in female apparel, chose, for the opportunity to enter her house, the moment when she was celebrating, by night, attended by the matrons, mysteries in honour of the Roman people.[1016] Now, it was forbidden to a male to be present at these religious ceremonies, which it was believed that his presence even would defile. Clodius, recognised by a female slave, was expelled with ignominy. The pontiffs uttered the cry of sacrilege, and it became the duty of the vestals to begin the mysteries anew. The nobles, who had already met with an enemy in Clodius, saw in this act a means to compass his overthrow, and at the same time to compromise Cæsar. The latter, without condescending to inquire whether Pompeia was guilty or not, repudiated her. A decree of the Senate, carried by four hundred votes against fifteen, decided that Clodius must take his trial.[1017] He defended himself by pleading an alibi; and, with the sole exception of Aurelia, not a witness came forward against him. Cæsar himself, when examined, declared that he knew nothing; and when asked to explain his own conduct, replied, with equal regard to his honour and his interest, "The wife of Cæsar must be above suspicion!" But Cicero, yielding to the malicious suggestions of his wife Terentia, came forward to assert that on the day of the event he had seen Clodius in Rome.[1018] The people showed its sympathy with the latter, either because they deemed the crime one that did not deserve a severe punishment, or because their religious scruples were not so strong as their political passions. Crassus, on his part, directed the whole intrigue, and lent the accused funds sufficient to buy his judges. They acquitted him by a majority of thirty-one to twenty-five.[1019]

The Senate, indignant at this contradiction, passed, on the motion of Cato, a bill of indictment against the judges who had suffered themselves to be bribed. But as they happened to be knights, the equestrian order made common cause with them, and openly separated themselves from the Senate. Thus the outrage of Clodius had two serious consequences: first, it proved in a striking manner the venality of justice; secondly, it once more threw the knights into the arms of the popular party. But far other steps were taken to alienate them. The farmers of the revenue demanded a reduction in the price of the rents of Asia, on the ground that they had been leased to them at a price that had become too high in consequence of the wars. The opposition of Cato caused their demand to be refused. This refusal, though doubtless legal, was, under the circumstances, in the highest degree impolitic.

Pompey's Triumphal Return (692).

IX. Whilst at Rome dissensions were breaking out on all occasions, Pompey had just brought the war in Asia to a close. Having defeated Mithridates in two battles, he had compelled him to fly towards the sources of the Euphrates, to pass thence into the north of Armenia, and finally to cross thence to Dioscurias, in Colchis, on the western shore of the Black Sea.[1020] Pompey had advanced as far as the Caucasus, where he had defeated two mountain tribes, the Albanians and the Iberians, who disputed his passage. When he had arrived within three days' march of the Caspian, having nothing more to fear from Mithridates, and surrounded by barbarians, he began his retreat through Armenia, where Tigranes came to tender his submission. Next, taking a southerly course, he crossed Mount Taurus, attacked the King of Commagene, fought a battle with the King of Media, invaded Syria, made alliance with the Parthians, received the submission of the Nabathæan Arabs and of Aristobulus, king of the Jews, and took Jerusalem.[1021]

During this period, Mithridates, whose energy and whose views appeared to expand in proportion to his dangers and his reverses, was executing a bold scheme. He had passed round by the eastern coast of the Black Sea, and, allying himself with the Scythians and the peoples of the Crimea, he had reached the shores of the Cimmerian Hellespont; but he had still more gigantic designs in his mind. His idea was to open communications with the Celts, and so reach the Danube, traverse Thrace, Macedonia, and Illyria, cross the Alps, and, like Hannibal, descend upon Italy. Alone, he was great enough to conceive this enterprise, but he was obliged to give it up; his army deserted him, Pharnaces his son betrayed him, and he committed suicide at Panticapæum (Kertch). By this event the vast and rich territories that lie between the Caspian and the Red Sea were placed at the disposal of Pompey. Pharnaces received the kingdom of the Bosphorus. Tigranes, deprived of a portion of his dominions, only preserved Armenia. Deiotarus, tetrarch of Galatia, obtained an increase of territory, and Ariobarzanes obtained an enlargement of the kingdom of Cappadocia, which was re-established in his favour. Various minor princes devoted to the Roman interests received endowments, and thirty-nine towns were rebuilt or founded. Finally, Pontus, Cilicia, Syria, Phœnicia, declared to be Roman provinces, were obliged to accept the constitution imposed upon them by the conqueror. These countries received institutions which they preserved through several centuries.[1022] All the shores of the Mediterranean, with the exception of Egypt, became tributaries of Rome.

The war in Asia terminated, Pompey sent before him his lieutenant, Pupius Piso Calpurnianus, who was soliciting the consulship, and who for that reason requested an adjournment of the elections. This adjournment was granted, and Piso unanimously elected consul for the year 693,[1023] with M. Valerius Messala; to such a degree did the terror of Pompey's name make every one eager to grant what he desired. For no one knew his designs; and it was feared lest, on his return, he should again march upon Rome at the head of his victorious army. But Pompey, having landed at Brundusium about the month of January, 693, disbanded his army, and arrived at Rome, escorted only by the citizens who had gone out in crowds to meet him.[1024]

After the first display of public gratitude, he found his reception different from that on which he had reckoned, and domestic griefs came to swell the catalogue of his disappointments. He had been informed of the scandalous conduct of his wife Mutia during his absence, and determined to repudiate her.[1025]

Envy, that scourge of a Republic, raged against him. The nobles did not conceal their jealousy: it seemed as though they were taking revenge for their own apprehensions, to which they were now adding their own feelings of personal resentment. Lucullus had not forgiven him for having frustrated his expectation of the command of the army of Asia. Crassus was jealous of his renown; Cato, always hostile to those who raised themselves above their fellows, could not be favourable to him, and had even refused him the hand of his niece; Metellus Creticus cherished a bitter remembrance of attempts which had been made to wrest from him the merit of conquering Crete;[1026] and Metellus Celer was offended at the repudiation of his sister Mutia.[1027] As for Cicero, whose opinion of men varied according to their more or less deference for his merit, he discovered that his hero of other days was destitute of rectitude and greatness of soul.[1028] Pompey, foreseeing the ill-feeling he was about to encounter, exerted all his influence, and spent a large sum of money to secure the election of Afranius, one of his old lieutenants, as consul. He reckoned upon him to obtain the two things which he desired most: a general approval of all his acts in the East, and a distribution of lands to his veterans. Notwithstanding violent opposition, Afranius was elected with Q. Metellus Celer. But, before proposing the laws which concerned him, Pompey, who till then had not entered Rome, demanded a triumph. It was granted him, but for two days only. However, the pageant was not less remarkable for its splendour. It was held on the 29th and 30th of September, 693.

Before him were carried boards on which were inscribed the names of the conquered countries, from Judæa to the Caucasus, and from the shores of the Bosphorus to the banks of the Euphrates; the names of the towns and the number of the vessels taken from the pirates; the names of thirty-nine towns re-peopled; the amount of wealth brought in to the treasury, amounting to 20,000 talents (more than 115 millions of francs [£4,600,000]), without counting his largesses to his soldiers, of whom he who received least had 1,500 drachmas (1,455 francs [£57]).[1029] The public revenues, which before Pompey's time amounted only to fifty millions of drachmas (forty-eight millions and a half of francs [nearly two millions sterling]), reached the amount of eighty-one millions and a half (seventy-nine millions of francs [£3,160,000]). Among the precious objects that were exposed before the eyes of the Romans was the Dactylotheca (or collection of engraved stones) belonging to the King of Pontus;[1030] a chessboard made of only two precious stones, but which, nevertheless, measured four feet in length by three in breadth, ornamented with a moon in gold, weighing thirty pounds; three couches for dinner, of immense value; vases of gold and precious stones numerous enough to load nine sideboards; thirty-three chaplets of pearls; three gold statues, representing Minerva, Mars, and Apollo; a mountain of the same metal, on a square base, decorated with fruits of all kinds, and with figures of stags and lions, the whole encircled by a golden vine, a present from King Aristobulus; a miniature temple dedicated to the Muses, and provided with a clock; a couch of gold, said to have belonged to Darius, son of Hystaspes; murrhine vases;[1031] a statue in silver of Pharnaces, king of Pontus, the conqueror of Sinope, and the contemporary of Philip III. of Macedon;[1032] a silver statue of the last Mithridates, and a colossal bust of him in gold, eight cubits high, together with his throne and sceptre; chariots armed with scythes, and enriched with gilt ornaments;[1033] then, the portrait of Pompey himself, embroidered in pearls. Lastly, trees were now introduced for the first time as rare and precious objects: these were the ebony-tree and the shrub which produces balsam.[1034] Before the chariot of Pompey came the Cretan Lasthenes and Panares, taken from the triumph of Metellus Creticus;[1035] the chiefs of the pirates; the son of Tigranes, king of Armenia, his wife, and his daughter; the widow of the elder Tigranes, called Zosima; Olthaces, chief of the Colchians; Aristobulus, king of the Jews; the sister of Mithridates, with five of his sons; the wives of the chieftains of Scythia; the hostages of the Iberians and Albanians, and those of the princes of Commagene. Pompey was in a chariot, adorned with jewels, and dressed in the costume of Alexander the Great;[1036] and as he had already three times obtained the honours of a triumph for his successes in Africa, Europe, and Asia, a grand trophy was displayed, with this inscription, "Over the whole world!"[1037]

So much splendour flattered the national pride, without disarming the envious. Victories in the East had always been obtained without extraordinary efforts, and therefore people had always depreciated their merit, and Cato went so far as to say that in Asia a general had only women to fight against.[1038] In the Senate, Lucullus, and other influential men of consular rank, threw out the decree that was to ratify all the acts of Pompey; and yet, to refuse to ratify either the treaties concluded with the kings, or the exchange of the provinces, or the amount of tribute imposed upon the vanquished, was as though they questioned all that he had done. But they went still farther.

Towards the month of January, 694, the tribune L. Flavius proposed[1039] to purchase and appropriate to Pompey's veterans, for purposes of colonisation, all the territory that had been declared public domain in the year 521, and since sold; and to divide among the poor citizens the ager publicus of Volaterræ and Arretium, cities of Etruria, which had been confiscated by Sylla, but not yet distributed.[1040] The expense entailed by these measures was to be defrayed by five years' revenue of the conquered provinces.[1041] Cicero, who wished to gratify Pompey, without damaging the interests of those he termed his rich friends,[1042] proposed that the ager publicus should be left intact, but that other lands of equal value should be purchased. Nevertheless, he was in favour of the establishment of colonies, though two years before he had called the attention of his hearers to the danger of such establishments; he was ready to admit that that dangerous populace, those dregs of the city (sentina urbis), must be removed to a distance from Rome, though in former days he had engaged that same populace to remain in Rome, and enjoy their festivals, their games, and their rights of suffrage.[1043] Finally, he proposed to buy private estates, and leave the ager publicus intact; whereas, in his speech against Rullus, he had blamed the establishment of colonies on private estates as a violation of all precedent.[1044] The eloquence of the orator, which had been powerful enough to cause the rejection of the law of Rullus, was unsuccessful in obtaining the adoption of that of Flavius; it was attacked with such violence by the consul Metellus, that the tribune caused him to be put in prison; but this act of severity having met with a general disapproval, Pompey was alarmed at the scandal, and bade Flavius set the consul at liberty, and abandoned the law. Sensitive to so many insults, and seeing his prestige diminish, the conqueror of Mithridates regretted that he had disbanded his army, and determined to make common cause with Clodius, who then enjoyed an extraordinary popularity.[1045]

About the same period, Metellus Nepos, who had returned a second time to Italy with Pompey, was elected prætor, and obtained a law to abolish tolls throughout Italy, the exaction of which had hitherto given rise to loud complaints. This measure, which had probably been suggested by Pompey and Cæsar, met with general approval; yet the Senate made an unsuccessful attempt to have the name of the proposer erased from the law: which shows, as Dio Cassius says, that that assembly accepted nothing from its adversaries, not even an act of kindness.[1046]

Destiny regulates Events.

X. Thus all the forces of society, paralysed by intestine divisions, and powerless for good, appeared to revive only for the purpose of throwing obstacles in its way. Military glory and eloquence, those two instruments of Roman power, inspired only distrust and envy. The triumph of the generals was regarded not so much as a success for the Republic as a source of personal gratification. The gift of eloquence still exercised its ancient empire, so long as the orator remained upon the tribune; but scarcely had he stepped down before the impression he had made was gone; the people remained indifferent to brilliant displays of rhetoric that were employed to encourage selfish passions, and not to defend, as heretofore, the great interests of the fatherland.

It is well worthy of our attention that, when destiny is driving a state of things towards an aim, there is, by a law of fate, a concurrence of all forces in the same direction. Thither tend alike the attacks and the hopes of those who seek change; thither tend the fears and the resistance of those who would put a stop to every movement. After the death of Sylla, Cæsar was the only man who persevered in his endeavours to raise the standard of Marius. Hence nothing more natural than that his acts and speeches should bend in the same direction. But the fact on which we ought to fix our attention is, the spectacle of the partisans of resistance and the system of Sylla, the opponents of all innovation, helping, unconsciously, the progress of the events which smoothed for Cæsar the way to supreme power.

Pompey, the representative of the cause of the Senate, gives the hardest blow to the ancient régime by re-establishing the tribuneship. The popularity which his prodigious successes in the East had won for him, had raised him above all others; by nature, as well as by his antecedents, he leaned to the aristocratic party; the jealousy of the nobles throws him into the popular party and into the arms of Cæsar.

The Senate, on its part, while professing to aim at the preservation of all the old institutions intact, abandons them in the presence of danger; through jealousy of Pompey, it leaves to the tribunes the initiative in all laws of general interest; through fear of Catiline, it lowers the barriers that had been raised between new men and the consulship, and confers that office upon Cicero. In the trial of the accomplices of Catiline, it violates both the forms of justice and the chief safeguard of the liberty of the citizens, the right of appeal to the people. Instead of remembering that the best policy in circumstances of peril is to confer upon men of importance some brilliant mark of acknowledgment for the services they have rendered to the State, either in good or bad fortune; instead of following, after victory, the example given after defeat by the ancient Senate, which thanked Varro because he had not despaired of the Republic, the Senate shows itself ungrateful to Pompey, gives him no credit for his moderation, and, when it can compromise him, and even bind him by the bonds of gratitude, it meets his most legitimate demands with a refusal, a refusal which will teach generals to come, that, when they return to Rome, though they have increased the territory of the Commonwealth, though they have doubled the revenues of the Republic, if they disband their army, the approval of their acts will be disputed, and an attempt made to bargain with their soldiers for the reward due to their glorious labours.

Cicero himself, who is desirous of maintaining the old state of things, undermines it by his language. In his speeches against Verres, he denounces the venality of the Senate, and the extortions of which the provinces complain; in others, he unveils in a most fearful manner the corruption of morals, the traffic in offices, and the dearth of patriotism among the upper classes; in pleading for the Manilian law, he maintains that there is need of a strong power in the hands of one individual to ensure order in Italy and glory abroad; and it is after he has exhausted all the eloquence at his command in pointing out the excess of the evil and the efficacy of the remedy, that he thinks it is possible to stay the stream of public opinion by the chilling counsel of immobility.

Cato declared that he was for no innovations whatever; yet he made them more than ever indispensable by his own opposition. No less than Cicero, he threw the blame on the vices of society; but whilst Cicero wavered often through the natural fickleness of his mind, Cato, with the systematic tenacity of a stoic, remained inflexible in the application of absolute rules. He opposed everything, even schemes of the greatest utility; and, standing in the way of all concession, rendered personal animosities as hard to reconcile as political factions. He had separated Pompey from the Senate by causing all his proposals to be rejected; he had refused him his niece, notwithstanding the advantage for his party of an alliance which would have impeded the designs of Cæsar.[1047] Regardless of the political consequences of a system of extreme rigour, he had caused Metellus to be deposed when he was tribune, and Cæsar when he was prætor; he caused Clodius to be put upon his trial; he impeached his judges, without any foresight of the fatal consequences of an investigation which called in question the honour of an entire order. This immoderate zeal had rendered the knights hostile to the Senate; they became still more so by the opposition offered by Cato to the reduction of the price of the farms of Asia.[1048] And thus Cicero, seeing things in their true light, wrote as follows to Atticus: "With the best intentions in the world, Cato is ruining us: he judges things as if we were living in Plato's Republic, while we are only the dregs of Romulus."[1049]

Nothing, then, arrested the march of events; the party of resistance hurried them forward more rapidly than any other. It was evident that they progressed towards a revolution; and a revolution is like a river, which overflows and inundates. Cæsar aimed at digging a bed for it. Pompey, seated proudly at the helm, thought he could command the waves that were sweeping him along. Cicero, always irresolute, at one moment allowed himself to drift with the stream, at another thought himself able to stem it with a fragile bark. Cato, immovable as a rock, flattered himself that alone he could resist the irresistible stream that was carrying away the old order of Roman society.

# CHAPTER IV
## (693-695)

Cæsar Proprætor in Spain (693).

I. WHILST at Rome ancient reputations were sinking in struggles destitute alike of greatness and patriotism, others, on the contrary, were rising in the camps, through the lustre of military glory. Cæsar, on quitting his prætorship, had gone to Ulterior Spain (Hispania Ulterior), which had been assigned to him by lot. His creditors had vainly attempted to retard his departure: he had had recourse to the credit of Crassus, who had been his security for the sum of 830 talents (nearly five millions of francs [£200,000]). [1050] He had not even waited for the instructions of the Senate,[1051] which, indeed, could not be ready for some time, as that body had deferred all affairs concerning the consular provinces till after the trial of Clodius, which was only terminated in April, 693.[1052] This eagerness to reach his post could not therefore be caused by fear of fresh prosecutions, as has been supposed; but its motive was the desire to carry assistance to the allies, who were imploring the protection of the Romans against the mountaineers of Lusitania. Always devoted without reserve to those whose cause he espoused,[1053] he took with him into Spain his client Masintha, a young African of high birth, whose cause he had recently defended at Rome with extreme zeal, and whom he had concealed in his house after his condemnation,[1054] to save him from the persecutions of Juba, son of Hiempsal, king of Numidia.

It is related that, in crossing the Alps, Cæsar halted at a village, and his officers asked him, jocularly, if he thought that even in that remote place there were solicitations and rivalries for offices. He answered, gravely, "I would rather be first among these savages than second in Rome."[1055] This anecdote, which is more or less authentic, is repeated as a proof of Cæsar's ambition. Who doubts his ambition? The important point to know is whether it were legitimate or not, and if it were to be exercised for the salvation or the ruin of the Roman world. After all, is it not more honourable to admit frankly the feelings which animate us, than to conceal, as Pompey did, the ardour of desire under the mask of disdain?

On his arrival in Spain, he promptly raised ten new cohorts, which, joined to the twenty others already in the country, furnished him with three legions, a force sufficient for the speedy pacification of the province. [1056] Its tranquillity was incessantly disturbed by the depredations of the inhabitants of Mount Herminium,[1057] who ravaged the plain. He required them to establish themselves there, but they refused. Cæsar then began a rough mountain war, and succeeded in reducing them to submission. Terrified by this example, and dreading a similar fate, the neighbouring tribes conveyed their families and their most precious effects across the River Durius (Douro). The Roman general hastened to profit by the opportunity, penetrated into the valley of the Mondego to take possession of the abandoned towns, and went in pursuit of the fugitives. The latter, on the point of being overtaken, turned, and resolved to accept battle, driving their flocks and herds before them, in the hope that, through this stratagem, the Romans would leave their ranks in their eagerness to secure the booty, and so be more easily overcome. But Cæsar was not the man to be caught in this clumsy trap; he left the cattle, went straight at the enemy, and routed them. Whilst occupied in the campaign in the north of Lusitania, he learnt that in his rear the inhabitants of Mount Herminium had revolted again with the design of closing the road by which he had come. He then took another; but they made a further attempt to intercept his passage by occupying the country between the Serra Albardos[1058] and the sea. Defeated, and their retreat cut off, they were forced to fly in the direction of the ocean, and took refuge in an island now called Peniche de Cima, which, being no longer entirely separated from the continent, has become a peninsula. It is situated about twenty-five leagues from Lisbon.[1059] As Cæsar had no ships, he ordered rafts to be constructed, on which some troops crossed. The rest thought that they might venture through some shallows, which, at low tide, formed a ford; but, desperately attacked by the enemy, they were, as they retreated, engulphed by the rising tide. Publius Scævius, their chief, was the only man who escaped, and he, notwithstanding his wounds, succeeded in reaching the mainland by swimming. Subsequently, Cæsar obtained some ships from Cadiz, crossed over to the island with his army, and defeated the barbarians. Thence he sailed in the direction of Brigantium (now La Corogne), the inhabitants of which, terrified at the sight of the vessels, which were strange to them, surrendered voluntarily.[1060] The whole of Lusitania became tributary to Rome.

Cæsar received from his soldiers the title of Imperator. When the news of his successes reached Rome, the Senate decreed in his honour a holiday,[1061] and granted him the right of a triumph on his return. The expedition ended, the conqueror of the Lusitanians took in hand the civil administration, and caused justice and concord to reign in his province. He merited the gratitude of the Spaniards by suppressing the tribute imposed by Metellus Pius during the war against Sertorius.[1062] Above all, he applied himself to putting an end to the differences that arose each day between debtors and creditors, by ordaining that the former should devote, every year, two-thirds of their income to the liquidation of their debts; a measure which, according to Plutarch, brought him great honour.[1063] This measure was, in fact, an act which tended to the preservation of property; it prevented the Roman usurers from taking possession of a debtor's entire capital to reimburse themselves; and we shall see that Cæsar made it of general application when he became dictator.[1064] Finally, having healed their dissensions, he loaded the inhabitants of Cadiz with benefits, and left behind him laws, the happy influence of which was felt for a long period. He abolished among the people of Lusitania their barbarous customs, some of which went as far as the sacrifice of human victims.[1065] It was there that he became intimate with a man of consideration in Cadiz, L. Cornelius Balbus, who became magister fabrorum (chief engineer) during his Gaulish wars, and who was defended by Cicero when his right of Roman citizen was called in question.[1066]

Though he administered his province with the greatest equity, yet, during his campaign, he had amassed a rich booty, which enabled him to reward his soldiers, and to pay considerable sums into the treasury without being accused of peculation or of arbitrary acts. His conduct as prætor of Spain[1067] was praised by all, and among others by Mark Antony, in a speech pronounced after Cæsar's death.

It was not then, as Suetonius pretends, by the begging of subsidies[1068] (for a general hardly begs at the head of an army), nor was it by an abuse of power, that he amassed such enormous riches; he obtained them by contributions of war, by a good administration, and even by the gratitude of those whom he had governed.

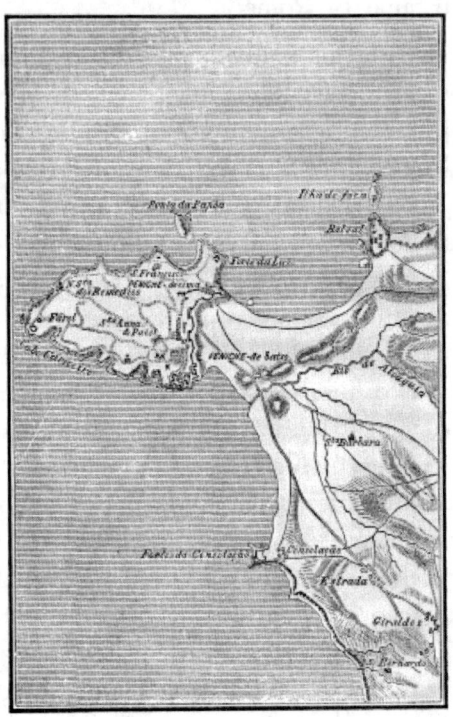

Cæsar demands a Triumph and the Consulship (694).

II. Cæsar returned to Rome towards the month of June[1069] without waiting for the arrival of his successor. This return, which the historians describe as hasty, was by no means so, since his regular authority had expired in the month of January, 694. But he was determined to be present at the approaching meeting of the consular comitia; he presented himself with confidence, and whilst preparing for his triumph, demanded at the same time permission to become a candidate for the consulship. Invested with the title of Imperator, having, by a rapid conquest, extended the limits of the empire to the northern shores of the Ocean, he might justly aspire to this double distinction; but it was granted with difficulty. To obtain a triumph, it was necessary to remain without the walls of Rome, to retain the lictors and continue the military uniform, and to wait till the Senate should fix the date of entry. To solicit for the consulship, it was necessary, on the contrary, to be present in Rome, clad in a white robe,[1070] the costume of those who were candidates for public offices, and to reside there several days previous to the election. The Senate had not always considered these two demands incompatible:[1071] it would perhaps even have granted this indulgence to Cæsar, had not Cato, by speaking till the end of the day, rendered all deliberation impossible.[1072] He had not, however, been so severe in 684; but it was because, on that occasion, Pompey was triumphing in reality over Sertorius, that foe to the aristocracy, though officially it was only talked of as a victory over the Spaniards.[1073] Constrained to choose between an idle pageant and real power, Cæsar did not hesitate.

The ground had been well prepared for his election. His popularity had been steadily on the increase; and the Senate, too much elated by its successes, had estranged those who possessed the greatest influence. Pompey, discontented at the uniform refusals with which his just demands had been met, knew well also that the recent law, declaring enemies of the State those who bribed the electors, was a direct attack against himself, since he had openly paid for the election of the consul Afranius; but, always infatuated with his own personal attractions, he consoled himself for his checks by strutting about in his gaudy embroidered robe.[1074] Crassus, who had long remained faithful to the aristocratic party, had become its enemy, on account of the ill-disguised jealousy of the nobles towards him, and their intrigues to implicate him with Cæsar in the conspiracy of Catiline. However, though he held in his hands the strings of many an intrigue, he was fearful of compromising himself, and shrank from declaring in public against any man in credit.[1075] Lucullus, weary of warfare and of intestine struggles, was withdrawing from politics in order to enjoy his vast wealth in tranquillity. Catulus was dead, and the majority of the nobles were ready to follow the impulse given them by certain enthusiastic senators who, caring little about public affairs, thought themselves the happiest of men if they had in their fishponds carp sufficiently tamed to come and eat out of their hands.[1076] Cicero felt his own solitary position. The nobles, whose angry feelings he had served, now that the peril was over, regarded him as no better than an upstart. Therefore he prudently changed his principles; he, the exterminator of conspirators, had become the defender of P. Sylla, one of Catiline's accomplices, and procured his acquittal in the teeth of the evidence;[1077] he, the energetic opponent of all partitions of land, had spoken in favour of the agrarian law of Flavius. He wrote to Atticus, "I have seen that those men whose happiness belongs to the passing hour, those illustrious lovers of fishponds, are no longer able to conceal their jealousy of me; so I have sought more solid support."[1078]

In a word, he had made overtures to Pompey, though in secret he admitted that he possessed neither greatness of mind nor nobleness of heart. "He only knows how to curry favour and flatter the people," he said; "and here am I bound to him on such terms that our interest, as individuals, is served thereby; and, as statesmen, we can both act with greater firmness.

The ill-will of our ardent and unprincipled youth had been excited against me. I have been so successful in bringing it round by my address, that at present it cares for no one but me. Finally, I am careful to wound no man's feelings, and that without servileness or popularity-hunting. My entire conduct is so well planned, that, as a public man, I yield in nothing; and as a private individual, who knows the weakness of honest men, the injustice of the envious, and the hatred of the wicked, I take my precautions, and act with prudence."[1079]

Cicero deceived himself with regard to the causes of his change of party, and did not acknowledge to himself the reasons that constrained him to look out for powerful patrons. Like all men destitute of force of character, instead of openly confessing the motives of his conduct, he justified himself to his friends by pretending that, so far from having altered his own opinions, it was he who was converting Pompey, and would soon make the same experiment upon Cæsar. "You rally me pleasantly," he wrote to Atticus, "on the subject of my intimacy with Pompey; but do not fancy that I have contracted it out of regard for my personal safety. It is all the effect of circumstances. When there was the slightest disagreement between us, there was trouble in the State. I have laid my plans and made my conditions, so that, without laying aside my own principles, which are good, I have led him to better sentiments. He is somewhat cured of his madness for popularity.... If I am equally successful with Cæsar, whose ship is now sailing under full canvas, shall I have done great harm to the State?"[1080] Cicero, like all men whose strength lies in eloquence, felt that he could play no important part, or even secure his own personal safety, unless he allied himself with men of the sword.

Whilst at Rome the masters of the world were wasting their time in mean quarrels, alarming news came suddenly to create a diversion in political intrigue. Information was brought that the Gaulish allies on the banks of the Saône had been defeated by the Germans, that the Helvetii were in arms, and making raids beyond the frontiers. The terror was universal. Fears were entertained of a fresh invasion of the Cimbri and Teutones; and, as always happened on such occasions, a general levy, without exception, was ordered. [1081] The consuls of the previous year drew lots for their provinces, and it was decided to dispatch commissioners to come to an understanding with the Gaulish tribes, with a view to resist foreign invasions. The names of Pompey and Cicero were at once pronounced; but the Senate, influenced by different motives, declared that their presence was too necessary in Rome to allow them to be sent away. They were unwilling to give the former an opportunity of again distinguishing himself, or to deprive themselves of the concurrence of the latter.

Alliance of Cæsar, Pompey, and Crassus.

III. News of a more re-assuring character having been received from Gaul, the fear of war ceased for a time, and things had returned to their customary course when Cæsar came home from Spain. In the midst of conflicting opinions and interests, the presence of a man of steady purpose and deeply-rooted convictions, and illustrious through recent victories, was, without any doubt, an event. He did not require long to form his estimate of the situation; and, as he could not as yet unite the masses by the realisation of a grand idea, he thought to unite the chiefs by a common interest.

All his endeavours from that time were devoted to making Pompey, Crassus, and Cicero share his ideas. The first had been rather ill disposed towards him. On his return from his campaign against Mithridates, Pompey had called Cæsar his Egistheus,[1082] in allusion to the intrigue which he had had with his wife Mutia, whilst he, like Agamemnon, was making war in Asia. Resentment, on this account, usually slight enough among the Romans, soon disappeared before the exigencies of political life. As for Crassus, who had long been separated from Pompey by a jealous feeling of rivalry, it needed all Cæsar's tact, and all the seduction of his manners, to induce him to become reconciled with his rival. But, to bring them both to follow the same line of conduct, it was necessary, over and above this, to tempt them with such powerful motives as would ensure conviction. The historians, in general, have given no other reason to account for the agreement of these three men than personal interest. Doubtless, Pompey and Crassus were not insensible to a combination that favoured their love of power and wealth; but we ought to lend Cæsar a more elevated motive, and suppose him inspired by a genuine patriotism.

The condition of the Republic must have appeared thus to his comprehensive grasp of thought:—The Roman dominion, stretched, like some vast figure, across the world, clasps it in her sinewy arms; and whilst her limbs are full of life and strength, the heart is wasting by decay. Unless some heroic remedy be applied, the contagion will soon spread from the centre to the extremities, and the mission of Rome will remain unfinished!— Compare with the present the prosperous days of the Republic. Recollect the time when envoys from foreign nations, doing homage to the policy of the Senate, declared openly that they preferred the protecting sovereignty of Rome to independence itself. Since that period, what a change has taken place! All nations execrate the power of Rome, and yet that power preserves them from still greater evils. Cicero is right, "Let Asia think well of it: there is not one of the woes that are bred of war and civil strife, that she would not experience did she cease to live under our laws."[1083] And this advice may be applied to all the countries whither the legions have penetrated. If, then, fate has willed that the nations are to be subject to the sway of a single people, it is the duty of that people, as charged with the execution of the eternal decrees, to be, towards the vanquished, as just and equitable as the Divinity, since he is as inexorable as destiny. How are we to fix a limit to the arbitrary conduct of proconsuls and proprætors, which all the laws promulgated for so many years have been powerless to check? How put a stop to the exactions committed at all points of the empire, if a firmer and stronger direction do not emanate from the central power?—The Republic pursues an irregular system of encroachment, which will exhaust its resources; it is impossible for her to fight against all nations at once, and at the same time to maintain her allies in their allegiance, if, by unjust treatment, they are driven to revolt. The enemies of the Republic must be diminished in number by restoring their freedom to the cities which are worthy of it,[1084] and acknowledging as friends of the Roman people those nations with whom there is a chance of living in peace.[1085] Our most dangerous enemies are the Gauls, and it is against this turbulent and warlike nation that all the strength of the State ought to be directed.—In Italy, and under this name Cisalpine Gaul must be included, how many citizens are deprived of political rights! At Rome, how many of the proletaries are living on the charity either of the rich or of the State! Why should we not extend the Roman commune as far as the Alps, and why not augment the race of labourers and soldiers by making them landowners? The Roman people must be raised in its own eyes, and the Republic in the eyes of the world!—Absolute liberty of speech and of vote was a great benefit, when, modified by morality, and restrained by a powerful aristocracy, it gave scope to individual faculties without damaging the general well-being; but, ever since the morality of ancient days disappeared with the aristocracy, we have seen the laws become weapons of war for the use of parties, the elections a traffic, the forum a battle-field; while liberty is nothing more than a never-ending cause of weakness and decay.—Our institutions cause such uncertainty in our councils, and such independence in our offices of State, that we search in vain for that spirit of order and control which are indispensable elements in the maintenance of so vast an empire. Without overthrowing institutions which have given five centuries of glory to the Republic, it is possible, by a close union of the most worthy citizens, to establish in the State a moral authority, which governs the passions, tempers the laws, gives a greater stability to power, directs the elections, maintains the representatives of the Roman people in their duty, and frees us from the two most serious dangers of the present: the selfishness of the nobles and the turbulence of the mob. This is what they may realise by their union; their disunion, on the contrary, will only encourage the fatal conduct of these men who are endangering the future equally, some by their opposition, the others by their headlong violence.

These considerations must have been easily understood by Pompey and Crassus, who had themselves been actors in such great events, witnesses of so much blood shed in civil wars, of so many noble ideas, triumphing at one moment and overthrown the next. They accepted Cæsar's proposal, and thus was concluded an alliance which is wrongly termed the First Triumvirate.[1086] As for Cicero, Cæsar tried to persuade him to join the compact which had just been formed, but he refused to become one of what he termed a party of friends.[1087] Always uncertain in his conduct, always divided between his admiration for those who held the sovereign power, and his engagements with the oligarchy, and uneasy for the future which his foresight could not penetrate, he set his mind to work to prevent the success of every measure which he approved as soon as it had succeeded. The alliance which these three persons ratified by their oaths,[1088] remained long a secret; and it was only during Cæsar's consulship that it became matter of public notoriety from the unanimity they displayed in all their political resolutions. Cæsar, then, set energetically to work to unite in his own favour every chance that could render his election certain.

Cæsar's Election.

IV. Among the candidates was L. Lucceius. Cæsar was desirous of attaching to his cause this person, who was distinguished alike by his writings and his character,[1089] and who, possessed of vast wealth, had promised to make abundant use of it for their common profit, in order to command the majority of votes in the centuries. "The aristocratic faction," says Suetonius, "on learning this arrangement, was seized with fear. They thought that there was nothing which Cæsar would not attempt in the exercise of the sovereign magistracy, if he had a colleague who agreed with him, and who would support all his designs."[1090] The nobles, unable to eject him, resolved to give him Bibulus for a colleague, who had already been his colleague in the edileship and the prætorship, and had constantly shown himself his opponent. They all made a pecuniary contribution to influence the elections; Bibulus spent large sums,[1091] and the incorruptible Cato himself, who had solemnly sworn to impeach any one who should be guilty of bribery, contributed his quota, owning that for the interest of the State his principles must for once yield.[1092] Neither was Cicero more inflexible: some time before, he expressed to Atticus the necessity of purchasing the concurrence of the equestrian order.[1093] We can see how even the most honourable were swept along, by the force of events, in the current of a corrupt society.

By the force of public opinion, and by the support of the two men of greatest influence, Cæsar was elected consul unanimously, and conducted, according to custom, from the Campus Martius to his own house by an enthusiastic crowd of his fellow-citizens, and a vast number of senators. [1094]

If the party opposed to Cæsar had been unable to stand in the way of his becoming consul, it did not despair of preventing his playing the important part he had a right to expect as proconsul. To effect this, the Senate determined to evade the law of Caius Gracchus, which, to prevent the assignment of provinces from personal considerations, provided that it should take place before the comitia were held. The assembly, therefore, departing from the rule, assigned to Cæsar and his colleague, by an act of flagrant ill-will, the supervision of the public roads and forests; an office somewhat similar, it is true, to that of governor of a province.[1095] This humiliating appointment, proof as it was of a persevering hostility, wounded him deeply; but the duties of his new office imposed silence upon his resentments. Cæsar the consul would forget the wrongs done to Cæsar the man, and generously attempt a policy of conciliation.

# CHAPTER V
## CONSULSHIP OF CÆSAR AND BIBULUS (695)

Attempts at Conciliation.

I. CÆSAR has arrived at the first magistracy of the Republic. Consul with Bibulus at the age of forty-one, he has not yet acquired the just celebrity of Pompey, nor does he enjoy the treasures of Crassus, and yet his influence is perhaps greater than that of those two personages. Political influence, indeed, does not depend solely on military successes or on the possession of immense riches; it is acquired especially by a conduct always in accord with fixed convictions. Cæsar alone represents a principle. From the age of eighteen, he has faced the anger of Sylla and the hostility of the aristocracy, in order to plead unceasingly the grievances of the oppressed and the rights of the provinces.

So long as he is not in power, being exempt from responsibility, he walks invariably in the way he has traced, listens to no compromise, pursues unsparingly the adherents of the opposite party, and maintains his opinions energetically, at the risk of wounding his adversaries; but, once consul, he lays aside all resentment, and makes a loyal appeal to all who will rally round him; he declares to the Senate that he will not act without its concurrence, that he will propose nothing contrary to its prerogatives. [1096] He offers his colleague Bibulus a generous reconciliation, conjuring him, in the presence of the senators, to put a term to differences of opinion, the effects of which, already so much to be regretted during their common edileship and prætorship, would become fatal in their new position.[1097] He makes advances to Cicero, and, after sending Cornelius Balbus to him in his villa of Antium to assure him that he is ready to follow his counsels and those of Pompey, offers to take him as an associate in his labours.[1098]

Cæsar must have believed that these offers of co-operation would be embraced. In face of the perils of a society deeply agitated, he supposed that others had the same sentiments which animated himself. Love of the public good, and the consciousness of having entirely devoted himself to it, gave him that confidence without reserve in the patriotism of others which admits neither mean rivalries nor the calculations of selfishness: he was deceived. The Senate showed nothing but prejudices, Bibulus, but rancours, Cicero, but a false pride.

It was essential for Cæsar to unite Pompey, who was wanting in firmness of character, more closely with his destinies; he gave him in marriage his daughter Julia, a young woman of twenty-three years of age, richly endowed with graces and intelligence, who had already been affianced to Servilius Cæpio. To compensate the latter, Pompey promised him his own daughter, though she also was engaged to another, to Faustus, the son of Sylla. Soon afterwards Cæsar espoused Calpurnia, the daughter of Lucius Piso.[1099] Cato protested energetically against these marriages, which he qualified as disgraceful traffics with the common weal.[1100] The nobles, and especially the two Curios, made themselves the echoes of this reprobation. Their party, nevertheless, did not neglect to strengthen themselves by such alliances. Doubtless, when Cato gave his daughter to Bibulus, it was for a political motive; and when he ceded his own wife to Hortensius,[1101] although the mother of three children, to take her back again when enriched by the death of her last husband, there was also an interest hardly honourable, which Cæsar subsequently unveiled in a book entitled Anti-Cato.[1102]

The first care of the new consul was to establish the practice of publishing daily the acts of the Senate and those of the people, in order that public opinion might bear with all its weight upon the resolutions of the conscript fathers, whose deliberations had previously been often secret.[1103] The initiative taken by Cæsar from the commencement of his consulship, in questioning the senators on the projects of laws, is an evidence that he had the fasces before Bibulus. We know, in fact, that the consuls enjoyed this honour alternately for a month, and it was in the period when they were invested with the signs distinctive of power that they were permitted to ask the advice of the senators.[1104]

Agrarian Laws.

II. He proposed next, in the month of January, an agrarian law founded upon wise principles, and which respected all legitimate rights. The following were its principal provisions:—

Partition of all the free part of the ager publicus, except that of Campania and that of Volaterræ; the first excepted originally on account of its great fertility,[1105] and the second guaranteed to all those who had got it into their possession.[1106]—In case of insufficiency of territory, new acquisitions, by means either of money coming from Pompey's conquests, or from the overplus of the public revenues.—Prohibition of all appropriation by force.—The nomination of twenty commissioners to preside at the distribution of the lands, with exclusion of the author of the proposal.— Estimate of private lands for sale, made according to the declaration at the last census, and not according to the valuation of the commissioners.— Obligation upon each senator to swear obedience to the law, and to engage never to propose anything contrary to it.

It was, as may be seen, the project of Rullus, relieved from the inconveniences pointed out with so much eloquence by Cicero. In fact, instead of ten commissioners, Cæsar proposed twenty, in order to distribute among a greater number a power of which men feared the abuse. He himself, to avoid all suspicion of personal interest, excluded himself from the possibility of forming part of it. The commissioners were not, as in the law of Rullus, authorised to act according to their will, and tax the properties arbitrarily. Acquired rights were respected; those territories only were distributed of which the State had still the full disposal. The sums arising from Pompey's conquests were to be employed in favour of the old soldiers; and Cæsar said himself that it was just to give the profit of that money to those who had gained it at the peril of their lives.[1107] As to the obligation of the oath imposed upon the senators, it was not an innovation, but an established custom. In the present case, the law having been voted before the elections, all the candidates, and especially the tribunes of the following year, had to take the engagement to observe it.[1108]

"Nobody," says Dio Cassius,[1109] "had reason for complaint on this subject. The population of Rome, the excessive increase of which had been the principal aliment of seditions, was called to labour and a country life; the greater part of the countries of Italy, which had lost their inhabitants, were re-peopled. This law insured means of existence not only to those who had supported the fatigues of the war, but also to all the other citizens, without causing expenditure to the State or loss to the nobles; on the contrary, it gave to several honours and power."

Thus, while some historians accuse Cæsar of seeking in the populace of Rome the point of support for his ambitious designs, he, on the contrary, obtains a measure, the effect of which is to transport the turbulent part of the inhabitants of the capital into the country.

Cæsar, then, read his project to the Senate; after which, calling the senators by their names, one after the other, he asked the opinion of each, declaring his readiness to modify the law, or withdraw it altogether, if it were not agreeable to them. But, according to Dio Cassius, "It was unassailable, and, if any disapproved of it, none dared to oppose it; what afflicted its opponents most was, that it was drawn up in such a manner as to leave no room for a complaint."[1110] So the opposition was limited to adjourning from time to time, under frivolous pretexts. Cato, without making a direct opposition, alleged the necessity of changing nothing in the constitution of the Republic, and declared himself the adversary of all kind of innovation; but, when the moment came for voting, he had recourse again to his old tactics, and rendered all deliberation impossible by speaking the entire day, by which he had already succeeded in depriving Cæsar of the triumph. [1111] The latter lost patience, and sent the obstinate orator to prison; Cato was followed by a great number of senators, and M. Petreius, one of them, replied to the consul, who reproached him for withdrawing before the meeting was closed: "I would rather be in prison with Cato than here with thee." Regretting, however, this first movement of anger, and struck by the attitude of the assembly, Cæsar immediately restored Cato to liberty; then he dismissed the Senate, addressing them in the following words: "I had made you supreme judges and arbiters of this law, in order that, if any one of its provisions displeased you, it should not be referred to the people; but, since you have refused the previous deliberation, the people alone shall decide it."

His attempt at conciliation having failed with the Senate, he renewed it towards his colleague, and, in the assembly of the tribes, adjured Bibulus to support his proposal. On their side, the people joined their entreaties with those of Cæsar; but Bibulus, inflexible, merely said: "You will not prevail with me, though you were all of one voice; and, as long as I shall be consul, I will suffer no innovation."[1112]

Then Cæsar, judging other influences necessary, appealed to Pompey and Crassus. Pompey seized happily this opportunity for speaking to the people: he said that he not only approved the agrarian law, but that the senators themselves had formerly admitted the principle, in decreeing, on his return from Spain, a distribution of lands to his soldiers and to those of Metellus; if this measure had been deferred, it was on account of the penury of the treasury, which, thanks to him, had now ceased. Then, replying to Cæsar, who asked him if he would support the law in case it were opposed by violence, "If any one dared to draw his sword," he cried, "I would take even my buckler;" meaning by that, that he would come into the public place armed as for the combat. This bold declaration of Pompey, supported by Crassus and Cæpio,[1113] silenced all opposition except that of Bibulus, who, with three tribunes his partisans, called an assembly of the Senate in his own house, where it was resolved that at all risk the law should be openly rejected.[1114]

The day of meeting of the comitia having been fixed, the populace occupied the Forum during the night. Bibulus hurried with his friends to the temple of Castor, where his colleague was addressing the multitude; he tried in vain to obtain a hearing, was thrown down from the top of the steps, and obliged to fly, after seeing his fasces broken to pieces and two tribunes wounded. Cato, in his turn, tried to mount the rostra; expelled by force, he returned, but, instead of treating of the question, seeing that nobody listened to him, he attacked Cæsar with bitterness, until he was dragged a second time from the tribune. Calm being restored, the law was adopted. Next day Bibulus tried to propose to the Senate its abrogation; but nobody supported him, such was the effect of this burst of popular enthusiasm;[1115] from this moment he took the part of shutting himself up at home during the residue of Cæsar's consulship. When the latter presented a new law on the days of the comitia, he contented himself with protesting, and with sending by his lictors to say that he was observing the sky, and that consequently all deliberation was illegal.[1116] This was to proclaim loudly the political aim of this formality.

Cæsar was far from yielding to this religious scruple, which, indeed, had lost its authority. At this very time Lucullus wrote a bold poem against the popular credulity, and for some time the observation of the auspices had been regarded as a puerile superstition; two centuries and a half before, a great captain had given a remarkable proof of this. Hannibal, then a refugee at the court of King Prusias, engaged the latter to accept his plans of campaign against the Romans; the king refused, because the auspices had not been favourable. "What!" cried Hannibal, "have you more confidence in a miserable calf's liver than in the experience of an old general like me?"[1117]

Be this as it may, the obligation not to hold the comitia while the magistrate was observing the sky was a law; and to excuse himself for not having observed it, as well as to prevent his acts from being declared null, Cæsar, before quitting his office, brought the question before the Senate, and thus obtained a legal ratification of his conduct.

The law being adopted by the people, each senator was called to take his oath to observe it. Several members, and, among others, Q. Metellus Celer, M. Cato, and M. Favonius,[1118] had declared that they would never submit to it; but when the day of taking the oath arrived, their protests vanished before the fear of the punishment decreed against those who abstained, and, except Laterensis, everybody, even Cato, took the oath.[1119]

Irritated at the obstacles which he had encountered, and sure of the approval of the people, Cæsar included, by a new law, in the distribution of the public domain, the lands of Campania and of Stella, omitted before out of deference to the Senate.[1120]

In carrying the law into effect, Pompey's veterans received lands at Casilinum, in Campania;[1121] at Minturnæ, Lanuvium, Volturnum, and Aufidena, in Samnium; and at Bovianum; Clibæ, and Veii, in Etruria;[1122]

twenty thousand fathers of families having more than three children were established in Campania, so that about a hundred thousand persons became husbandmen, and re-peopled with free men a great portion of the territory, while Rome was relieved from a populace which was inconvenient and debased. Capua became a Roman colony, which was a restoration of the democratic work of Marius, destroyed by Sylla.[1123] It appears that the ager of Leontinum, in Sicily, was also comprised in the agrarian law.[1124] The nomination of the twenty commissioners, chosen among the most commendable of the consulars, was next proceeded with.[1125] Of the number were C. Cosconius and Atius Balbus, the husband of Cæsar's sister. Clodius could not obtain admission among them,[1126] and Cicero, after the death of Cosconius, refused to take his place.[1127] The latter, in his letters to Atticus, blames especially the distribution of the territory of Capua, as depriving the Republic of an important revenue; and inquires what will remain to the State, unless it be the twentieth on the enfranchisement of slaves, since the rights of toll had already been abandoned through the whole of Italy; but it was objected with reason that, on the other hand, the State was relieved from the enormous charges imposed by the necessity of distributing wheat to all the poor of Rome.

Nevertheless, the allotment of the ager Campanus and of the ager of Stella met with many delays; it was not yet terminated in 703, since at that epoch Pompey was advised to hasten the distribution of the last-mentioned lands, in order that Cæsar, on his return from Gaul, might not have the merit of it.[1128]

Cæsar's various Laws.

III. We have seen how, in previous years, Cato was instrumental in refusing the request of those who farmed the taxes of Asia to have the terms of their leases lowered. By this rigorous measure, the Senate had estranged from itself the equestrian order, whose complaints had been far from unreasonable. In fact, the price paid for the farming of the revenues of Asia had been heavy during the war against Mithridates, as may be learnt from the speech of Cicero against the Manilian Law; and the remission of a portion of the money due to the State was a measure not without some show of justice to excuse it. Cæsar, when he became consul, influenced by a sense of justice no less than by policy, lost no time in proposing a law to remit to the farmers of the revenue one-third of the sums for which they were responsible.[1129] He first addressed himself to the Senate; but that body having refused to deliberate on the question, he found himself compelled to submit it to the people,[1130] who adopted his opinion. This liberality, so far beyond what they had hoped for, filled the farmers of the revenue with joy, and rendered them devoted to the man who showed himself so generous: he advised them, however, publicly, to be more careful in future, and not overbid in an inconsiderate manner at the time of the sale of the taxes.[1131]

The agrarian law, and the law concerning the rents, having satisfied the interests of the proletaries, the veterans, and the knights, it became important to settle the just demands of Pompey. Therefore Cæsar obtained from the people their approbation of all the acts of the conqueror of Mithridates. [1132] Lucullus had been till then one of the most earnest adversaries of this measure. He could not forget the glory of which Pompey had frustrated him; but his dread of a prosecution for peculation was so great, that he fell at Cæsar's feet, and forswore all opposition.[1133]

The activity of the consul did not confine itself to internal reforms; it extended to questions which were raised abroad. The condition of Egypt was precarious: King Ptolemy Auletes, natural son of Ptolemy Lathyrus, was afraid lest, in virtue of a forged will of Ptolemy Alexander, or Alexas, to whose fall he had contributed, his kingdom might be incorporated with the Roman Empire.[1134] Auletes, perceiving his authority shaken in Alexandria, had sought the support of Pompey during the war in Judæa, and had sent him presents, and a large sum of money, to engage him to maintain his cause before the Senate.[1135] Pompey had offered himself as his advocate; and Cæsar, whether from policy, or from a wish to please his son-in-law, caused Ptolemy Auletes to be declared a friend and ally of Rome. [1136] At his demand, the same favour was granted to Ariovistus, king of the Germans, who, after having made war upon the Ædui, had withdrawn from their country at the invitation of the Senate, and had expressed a desire to become an ally of Rome. It was entirely the interest of the Republic to conciliate the Germans, and send them to the other bank of the Rhine, whatever might be the views of the consul regarding his future command in Gaul.[1137] Next, he conferred some privileges on certain municipia and satisfied many ambitions; "for," says Suetonius, "he granted everything that was asked of him: no man dared oppose him, and, if any one attempted, he knew how to intimidate him."[1138]

Among the cares of the consul was the nomination of tribunes devoted to him, since it was they generally who proposed the laws for the people to ratify.

Clodius, on account of his popularity, was one of the candidates who could be most useful to him; but his rank of patrician obliged him to pass by adoption into a plebeian family before he could be elected, and that he could only do in virtue of a law. Cæsar hesitated in bringing it forward; for if, on the one hand, he sought to conciliate Clodius himself, on the other, he knew his designs of vengeance against Cicero, and was unwilling to put into his hands an authority which he might abuse. But when, towards the month of March, at the trial of C. Antonius, charged with disgraceful conduct in Macedonia, Cicero, in defending his former colleague, indulged in a violent attack upon those in power, on that same day Clodius was received into the ranks of the plebeians,[1139] and soon afterwards became, together with Vatinius, tribune-elect.[1140] There was a third tribune, whose name is unknown, but who was equally won over to the interests of the consul.[1141]

Thus Cæsar, as even Cicero admits, was alone more powerful already than the Republic.[1142] Of some he was the hope; of others, the terror; of all, master irrevocably. The inactivity of Bibulus had only served to increase his power.[1143] Thus it was said in Rome, as a jest, that men knew of no other consulship than that of Julius and Caius Cæsar, making two persons out of a single name; and the following verses were handed about:—

"Non Bibulo quidquam nuper sed Cæsare factum est:
Nam Bibulo fieri consule nil memini."[1144]

And as popular favour, when it declares itself in favour of a man in a conspicuous position, sees something marvellous in everything that concerns his person, the populace drew a favourable augury from the existence of an extraordinary horse born in his stables. Its hoofs were forked, and shaped like fingers. Cæsar was the only man who could tame this strange animal, the docility of which, it was said, foreboded to him the empire of the world.[1145]

During his first consulship, Cæsar caused a number of laws to be passed, the greater part of which have not descended to us. Some valuable fragments, however, of the most important ones have been preserved, and among others, the modifications in the sacerdotal privileges. The tribune Labienus, as we have seen, in order to secure Cæsar's election to the office of pontiff, had granted the right of election to seventeen tribes selected by lot. Although this law seemed to authorise absentees to become candidates for the priesthood, the people and the priests disputed the right of those who did not solicit the dignity in person. Endless quarrels and disturbances were the result. To put an end to these, Cæsar, while confirming the law of Labienus, announced that not only those candidates who appeared in person, but those at a distance also, who had any title whatever to that honour, might offer themselves as candidates.[1146]

He turned his attention next to the provinces, whose condition had always excited his sympathy. The law intended to reform the vices of the administration (De provinciis ordinandis) is of uncertain date; it bears the same title as that of Sylla, and resembles it considerably. Its provisions guaranteed the inhabitants against the violence, the arbitrary conduct, and the corruption of the proconsuls and propraetors, and fixed the allotments to which these were entitled.[1147]

It released the free states, liberæ civitates, from dependence upon governors, and authorised them to govern themselves by their own laws and their own magistrates.[1148] Cicero himself considered this measure as the guarantee of the liberty of the provinces;[1149] for, in his speech against Piso, he reproaches him with having violated it by including free nations in his government of Macedonia.[1150] Lastly, a separate proviso regulated the responsibility and expenses of the administration, by requiring that on going out of office the governors should deliver, at the end of thirty days, an account explaining their administration and their expenses, of which three copies were to be deposited, one in the treasury (ærarium) at Rome, and the others in the two principal towns of the province.[1151] The propraetors were to remain one year, and the proconsuls two, at the head of their governments.[1152]

The generals were in the habit of burdening the people they governed with exorbitant exactions. They extorted from them crowns of gold (aurum coronarium), of considerable value, under pretence of the triumph, and obliged the countries through which they passed to bear the expenses of themselves and their attendants. Cæsar remedied these abuses, by forbidding the proconsuls to demand the crown before the triumph had been decreed,[1153] and by subjecting to the most rigorous restrictions the contributions in kind which were to be furnished.[1154] We may judge how necessary these regulations were from the fact that Cicero, whose government was justly considered an honest one, admits that he drew large sums from his province of Cilicia eight years after the passing of the law Julia.[1155]

The same law forbad all governors to leave their provinces, or to send their troops out of them to interfere in the affairs of any neighbouring State, without permission of the Senate and the people,[1156] or to extort any money from the inhabitants of the provinces.[1157]

The law by similar provisions diminished the abuse of free legations (legationes liberæ). This was the name given to the missions of senators, who, travelling into the provinces on their own affairs, obtained by an abuse the title of envoy of the Roman people, to which they had no right, in order to be defrayed the expenses and costs of travelling. These missions, which were for an indefinite time, were the subject of incessant[1158] complaints. Cicero had limited them to a year: Cæsar prescribed a still narrower limit, but its exact length is unknown.[1159]

As a supplement to the preceding measures he brought in a law (De pecuniis repetundis), the provisions of which have often been confounded with those of the law De provinciis ordinandis. Cicero boasts of its perfection[1160] and justice. It contained a great number of sections. In a letter from Cœlius to Cicero, the 101st chapter of the law is referred to. Its object was to meet all cases of peculation, out of Italy as well as in Rome. Persons who had been wronged could demand restitution before a legal tribunal of the sums unjustly collected.[1161] Though the principal provisions of it were borrowed from the law of Sylla on the same subject, the penalty was more severe and the proceedings more expeditious. For instance, as the rich contrived, by going into voluntary exile before the verdict, to elude the punishment, it was provided that in that case their goods should be confiscated, in part or wholly, according to the nature of the crime.[1162] If the fortune of the defendant was not sufficient for the repayment of the money claimed, all those who had profited by the embezzlement were sought out and jointly condemned.[1163] Finally, corruption was attacked in all its forms,[1164] and the law went so far as to watch over the honesty of business transactions. One article deserves special remark, that which forbad a public work to be accepted as completed if it were not absolutely finished. Cæsar had doubtless in mind the process which he had unsuccessfully instituted against Catulus for his failure to complete the temple of Jupiter Capitolinus.

We may for the most part consider as Cæsar's laws those which were passed at his instigation, whether by the tribune P. Vatinius, or the prætor Q. Fufius Calenus.[1165]

One of the laws of the former authorised the accuser in a suit, as well as the accused, to challenge for once all the judges: down to this time they had only been permitted to challenge a certain number.[1166] Its object was to give to all the same guarantee which Sylla had reserved exclusively to the senators, since for the knights and plebeians he limited the challenge to three. [1167] Vatinius had also conferred on five thousand colonists, established at Como (Novum Comum), the rights of a Roman city. This measure[1168] flattered the pride of Pompey, whose father, Pompeius Strabo, had rebuilt the town of Comum; and it offered to other colonists the hope of obtaining the qualification of Roman citizens, which Cæsar subsequently granted to them.[1169]

Another devoted partisan of the consul, the prætor Q. Fufius Calenus,[1170] proposed a law which in judicial deliberations laid the responsibility upon each of the three orders of which the tribunal was composed: the senators, the knights, and the tribunes of the treasury. Instead of pronouncing a collective judgment, they were called upon to express their opinion separately. Dio Cassius explains the law in these terms: "Seeing that in a process all the votes were mixed together, and that each order took to itself the credit of the good decisions, and threw the bad ones to the account of the others, Calenus had a law made that the different orders should vote independently, in order to know thus, not the opinion of individuals, since the vote was secret, but that of each order."[1171]

All the laws of Cæsar were styled "Julian laws;" they received the sanction of the Senate, and were adopted without opposition,[1172] and even Cato himself did not oppose them; but when he became prætor, and found himself obliged to put them into execution, he was little-minded enough to object to call them by their name.[1173]

We may be convinced by the above facts, that, during his first consulship, Cæsar was animated by a single motive, the public interest. His ruling thought was to remedy the evils which afflicted the country. His acts, which several historians have impeached as subversive and inspired by boundless ambition, we find, on an attentive examination, to be the result of a wise policy, and the carrying out of a well-known plan, proclaimed formerly by the Gracchi, and recently by Pompey himself. Like the Gracchi, Cæsar desired a distribution of the public domain, the reform of justice, the relief of the provinces, and the extension of the rights of city; like them, he had protected the knightly order, so that he might oppose it to the formidable resistance of the Senate; but he, more fortunate, accomplished that which the Gracchi had been unable to realise. Plutarch, in the life of Crassus,[1174] pronounces a eulogium on the wisdom of his government, although an intemperate judgment had led that writer, elsewhere, to compare his conduct to that of a factious tribune.[1175]

Following the taste of the age, and especially as a means of popularity, Cæsar gave splendid games, shows, and gladiatorial combats, borrowing from Pompey and Atticus considerable sums to meet his love of display, his profusion, and his largesses.[1176] Suetonius, ever ready to record, without distinction, the reports, true and false, current at the time, relates that Cæsar had taken from the treasury three thousand pounds of gold, for which he substituted gilt metal; but his high character is sufficient to refute this calumny. Cicero, who had not, at this time, any reason to spare him, makes no mention of it in his letters, where his ill-humour displays itself, nor in his speech against Vatinius, one of Cæsar's devoted friends. On the other hand, Pliny[1177] mentions a similar fact which happened during Pompey's consulate.

Cæsar receives the Government of the Gauls.

IV. Cæsar did not confine his ambition to discharging the functions of a consul and legislator: he desired to obtain a command worthy of the elevation of his genius, to extend the frontiers of the Republic, and to preserve them from the invasion of their most powerful enemies. It will be remembered that at the time of the election of the consuls, the Senate had conferred upon them the superintendence of the woods and public roads. He had, therefore, slender grounds to expect a return of friendly feeling on the part of that assembly, and, if the distribution of governments was vested in them, history offered examples of provinces given by vote of the people. Numidia was assigned to Marius on the proposal of the tribune L. Manlius; and L. Lucullus, having received Cisalpine Gaul from the Senate, obtained Cilicia from the people.[1178] It was thus that the command of Asia had been conferred upon Pompey. Strong in these precedents, Vatinius proposed to the people to confer upon Cæsar, for five years, the command of Cisalpine Gaul and Illyria, with three legions.[1179] Pompey supported this proposal with all his influence. The friends of Crassus,[1180] Claudius[1181] and L. Piso, gave their votes in favour of this law.

At first, it appeared strange that the proposal of the tribune only included Cisalpine Gaul, without reference to the other side of the Alps, which alone offered chances of acquiring glory. But, on reflection, we discover how skilful and politic was this manner of putting the question. To solicit at the same time the government of both the Gauls might have seemed exorbitant, and likely to expose him to failure. To demand the government of Gaul proper was dangerous, for if he had obtained it without Cisalpine Gaul, which would have devolved upon another proconsul, Cæsar would have found himself completely separated from Italy, inasmuch as it would have been impossible for him to repair thither during the winter, and so preserve continuous relations with Rome. The proposal of Vatinius, on the contrary, having for its object only Cisalpine Gaul and Illyria, they could scarcely refuse a command limited to the ordinary bounds, and Cæsar acquired thereby a solid basis for operations in the midst of devoted populations, where his legions could be easily recruited. As to the province beyond the Alps, it was probable that some fortuitous circumstance, or new proposal, would place it under his orders. This happened sooner than he expected, for the Senate, by a skilful, but at this time unusual, determination, added to his command a third province, Gallia Comata, or Transalpine, and a fourth legion. The Senate thus obtained for itself the credit of an initiative, which the people would have taken of itself had it not been anticipated.[1182]

Transported with joy at this news, Cæsar, according to Suetonius, exclaimed in the full Senate, that now, having succeeded to the utmost of his desire in spite of his enemies, he would march over their heads.[1183] This story is not probable. He was too prudent to provoke his enemies in their face at the moment he was going to a distance from Rome. "Always master of himself," says an old writer, "he never needlessly ran against anybody."[1184]

Opposition of the Patricians.

V. Whilst, contending with the most serious difficulties, Cæsar endeavoured to establish the Republic on the securest foundations, the aristocratic party consoled itself for its successive defeats by a petty war of sarcasm and chicanery. At the theatre they applauded all the injurious allusions of Pompey, and received Cæsar with coldness.[1185] Bibulus, the son-in-law of Cato, published libels containing the grossest attacks. He renewed the accusation of plotting against the Republic, and of the pretended shameful relations with Nicomedes.[1186] People rushed to read and copy these insulting placards. Cicero gladly sent them to Atticus. [1187] The party, too, to which Bibulus belonged, extolled him to the skies, and made him a great man.[1188] His opposition, however, had only succeeded in postponing the consular comitia until the month of October. This prorogation was made in the hope of preventing the election of consuls friendly to the triumvirs. Cæsar, on this occasion, attacked him in a violent speech, and Vatinius proposed to arrest him. Pompey, on his part, moved by invectives to which he was unaccustomed, complained to the people of the animosity of which he was the object; but his speech does not appear to have been attended with much success.

It is sad to see the accomplishment of great things often thwarted by the little passions of short-sighted men, who only know the world in the small circle to which their life is confined. By seconding Cæsar, Bibulus might have obtained an honourable reputation. He preferred being the hero of a coterie, and sought to obtain the interested applause of a few selfish senators, rather than, with his colleague, to merit public gratitude. Cicero, on his part, mistook for a true expression of opinion the clamours of a desperate faction. He was, moreover, one of those who find that all fares well while they are themselves in power, and that everything is endangered when they are out. In his letters to Atticus he speaks of the general hatred to these new kings, predicts their approaching fall, and exclaims,[1189] "What murmurs! what irritation! what hatred against our friend Pompey! His name of great is growing old like that of rich Crassus."[1190]

He explains, with a perfect naïveté, the consolation which his self-love finds in the abasement of him who was formerly the object of his admiration. "I was tormented with fear that the services which Pompey rendered to our country should hereafter appear greater than mine. I have quite recovered from it. He is so low, so very low, that Curius himself appears to me a giant beside him."[1191] And he adds, "Now there is nothing more popular than to hate the popular men; they have no one on their side. They know it, and it is this which makes me fear a resort to violence. I cannot think without shuddering of the explosions which are inevitable."[1192] The hatred which he bore to Clodius and Valerius misled his judgment.

Whilst Cæsar laboriously pursued the course of his destiny, the genius of Cicero, instead of understanding the future and hastening progress by his co-operation, resisted the general impulse, denied its evidence, and could not perceive the greatness of the cause through the faults of certain adherents to power.

Cæsar bore uneasily the attacks of Cicero; but, like all who are guided by great political views, superior to resentment, he conciliated everything which might exercise an ascendency over people's minds; and the eloquence of Cicero was a power. Dio Cassius thus explains the conduct of Cæsar: "He did not wound Cicero either by his words or his acts. He said that often many men designedly throw vain sarcasm against those who are above them in order to drive them to dispute, in the hope of appearing to have some resemblance to them, and be put in the same rank if they succeed in being abused in return. Cæsar therefore judged that he ought not to enter the lists with anybody. Such was his rule of conduct towards those who insulted him, and, as he saw very well that Cicero sought less to offend him than to provoke him to make some injurious reply, from the desire which he had to be looked upon as his equal, he took no notice of him, made no account of what he said, and even allowed Cicero to insult him as he liked, and to praise himself beyond measure. However, he was far from despising him, but, naturally gentle, his anger was not easily aroused. He had much to punish, as must be the case with one mixed up with great affairs, but he never yielded to passion."[1193]

An incident occurred which showed all the animosity of a certain party. L. Vettius, an old spy of Cicero's in the Catiline conspiracy, punished for having falsely accused Cæsar, was arrested on suspicion of wishing to attempt his life, as well as that of Pompey. A poniard was found upon him; and, being interrogated before the Senate, he denounced, as the instigators of his crime, the young Curio, Cæpio, Brutus, Lentulus, Cato, Lucullus, Piso, son-in-law of Cicero, Cicero himself, M. Laterensis, and others. He also named Bibulus, which removed all air of probability from his accusations, Bibulus having already warned Pompey to be on his guard. [1194] Historians, such as Dio Cassius, Appian, and Plutarch, treat this plot seriously; the first maintains expressly that Cicero and Lucullus had armed the hand of the assassin. Suetonius, on the contrary, reproaches Cæsar with having suborned Vettius in order to throw the blame upon his adversaries.

In face of these contradictory informations, it is best, as in the case of an ordinary lawsuit, to estimate the worth of the charge according to the previous character of the accused. Now, Cicero, notwithstanding his instability, was too honest to have a hand in a plot for assassination, and Cæsar had too elevated a character and too great a consciousness of his power to lower himself so far as to seek, in a miserable intrigue, the means of augmenting his influence. A senatus-consultum caused Vettius to be thrown into prison; but Cæsar, interested in, and resolved on, the discovery of the truth, referred the matter to the people, and forced Vettius to mount the tribune of the orators. He, with a suspicious versatility, denounced those whom he had before acquitted, and cleared those whom he had denounced, and among others, Brutus. With regard to the latter, it was pretended that this change was due to Cæsar's connection with his mother. Vettius was remanded to prison, and found dead next day. Cicero accused Vatinius of killing him;[1195] but, according to others, the true authors of his death were those who had urged him into this disgraceful intrigue, and were in fear of his revelations.[1196]

The comparison of these various accounts leads us to conclude that this obscure agent of dark intrigues had made himself the instigator of a plot, in order to have the merit of revealing it, and to attract the favour of Cæsar by pointing to his political adversaries as accomplices. Nevertheless, the event turned to the profit of Cæsar, and the people permitted him to take measures for his personal safety.[1197] It was doubtless at this period that the ancient custom was re-established of allowing a consul, during the month when he had not the fasces, the right of being preceded by a beadle (accensus) and followed by lictors.[1198]

Without changing the fundamental laws of the Republic, Cæsar had obtained a great result: he had replaced anarchy by an energetic power, ruling at the same time the Senate and the comitia; by the mutual understanding between the three most important men, he had substituted for personal rivalries a moral authority which enabled him to establish laws conducive to the prosperity of the empire. But it was essential that his departure should not entail the fall of the edifice so laboriously raised. He was not ignorant of the number and power of his enemies; he knew that if he abandoned to them the forum and the curia, not only would they reverse his enactments, but they would even deprive him of his command. If there was any doubt of the degree of hatred of which he was the object, it would be sufficient to be reminded, that a year afterwards Ariovistus confessed to him, in an interview on the banks of the Rhine, that many of the important nobles of Rome had designs against his life.[1199] Against such animosities he had the task, no easy one, of directing the elections. The Roman constitution caused new candidates to spring up every year for honours; and it was indispensable to have partisans amongst the two consuls, the eight prætors, and the ten tribunes named in the comitia. At all epochs, even at the time when the aristocracy exercised the greatest influence, it could not prevent its opponents from introducing themselves into the public offices. Moreover, the three who had made common cause had reason to fear the ambition and ingratitude of the men whom they had raised, and who would soon seek to become their equals. There was still a last danger, and perhaps the most serious: it was the impatience and want of discipline of the democratic party, of which they were the chiefs.

In face of these dangers, the triumvirs agreed to cause L. Piso, the father-in-law of Cæsar, and A. Gabinius, the devoted partisan of Pompey, to be elected to the consulship the following year. They were, in fact, designated consuls on the 18th of October, in spite of the efforts of the nobles and the accusation of Cato against Gabinius.

At the end of the year 695, Cæsar and Bibulus ceased their functions. The latter, in reporting his conduct according to custom, endeavoured to paint in the blackest colours the state of the Republic; but Clodius prevented him from speaking.[1200] As for Cæsar, his presentiment of the attacks to which he was to be subjected was only too well founded; for he had hardly quitted office, when the prætor L. Domitius Ahenobarbus, and C. Memmius, friends of Cicero,[1201] proposed to the Senate to prosecute him for the acts committed during his consulate, and especially for not having paid attention to the omens. From this proposal the Senate recoiled.[1202] Still, they brought Cæsar's questor to trial. He himself was cited by the tribune L. Antistius. But the whole college refused to entertain the charge, in virtue of the law Memmia, which forbad an accusation to be entertained against a citizen while absent on the public service.[1203]

Cæsar found himself once more at the gates of Rome, invested with the imperium, and, according to Cicero's letters,[1204] at the head of numerous troops, composed apparently of veteran volunteers.[1205] He even remained there more than two months, in order to watch that his departure should not become the signal for the overthrow of his work.

Law of Clodius. Exile of Cicero.

VI. During this time, Clodius, a restless and turbulent spirit,[1206] proud of the support which he had lent the triumvirs, as well as of that he had received from them, listened only to his passion, and caused laws to be enacted, some of which, flattering the populace and even the slaves, menaced the State with anarchy. In virtue of these laws, he re-established political associations (collegia), clubs dangerous to public tranquillity,[1207] which Sylla had dissolved, but which were subsequently reorganised to be again suppressed in 690;[1208] he made gratuitous distributions of wheat to the people; took from the censors the right of excluding from the Senate anybody they wished, allowing them only to reject those who were under condemnation;[1209] forbad the magistrates taking omens, or observing the sky on the day of the deliberation of the comitia;[1210] and, lastly, he inflicted severe penalties on those who had condemned Roman citizens to death unheard. This last enactment was evidently directed against Cicero, although his name was not mentioned in it. In order to ensure its adoption, its author desired the acquiescence of Cæsar, who was detained at the gates of Rome by the military command, which forbad him to enter. Clodius then convoked the people outside the walls, and when he asked the proconsul his opinion, the latter replied that it was well known by his vote in the affair of the accomplices of Catiline; that, nevertheless, he disapproved of a law which pronounced penalties upon facts which belonged to the past.[1211]

On this occasion the Senate went into mourning, in order to exhibit its discontent to all eyes; but the consuls Gabinius and Piso obliged the Senate to relinquish this ill-timed demonstration.

Cæsar, in order to defend Cicero from the danger which threatened him, offered to take him with him to Gaul as his lieutenant.[1212] Cicero rejected the offer, deceiving himself through his confidence in his own influence,[1213] and reckoning, moreover, on the protection of Pompey. It appears positive from this that Clodius exceeded Cæsar's views, a new proof that such instruments when employed are two-edged swords, which even the most skilful hands find it difficult to direct. It is thus that later, Vatinius, aspiring to become prætor, received from his old patron this strong warning: "Vatinius has done nothing gratuitously during his tribuneship; he who only looks for money ought to dispense with honours."[1214] In fact, Cæsar, whose efforts to re-establish the popular institutions had never slackened, desired neither anarchy nor democratic laws; and just as he had not approved of the proposal of Manilius for the emancipation of the freedmen, so he opposed the reorganisation of the corporations, the gratuitous distributions of wheat, and the projects of vengeance entertained by Clodius, who, however, continually boasted of his support.

Crassus, on his part, desiring to be useful to Cicero without compromising himself,[1215] engaged his son to go to his aid. As for Pompey, wavering between fear and friendship, he devised a pretext not to receive Cicero when he came to seek his support. Deprived of this last resource, the great orator abandoned his delusions, and after some show of resistance voluntarily withdrew. Scarcely had he quitted Rome when the law against him was passed without opposition, with the concurrence of those whom Cicero had looked upon as his friends.[1216] His goods were confiscated, his house razed, and he was exiled to a distance of four hundred miles.

Cæsar had skilfully taken precautions that his influence should be felt at Rome during his absence, as much as the instability of the magistracy would permit. By the aid of his daughter Julia, whose charms and mental accomplishments captivated her husband, Cæsar retained his influence over Pompey. By his favours to the son of Crassus, a young man of great merit, who was appointed his lieutenant, he assured himself of his father. Cicero is removed, but soon Cæsar will consent to his return, and will conciliate him again by taking into his favour his brother Quintus. There remains the opposition of Cato. Clodius undertakes to remove him under the pretence of an honourable mission: he is sent to Cyprus to dethrone King Ptolemy, whose irregularities excited the hatred of his subjects.[1217] Finally, all the men of importance who had any chance of obtaining employment are gained to the cause of Cæsar; some even engage themselves to him by writing. [1218] He can thus proceed to his province; Destiny is about to open a new path; immortal glory awaits him beyond the Alps, and this glory, reflected upon Rome, will change the face of the world.

The Explanation of Cæsar's Conduct.

VII. We have shown Cæsar obeying only his political convictions, whether as the ardent promoter of all popular measures, or as the declared partisan of Pompey; we have shown him aspiring with a noble ambition to power and honours; but we are not ignorant that historians in general give other motives for his conduct. They represent him, in 684, as having already his plans defined, his schemes arranged, his instruments all prepared. They attribute to him an absolute prescience of the future, the faculty of directing men and things at his will, and of rendering each one, unknowingly, the accomplice of his profound designs. All his actions have a hidden motive, which the historian boasts of having discovered. If Cæsar raises up again the standard of Marius, makes himself the defender of the oppressed, and the persecutor of the hired assassins of past tyranny, it is to acquire a concurrence necessary to his ambition; if he contends with Cicero in favour of legality in the trial of the accomplices of Catiline, or to maintain an agrarian law of which he approves the political aim, or if, to repair a great injustice of Sylla, he supports the restoration of the children of the proscribed to their rights, it is for the purpose of compromising the great orator with the popular party. If, on the contrary, he places his influence at the service of Pompey; if, on the occasion of the war against the pirates, he contributes to obtain for him an authority considered exorbitant; if he seconds the plebiscitum which further confers upon him the command of the army against Mithridates; if subsequently he causes extraordinary honours to be awarded him, though absent, it is still with the Machiavellian aim of making the greatness of Pompey redound to his own profit. So that, if he defends liberty, it is to ruin his adversaries; if he defends power, it is to accustom the Romans to tyranny. Finally, if Cæsar seeks the consulate, like all the members of the Roman nobility, it is, say they, because he already foresees, beyond the fasces of the consul and the dust of battles, the dictatorship and even the throne. Such an interpretation results from the too common fault of not being able to appreciate facts in themselves, but according to the complexion which subsequent events have given them.

Strange inconsistency, to impute to great men at the same time mean motives and superhuman forethought! No, it was not the miserable thought of checking Cicero which guided Cæsar; he had not recourse to a tactic more or less skilful: he obeyed a profound conviction, and what proves it indisputably is, that, once elevated to power, his first acts are to execute, as consul or dictator, what as a citizen he had supported: witness the agrarian law and the restoration of the proscribed. No, if he supports Pompey, it is not because he thinks that he can degrade him after having once elevated him, but because this illustrious captain had embraced the same cause as himself; for it would not have been given to any one to read so far into the future as to predict the use which the conqueror of Mithridates would make of his triumphs and veritable popularity. In fact, when he disembarked in Italy, Rome was in anxiety: will he disband his army?[1219] Such was from all quarters the cry of alarm. If he returns as a master, no one is able to resist him. Contrary to the general expectation, Pompey disbanded his troops. How then could Cæsar foresee beforehand a moderation then so unusual?

Is it truer to say that Cæsar, having become proconsul, aspired to the sovereign power? No; in departing for Gaul, he could no more have thought of reigning over Rome, than could General Buonaparte, starting for Italy in 1796, have dreamed of the Empire. Was it possible for Cæsar to foresee that, during a sojourn of ten years in Gaul, he would there link Fortune to him for ever, and that, at the end of this long space of time, the public mind at Rome would still be favourable to his projects? Could he foresee that the death of his daughter would break the ties which attached him to Pompey? that Crassus, instead of returning in triumph from the East, would be conquered and slain by the Parthians? that the murder of Clodius would throw all Italy into commotion? and, finally, that anarchy, which he had sought to stifle by the triumvirate, would be the cause of his own elevation? Cæsar had before his eyes great examples for his guidance; he marched in the track of the

Scipios and of Paulus Æmilius; the hatred of his enemies forced him, like Sylla, to seize upon the dictatorship, but for a more noble cause, and by a course of proceeding exempt from vengeance and cruelty.

Let us not continually seek little passions in great souls. The success of superior men, and it is a consoling thought, is due rather to the loftiness of their sentiments than to the speculations of selfishness and cunning; this success depends much more on their skill in taking advantage of circumstances, than on that presumption, blind enough to believe itself capable of creating events, which are in the hands of God alone. Certainly, Cæsar had faith in his destiny, and confidence in his genius; but faith is an instinct, not a calculation, and genius foresees the future without understanding its mysterious progress.

# FOOTNOTES:

[1]  Montesquieu, Grandeur et Décadence des Romains, xviii.

[2]  Suetonius, Cæsar, 22.

[3]  "Cæsar resolved to pass into Britain, the people of which had, in nearly all wars, assisted the Gauls." (Cæsar, Gallic War, IV. 20.)

[4]  Suetonius, Cæsar, 47.

[5]  Appian, Civil Wars, I. 110, 326, edit. Schweighæuser.

[6]  Cicero, Epistolæ ad Atticum, XIV. 10.

[7]  In fact, how many disturbances, civil wars, and revolutions in Europe since 1815! in France, Spain, Italy, Poland, Belgium, Hungary, Greece, and Germany!

[8]  Grandeur et Décadence des Romains.

[9]  Titus Livius I. 44.—Dionysius of Halicarnassus, speaking of the portion of the rampart between the Porta Æsquilina and the Porta Collina, says, "Rome is fortified by a fosse thirty feet deep and a hundred or more wide in the narrowest part. Above this fosse rises a wall supported internally by a lofty and wide terrace, so that it cannot be shaken by battering rams, or overthrown by undermining." (Antiq. Roman., IX. 68.)

[10]  "Since that time (the time of Servius Tullius) Rome has been no farther enlarged ... and if, in face of this spectacle, any one would form a notion of the magnitude of Rome, he would certainly fall into error, for he would not be able to distinguish where the town ends and where it is limited, so close the suburbs come up to the town.... The Aventine, till the reign of Claudius, remained outside the Pomœrium, notwithstanding its numerous inhabitants." (Aulus Gellius, XIII. 14.—Dionysius of Halicarnassus, IV. 13.)

[11]  Dionysius of Halicarnassus, IV. 49.

[12]  "By this treaty, the Romans and their allies engage not to navigate beyond the Bonum Promontorium (a cape situated to the north and opposite Carthage, and now called by navigators the Cape of Porto-

Farino).... The Carthaginians undertake to respect the Ardeates, the Antiates, the Laurentes, the Circeii, the Tarracinians, and indeed all the Latin peoples subject to Rome." (Polybius, III. 22.)

[13] "When Tarquinius Priscus regulated, with the foresight of a skilful prince, the state of the citizens, he attached great importance to the dress of children of condition; and he decreed that the sons of patricians should wear the bulla with the robe hemmed with purple: but even this privilege was restricted to the children of those fathers who had exercised a curule dignity; the sons of other patricians had merely the prætexta, and it was necessary that even their fathers should have served the prescribed time in the cavalry." (Macrobius, Saturnalia, I. 6.)

[14] "The plebeians were excluded from all offices, and put only to agriculture, the breeding of cattle, and mercantile occupations." (Dionysius of Halicarnassus, II. 9.)—"Numa encouraged the agriculturists; they were excused from service in war, and discharged from the care of municipal affairs." (Dionysius of Halicarnassus, II. 76.)

[15] Dionysius of Halicarnassus, II. 9.—Plutarch, Romulus, 13.

[16] "Agrorum partes attribuerant tenuioribus." (Festus, under the word Patres, p. 246, edit. O. Müller.)

[17] Dionysius of Halicarnassus, IV. 24.

[18] These questions have been the object of learned researches; but, after an attentive perusal of the works of Beaufort, Niebuhr, Gœttling, Duruy, Marquardt, Mommsen, Lange, &c., the difference of opinions is discouraging: we have adopted those which appeared most probable.

[19] Dionysius of Halicarnassus, V. 40.—Titus Livius, II. 16.

[20] Titus Livius, II. 48.—Dionysius of Halicarnassus, IX. 15.

[21] Titus Livius, II. 64.

[22] Dionysius of Halicarnassus, X. 15.

[23] "They called a decree of the people (scitum populi) the measure which the order of patricians had voted, on the proposal of a patrician, without the participation of the plebs." (See Festus, under the words Scitum populi, p. 330.)—Titus Livius, speaking of the tribunes, puts the following words into the mouth of Appius Claudius: "Non enim populi, sed plebis, eum magistratum esse." (Titus Livius, II. 56.)

[24] "The plebs was composed of all the mass of the people which was neither senator nor patrician." (See Festus, under the words Scitum populi.)

[25] "Populus autem non omnis hominum cœtus quoquo modo congregatus, sed cœtus multitudinis juris consensu et utilitatis communione sociatus." — (Cicero, De Republica, I. 25.)

[26] "Populus curiatis eum (Numam) comitiis regem esse jusserat. Tullum Hostilium populus regem, interrege rogante, comitiis curiatis creavit. Servius, Tarquinio sepulto, populum de se ipse consuluit jussusque regnare legem de imperio suo curiatam tulit." (Cicero, De Republica, II. 13-21.)

[27] "The predecessors of Servius Tullius brought all causes before their tribunal, and pronounced judgment themselves in all disputes which regarded the State or individuals. He separated these two things, and, reserving to himself the cognizance of affairs which concerned the State, abandoned to other judges the causes of individuals, with injunctions, nevertheless, to regulate their judgments according to the laws which he had passed." (Dionysius of Halicarnassus, IV. 25.)

[28] "The consuls, like the ancient kings, have twelve lictors carrying axes and twelve lictors carrying rods." (Appian, Syrian Wars, 15.)

[29] "From that time Tarquinius Superbus carried, during the rest of his life, a crown of gold, a toga of embroidered purple, and a sceptre of ivory, and his throne was also of ivory; when he administered justice, or walked abroad in the town, he was preceded by twelve lictors, who carried axes surrounded with rods. (Dionysius overlooks the twelve other lictors who carried rods only.) After the kings had been expelled from Rome, the annual consuls continued to use all these insignia, except the crown and the robe with purple embroidery. These two only were withdrawn, because they were odious and disagreeable to the people. But even these were not entirely abolished, since they still used ornaments of gold and dress of embroidered purple, when, after a victory, the Senate decreed them the honours of the triumph." (Dionysius of Halicarnassus, III. 62.)

[30] "The soldiers of Romulus, to the number of three thousand, were divided into three bodies, called 'tribes.'" (Dio Cassius, Fragm., XIV., edit. Gros. — Dionysius of Halicarnassus, II. 7. — Plutarch, Romulus, 25.) — "The name of tribune of the soldiers is derived from the circumstance that the three tribes of the Ramnes, the Luceres, and the Tatiens each sent three to the army." (Varro, De Lingua Latina, V. § 81, p. 32, edit. O. Müller.)

[31] Dionysius of Halicarnassus, II. 35. Attempts have been made to explain in different ways the origin of the word curia. Some have derived it from the word curare, or from the name of the town of Cures, or from

κύριος, "a lord:" it seems more natural to trace it to quiris (curis), which had the signification of a lance (Dionysius of Halicarnassus, II. 48.—Plutarch, Romulus, for thus we obtain a term analogous with that of the Middle Ages, where spear signified a man-at-arms, accompanied by six or eight armed followers. And as the principal aim of the formation of the curia was to furnish a certain number of armed citizens, it is possible that they may have given to the whole the name of a part. We read in Ovid, Fasti, II. lines 477-480:—

> "Sive quod hasta curis priscis est dicta Sabinis,
> Bellicus a telo venit in astra deus:
> Sive suo regi nomen posuere Quirites,
> Seu quis Romanis junxerat ille Cures."

[32] Titus Livius, 1. 43.

[33] Dionysius of Halicarnassus, II. 14, and IV. 20.

[34] "The appeal to the people existed even under the kings, as the books of the pontiffs show." (Cicero, De Republica, II. 31.)

[35] Plutarch, Numa, 17.—Pliny, Natural History, XXXIV. 1.

[36] "Servius Tullius conformed no longer as aforetime to the ancient order of three tribes, distinguished by origin, but to the four new tribes which he had established by quarters." (Dionysius of Halicarnassus, IV. 14.)

[37] Dionysius of Halicarnassus, III. 61.—Titus Livius, I. 35.

[38] Dionysius of Halicarnassus, IV. 22.

[39] Dionysius of Halicarnassus, IV. 19. "Servius Tullius, by these means, threw back upon the richest all the costs and dangers of war." (Dionysius of Halicarnassus, IV. 20.)

[40] "If Numa was the legislator of the religious institutions, posterity proclaims Servius as the founder of the order which distinguishes in the Republic the difference of rank, dignity, and fortune. It was he who established the census, the most salutary of all institutions for a people destined to so much greatness. Fortunes, and not individuals, were called upon to support the burdens of the State. The census established the classes, the centuries, and that order which constitutes the ornament of Rome during peace and its strength daring war." (Titus Livius, I. 42.)

[41] Dionysius of Halicarnassus, IV. 16.

[42]  "When Servius Tullius had completed the taking of the census, he ordered all the citizens to assemble in arms in the greatest of the fields situated near the town, and, having arranged the horsemen in squadrons, the footmen in phalanx, and the light-armed men in respective orders, he submitted them to a lustration, by the immolation of a bull, a ram, and a he-goat. He ordered that the victims should be led thrice round about the army, after which he sacrificed to Mars, to whom this field was dedicated. From that epoch to the present time the Romans have continued to have the same ceremony performed, by the most holy of magistracies, at the completion of each census; it is what they call a lustrum. The total number of all the Romans enumerated, according to the writing of the tables of the census, gave 300 men less than 85,000." (Dionysius of Halicarnassus, IV. 22.)

[43]  "This good order of government (under Servius Tullius) was sustained among the Romans during several centuries, but in our days it has been changed, and, by force of circumstances, has given place to a more democratic system. It is not that the centuries have been abolished, but the voters were no longer called together with the ancient regularity, and their judgments have no longer the same equity, as I have observed in my frequent attendance at the comitia." (Dionysius of Halicarnassus, IV. 21.)

[44]  "The poorest citizens, in spite of their great number, were the last to give their vote, and made but one century." (Dionysius of Halicarnassus, IV. 21.)

[45]  Titus Livius, I. 43.

[46]  "From the age of seventeen years, they were called to be soldiers. Youth began with that age, and continued to the age of forty-six. At that date old age began." (Aulus Gellius, X. 28.—Dionysius of Halicarnassus, IV. 16.)

[47]  Titus Livius speaks only of a hundred and ninety-two centuries; Dionysius of Halicarnassus reckons a hundred and ninety-three. "In the Roman plebs, the poorest citizens, those who reported to the census not more than fifteen hundred ases, were called proletarii; those who were not worth more than three hundred and seventy-five ases, and who thus possessed hardly anything, were called capite censi. Now, the fortune and patrimony of the citizen being for the State a sort of guarantee, the pledge and foundation of his love for his country, the men of the two last classes were only enrolled in case of extreme danger. Yet the position of the proletarii was a little more honourable than that of the capite censi; in times of difficulty, when there was

want of young men, they were incorporated in the hastily-formed militia, and equipped at the cost of the State; their name contained no allusion to the mere poll-tax to which they were subjected; less humiliating, it reminded one only of their destination to give children to their country. The scantiness of their patrimony preventing them from contributing to the aid of the State, they at least contributed to the population of the city." (Aulus Gellius, XVI. 10.)

[48] "Tarquinius Priscus afterwards gave to the knights the organisation which they have preserved to the present time." (Cicero, De Republica, II. 20.)

[49] "It is said that the number of citizens inscribed under this title was 80,000. Fabius Pictor, the most ancient of our historians, adds that this number only includes the citizens in condition to bear arms." (Titus Livius, I. 44.)

[50] The different censuses of the people furnished by the ancient historians have been explained in different manners. Did the numbers given designate all the citizens, or only the heads of families, or those who had attained the age of puberty? In my opinion, these numbers in Livy, Dionysius of Halicarnassus, and Plutarch, applied to all the men in a condition to carry arms, that is, according to the organisation of Servius Tullius, to those from seventeen to sixty years old. This category formed, in fact, the true Roman citizens. Under seventeen, they were too young to count in the State; above sixty, they were too old.

We know that the aged sexagenarians were called *depontani*, because they were forbidden the bridges over which they must go to the place of voting. (Festus, under the word *sexagenarius*, p. 834.—Cicero, *Pro S. Roscio Amerino*, 35.)

80,000 men in condition to carry arms represent, according to the statistics of the present time, fifty-five hundredths of the male part of the population, say 145,000 men, and for the two sexes, supposing them equal in number, 290,000 souls. In fact, in France, in a hundred inhabitants, there are 35 who have not passed the age of seventeen, 55 aged from seventeen to sixty years, and 10 of more than sixty.

In support of the above calculation, Dionysius of Halicarnassus relates that in the year 247 of Rome a subscription was made in honour of Horatius Cocles: 300,000 persons, men and women, gave the value of what each might expend in one day for his food. (V. 25.)

As to the number of slaves, we find in another passage of Dionysius of Halicarnassus (IX. 25) that the women, children, slaves, merchants, and artisans amounted to a number triple of that of the citizens.

If, then, the number of citizens in condition to carry arms was 80,000, and the rest of the population equalled three times that number, we should have for the total 4 x 80,000 = 320,000 souls. And, subtracting from this number the 290,000 obtained above, there would remain 30,000 for the slaves and artisans.

Whatever proportion we admit between these two last classes, the result will be that the slaves were at that period not numerous.

[51] Dionysius of Halicarnassus, IV. 9, 23.

[52] "Within the town, the buildings were not allowed to approach the ramparts, which they now ordinarily touch, and outside a space extended which it was forbidden to cultivate. To all this space, which it was not permitted to inhabit or cultivate, the Romans gave the name of Pomœrium. When, in consequence of the increase of the town, the rampart was carried farther out, this consecrated zone on each side was still preserved." (Titus Livius, I. 44.)

[53] "Founded on the testimony of the sacred books which are preserved with great care in the temples." (Dionysius of Halicarnassus, XI. 62.)

[54] "These precious pledges, which they regard as so many images of the gods." (Dionysius of Halicarnassus, VI. 45.)

[55] "Hence is explained the origin of the name given to the Capitol: in digging the foundation of the temple, they found a human head; and the augurs declared that Rome would become the head of all Italy." (Dionysius of Halicarnassus, IV. 61.)

[56] "This recourse to the opinions of the priests and the observations of religious worship made the people forget their habits of violence and their taste for arms. Their minds, incessantly occupied with religious ideas, acknowledged the intervention of Providence in human affairs, and all hearts were penetrated with a piety so lively that good faith and fidelity to an oath reigned in Rome more than fear of laws or punishments." (Titus Livius, I. 21.)

[57] Titus Livius, I. 45.

[58] "Assemblies of people, levies of troops—indeed, the most important operations—were abandoned, if the birds did not approve them." (Titus Livius, I. 36.)

[59] "Numa established also the auspicious and inauspicious days, for with the people an adjournment might sometimes be useful." (Titus Livius, I. 19.)

[60] "We have a town, founded on the faith of auspices and auguries; not a spot within these walls which is not full of gods and their worshippers; our solemn sacrifices have their days fixed as well as the place where they are to be made." (Titus Livius, V. 52, Speech of Camillus, VI. &c.)

[61] Cicero, De Republica, II. 14.

[62] "All religious acts, public and private, were submitted to the decision of the pontiff; thus the people knew to whom to address themselves, and disorders were prevented which might have brought into religion the neglect of the national rites or the introduction of foreign ones. It was the same pontiff's duty also to regulate what concerned funerals, and the means of appeasing the Manes, and to distinguish, among prodigies announced by thunder and other phenomena, those which required an expiation." (Titus Livius, I. 20.)

[63] "The grand pontiff exercises the functions of interpreter and diviner, or rather of hierophant. He not only presides at the public sacrifices, but he also inspects those which are made in private, and takes care that the ordinances of religious worship are not transgressed. Lastly, it is he who teaches what each individual ought to do to honour the gods and to appease them." (Plutarch, Numa, 12.)

[64] "Numa divided the year into twelve months, according to the moon's courses; he added January and February to the year." (Titus Livius, I. 19.—Plutarch, Numa, 18.)

[65] Dionysius of Halicarnassus, II. 73.

[66] Dionysius of Halicarnassus, II. 64.

[67] Salian is derived from salire (to leap, to dance). (Dionysius of Halicarnassus, II. 70.)—It was their duty, on certain occasions, to execute sacred dances, and to chant hymns in honour of the god of war.

[68] Dionysius of Halicarnassus, II. 72.—"The name of feciales is derived from the circumstance that they presided over the public faith between peoples; for it was by their intervention that war when undertaken assumed the character of a just war, and, that once terminated, peace was guaranteed by a treaty. Before war was undertaken, some of the feciales were sent to make whatever demands had to be made." (Varro, De Lingua Latina, V. § 86.)—"If allies complained that the Romans had done them wrong, and demanded reparation for it, it was the business of the feciales to examine if there were any violation of treaty." (Dionysius of Halicarnassus, II. 72.)—Those fecial priests had been instituted by Numa, the mildest and most just of kings, to

be guardians of peace, and the judges and arbiters of the legitimate motives for undertaking war. (Plutarch, Camillus, 20.)

[69] Dionysius of Halicarnassus, IV. 14.—Pliny, Natural History, XXI. 8.

[70] Numa raised a temple to Romulus, whom he deified under the name of Quirinus. (Dionysius of Halicarnassus, II. 63)

[71] "Temple of Vesta, emblem of chastity; temple to Public Faith; raised by Numa." (Dionysius of Halicarnassus, II. 65 and 75.)

[72] "The god Terminus; the festival in honour of Pales, the goddess of shepherds; Saturn, the god of agriculture; the god of fallow-grounds, pasture," &c. (Dionysius of Halicarnassus, II. 74.)

[73] "After having done these things in peace and war, Servius Tullius erected two temples to Fortune, who appeared to have been favourable to him all his life, one in the oxen-market, the other on the banks of the Tiber, and he gave her the surname of Virilis, which she has preserved to the present day among the Romans." (Dionysius of Halicarnassus, IV. 27.)

[74] "The Temple of Janus had been closed twice since the reign of Numa: the first time by the consul Titus Manlius, at the end of the first Punic war; the second, when the gods granted to our age to see, after the battle of Actium, Cæsar Augustus Imperator give peace to the universe." (Titus Livius, I. 19.)—And Plutarch says, in his Life of Numa, XX., "Nevertheless, this temple was closed after the victory of Cæsar Augustus over Antony, and it had previously been closed under the consulate of Marcus Atilius and of Titus Manlius, for a short time, it is true; it was almost immediately opened again, for a new war broke out. But, during the reign of Numa, it was not seen open a single day."

[75] We employ intentionally the word republic, because all the ancient authors give this name to the State, under the kings as well as under the emperors. It is only by translating faithfully these denominations that we can form an exact idea of ancient societies.

[76] "We acknowledge how many good and useful institutions the Republic owed to each of our kings." (Cicero, De Republica, II. 21.)

[77] "Among the Romans, the children possess nothing of their own during their father's life. He can dispose not only of all the goods, but even of the lives of his children." (Dionysius of Halicarnassus, VIII. 79; II. 25.)

[78] Dionysius of Halicarnassus, II., 25, 26.—"From the beginning," says Mommsen, "the Roman family presented, in the moral order which reigned among its members, and their mutual subordination, the conditions of a superior civilisation." (Roman History, 2nd edit., I., p. 54.)

[79]   "Morals were so pure that, during two hundred and thirty years, no husband was known to repudiate his wife, nor any woman to separate from her husband." (Plutarch, Parallel of Theseus and Romulus.)

[80]   Cicero admires the profound wisdom of the first kings in admitting the conquered enemies to the number of the citizens. "Their example," he says, "has become an authority, and our ancestors have never ceased granting the rights of citizens to conquered enemies." (Oration for Balbus, xxxi.)

[81]   Roman colonies (coloniæ civium cum jure suffragii et honorum).— First period: 1-244 (under the kings).

*Cænina* (Sabine). Unknown.
*Antemnæ* (Sabine). Unknown.
*Cameria* (Sabine). Destroyed in 252. Unknown.
*Medullia* (Sabine). *Sant'-Angelo.*—See Gell., *Topogr. of Rome*, 100.
*Crustumeria* (Sabine). Unknown.
*Fidenæ* (Sabine). Ruins near *Giubileo* and *Serpentina*. Re-colonised in 326. Destroyed, according to an hypothesis of M. Madvig.
*Collatia.*
*Ostia* (the mouth of the Tiber). Ruins between
*Torre Bovacciano* and *Ostia.*

Latin colonies (coloniæ Latinæ).—First period: 1-244 (under the kings).

We cannot mention with certainty any Latin colony founded at this epoch, from ancient authorities. The colonies of *Signia* and *Circeii* were both re-colonized in the following period, and we shall place them there.

[82]   "Tarquin embellished also the great circus between the Aventine and Palatine hills; he was the first who caused the covered seats to be made round this circus." (Dionysius of Halicarnassus, III. 68.)

[83]   Titus Livius, I. 44.—"Immediately the centurions, whose centuries had taken flight, and the antesignani who had lost their standard, were condemned to death: some had their heads cut off; others were beaten to death. As to the rest of the troops, the consul caused them to be decimated; in every ten soldiers, he upon whom the lot fell was conducted to the place of execution, and suffered for the others. It is the usual punishment among the Romans for those who have quitted their ranks or abandoned their standards." (Dionysius of Halicarnassus, IX. 1.)

[84]   "Romulus placed upon their hair a crown of laurels." (Plutarch, Romulus, XX.)

[85] "The Senate and the people decreed to King Tarquin the honours of the triumph." (Combat of the Romans and Etruscans, Dionysius of Halicarnassus, III. 60.)—"An ovation differs from a triumph, first, because he who receives the honours of it enters on foot at the head of the army, and not mounted in a car; secondly, that he has neither the crown of gold, nor the toga embroidered with gold and of different colours, but he carries only a white trabea bordered with purple, the ordinary costume of the generals and consuls. Besides having only a crown of laurel, he does not carry a sceptre. This is what the little triumph has less than the great; in all other respects there is no difference." (Dionysius of Halicarnassus, V. 47.)

[86] Romulus kills Acron, routs the enemies, and returns to offer to Jupiter Feretrius the opima spolia taken from that prince.

"After Romulus, Cornelius Cossus was the first who consecrated to the same gods similar spoils, having slain with his own hand, in a combat where he commanded the cavalry, the general of the Fidenates.

"We must not separate the example of M. Marcellus from the two preceding. He had the courage and intrepidity to attack on the banks of the Pô, at the head of a handful of horsemen, the king of the Gauls, though protected by a numerous army; he struck off his head, and *carried off his armour*, of which he made an offering to Jupiter Feretrius. (Year of Rome 531.)

"The same kind of bravery and combat signalised T. Manilius Torquatus, Valerius Corvus, and Scipio Æmilianus. These warriors, challenged by the chieftains of the enemies, made them bite the dust; but, as they had fought under the auspices of a superior chief, they did not offer their spoils to Jupiter." (Year of Rome 392, 404, 602.) (Valerius Maximus, III. 2, §§ 3, 4, 5, 6.)

[87] "Tarquin divided the seats (of the great circus) among the thirty curiæ, assigning to each the place which belonged to him." (Dionysius of Halicarnassus, III. 68.)—"It was then (after the war against the Latins) that the site was chosen which is now called the great circus. They marked out in it the particular places for the senators and for the knights." (Titus Livius, I. 35.)

[88] "The hundred senators were divided into ten decaries, and each chose one of its members to exercise this authority. The power was collective: one alone carried the insignia of it, and walked preceded by the lictors. The duration of this power was for five days, and each exercised it in turn ... The plebs was not long before it began to murmur. Its servitude had only been aggravated; instead of one master, it had a hundred. It appeared disposed to suffer only one king, and to choose him itself." (Titus Livius, I. 17.)

[89] "For the rest, this liberty consisted at first rather in the annual election of the consuls than in the weakening of the royal power. The first consuls assumed all its prerogatives and all its insignia; only it was feared that, if both possessed the fasciæ, this solemnity might inspire too much terror, and Brutus owed to the deference of his colleague the circumstance of possessing them first." (Titus Livius, II. 1.)

[90] "The death of Melius was justified," said Quinctius, "to appease the people, although he might be innocent of the crime of aspiring to the kingly power." (Titus Livius, IV. 15.)

[91] "From these inflexible hearts came a sentence of death, which was odious to the judges themselves." (Titus Livius, VI. 20.)

[92] Discourse on Titus Livius, I. 5.

[93]  Proofs of the disagreement of the two consuls: "Cassius brought secretly as many Latins and Hernici as he possibly could to have their suffrages; there arrived in Rome such a great number, that in a short time the town was full of strangers. Virginius, who was informed of it, caused a herald to proclaim in all the public places that all those who had no domicile in Rome should withdraw immediately; but Cassius gave orders contrary to those of his colleague, forbidding any one who had the right of Roman freedom to quit the town until the law was confirmed and received." (Year of Rome 268.) (Dionysius of Halicarnassus, VIII. 72.)—"Quinctius, more indulgent than his colleague, willed the concession to the people of all their just and reasonable demands; Appius, on the contrary, was willing to die rather than to yield." (Year of Rome 283.) (Dionysius of Halicarnassus, IX. 48.)

[94] "The two consuls were of the most opposite tempers, and were always in discord (dissimiles discordesque)." (Titus Livius, XXII. 41.)—"While they lost their time in quarrels rather than in deliberations." (Titus Livius, XXII. 45.)

[95] Titus Livius, XXI. 52.—Dio Cassius, Fragments, CCLXXI. edit. Gros.

[96] Titus Livius, XXI. 52.

[97] "In the Roman army the two consuls enjoyed an equal power; but the deference of Agrippa in concentrating the authority in the hands of his colleague, established the unity so necessary for the success of great enterprises." (Titus Livius, III. 70.)—"The two consuls commanded often both in the day of battle." (Titus Livius, Battle of Mount Vesuvius, VIII. 9; Battle of Sentinum, X. 27.)—"A fatal innovation; from that time each had in view his personal interest, and not the

general interest, preferring to see the Republic experience a check than his colleague covered with glory, and evils without number afflicted the fatherland." (Dio Cassius, Fragments, LI. edit. Gros.)

[98] "They called tribunes of the people those who, from tribunes of the soldiers, which they were first, were charged with the defence of the people during its retreat at Crustumerium." (Varro, De Lingua Latina, V. 81, edition of O. Müller.)

[99] "The discontented obtained from the patricians the confirmation of their magistrates; afterwards they demanded of the Senate the permission to elect annually two plebeians (ediles) to second the tribunes in all things in which they might have need of aid, to judge the causes which these might entrust into their hands, to have care of the sacred and public edifices, and to ensure the supplying of the market with provisions." (Year of Rome 260.) (Dionysius of Halicarnassus, VI. 90.)

[100] Dionysius of Halicarnassus, VI. 89.

[101] The tribunes oppose the enrolment of troops. (Year of Rome 269.) (Dionysius of Halicarnassus, VIII. 81.)—"Licinius and Sextius re-elected tribunes of the people, allowed no curule magistrate to be elected; and, as the people continued to re-appoint the two tribunes, who always threw out the elections of the military tribunes, the town remained five years deprived of magistrates." (Year of Rome 378.) (Titus Livius, VI. 35.)—"Each time the consuls convoked the people to confer the consulship on the candidates, the tribunes, in virtue of their powers, prevented the holding of the assemblies. So also, when these assembled the people to make the election, the consuls opposed it, pretending that the right of convoking the people and collecting the suffrages belonged to them alone." (Year of Rome 271.) (Dionysius of Halicarnassus, VIII. 90.)—"Sometimes the tribunes prevented the patricians from assembling for the election of the interrex, sometimes they forbade the interrex himself making the senatus consultus for the consular comitia." (Year of Rome 333.) (Titus Livius, IV. 43.)

[102] Titus Livius, III. 30.

[103] Dionysius of Halicarnassus, X. 31.

[104] "The most remarkable event of this year (the year of Rome 282), in which military successes were so nearly balanced, and in which discord broke out in the camp and in the town with so much fury, was the establishment of the comitia by tribes, an innovation which gave to the plebeians the honour of the victory, but little real advantage. In fact, the exclusion of the patricians deprived the comitia of all their pomp, without augmenting the power of the people or diminishing that of the Senate." (Titus Livius, II. 60.)

[105] Assembly of the people both of the town and country; the suffrages were given in it, not by centuries, but by tribes:—"The day of the third market, from an early hour in the morning, the public place was occupied by so great a crowd of country people as had never been seen before. The tribunes assembled the people by tribes, and, dividing the Forum by ropes stretched across, formed as many distinct spaces as there were tribes. Then, for the first time, the Roman people gave its suffrages by tribes, in spite of the opposition of the patricians, who tried to prevent it, and demanded that they should assemble by centuries, according to the ancient custom." (Year of Rome 263.) (Dionysius of Halicarnassus, VII. 59.)—"From that period (the year 283, consulate of Appius) to our days, the comitia by tribes have elected the tribunes and ediles, without auspices or observation of other auguries. Thus ended the troubles which agitated Rome." (Dionysius of Halicarnassus, IX. 49.)—"The Roman people, more irritated than ever, demanded that for each tribe a third urn should be added for the town of Rome, in order to put the suffrages in it." (Year of Rome 308.) (Dionysius of Halicarnassus, XI. 52.)

[106] "Duas civitates ex una factas: suos cuique parti magistratus, suas leges esse." (Titus Livius, II. 44.)—"In fact, we are, as you see yourselves, divided into two towns, one of which is governed by poverty and necessity, and the other by abundance of all things and by pride and insolence." (Year of Rome 260). (Speech of Titus Larcius to the envoys of the Volsci, Dionysius of Halicarnassus, VI. 36,)

[107] The clients began to vote in the comitia by tribes after the law Valeria Horatia; we see, by the account of Titus Livius (V. 30, 32), that in the time of Camillus the clients and the patricians had already entered the comitia by tribes.

[108] Appian, Civil Wars, I. 1.

[109] Titus Livius, III. 9.

[110] Lectorius, the most aged of the tribunes of the people, spoke of laws which had not been long made. "By the first, which concerned the translation of judgments, the Senate granted to the people the power of judging any one of the patricians." (Year of Rome 283.) (Dionysius of Halicarnassus, IX. 46.)

[111] "The laws voted by the people in the comitia by tribes were to be obligatory on all Romans, and have the same force as those which were made in the comitia by centuries. The pain of death and confiscation was even pronounced against any one who should be convicted of having in anything abrogated or violated this regulation. This new

ordinance cut short the old quarrels between the plebeians and the patricians, who refused to obey the laws made by the people, under the pretext that what was decided in the assemblies by tribes was not obligatory on all the town, but only on the plebeians; and that, on the contrary, what was decided in the comitia by centuries became law as well for themselves as for the other citizens." (Year of Rome 305.) (Dionysius of Halicarnassus, XI. 45.)—"One point always contested between the two orders was to know if the patricians were subjected to the plebiscita. The first care of the consuls was to propose to the comitia assembled by centuries a law to the effect that the decrees of the people assembled by tribes should be laws of the State." (Year of Rome 305.) (Titus Livius, III. 55.)—"The patricians pretended that they alone had the power of giving laws." (Titus Livius, III. 31.)

[112] "The comitia by curiæ for everything which concerns military affairs; the comitia by centuries for the election of your consuls and of your military tribunes, &c." (Titus Livius, V. 52.)

[113] Aulus Gellius, XV. 27.—Festus, under the words Scitum populi.

[114] Titus Livius, IV. 3.

[115] "The indignation of the people was extreme, on account of the refusal to take the auspices, as if it had been an object for the reprobation of the immortal gods."—"The tribune demanded for what reason a plebeian could not be consul, and was told in reply that the plebeians had not the auspices, and that the decemvirs had interdicted marriage between the two orders only to hinder the auspices from being troubled by men of equivocal birth." (Titus Livius, IV. 6.)—"Now in what hands are the auspices according to the custom of our ancestors? In the hands of the patricians, I think; for the auspices are never taken for the nomination of a plebeian magistrate."—"Is it not then the same thing as to annihilate the auspices in this city, to take them, in electing plebeian consuls, from the patricians, who alone can observe them?" (Year of Rome 386.) (Titus Livius, VI. 41.)

To the consul, the prætor, and the censor was reserved the right of taking the great auspices; to the less elevated magistracies that of taking the lesser ones. The great auspices appear, in fact, to have been those of which the exercise was of most importance to the rights of the aristocracy. The ancients have not left us a precise definition of the two classes of auspices; but it appears to result from what Cicero says of them (De Legibus, II. 12), that by the great auspices were understood those for which the intervention of the augurs was indispensable; the little auspices, on the contrary, were those which were taken without them. (See Aulus Gellius, XIII. 15.)

As to the auspices taken in the comitia where the consular tribunes were elected, passages of Titus Livius (V. 14, 52; VI. 11) prove that they were the same as for the election of the consuls, and consequently that they were the great auspices; for we know from Cicero (*De Divinatione*, I. 17; II. 35—compare Titus Livius, IV. 7) that it was the duty of the magistrate who held the comitia to bring there an augur, of whom he demanded what the presages announced. The privileges of the nobility were maintained by causing the comitia for the election of the consular tribunes to be held by an interrex chosen by the aristocracy.

[116] Titus Livius, VI. 5.

[117] Titus Livius, VII. 17.

[118] In 333, the number was increased to four. Two, overseers for the guard of the treasury and the disposition of the public money, were appointed by the consuls; the two others, charged with the administration of the military chest, were appointed by the tribes.

[119] "The master of the knights was so called because he exercised the supreme power over the knights and the accensi, as the dictator exercised it over the whole Roman people; whence the name of master of the people, which was also given to him." (Varro, De Lingua Latina, V. 82, edit. Müller.)

[120] "The duumvirs charged with the sacred rites were replaced by the decemvirs, half plebeians, half patricians." (Titus Livius, VI. 37.)

[121] Titus Livius, VII. 5.

[122] "Appius convokes an assembly, accuses Valerius and Horatius of the crime of perduellio, calculating entirely on the tribunian power with which he was invested." (Year of Rome 305.) (Dionysius of Halicarnassus, XI. 39.)

[123] "In the interim, there was at Rome a conspiracy of several slaves, who formed together the design of seizing the forts and setting fire to the different quarters of the town." (Year of Rome 253.) (Dionysius of Halicarnassus, V. 51.)—"From the summit of the Capitol, Herdonius called the slaves to liberty. He had taken up the cause of misfortune; he had just restored to their country those whom injustice had banished, and delivered the slaves from a heavy yoke; it is to the Roman people that he wishes to give the honour of this enterprise." (Year of Rome 294.) (Titus Livius, III. 15.)—"The slaves who had entered into the conspiracy were, at different points, to set fire to the town, and, while the people were occupied in carrying assistance to the houses which were in flames, to seize by force of arms the citadel and the Capitol.

Jupiter baffled these criminal designs. On the denunciation of two slaves, the guilty were arrested and punished." (Year of Rome 336.) (Titus Livius, IV. 45.)

[124] "Finally, under the consulship of M. Minucius and A. Sempronius, wheat arrived in abundance from Sicily, and the Senate deliberated on the price at which it must be delivered to the citizens." (Year of Rome 263.) (Titus Livius, II. 34.)—"As the want of cultivators gave rise to the fear of a famine, people were sent to search for wheat in Etruria, in the Pomptinum, at Cumæ, and even as far as Sicily." (Year of Rome 321.) (Titus Livius, IV. 25.)

[125] "When Romulus had distributed all the people in tribes and curiæ, he also divided the lands into thirty equal portions, of which he gave one to each curia, reserving, nevertheless, what was necessary for the temples and the sacrifices, and a certain portion for the domain of the Republic." (Dionysius of Halicarnassus, II. 7.)

[126] "Numa distributed to the poorest of the plebeians the lands which Romulus had conquered and a small portion of the lands of the public domain." (Dionysius of Halicarnassus, II. 62.)—" Similar measures are attributed to Tullius Hostilius and Ancus Martius." (Dionysius of Halicarnassus, III. 1, 48.)—"As soon as he was mounted on the throne, Servius Tullius distributed the lands of the public domain to the thetes (mercenaries) of the Romans." (Dionysius of Halicarnassus, IV. 13.)

[127] Romulus, according to Dionysus of Halicarnassus, sent two colonies to Cænina and Antemnæ, having taken from those two towns the third of their lands. (II. 35.)—In the year 252, the Sabines lost ten thousand acres (jugera) of arable land. (Dionysius of Halicarnassus, V. 49.)—A treaty concluded with the Hernici, in 268, deprived them of two-thirds of their territory. (Titus Livius, II. 41.)—"In 413, the Privernates lost two-thirds of their territory; in 416, the Tiburtines and Prenestines lost a part of their territory." (Titus Livius, VIII. I, 14.)—"In 563, P. Cornelius Scipio Nasica took from the Boians nearly half their territory." (Titus Livius, XXXVI. 39.)

[128] Appian, Civil Wars, I. vii.—This citation, though belonging to a posterior date, applies nevertheless to the epoch of which we are speaking.

[129] "Servius published an edict to oblige all who had appropriated, under the title of usufructuaries or proprietors, the lands of the public domain, to restore them within a certain time, and, by the same edict, the citizens who possessed no heritage were ordered to bring him their names." (Dionysius of Halicarnassus, IV. 10.)

[130] "We need not be astonished if the poor prefer the lands of the domain to be distributed (to all the citizens) than to suffer that a small number of the most shameless should remain sole possessors. But if they see that they are taken from those who gather their revenues, and that the public is restored to the possession of its domain, they will cease to be jealous of us, and the desire to see them distributed to each citizen would diminish, when it shall be demonstrated to them that these lands will be of greater utility when possessed in common by the Republic." (Year of Rome 268.) (Speech of Appius, Dionysius of Halicarnassus, VIII. 73.)

[131] Agannius Urbicus, De Controversiiss agrorum, in the Gromatici veteres, ed. Lachmann, vol. I, p. 82.

[132] Titus Livius, II. 48.

[133] "Lucius Æmilius said that it was just that the common goods should be shared among all the citizens, rather than leave the enjoyment of them to a small number of individuals; that in regard to those who had seized upon the public lands, they ought to be sufficiently satisfied that they had been left to enjoy them during so long a time without being disturbed in their possession, and that if afterwards they were deprived of them, it ill became them to be obstinate in retaining them. He added that, besides the public law acknowledged by general opinion, and according to which the public goods are common to all the citizens, just as the goods of individuals belong to those who have acquired them legitimately, the Senate was obliged, by a special reason, to distribute the lands to the people, since it had passed an ordinance for that purpose already seventeen years ago." (Dionysius of Halicarnassus, IX. 51.)

[134] Titus Livius, III. 31.—Dionysius of Halicarnassus, X. 33 et seq.

[135] "The plebeians complain loudly that their conquests have been taken from them; that it is disgraceful that, having conquered so many lands from the enemy, not the least portion of it remains to them; that the ager publicus is possessed by rich and influential men who take the revenue unjustly, without other title than their power and unexampled acts of violence. They demand finally that, sharing with the patricians all the dangers, they may also have their share in the advantages and profit derived from them." (Year of Rome 298.) (Dionysius of Halicarnassus, X. 36.)

[136] "The moment would have been well chosen, after having taken vengeance on the seditious, to propose, in order to soothe people's minds, the partition of the territory of the Bolani; they would thus

have weakened the desire for an agrarian law which would expel the patricians from the public estates they had unjustly usurped. For it was an indignity which cut the people to the heart, this rage of the nobility to retain the public lands they occupied by force, and, above all, their refusal to distribute to the people even the vacant lands recently taken from the enemy, which, indeed, would soon become, like the rest, the prey of some of the nobles," (Year of Rome 341.) (Titus Livius, IV. 51.)

[137] Titus Livius, V. 30.

[138] Titus Livius, VI. 21.—It appears that the Pontine Marshes were then very fertile, since Pliny relates, after Licinius Mucianus, that they included upwards of twenty-four flourishing towns. (Natural History, III. v. 56, edit. Sillig.)

[139] Titus Livius, VI. 35-42.—Appian, Civil Wars, I. 8.

[140] See the remarkable work of M. A. Mace, Sur les Lois Agraires, Paris, 1846.

[141] Roman Colonies.—Second period: 244-416

> *Lavici* (Labicum) (336). Latium. (*Via Lavicana.*) *La Colonna.*
> *Vitellia* (359). The Volscians. (*Via Prænestina.*) Uncertain. *Civitella* or *Valmontone.*
> *Satricum* (370). The Volscians. Banks of the Astura. *Casale di Conca,* between *Anzo* and *Velletri.*
>
> Latin Colonies.—Second period: 244-416.
>
> *Antium* (287). Volscians. *Torre d'Anzio* or *Porto d'Anzio.*
> *Suessa Pometia* (287). Near the Pontine Marshes. Disappeared at an early period.
> *Cora.* Volscians (287). *Cori.*
> *Signia* (259). Volscians. *Segni.*
> *Velitræ* (260). Volscians. *Velletri.*
> *Norba* (262). Volscians. Near the modern village of *Norma.*
> *Ardea* (312). Rutuli. *Ardea.*
> *Circeii* (361). Aurunces. *Monte Circello: San Felice* or *Porto di Paolo.*
> *Satricum* (369). Volscians. *Casale di Conca.*
> *Sutrium* (371). Etruria. (*Via Cassia.*) *Sutri.*
> *Setia* (372) Volscians. *Sezze.*
> *Nepete* (381). Etruria. *Nepi.*

[142] It is thus that we see, in 416, each poor citizen receiving two jugera, taken from the land of the Latins and their allies. In 479, after the departure of Pyrrhus, the Senate caused lands to be distributed to those who had fought against the King of Epirus. In 531, the Flaminian

law, which Polybius accuses wrongly of having introduced corruption into Rome, distributed by head the Roman territory situated between Rimini and the Picenum; in 554, after the capture of Carthage, the Senate made a distribution of land to the soldiers of Scipio. For each year of service in Spain or Africa, each soldier received two jugera, and the distribution was made by decemvirs. (Titus Livius, XXXI. 49.)

[143] "Marcus Valerius demonstrated to them that prudence did not permit them to refuse a thing of small importance to citizens who, under the government of the kings, had distinguished themselves in so many battles for the defence of the Republic." (Year of Rome 256.) (Dionysius of Halicarnassus, V. 65.)—"On one hand, the plebeians pretended not to be in a condition to pay their debts; they complained that, during so many years of war, their lands had produced nothing, that their cattle had perished, that their slaves had escaped or had been carried away in the different incursions of the enemies, and that all they possessed at Rome was expended for the cost of the war. On the other hand, the creditors said that the losses were common to everybody; that they had suffered no less than their debtors; that they could not consent to lose what they had lent in time of peace to some indigent citizens in addition to what the enemies had taken from them in time of war." (Year of Rome 258.) (Dionysius of Halicarnassus, VI. 22.)

[144] Those who pleaded the causes of individuals were nearly all senators, and exacted for this service very heavy sums under the title of fees. (Titus Livius, XXXIV. 4.)

[145] "The days following, Servius Tullius caused a report to be drawn up of the insolvent debtors, of their creditors, and of the respective amount of their debts. When this was prepared, he caused counters to be established in the Forum, and, in public view, repaid the lenders whatever was due to them." (Dionysius of Halicarnassus, IV. 10.)

[146] "Servilius caused a herald to proclaim that all persons were forbidden to seize, sell, or retain in pledge the goods of Romans who served against the Volsci, or to take away their children, or any one of their family, for any contract whatever." — "An old man complains that his creditor has reduced him to slavery: he declares loudly that he was born free, that he had served in all the campaigns as long as his age permitted, that he was in twenty-eight battles, where he had several times gained the prize of valour; but that, since the times had become bad, and the Republic was reduced to the last extremity, he had been constrained to borrow money to pay the taxes. After that, he added, having no longer wherewith to pay my debts, my merciless creditor has reduced me to slavery with my two children, and, because I expostulated slightly

when he ordered me to do things which were too difficult, caused me to be disgracefully beaten with several blows." (Year of Rome 259.) (Dionysius of Halicarnassus, VI. 29.)—"The creditors contributed to the insurrection of the populace, they cast aside all moderation, but threw their debtors into prison, and treated them like the slaves whom they would have bought for money." (Year of Rome 254.) (Dionysius of Halicarnassus, V. 53.)

[147] "The poor, especially those who were not in condition to pay their debts, who formed the greatest number, refused to take arms, and would hold no communication with the patricians, until the Senate should pass a law for the abolition of debts." (Year of Rome 256.) (Dionysius of Halicarnassus, V. 63.)

[148] Dionysius of Halicarnassus, V. 64.

[149] Appius Claudius Sabinus expressed an opinion quite contrary to that of Marcus Valerius: he said that "there could be no doubt that the rich, who were not less citizens than the poor, and who held the first rank in the Republic, occupied the public offices, and had served in all the wars, would take it very ill if they discharged their debtors from the obligation of paying what was due." (Year of Rome 256.) (Dionysius of Halicarnassus, V. 66.)

[150] It results from the testimony of Polybius, Dionysius of Halicarnassus, Livy, Florus, and Eutropius, that at the moment of the fall of Tarquinius Superbus, the domination of Rome extended over all Latium, over the greater part of the country of the Sabines, and even as far as Ocriculum (Otricoli) in Umbria; that Etruria, the country of the Hernici, and the territory of Cære (Cervetri), were united with the Romans by alliances which placed them, with regard to these, in a state of subjection.

The establishment of the consular government was, for the peoples subject to Rome, the signal of revolt. In 253, all the peoples of Latium were leagued against Rome; with the victory of Lake Regillus, in 258, that is, fourteen years after the overthrow of the Tarquins, the submission of Latium began, and it was finished by the treaty concluded by Spurius Cassius with the Latins in the year of Rome 268. The Sabines were only finally reduced by the consul Horatius in 305. Fidenæ, which had acknowledged the supremacy of Tarquin, was taken in the year 319, then taken again, after an insurrection, in 328. Anxur (*Terracina*) was only finally subjected after the defeat of the Volsci; and Veii and Falerium only fell under the power of the Romans in the year 358 and 359. Circci, where a Latin colony had been established in the times of the kings, only received a new one in the year 360. Cære was reunited to the Roman territory in the year 364, and it was only at the time of the Gallic invasion that Antium and Ecetra were finally annexed to the Roman territory. In 408, the capture of Satricum, at the entrance of the country of the Volscians, prevented that people from supporting an insurrection which had already begun among the Latins. In 411, the whole plain of Latium was occupied by Roman citizens or allies, but in the mountains there remained Volscian and Latin cities which were independent and secretly enemies. Nevertheless it may be said that, towards that period, the Republic had re-conquered the territory which it possessed under the kings, although Rome had again, in 416, to suppress a last insurrection of the Latins.

[151] Mommsen, Roman History, I., p. 241, 2nd edit.

[152] In fourteen years, from 399 to 412, the patricians allowed only six plebeians to arrive at the consulship.

[153] Titus Livius, X. 23.

[154] Titus Livius, X. 9.

[155] "Who does not see clearly that the vice of the dictator (Marcellus) in the eyes of the augurs was that he was a plebeian?" (Titus Livius, VIII. 23.—Cicero, De Divinatione, II. 35, 37; De Legibus, II. 13.)

[156] The consuls and prætors could only assemble the comitia, command the armies, or give final judgment in civil affairs, after having been invested with the imperium and with the right of taking the auspices (jus auspiciorum) by a curiate law.

[157] Second Oration on the Agrarian Law, 9.

[158] Titus Livius, IV. 3.

[159] If a citizen refused to give his name for the recruitment, his goods were confiscated; if he did not pay his creditors, he was sold for a slave. Women were forbidden the use of wine. (Polybius, VI. 2.)—The number of guests who could be admitted to feasts was limited. (Athenæus, VI. p. 274.)—The magistrates also, on entering on office, could not accept invitations to dinner, except from certain persons who were named. (Aulus Gellius, II. 24.—Macrobius, II. 13.)—"Marriage with a plebeian or a stranger was surrounded with restrictive measures; it was forbidden with a slave or with a freedman. Celibacy, at a certain age, was punished with a fine." (Valerius Maximus, II. ix. 1.)—There were regulations also for mourning and funerals. (Cicero, De Legibus, II. 24.)

[160] Aulus Gellius, IV. 12.

[161] Plutarch, Cato the Censor, 23.

[162] Historians have always assigned as the northern frontier of Italy, under the Republic, the River Macra, in Etruria; but that the limit was farther south is proved by the fact that Cæsar went to Lucca to take his winter quarters; this town, therefore, must have been in his command and made part of Cisalpine Gaul. Under Augustus, the northern frontier of Italy extended to the Macra.

[163] Speech of Cæsar to the Senate, reported by Sallust. (Conspiracy of Catilina, li.)

[164] This paragraph, expressing with great clearness the policy of the Roman Senate, is extracted from the excellent Hist. Romaine of M. Duruy, t. I., c. xi.

[165] As, for example, to put the wife in complete obedience to her husband; to give the father absolute authority over his children, etc.

[166] In the origin, the municipia were the allied towns preserving their autonomy, but engaging to render to Rome certain services (munus); whence the name of municipia. (Aulus Gellius, XVI. 13.)

[167] To be able to enjoy the right of city, it was necessary to be domiciliated at Rome, to have left a son in his majority in the municipium, or to have exercised there a magistracy.

[168] Aul. Gellius, XVI. xiii.—Paulus Diaconus, on the word Municipium, p. 127.

[169] In this category were sometimes found municipia of the third degree, such as Cære. (See Festus, under the word Præfecturæ, p. 233.)— Several of these towns, such as Fundi, Formiæ, and Arpinum, obtained in the sequel the right of suffrage; they continued, however, by an ancient usage, to be called by the name of præfecturæ, which was also applied by abuse to the colonies.

[170] Socius et amicus (Titus Livius, XXXI. 11).—Compare Dionysius of Halicarnassus, VI. 95; X. 21.

[171] With Carthage, for example. (Polybius, III. 22.—Titus Livius, VII. 27; IX. 19, 43.)

[172] Thus with the Latins. "Ut eosdem quos populus Romanus amicos atque hostes habeant." (Titus Livius, XXXVIII. 8.)

[173] Cicero, Oration for Balbus, xvi.

[174] The freedmen were, in fact, either Roman citizens, or Latins, or ranged in the number of the dediticii; slaves who had, while they were in servitude, undergone a grave chastisement, if they arrived at freedom, obtained only the assimilation to the dediticii. If, on the contrary, the slave had undergone no punishment, if he was more than thirty years of age, if, at the same time, he belonged to his master according to the law of the quirites, and if the formalities of manumission or affranchisement exacted by the Roman law had been observed, he was a Roman citizen. He was only Latin if one of these circumstances failed. (Institutes of Gaius, I. § 12, 13, 15, 16, 17.)

[175] "Valerius sent upon the lands conquered from the Volsci a colony of a certain number of citizens chosen from among the poor, both to serve as a garrison against the enemies, and to diminish at Rome the party of the seditious." (Year of Rome 260.) (Dionysius of Halicarnassus, VI. 43.)—This great number of colonies, by clearing the population of Rome of a multitude of indigent citizens, had maintained tranquillity (452). (Titus Livius, X. 6.)

[176] Modern authors are not agreed on this point, which would require a long discussion; but we may consider the question as solved in the sense of our text by Madvig, Opuscula, I. pp. 244-254.

[177] "There the people (populus) named their magistrates; the duumviri performed the functions of consuls or prætors, whose title they sometimes took (Corpus Inscriptionum Latin., passim); the quinquennales corresponded to the censors. Finally, there were questors and ediles. The Senate, as at Rome, was composed of members, elected for life, to the number of a hundred; the number was filled up every five years (lectio senatus)." (Tabula Heracleensis, cap. x. et seq.)

[178] A certain number of colonies figure in the list given by Dionysius of Halicarnassus of the members of the confederacy (V. 61).

[179] Pliny, Natural History, III. iv. § 7.

[180] Because it named its magistrates, struck money (Mommsen, Münzwesen, p. 317), privileges refused to the Roman colonies, and preserved its own peculiar laws according to the principle: "Nulla populi Romani lege adstricti, nisi in quam populus eorum fundus factus est." (Aulus Gellius, XVI. xiii. 6.—Compare Cicero, Oration for Balbus, viii. 21.)

[181] Cicero, Oration on the Agrarian Law, ii. 27.

[182] Titus Livius, XXVII. 9.

[183] Florus, I. 16.

[184] Titus Livius, VIII. 13, 14.

[185] Titus Livius, VIII. 14. These towns had the right of city without suffrage; of this number were Capua (in consideration of its knights, who had refused to take part in the revolt), Cumæ, Fundi, and Formiæ.

[186] Velleius Paterculus, I. 15.

[187] Titus Livius, VIII. 14.

[188] Titus Livius, VIII. 14, et seq.—Valerius Maximus, VI. ii. 1.

[189] Florus, I. 16.

[190] Titus Livius, VIII. 26; XXI. 49; XXII. 11.

[191] "Eam solam gentem restare." (Titus Livius, VIII. 27.)

[192] Cicero, de Officiis, iii. 30.

[193] Titus Livius, IX. 24, 28.

[194] Diodorus Siculus, XX. 36.—Titus Livius, IX. 29.

[195] Diodorus Siculus, XIX. 101.

[196] Titus Livius, IX. 31.

[197] Diodorus Siculus, XX. 35.

[198] Now Lago di Vadimone or Bagnaccio, situated on the right bank and three miles from the Tiber, between that river and the Lake Ciminius, about the latitude of Narni.

[199] Titus Livius, IX. 43.—Cicero, Oration for Balbus, 13.—Festus, under the word Præfecturæ, p. 233.

[200] Titus Livius, IX. 45.—Diodorus Siculus, XX. 101.

[201] Titus Livius, IX. 45; X. 3, 10.

[202] Appian, Samnite Wars, § vii., p. 56, edit. Schweighæuser.

[203] Diodorus Siculus, XIX. 10.

[204] Titus Livius, X. 11, et seq.

[205] Titus Livius, X. 22, et seq.—Polybius, II. 19.—Florus, I. 17.

[206] Volsiniæ, Perusia, and Arretium. (Titus Livius, X. 37.)

[207] Orosius, III. 22.—Zonaras, VII. 2.—Eutropius, II. 9.

[208] Velleius Paterculus, I. 14.—Festus, under the word Præfecturæ, p. 233.

[209] Dionysius of Halicarnassus, Excerpta, p. 2335, edit. Schweighæuser.

[210] Polybius, II. 19, 24.

[211] Titus Livius, Epitome, XII., XIII., XIV.—Plutarch, Pyrrhus, et seq.—
Florus, I. 18.—Eutropius, II. 11, et seq.—Zonaras, VIII. 2.

[212] Valerius Maximus, III. vii. 10.

[213] Appian (Samnite Wars, X. iii., p. 65) says that Pyrrhus advanced as far
as Anagnia.

[214] Cicero, Oration for Balbus, xxii.

[215] Titus Livius, Epitome, XIV.—Orosius, IV. 3.

[216] Florus, I. 20.

[217] Titus Livius, Epitome, XV.—Fasti Capitolini, an. 487.

[218] Roman Colonies.—Third period: 416-488.

> *Antium* (416). A maritime colony (Volsci). *Torre d'Anzo* or *Porto d'Anzo.*
> *Terracina* (425). A maritime colony (Aurunci). (*Via Appia.*) *Terracina.*
> *Minturnæ* (459). A maritime colony (Aurunci). (*Via Appia.*) Ruins near
> *Trajetta.*
> *Sinuessa* (459). A maritime colony (Campania). (*Via Appia.*) Near
> *Rocca di Mondragone.*
> *Sena Gallica* (465). A maritime colony (Umbria, *in agro Gallico*). (*Via
> Valeria.*) *Sinigaglia.*
> *Castrum Novum* (465). A maritime colony
> (Picenum). (*Via Valeria.*) *Giulia Nuova.*
>
> Latin Colonies.
>
> *Cales* (420). Campania. (*Via Appia.*) *Calvi.*
> *Fregellæ* (426). Volsci. In the valley of the Liris. *Ceprano*(?). Destroyed
> in 629.
> *Luceria* (440). Apulia. *Lucera.*
> *Suessa Aurunca* (441). Aurunci. (*Via Appia.*) *Sessa.*
> *Pontiæ* (441). Island opposite Circeii. *Ponza.*
> *Saticula* (441). On the boundary between Samnium and Campania.
> *Prestia*, near *Santa Agata de' Goti.* Disappeared early.
> *Interamna* (Lirinas) (442). Volsci. *Terame.* Not inhabited.
> *Sora* (451). On the boundary between the Volsci and the Samnites.
> *Sora.* Already colonised in a previous period.
> *Alba Fucensis* (451). Marsi. (*Via Valeria.*) *Alba*, a village near *Avezzano.*
> *Narnia* (455). Umbria. (*Via Flaminia.*) *Narni.* Strengthened in 555.
> *Carseoli* (456). Æqui. (*Via Valeria.*) *Cerita, Osteria del Cavaliere*, near
> *Carsoli.*

*Venusia* (463). Frontier between Lucania and Apulia. (*Via Appia*.) *Venosa*. Re-fortified in 554.

*Adria* (or *Hatria*) (465). Picenum. (*Via Valeria* and *Salaria*). *Adri*.

*Cosa* (481). Etruria or Campania. *Ansedonia*(?), near *Orbitello*. Re-fortified in 557.

*Pæstum* (481). Lucania, *Pesto*. Ruins.

*Ariminum* (486). Umbria, *in agro Gallico*. (*Via Flaminia*.) *Rimini*.

*Beneventum* (486). Samnium. (*Via Appia*.) *Benevento*.

[219] Campanians: Stellatina. Etruscans: Tromentina, Sabatina, Arniensis, in 367 (Titus Livius, VI. 5). Latins: Mœcia, and Scaptia, in 422 (Titus Livius, VIII. 17). Volsci: Pomptina, and Publilia, in 396 (Titus Livius, VII. 15). Ausones: Ufentina and Falerna, in 436 (Titus Livius, IX. 20). Æqui: Aniensis and Terentina, in 455 (Titus Livius, X. 9). Sabines: Velina and Quirina, in 513 (Titus Livius, Epitome, XIX.).

[220] At the beginning of each consular year, the magistrates or deputies of the towns were obliged to repair to Rome, and the consuls there fixed the contingent which each of them was to furnish according to the list of the census. These lists were drawn up by the local magistrates, who sent them to the Senate, and were renewed every five years, except in the Latin colonies, where they seem to have taken for a constant basis the number of primitive colonists.

[221] The country of the Samnites, among others, was completely cut up by these domains.

[222] Titus Livius places in the mouth of the consul Decius, in 452, these remarkable words: "Jam ne nobilitatis quidem suæ plebeios pœnitere" (Titus Livius, X. 7); and later still, towards 538, a tribune expresses himself thus: "Nam plebeios nobiles jam eisdem initiatos esse sacris, et contemnere plebem, ex quo contemni desierint a patribus, cœpisse." (Titus Livius, XXII. 34.)

[223] Titus Livius, XIV. 48.

[224] We have the proof of this in the condemnation of those who transgressed the law of Stolo. (Titus Livius, X. 13.)

[225] Valerius Maximus, IV. iii. 5.—Plutarch, Cato, iii.

[226] Valerius Maximus, IV. iii. 6.

[227] Valerius Maximus, IV. iii. 9.

[228] Titus Livius, IX. 46.

[229] "The goods of the debtor, not his body, should be responsible for the debt. Thus all the captured citizens were free, and it was forbidden for ever to put in bonds a debtor." (Titus Livius, VIII. 28.)

[230] Ignorance of the calendar, and of the method of fixing the festivals, left to the pontiffs alone the knowledge of the days when it was permitted to plead.

[231] "The lawyers, for fear that their services might become useless in judicial proceedings, invented certain formulæ, in order to make themselves necessary." (Cicero, Pro Murena, xi.)

[232] Titus Livius, Epitome, XI.—Pliny, XVI. x. 37.

[233] Cicero, Brutus, C. xiv.—Zonaras, Annales, VIII. 2.

[234] "You see here all the principal senators who set you the example. They will partake with you the fatigues and perils of war, although the laws and their age exempt them from carrying arms." (Speech of the Dictator Postumius to his troops; Dionysius of Halicarnassus, VI. 9.)

[235] Titus Livius, X., XII. 49.

[236] Valerius Maximus, II. viii. 4, 7.

[237] Plutarch, Flamininus, xxviii.

[238] Aur. Victor, Ill. Men, xxxvi. and xxvii.

[239] Titus Livius, IX. 10

[240] "A sedition was already rising between the patricians and the people, and the terror of so sudden a war (with the Tiburtini) stifled it." (Titus Livius, VII. 12.)—"Appius Sabinus, to prevent the evils which are an inevitable consequence of idleness, joined with want, determined to occupy the people in external wars, in order that, gaining their living for themselves, by finding on the lands of the enemy abundant provisions which were not to be had in Rome, they might render at the same time some service to the State, instead of troubling at an unseasonable moment the senators in the administration of affairs. He said that a town which, like Rome, disputed empire with all others, and was hated by them, could not want a decent pretext for making war; that, if they would judge the future by the past, they would see clearly that all the seditions which had hitherto torn the Republic had never arrived except in time of peace, when people no longer feared anything from without." (Dionysius of Halicarnassus, IX. 43.)

[241] Claudius made war thus in Umbria, and took the town of Camerinum, the inhabitants of which he sold for slaves. (See Valerius Maximus, VI. v. § 1.—Titus Livius, Epitome, XV.)—Camillus, after the capture of Veii, caused the free men to be sold by auction. (Titus Livius, V. 22.)—In 365, the prisoners, the greater part Etruscans, were sold in the

same manner. (Titus Livius, VI. 4.)—The auxiliaries of the Samnites, after the battle of Allifæ (447), were sold as slaves to the number of 7,000. (Titus Livius, IX. 42.)

[242] "The military port alone contained two hundred and twenty vessels." (Appian, Punic Wars, VIII. 96, p. 437, ed. Schweighæuser.)

[243] Appian, Punic Wars, VIII. 95, p. 436.

[244] Strabo, XVII. iii. § 15.

[245] Appian, Punic Wars, VIII. 130, p. 490.

[246] 5,820,000 francs [£232,800]. (Appian, Punic Wars, CXXVII. 486.) Following the labours of MM. Letronne, Böckh, Mommsen, &c., we have admitted for the sums indicated in the course of the present work the following reckonings:—

The *as* of copper = 1/10 deniers = 5 centimes.
The *sestertius* = 0.975 grammes = 19 centimes.
The *denarius* = 3.898 grammes = 75 centimes.
The *great sestertius* = 100,000 sestertii = 19,000 francs [£760].
The Attic or Euboic *talent*, of 26 kilogrammes, 196 grammes = 5,821 francs [£232 16s.].
The *mina*, of 436 grammes = 97 francs.
The *drachma*, of 4.37 grammes = 97 centimes.
The *obolus*, of 0.73 grammes = 16 centimes.

The Æginetic talent was equivalent to 8,500 Attic drachmas (37 kilogrammes, 2 gr.) = 8,270 francs [£330 16s.]. The Babylonic silver talent is of 33 kilogrammes, 42 = 7,426 francs [£297]. (See, for details, Mommsen, *Römisches Münzwesen*, pp. 24-26, 55. Hultsch, *Griechische und Römische Metrologie*, pp. 135-137.)

[247] Nearly 700,000 francs [£28,000]. (Athenæus, XII. lviii. 509, ed. Schweighæuser.)

[248] Strabo, XVII. iii. § 15.

[249] Scylax of Caryanda, Periplus, p. 51 et seq., ed. Hudson.

[250] See the work of Heeren, Ideen über die Politik, den Verkehr, und den Handel der vornehmsten Völker der alten Welt, Part I., Vol. II., secs. v. and vi., p. 163 et seq., 188 et seq. 3rd edit.

[251] Athenæus informs us that Polemon had composed an entire treatise on the mantles of the divinities of Carthage. (XII. lviii. 541.)

[252] Herodotus, VII. 145.—Polybius, I. 67.—Titus Livius, XXVIII. 41.

[253] Reckoning, after Titus Livius, her troops at the time of the second Punic War, we find a force of 291,000 foot and 9,500 horse. (Titus Livius, Books XXI. to XXIX.)

[254] Carthage, under certain circumstances, could make daily a hundred and forty shields, three hundred swords, five hundred lances, and a thousand darts for catapults. (Strabo, XVII. iii. § 15.)

[255] Strabo, XVII. iii. § 15.

[256] In 513, 3,200 Euboic talents (18,627,200 francs [£745,088]); in 516, 1,200 talents (6,985,200 francs [£279,408]); in 552, 10,000 talents (58,210,000 francs [£2,328,400]). Scipio, the first Africanus, brought, besides this, 123,000 pounds weight of gold from this town. (Polybius, I. 62, 63, 88; XV. 18.—Titus Livius, XXX. 37, 45.)

[257] Aristotle, Politics, VII. iii. § 5.—Polybius, I. 72.

[258] Diodorus Siculus, XX. 17.

[259] Pliny, Natural History, V. iii. 24.

[260] Scylax of Caryanda, Periplus, p. 49. edit. Hudson.

[261] Polybius, XII. 3.

[262] Titus Livius, XXXIV. 62.

[263] 58,200 francs (£2,328). (Titus Livius, XXII. 31.)

[264] Sallust, Jugurtha, xix.

[265] Pliny, citing this fact, throws doubt upon it. (Natural History, V. i. 8.)—See the Periplus of Hanno, in the collection of the minor Greek geographers.

[266] Strabo, III. v. § 3.

[267] Strabo, III. ii. § 1.

[268] Pliny, Natural History, III. iii. 30.—Strabo, III. ii. § 8.

[269] Strabo, III. ii. § 3.—Pliny, III. i. 3; XXXIII. vii. 40.

[270] Above 25,000 francs [£1,000]. (Strabo, III. ii. § 10.)

[271] 767,695 pounds of silver and 10,918 pounds of gold, without reckoning what was furnished by certain partial impositions, sometimes very heavy, such as those of Marcolica, one million of sestertii (230,000 francs [£9,200]), and of Certima, 2,400,000 sestertii (550,000 francs [£22,000]). (See Books XXVIII. to XLVI. of Titus Livius.) Such were the resources of Spain, even in the smallest localities, that in 602, C. Marcellus imposed on a little town of the Celtiberians (Ocilis) a

contribution of thirty talents of silver (about 174,600 francs [£6,984]); and this contribution was regarded by the neighbouring cities as most moderate. (Appian, Wars of Spain, VI. xlviii. 158, ed. Schweighæuser.) Posidonius, cited by Strabo (III. iv., p. 135), relates that M. Marcellus extorted from the Celtiberians a tribute of six hundred talents (about 3,492,600 francs [£139,704]).

[272] A fabulous people, spoken of by Homer. (Athenæus, I. xxviii. 60, edit. Schweighæuser.)

[273] Diodorus Siculus, V. 34, 35.

[274] Pliny, Natural History, XIX. i. 10.

[275] In the time of Hannibal, this town was one of the richest in the peninsula. (Appian, Wars of Spain, xii. 113.)

[276] Strabo, III. iv. § 2.

[277] Polybius, XXXIV., Fragm., 8.

[278] The medimnus of barley (52 litres) sold for one drachma (97 centimes); the medimnus of wheat, 9 oboli (about 1 franc 45 centimes). (The medium value of 52 litres in France is 10 francs.) A metretes of wine (39 litres) was worth one drachma (97 centimes); a hare, one obolus (16 centimes); a goat, one obolus (16 centimes); a lamb, from 3 to 4 oboli (50 to 60 centimes); a pig of a hundred pounds weight, 5 drachmas (4 francs 85 centimes); a sheep, 2 drachmas (1 franc 95 centimes); an ox for drawing, 10 drachmas (9 francs 70 centimes); a calf, 5 drachmas (4 francs 85 centimes); a talent (26 kilogrammes) of figs, 3 oboli (45 centimes).

[279] Strabo, III. ii. § 1.

[280] Appian, Wars of Spain, i. 102.—Pompey, in the trophies which he raised to himself on the coast of Catalonia, affirmed that he had received the submission of eight hundred and seventy-seven oppida. (Pliny, Natural History, III. iii. 18.)—Pliny reckoned two hundred and ninety-three in Hispania Citerior, and a hundred and seventy-nine in Bætica. (Natural History, III. iii. 18.)—We may, moreover, form an idea of the number of inhabitants by the amount of troops raised to resist the Scipios. In adding together the numbers furnished by the historians, we arrive at the fearful total of 317,700 men killed or made prisoners. (Titus Livius, XXX. et. seq.)—In 548, we see two nations of Spain, the Ilergetes and the Ausetani, joined with some other petty tribes, put on foot an army of 30,000 infantry and 4,000 cavalry. (Titus Livius, XXIX. 1.)—We remark fifteen to twenty others whose forces are

equal or superior. After the battle of Zama, Spain furnished Hasdrubal with 50,000 footmen and 4,500 horsemen. (Titus Livius, XXVIII. 12, 13.)—Cato has no sooner appeared with his fleet before Emporiæ, than an army of 40,000 Spaniards, who could only have been collected in the surrounding country, is ready prepared to resist him. (Appian, Wars of Spain, 40, p. 147.)—In Lusitania itself, a country of which the population was much less, we see Servius Galba and Lucullus killing 12,500 men. (Appian, Wars of Spain, 58, 59, p. 170 et. seq.)—Although laid waste and depopulated by these two generals, the country, at the end of a few years, furnished again to Viriathus considerable forces.

[281] Titus Livius, XXII. 20.

[282] Strabo, IV. i. § 11; ii. § 14; iii. § 3.

[283] See what M. Amedée Thierry says, Hist. des Gaul., II. 134 et seq. 3d edit.

[284] Pliny, XXI. 31.

[285] Diodorus Siculus, V. 26.—Athenæus, IV. xxxvi. 94.

[286] Demosthenes, Thirty-second Oration against Zenothemis, 980, edit. Bekker.

[287] Strabo, IV. vi. § 2, 3.

[288] Diodorus Siculus, V. xxxix.

[289] See Titus Livius, XXXII. to XLII.

[290] See Strabo, V. i. § 10, 11.

[291] Strabo, V. i. § 12.

[292] Gold was originally very abundant in Gaul; but the mines whence it was extracted, and the rivers which carried it, must have been soon exhausted, for the quality of the Gaulish gold coins becomes more and more abased as the date of their fabrication approaches that of the Roman conquest.

[293] Strabo, V. i. § 7.—Titus Livius, X. 2.

[294] Pliny, Natural History, III. xvi. 119.—Martial, Epigr., IV. xxv.— Antonine Itinerary, 126.

[295] Pliny, Natural History, XXXVII. iii. § 11.

[296] Small vessels, quick sailers, and rapid in their movements, excellent for piracy; also called liburnæ, from the name of the people who employed them.

[297] Polybius, II. 5.

[298] Titus Livius, XLI. 2, 4, 11.

[299] Polybius, II. 8.

[300] Titus Livius, XXXIX. 5.

[301] Pliny, XXXV. 60.

[302] Polybius, XXII. 13.

[303] Polybius, XXX. xv. § 5.—Titus Livius, XLV. 34.

[304] Plutarch, Flamininus, 2.

[305] Polybius, V. 9.

[306] Aristides, Panathen., p. 149.

[307] Pausanias, Attica, xxviii.

[308] Plutarch, Sylla, 20.

[309] Pausanias, Laconia, xi. We must further mention the famous temple of bronze of Minerva, the two gymnasia, and the Platanistum, a spacious place where the competitions of the youths took place, (Pausanias, Laconia, xiv.)

[310] Stephanus of Byzantium, under the word Λακεδαίμων, p. 413.

[311] Pausanias, Laconia, xxi.

[312] Titus Livius, XXXIV. 29.

[313] Pausanias, Arcadia, xlv.

[314] Pausanias, Arcadia, xli. Thirty-six columns out of thirty-eight are still standing.

[315] Pliny, Natural History, XIX. i. 4.

[316] Pausanias, Elis, II. 23 and 24.

[317] Pausanias, Elis, I. ii.

[318] Strabo, VIII. § 10, 19.

[319] Pausanias, Corinth, xxviii. 1.

[320] Pausanias, Corinth, xxvii.

[321] "Goods were not obliged to make the circuit by Corinth; a direct road crossed the isthmus in the narrowest part, and they had even established there a system of rollers on which vessels of small tonnage were transported from one sea to the other." (Strabo, VIII. ii. § 3.— Polybius, IV. 19.)

[322] Pausanias, Attica, ii.

[323] Cicero, De Republica, II. 4.—Strabo, VIII. vi. § 20.

[324] Strabo, VIII. vi. § 23.—Pliny, Natural History, XXXV. x. § 36.

[325] Arrian, Expedition of Alexander, I. xvi. 4.—Velleius Paterculus, I. 40.—Plutarch, Alexander, 16.

[326] Athenæus, VI. 272.

[327] Titus Livius, XXXII. 16.

[328] Titus Livius, XLV. 18, 29.

[329] Titus Livius, XLII. 12.

[330] "These were, in money, 100 talents (582,000 francs [£23,280]), and in wheat, 100,000 artabæ (52,500 hectolitres); and also considerable quantities of ship-building timber, tar, lead, and iron." (Polybius, V. 89.)

[331] About 1,164,000 francs [£46,560]. Perseus had promised him twice as much. (Titus Livius, XLII. 67.)

[332] Titus Livius, XLIV. 42.

[333] Titus Livius, XLIV. 41.

[334] Titus Livius, XLV. 82.

[335] Titus Livius, XLV. 33.

[336] It lasted three days: the first was hardly sufficient to pass in review the 250 chariots laden with statues and paintings; the second day, it was the turn of the arms, placed on cars, which were followed by 3,000 warriors carrying 750 urns full of money; each, borne by four men, contained three talents (the whole amounting to more than 13 millions of francs [£520,000]). After them came those who carried vessels of silver, chased and wrought. On the third day appeared in the triumphal procession those who carried the gold coins, with 77 urns, each of which contained three talents (the total about 17 millions [£680,000]); next came a consecrated cup, of the weight of ten talents, and enriched with precious stones, made by order of the Roman general. All this preceded the prisoners, Perseus and his household; and, lastly, came the car of the triumphant general. (Plutarch, Paulus Æmilius, 32, 33.)

[337] Titus Livius, XLV. 40.

[338] Polybius, IV. 38, 44, 45.

[339] Aristotle, Politics, VI. 4, § 1.—Ælian, Various Histories, III. 14.

[340] Strabo, VII. vi. § 2; XII. iii. § 11.

[341] Cicero, Oration for the Law Manilia, vi.

[342] Plutarch, Sylla, xxv.

[343] Especially the fish called pelamydes, objects of research throughout Greece. (Strabo, VII. vi. § 2; XII. iii. § 11, § 19.)

[344] Strabo, XII. iii. § 19.

[345] Strabo, XII. iii. § 13. Gadilonitis extended to the south-west of Amisus (Samsoun).

[346] Polybius, V. 44, 55.—Ezekiel xxvii. 13, 14.

[347] Xenophon, Retreat of the Ten Thousand, V. v. 34.—Homer, Iliad, II. 857.

[348] Strabo, XII. iii. § 19.

[349] There passed in the procession a statue of gold of the King of Pontus, six feet high, with his shield set with precious stones, twenty stands covered with vases of silver, thirty-two others full of vases of gold, with arms of the same metal, and with gold coinage; these stands were carried by men followed by eight mules loaded with golden beds, and after whom came fifty-six others carrying ingots of silver, and a hundred and seven carrying all the silver money, amounting to 2,700,000 drachmas (2,619,000 francs [£104,760]). (Plutarch, Lucullus, xxxvii.)

[350] Plutarch, Lucullus, xxiii.

[351] Strabo, XII. iii. § 13, 14.

[352] Appian, War against Mithridates, lxxviii.

[353] Plutarch, Lucullus, xiv.

[354] See what is reported by Plutarch (Lucullus, xxix.) of the riches and objects of art of every species with which Tigranocerta was crammed.

[355] Appian, Wars of Mithridates, xiii. p. 658; xv. p. 662; xvii. p. 664.

[356] Appian, Wars of Mithridates, xvii. 664. Lesser Armenia furnished 1,000 horsemen. Mithridates had a hundred and thirty chariots armed with scythes.

[357] Strabo, XII. iv. § 2.—Stephanus Byzantinus, under the word Νικομήδειον.—Pliny, Natural History, V. xxxii. 149.

[358] Strabo, XII. iii. § 6.

[359] Appian, Wars of Mithridates, xvii.

[360] Strabo, XII. v. § 7.

[361] Strabo (XII. v. § 3) tells us that Pessinus was the greatest mart of the province.

[362] Titus Livius, XXXVIII. 23.

[363] Titus Livius, XXXVIII. 26.

[364] Diodorus Siculus, XVIII. 16.

[365] Strabo, XII. ii. § 10.

[366] About 3,500,000 francs [£140,000]. (Titus Livius, XXXVIII. 37.) See Appian, Wars of Syria, xlii.—"Demetrius obtained soon afterwards a thousand talents (5,821,000 francs [£232,840]) from Olophernes for having established him on the throne of Cappadocia." (Appian, Wars of Syria, xlvii.)

[367] Strabo, XII. ii. 7, 8.

[368] Falkener, Ephesus: London, 1862.

[369] Natural History, V. xxx. 126.

[370] It was thence that the fleets of the kings of Pergamus put to sea. (Titus Livius, XXXVIII. 40; XLIV. 28.)

[371] The name of Pergamus is preserved in our modern languages in the word "parchment" (pergamena), which was used to designate the skin which was prepared in that town to serve as paper, after the Ptolemies had prohibited the exportation of Egyptian papyrus.

[372] Attalus I., King of Pergamus, gave to the Sicyonians 11,000 medimni of wheat. (Titus Livius, XXXII. 40.)—Eumenius II. lent 80,000 to the Rhodians. (Polybius, XXXI. xvii. 2.)

[373] Strabo, XII. viii. § 11.

[374] Athenæus, XV. xxxviii. 513, ed. Schweighæuser.

[375] The Sea of Marmora took its name from these quarries of marble.

[376] Κυξικηνοί στατῆρες, whence the word sequins.

[377] Strabo, XIII. i. § 23.

[378] Strabo, XV. iii. § 22.

[379] Titus Livius, XXXII. 16; XXXVI. 43.

[380] Titus Livius, XXXVII. 8.

[381] The petty king Moagetes, who reigned at Cibyra, in Phrygia, gave a hundred talents and 10,000 medimni of corn (Polybius, XXII. 17.—Titus Livius, XXXVIII. 14 and 15); Termessus, fifty talents; Aspendus,

Sagalassus, and all the cities of Pamphylia, paid the same (Polybius, XXII. 18 and 19); and the towns of this part of Asia contributed, at the first summons of the Roman general, for about 600 talents (3,500,000 francs [£140,000]); they also delivered to him about 60,000 medimni of corn.

[382] Titus Livius, XXXIX. 6.

[383] Manlius, although he had been despoiled on his way home of a part of his immense booty by the mountaineers of Thrace, displayed, at his triumph, crowns of gold to the weight of 212 pounds, 220,000 pounds of silver, 2,103 pounds of gold, more than 127,000 Attic tetradrachms, 250,000 cistophori, and 16,320 gold coins of Philip. (Titus Livius, XXXIX. 7.)

[384] Appian, Wars of Mithridates, lxiii.

[385] Arrian, Campaigns of Alexander, I. xx. § 3.—Diodorus, XVII. 23.

[386] Strabo, XIV. ii. 565.

[387] Strabo, XIV. i. § 6.

[388] Pliny, Natural History, V. 31.

[389] Strabo, XIV. iii. § 6.

[390] Titus Livius, XXXVIII. 39.

[391] Scylax, Periplus, 39, ed. Hudson.—Dio Cassius, XLVII. 34.

[392] Herodotus, I. 176.

[393] Pliny, Natural History, V. 28.

[394] Strabo, XIV. v. § 2.

[395] Strabo, XIV. v. § 2.

[396] Tarsus had still naval arsenals in the time of Strabo (XIV. v. § 12 et seq.).

[397] Arrian, Anabasis, II. 5.

[398] Polybius, XXII. 7.

[399] Seleucus founded sixteen towns of the name of Antiochia, five of the name of Laodicea, nine of the name of Seleucia, three of the name of Apamea, one of the name of Stratonicea, and a great number of others which equally received Greek names. (Appian, Wars of Syria, lvii. 622.)—Pliny (Natural History, VI. xxvi. 117) informs us that it was the Seleucides who collected into towns the inhabitants of Babylonia, who before only inhabited villages (vici), and had no other cities than Nineveh and Babylon.

[400] Pliny (Natural History, VI. 26, 119) mentions one of these towns which was 70 stadia in circuit, and in his time was reduced to a mere fortress.

[401] Strabo, XVI. ii. § 5.—Pausanias, VI. ii. § 7.

[402] John Malalas, Chronicle, VIII. 200 and 202, ed. Dindorf.

[403] Strabo, XVI. ii. § 4.

[404] Strabo, XVI. ii. § 6.

[405] Strabo, XVI. ii. § 10.

[406] It was raised on a terrace a thousand feet long by three hundred feet broad, and was built with stones 70 feet long.

[407] The empire of Seleucus comprised seventy-two satrapies. (Appian, Wars of Syria, lxii. 630.)

[408] Polybius, X. 27. Ecbatana paid to Antiochus III. a tribute of 4,000 talents (Attic talents = 23,284,000 francs [£931,360]), the produce of the casting of silver tiles which roofed one of its temples. Alexander the Great had already carried away those of the roof of the palace of the kings.

[409] The country of Gerra, among the Arabians, paid 500 talents to Antiochus (Attic talents = 2,910,500 francs [£116,420]). (Polybius, XIII. 9.)—There was formerly a great quantity of gold in Arabia. (Job xxviii. 1, 2.—Diodorus Siculus, II. 50.)

[410] Strabo, XVI. iii. § 3.

[411] Strabo, XI. ii. 426 et seq.

[412] Pliny, Natural History, VI. 11.

[413] Polybius, V. 54. If, as is probable, Babylonian talents are intended, this would make about 7,426,000 francs [£297,040], Seleucia, on the Tigris, was very populous. Pliny (Natural History, VI. 26) estimates the number of its inhabitants at 600,000. Strabo (XVI. ii. § 5) tells us that Seleucia was even greater than Antioch. This town, which had succeeded Babylon, appears to have inherited a part of its population.

[414] In 565, Antiochus III. gives 15,000 talents (Euboic talents = 87,315,000 francs [£3,492,600]). (Polybius, XXI. 14.—Titus Livius, XXXVIII. 37.) In the treaty of the following year, the Romans stipulated for a tribute of 12,000 Attic talents of the purest gold, payable in twelve years, each talent of 80 pounds Roman (69,852,000 francs [£2,794,080]). (Polybius, XXII. 26, § 19.) In addition to this, Eumenes was to receive 359 talents (2,089,739 francs [£83,589]), payable in five years (Polybius, XXII. 26, § 20).—Titus Livius (XXXVIII. 38) says only 350 talents.

[415] The father of Antiochus, Seleucus Callinicus, sent to the Rhodians 200,000 medimni of wheat (104,000 hectolitres). (Polybius, V. 89.) In 556, Antiochus gave 540,000 measures of wheat to the Romans. (Polybius, XXII. 26, § 19.)

[416] According to Strabo (XV. 3), wheat and barley produced there a hundredfold, and even twice as much, which is hardly probable.

[417] Strabo, XVI. 2.

[418] Athenæus, XII. 35, p. 460, ed. Schweighæuser.

[419] Polybius, XXXI. 3.—There were seen in these festivals a thousand slaves carrying silver vases, the least of which weighed 1,000 drachmas; a thousand slaves carrying golden vases and a profusion of plate of extraordinary richness. Antiochus received every day at his table a crowd of guests whom he allowed to carry away with them in chariots innumerable provisions of all sorts. (Athenæus, V. 46, p. 311, ed. Schweighæuser.)

[420] Polybius, V. 79.

[421] Titus Livius, XXXVII. 37.

[422] Strabo, XVI. 2.

[423] Polybius, V. 70.

[424] Titus Livius, XXXIII. 41.—Polybius, V. 59.—Strabo, XVI. 2.

[425] Strabo, XVI. 2.

[426] Strabo, XIV. 5.

[427] In 558, Antiochus sent to sea a hundred covered vessels and two hundred light ships. (Titus Livius, XXXIII. 19.)—It is the greatest Syrian fleet mentioned in these wars. At the battle of Myonnesus, the fleet commanded by Polyxenus was composed of ninety decked ships (574). (Appian, Wars of Syria, 27.)—In 563, before the final struggle against the Romans, that prince had forty decked vessels, sixty without decks, and two hundred transport ships. (Titus Livius, XXXV. 43.)—Finally, the next year, a little before the battle of Magnesia, Antiochus possessed, not including the Phœnician fleet, a hundred vessels of moderate size, of which seventy had decks. (Titus Livius, XXXVI. 43; XXXVII. 8.)—This navy was destroyed by the Romans.

[428] Herodotus, II. 177.—Diodorus Siculus, I. 31.

[429] A measure great enough to make thirty loaves. (Franz, Corpus Inscript. Græcarum, III. 303.—Polybius, V. 79.)

[430] Böckh, Staatshaushaltung der Athener, I. xiv. 15.

[431] Flavius Josephus, Jewish Antiquities, XII. 4.

[432] Athenæus, V. p. 203.

[433] Appian (Preface, § 10).—We may, nevertheless, judge from the following data of the enormity of the sums accumulated in the treasuries of the kings of Persia. Cyrus had gained, by the conquest of Asia, 34,000 pounds weight of gold coined, and 500,000 of silver. (Pliny, XXXIII. 15.)—Under Darius, son of Hystaspes, 7,600 Babylonian talents of silver (the Babylonian talent = 7,426 francs [£297]) were poured annually into the royal treasury, besides 140 talents devoted to the pay of the Cilician cavalry, and 360 talents of gold (14,680 talents of silver), paid by the Indies. (Herodotus, III. 94.)—This king had thus an annual revenue of 14,500 talents (108 millions of francs [£4,320,000]). Darius carried with him in campaign two hundred camels loaded with gold and precious objects. (Demosthenes, On the Symmories, p. 185, xv. p. 622, ed. Müller.)—Thus, according to Strabo, Alexander the Great found in the four great treasuries of that king (at Susa, Persia, Pasargades, and Persepolis) 180,000 talents (about 1,337 millions of francs [£53,480,000]).

[434] Polybius, V. 89.

[435] Strabo, XVII. 1.

[436] Strabo, XVII. 1.

[437] Strabo, XVI. 4; XVII.

[438] Strabo, XVII. 1.

[439] Diodorus Siculus, III. 43.

[440] Appian, Preface, § 10.—In 537, at Raphia, the Egyptian army amounted to 70,000 foot, 5,000 cavalry, and 73 elephants. (Polybius, V. 79; see also V. 65.)—Polybius, who gives us these details, adds that the pay of the officers was one mina (97 francs [£3 17s. 7d.]) a day. (XIII. ii.)

[441] Theocritus, Idylls, XVII. lines 90-102.—Athenæus (V. 36, p. 284) and Appian, Preface, § 10, give the details of this fleet.—Ptolemy IV. Philopator went so far as to construct a ship of forty ranges of rowers, which was 280 cubits long and 30 broad. (Athenæus, V. 37, p. 285.)

[442] Herodotus, IV. 199. The plateau of Barca, now desert, was then cultivated and well watered.

[443] The most important object of commerce of the Cyrenaica was the silphium, a plant the root of which sold for its weight in silver. A

kind of milky gum was extracted from it, which served as a panacea with the apothecaries and as a seasoning in the kitchen. When, in 658, Cyrenaica was incorporated with the Roman Republic, the province paid an annual tribute in silphium. Thirty pounds of this juice, brought to Rome in 667, were regarded as a miracle; and when Cæsar, at the beginning of the civil war, seized upon the public treasury, he found in the treasury chest 1,500 pounds of silphium locked up with the gold and silver. (Pliny, XIX. 3.)

[444] Diodorus Siculus, III. 49.—Herodotus, IV. 169.—Athenæus, XV. 22, p. 487; 38, p. 514.—Strabo, XVII. iii. 712.—Pliny, Natural History, XVI. 33; XIX. 3.

[445] Pindar, Pythian Odes, IV. 2.—Athenæus, III. 58, p. 392.

[446] Diodorus Siculus, XVII. 49.

[447] Aristotle, Politics, VII. 2, § 10.

[448] Josephus, Jewish Antiquities, XIII. 12, § 2, 3.

[449] Ælian, History of Animals, V. lvi.—Eustathius, Comment. on Dionysius Periegetes, 508, 198, edit. Bernhardy.

[450] Strabo, XIV. 6.—Pliny, Natural History, XXXIV. 2.

[451] Virgil, Æneid, I. 415.—Statius, Thebais, V. 61.

[452] Strabo, X. 4.

[453] Polybius, XIII. 8.

[454] Cretan mercenaries are found in the service of Flamininus in 557 (Titus Livius, XXXIII. 3), in that of Antiochus in 564 (Titus Livius, XXXVII. 40), in that of Perseus in 583 (Titus Livius, XLII. 51), and in the service of Rome in 633.

[455] Iliad, II. 656.

[456] Polybius, XXX. 7, year of Rome 590.

[457] Strabo, XIV. 2. The town of Rhoda in Spain, establishments in the Baleares, Gela in Sicily, Sybaris and Palæopolis in Italy, were Rhodian colonies.

[458] This happened especially at the epoch when the famous Colossus of Rhodes fell, and when the town was violently shaken by an earthquake. Hiero, tyrant of Syracuse, Ptolemy, king of Egypt, Antigonus Doson, king of Macedonia, and Seleucus, king of Syria, sent succours to the Rhodians. (Polybius, V. 88, 89.)

[459] We see, in fact, with what care the Rhodians spared their allies on the coast of the Pontus Euxinus. (Polybius, XXVII. 6.)

[460] Polybius, IV. 38.

[461] Strabo, VII. 4.

[462] Titus Livius, XXXIII. 18.

[463] During the siege of Rhodes, Demetrius had formed the design of delivering to the flames all the public buildings, one of which contained the famous painting of Ialysus, by Protogenes. The Rhodians sent a deputation to Demetrius to ask him to spare this masterpiece. After this interview, Demetrius raised the siege, sparing thus at the same time the town and the picture. (Aulus Gellius, XV. 31.)

[464] In 555, twenty ships; in 556, twenty vessels with decks; in 563, twenty-five ships with decks, and thirty-six vessels. This last fleet of thirty-six vessels was destroyed, and yet the Rhodians were able to send to sea again, the same year, twenty vessels. In 584 they had forty vessels. (Titus Livius, XXXI. 46; XXXII. 16; XXXVI. 45; XXXVII. 9, 11, 12; XLII. 45.)

[465] Pliny, XXXIV. 17.

[466] Strabo, XIV. 2.

[467] Athenæus, XII. 35, p. 461.

[468] Titus Livius, XXIII. 34.

[469] Titus Livius, XXIII. 40.

[470] Titus Livius, XLI. 12, 17, 28.—The number of 80,000 men whom the Sardinians lost in the campaign of T. Gracchus, in 578 and 579, was given by the official inscription which was seen at Rome in the temple of the goddess Matuta. (Titus Livius, XLI. 28.)

[471] Festus, p. 322, edit. O. Müller.—Titus Livius, XLI. 21.

[472] See Heeren, vol. IV. sect. I. chap. ii.—Polybius, I. 79.—Strabo, V. ii. 187.—Diodorus Siculus, V. 15.—Titus Livius, XXIX. 36.

[473] Titus Livius, XXX. 38.

[474] Strabo, V. 2.

[475] Diodorus Siculus, V. 14.—The Corsicans having revolted, in 573, had 2,000 slain. (Titus Livius, XL. 34.)—In 581, they lost 7,000 men, and had more than 1,700 prisoners. (Titus Livius, XLII. 7.)

[476] Strabo, V. 2.

[477] Pliny, Natural History, III. 6.

[478] Diodorus Siculus, V. 13.—In 573, the Corsicans were taxed by the Romans at 1,000,000 pounds of wax, and at 200,000 in 581. (Titus Livius, XL. 34; XLII. 7.)

[479] Cicero, Second Oration against Verres, II. ii. 74.—The oxen furnished hides, employed especially for the tents; the sheep, an excellent wool for clothing.

[480] Cicero, Second Oration against Verres, II. III. 70.

[481] Titus Livius, XXV. 31.

[482] Polybius, I. 17, 18.

[483] Polybius, IX. 27.—Strabo, VI. 2.

[484] See what is said by Titus Livius (XXIX. 26) and Polybius (I. 41, 43, 46).—Florus, II. 2.

[485] See the work of the Duke of Serra di Falco, Antichità della Sicilia.

[486] Thus the Jupiter of the Capitol and the Italic Juno, at least in their official worship, were the protectors of virtuous morals and punished the wicked, while the Phœnician Moloch and Hercules, worshipped at Carthage, granted their favours to those who made innocent blood run upon their altars. (Diodorus Siculus, XX. 14.)—See the remarkable figures of Moloch holding a gridiron destined for human sacrifices. (Alb. della Marmora, Sardinian Antiquities, pl. 23, 53, tom. ii. 254.)

[487] Polybius, I. 7, 11.

[488] Polybius, I. 16.—Zonaras, VIII. 16 et seq.

[489] We have seen before that Rome, after the capture of Antium (Porto d'Anzo), had already a navy, but she had no galleys of three ranks or five ranks of oars. Nothing, therefore, is more probable than the relation of Titus Livius, who states that the Romans took for a model a Carthaginian quinquireme wrecked on their coast. In spite of the advanced state of science, we have not yet obtained a perfect knowledge of the construction of the ancient galleys, and, even at the present day, the problem will not be completely solved until chance furnishes us with a model.

[490] The Romans employed the triremes of Tarentum, Locri, Elea, and Naples to cross the Strait of Messina. The use of quinquiremes was entirely unknown in Italy.

[491] Polybius, I. 20, 21.

[492] Each vessel carried 300 rowers and 120 soldiers, or 420 men, which makes, for the Carthaginian fleet, 147,000 men, and, for the Roman fleet, 138,600. (Polybius, I. 25 and 26.)

[493] Nearly thirteen millions of francs [£520,000]. (Polybius, I. 62.)

[494] Polybius, I. 36.

[495] Valerius Maximus, V. i. 2.

[496] Titus Livius, Epitome, XIX.

[497] Polybius, III. 10, 27, 28.

[498] The Sardinians owed their civilisation to the Phœnicians; the Sicilians had received theirs from the Greeks. This difference explains the attachment of the first for Carthage, and the repulsion of the others for the Punic rule.

[499] Polybius, II. 4, 5, 10.

[500] Hahn, Albanesische Studien.

[501] Florus, II. 5.—Appian, Wars of Illyria, 7.

[502] Polybius, II. 11 et seq.

[503] Titus Livius, Epitome, XX., year of Rome 533.—Orosius, IV. xiii.

[504] Polybius, III. 16 et seq.

[505] A people situated between the Rhone and the Alps. (Polyb., II. 22, 34.)

[506] "It was not Rome alone that the Italians, terrified by the Gaulish invasion, believed they had thus to defend; they understood that it was their own safety which was in danger." (Polybius, II. 23.)

[507] The following, according to Polybius (II. 24), was the number of the forces of Italy:—

| | FOOT. | | HORSE. |
|---|---|---|---|
| Two consular armies, each of two legions, of 5,200 foot and 300 cavalry | 20,800 | | 1,200 |
| Allied troops | 30,000 | | 2,000 |
| Sabines and Etruscans | 50,000 | more than | 4,000 |
| Umbrians and Sarsinates, inhabitants of the Apennines | 20,000 | | — |
| Cenomani and Veneti | 30,000 | | — |
| At Rome | 20,000 | | 1,500 |
| Allies (of the reserve) | 30,000 | | 2,000 |
| Latins | 80,000 | | 5,000 |
| Samnites | 70,000 | | 7,000 |
| Iapygians and Messapians | 50,000 | | 16,000 |

| | | |
|---|---|---|
| Lucanians | 30,000 | 3,000 |
| Marsi, Marrucini, Frentani, and Vestinic | 20,000 | 4,000 |
| In Sicily and at Tarentum, two legions of 4,200 foot and 200 horse | 8,400 | 400 |
| Roman and Campanian citizens | 250,000 | 23,000 |
| | 699,200 | 69,100 |

[508] See the Memoir of Zumpt, Stand der Bevölkerung im Alterthum. Berlin, 1841.

[509] Polybius, III. 30.

[510] Titus Livius, XXI. 7.

[511] Appian, Wars of Spain, 10.

[512] Polybius, III. 90.—"The allies had till then remained firm in their attachment." (Titus Livius, XXII. 61.)—"This fidelity which they have preserved towards us in the midst of our reverses." (Speech of Fabius, Titus Livius, XXII. 39.)

[513] There were among the Roman troops Samnite cavalry. (Titus Livius, XXVII. 43.)

[514] Titus Livius, XXII. 49; XXIII. 12.—"In the second Punic war, the use of rings had already become common; otherwise it would have been impossible for Hannibal to send three modii of rings to Carthage." (Pliny, XXXIII. 6.)—We read in Appian: "The tribunes of the soldiers wear the gold ring, their inferiors have it of ivory." (Punic Wars, VIII. cv.)

[515] "The Greek towns, inclined to maintain their alliance with Rome." (Titus Livius, XXIV. 1.)—Even in Bruttium, the small town of Petelia defended itself against Hannibal with the greatest energy; the women fought like the men. (Appian, VII. 29.)

[516] Eutropius, III. 6.

[517] Titus Livius, XXVI. 1.

[518] Titus Livius, XXIV. 14.

[519] "The Oppian law, proposed by the tribune C. Oppius, under the consulship of Q. Fabius and Tiberius Sempronius (539), in the height of the second Punic war, forbad the women to have for their use more than half an ounce of gold, to wear dresses of different colours, &c., to

be driven or carried about Rome, within a radius of seven miles, in a chariot drawn by horses, except to attend the public sacrifices." This law, being only temporary, was revoked, in spite of the opposition of P. Cato, in 559. (Titus Livius, XXXIV. 1, 6.)

[520] Valerius Maximus, I. i. 15.

[521] "It was in his cavalry that Hannibal placed all his hopes." (Polybius, III. 101.)—"Hannibal's cavalry alone caused the victories of Carthage and the defeats of Rome." (Polybius, IX. 3.)—"The loss of 500 Numidians was felt more by Hannibal than any other check, and from that time he had no longer the superiority in cavalry which had previously given him so much advantage" (543). (Titus Livius, XXVI. 38.)

[522] "Hannibal remembered how he had failed before Placentia." (Titus Livius, XXVII. 39.)

[523] Titus Livius, XXIII. 15 and 18.—Hannibal reduced by famine the fortresses of Casilinum and Nuceria; as to the citadel of Tarentum, it resisted five years, and could not be taken by force. (Titus Livius, XXVII. 25.)

[524] "Hannibal descends towards Naples, having at heart to secure a maritime place to receive succours from Africa." (Titus Livius, XXIII. 15.)

[525] Polybius, III. 106.

[526] Appian, Wars of Hannibal, 26.

[527] Plutarch, Marcellus, 11, 33.

[528] Titus Livius, XXVII. 49.

[529] Appian, Wars of Hannibal, 54.

[530] In 536, Rome had at sea 220 quinquiremes and 20 small vessels (Titus Livius, XXI. 17), with which she protected efficiently the coasts of Sicily and Italy. (Titus Livius, XXI. 49, 51.)—In 537, Scipio, with 35 vessels, destroyed a Carthaginian fleet at the mouth of the Ebro (Titus Livius, XXII. 19), and the consul Servilius Geminus effected a landing in Africa with 120 vessels, in order to prevent Carthage from sending reinforcements to Hannibal. (Titus Livius, XXII. 31.)—In 538, the fleet of Sicily is reinforced with 25 ships. (Titus Livius, XXII. 37.)—In 539, Valerius Lævinus had 25 vessels to protect the coast of the Adriatic, and Fluvius the same number to watch the coast of Ostia (Titus Livius, XXIII. 32) after which the Adriatic fleet, raised to 55 sails, is sent to act as a check upon Macedonia. (Titus Livius, XXIII. 38.)—The same year, the fleet of Sicily, under Titus Otacilius, defeats the Carthaginians.

(Titus Livius, XXIII. 41.)—In 540 Rome has 150 vessels (Titus Livius, XXIV. 11) this year and the following, the Roman fleet defends Apollonia, attacked by the King of Macedonia, and lands troops which ravage the territory of Utica. The effective strength of the Roman fleet appears not to have varied until 543, the epoch at which Greece again required the presence of 50 Roman ships and Sicily 100. (Titus Livius, XXVI. 1.)—In 544, 20 vessels were stationed in the waters of Rhegium, to secure the passage of provisions between Sicily and the garrison of Tarentum. (Titus Livius, XXVI. 39.)—In 545, 30 sails are detached from the fleet of Sicily to cruise before that town. (Titus Livius, XXVII. 22.)— In 546, Carthage was preparing a formidable fleet of 200 sails (Titus Livius, XXVII. 22); Rome opposes it with 280 ships: 30 defend the coast of Spain, 50 guard Sardinia, 50 the mouths of the Tiber, 50 Macedonia, 100 are stationed in Sicily, ready to make a descent in Africa, and the Carthaginian fleet is beaten before Clupea. (Titus Livius, XXVII. 29.)— Lastly, in 547, a second victory gained by Valerius Lævinus renders the sea entirely free. (Titus Livius, XXVIII. 4.)

[531] "The Carthaginians, occupied only with the care of maintaining themselves in Spain, sent no succour to Hannibal, as though he had had nothing but successes in Italy." (Titus Livius, XXVIII. 12.)

[532] Titus Livius, XXIII. 13 and 41.

[533] Appian, Wars of Hannibal, liv.

[534] In 540, Rome had on foot eighteen legions; in 541, twenty legions; in 542 and 543, twenty-three legions; in 544 and 546, twenty-one; in 547, twenty-three; in 551, twenty; in 552, sixteen; in 553, fourteen; in 554, the number is reduced to six. (Titus Livius, XXIV. 11-44; XXV. 3; XXVI. 1, 28; XXVII. 22, 36; XXX. 2, 27, 41; XXXI. 8.)

[535] "The Romans raised their infantry and cavalry only in Rome and Latium." (Titus Livius, XXII. 37.)

[536] Titus Livius, XXIII. 23.

[537] Q. Metellus said "that the invasion of Hannibal had re-awakened the slumbering virtue of the Roman people." (Valerius Maximus, VII. ii. 3.)

[538] The Senate demanded of thirty colonies men and money. Eighteen gave both with eagerness, namely, Signia, Norba, Saticulum, Brundusium, Fregellæ, Luceria, Venusia, Adria, Firmum, Ariminum, Pontia, Pæstum, Cosa, Beneventum, Isernia, Spoletum, Placentia, and Cremona. The twelve colonies which refused to give any succours, pretending that they had neither men nor money, were: Nepete,

Sutrium, Ardea, Cales, Alba, Carseoli, Cora, Suessa, Setia, Circeii, Narnia, Interamna. (Titus Livius, XXVII. 9.)

[539] "The quarrels and struggles between the two parties ended in the second Punic war." (Sallust, Fragments, I. vii.)

[540] "Four tribes referred it to the Senate to grant the right of suffrage to Formiæ, Fundi, and Arpinum; but they were told in reply that to the people alone belonged the right of suffrage." (Titus Livius, XXXVIII. 36.)

[541] "The annual change of generals was disastrous to the Romans. They recalled all those who had experience in war, as though they had been sent not to fight, but only to practice." (Zonaras, Annales, VIII. 16.)

[542] Titus Livius, XXII. 29.

[543] Titus Livius, XXVII. 5, 7.

[544] Titus Livius, XXXII. 28.

[545] Titus Livius, XXXI. 4, 49.

[546] Titus Livius, XXIV. 49.—Polybius, III. 75.

[547] Zonaras, Annales, VIII. 16.

[548] Titus Livius, XXXIX. 3.

[549] Plutarch, Marcellus, 28.

[550] Titus Livius, XXIII. 30.

[551] Titus Livius, XXXIV. 54.

[552] "Et equites Romanos milites et negociatores." (Sallust, Jugurtha, 65.)

[553] "In 342, a senator and two knights were charged, during a famine, with the provisioning of Rome." (Titus Livius, IV. 3.)

[554] Seminarium senatus. (Titus Livius, XLII. 61.)

[555] Titus Livius, XXIII. 49.—Valerius Maximus, V. vi. 8.

[556] Titus Livius, XXI. 63; XXV. 3.

[557] Valerius Maximus, IV. viii. 2.

[558] Valerius Maximus, IV. v. 1.

[559] They had no deliberative voice, because, according to the public Roman law, no acting magistrate could vote. (See Mommsen, i. 187.)

[560] "Now you have still the comitia by centuries, and the comitia by tribes. As for the comitia by curiæ, they are observed only for the auspices." (Cicero, Second Oration on the Agrarian Law, 9.)

[561] The ancient mode of division by curiæ had lost all significance and ceased to be in use. (Ovid, Fasti, II. 1. 531.) So Cicero says, speaking of them: "The comitia, which are retained only for the sake of form, and because of the auspices, and which, represented by the thirty lictors, are but the appearance of what was before. Ad speciem atque usurpationem vetustatis." (Oration on the Agrarian Law, II. 12.)— In the latter times of the Republic, the curiæ, in the election of the magistrates, had only the inauguration of the flamens, of the king of the sacrifices (rex sacrificulus), and probably the choice of the grand curion (curio maximus). (Titus Livius, XXVII. 8.—Dionysius of Halicarnassus, V. 1.—Aulus Gellius, XV. 27.—Titus Livius, XXVII. vi. 36.)

[562] "Achaia alone had twelve hundred for her share." (Titus Livius, XXXIV. 50.)

[563] Titus Livius, XXXIII. 32.

[564] "The allies exclaimed that the war must be continued, and the tyrant exterminated, without which the liberty of Greece would be always in danger. It would have been better not to have taken up arms at all than to lay them down without having attained the end. The consul replied, 'If the siege of Lacedæmon retained the army a long time, what other troops could Rome oppose to a monarch (Antiochus) so powerful and so formidable?'" (Titus Livius, XXXIV. 33.)

[565] Titus Livius, XXXIII. 12.

[566] Titus Livius, XXXIV. 58.

[567] "Other peoples of Greece had shown in this way a no less culpable forgetfulness of the benefits of the Roman people." (Titus Livius, XXXVI. 22.)

[568] Titus Livius, XXXVII. 45.

[569] Appian, Wars of Hannibal, 43.

[570] Titus Livius, XL. 38; XLII. 22.

[571] Roads from Arezzo to Bologna, from Placentia to Rimini (Titus Livius, XXXIX. 2), and from Bologna to Aquileia.

[572] Roman Colonies—488-608.

> Æsulum (507), or Æsium, according to Mommsen, Jesi in Umbria, on the River Æsis.
> Alsium (507), a maritime colony, Etruria (Via Aurelia); Palo, near Porto.
> Fregenæ (509), a maritime colony, Etruria (Via Aurelia); Torre

*Maccarese.*

*Pyrgi* (before 536), maritime colony, Etruria (*Via Aurelia*); *Santa Severa.*

*Castrum* (555), *Pagus,* near Sylaceum; Bruttium, near *Squillace;* united in 631 to the colony Minerviæ.

*Puteoli* (560), maritime colony, Campania; *Pozzuoli;* Prefecture.

*Vulturnum* (560), maritime colony, Campania; *Castelamare,* or *Castel di Volturno;* Prefecture.

*Liternum* (560), maritime colony, Campania; *Tor di Patria,* near the *Lago di Patria;* Prefecture.

*Salernum* (560), maritime colony, Campania; *Salerno;* decreed three years before.

*Buxentum* (560), maritime colony, Lucania; *Policastro.*

*Sipontum* (560), maritime colony, Apulia; *Santa Maria di Siponto;* recolonised.

*Tempsa* (Temesa) (560), maritime colony, Bruttium; perhaps near to *Torre del Piano del Casale.*

*Croton* (560), maritime colony, Bruttium; *Cotrone.*

*Potentia* (570), maritime colony, Picenum; *Porto di Potenza,* or *di Ricanati.*

*Pisaurum* (570), maritime colony, Gaulish Umbria (*Via Flaminia*); *Pesaro.*

*Parma* (571), Cispadane Gaul (*Via Æmilia*); *Parma;* Prefecture.

*Mutina* (571), Cispadane Gaul (*Via Æmilia*); *Modena;* Prefecture.

*Saturnia* (571), Etruria (centre); *Saturnia.*

*Graviscæ* (573), maritime colony, Etruria (south) (*Via Aurelia*); *San Clementino* or *Le Saline* (?).

*Luna* (577), Etruria (north), (*Via Aurelia*); *Luni,* near *Sarzana.*

*Auximum* (597), maritime colony, Picenum; *Osimo.*

Latin Colonies: 488-608.

*Firmum* (490), Picenum (*Via Valeria*); *Fermo.*

*Æsernia* (491), Samnium; *Isernia.*

*Brundisium* (510), Iapygian Calabria (*Via Egnatia*); *Brindisi.*

*Spoletum* (513), Umbria (*Via Flaminia*); *Spoleto.*

*Cremona* (536), Transpadane Gaul; *Cremona;* reinforced in 560.

*Placentia* (536), Cispadane Gaul (*Via Æmilia*); *Piacenza.*

*Copiæ* (territory of Thurium) (561), Lucania.

*Vibo,* or *Vibona Valentia,* called also *Hipponium,* Bruttium (565, or perhaps 515); *Bibona. Monte-Leone.*

*Bononia* (565), Cispadane Gaul (*Via Æmilia*); *Bologna.*

*Aquileia* (573), Transpadane Gaul; *Aquileia.*

*Carteia* (573), Spain; St. Roque, in the Bay of Gibraltar.

[573] Titus Livius, XXXIX. 26.

[574] Titus Livius, XLI. 19.

[575] Titus Livius, XLI. 22.

[576] Titus Livius, XLII. 62.

[577] Titus Livius, XLI. 5.

[578] Titus Livius, XLV. 21 et seq.

[579] Titus Livius, XLV. 29.

[580] Titus Livius, XLV. 26.

[581] Titus Livius, XLV. 18. — "The laws given to the Macedonians by Paulus Æmilius were so wisely framed, that they seemed to have been made not for vanquished enemies, but for allies whose services it was desired to reward; and in which, after a long course of years, use, the sole reformer of laws, showed nothing defective." (Titus Livius, XLV. 32.)

[582] Polybius, XXX. 10; XXXV. 6.

[583] Titus Livius, XLII. 24. — We see by the following passage in Livy that Masinissa feared the justice of the Senate as against his own interest: "If Perseus had had the advantage, and if Carthage had been deprived of the Roman protection, nothing would then have hindered Masinissa from conquering all Africa." (Titus Livius, XLII. 29.)

[584] Titus Livius, XLV. 13.

[585] Titus Livius, XLV. 42.

[586] Titus Livius, XLV. 44.

[587] Titus Livius, XXXVIII. 45.

[588] Titus Livius, XLI. 7.

[589] Titus Livius, XLIII. 1.

[590] Titus Livius, XXXIX. 3.

[591] "It was commonly said that the masters of the Spanish provinces themselves opposed the prosecution of noble and powerful persons." (Titus Livius, XLIII. 2.)

[592] Valerius Maximus, VI. ix. 10.

[593] Montesquieu, Grandeur et Décadence des Romains, ix. 66.

[594] Scipio reproves the people, who wished to make him perpetual consul and dictator. (Titus Livius, XXXVIII. 56.)

[595] Cato used interpreters in speaking to the Athenians, though he understood Greek perfectly. (Plutarch, Cato the Censor, 18.)—It was an old habit of the Romans, indeed, to address strangers only in Latin. (Valerius Maximus, II. ii. 2.)

[596] Plutarch, Cato the Censor, 8, 25.

[597] Titus Livius, Epitome, XLVIII.—Valerius Maximus, IV. i. 10.

[598] Plutarch, Cato the Censor, 34.—Aulus Gellius, VI. 14.

[599] Titus Livius, Epitome, XLIX.

[600] "Cato barked without ceasing at the greatness of Scipio." (Titus Livius, XXXVIII. 54.)

[601] "P. Cato had a bitter mind, a sharp and unmeasured tongue." (Titus Livius, XXXIX. 40.)

[602] "He declaimed against usurers, and he himself lent out, at high interest, the money which he got from his estates. He condemned the sale of young slaves, yet trafficked in the same under an assumed name." (Plutarch, Cato the Censor, 33.)

[603] Drumann, Geschichte Roms, v., p. 148.

[604] "The last act of his political life was to cause the ruin of Carthage to be determined on." (Plutarch, Cato the Censor, 39.)

[605] Titus Livius, Epitome, XLVIII.

[606] At Carthage, the multitude governed; at Rome, the power of the Senate was absolute. (Polybius, VI. 51.)

[607] Titus Livius, L. 16.

[608] Appian, Punic Wars, 93 et seq.

[609] Justin, XXXIV. 1.—Titus Livius, Epitome, LI.—Polybius, I. 2, 3.

[610] Pausanias, VII. 16.—Justin, XXXIV. 2.

[611] Polybius, XL. 11.

[612] Appian, Wars of Spain, 52.

[613] Eutropius, IV. 7.

[614] The town of Garray, in Spain, situated about a league from Soria, on the Duero, is built on the site of ancient Numantia. (Miñano, Diccionario Geográfico de España.)

[615] Appian, Civil Wars, V. iv. 38.

[616] Velleius Paterculus, II. 20.

[617] Titus Livius, XXXIV. 31.

[618] Titus Livius, XLV. 21.

[619] Titus Livius, VII. 43.

[620] In 555, 585, and 639. (Titus Livius, XLV. 15.)—Aurelius Victor, Illustrious Men, lxii.

[621] The tribune Licinius Crassus proposed, in 609, to transfer to the people the election of the pontiffs, until then nominated by the sacerdotal college. This proposition was adopted only in 650 by the law Domitia, and was anew abolished by Sylla.

[622] Titus Livius, Epitome, LVII.

[623] The expedition against the Scordisci, in 619.

[624] Sallust, Fragm., I. 8.

[625] "Corruption especially had increased, because, Macedonia destroyed, the empire of the world seemed thenceforth assured to Rome." (Polybius, XI. 32.)

[626] Sallust, Fragm., I. 10.

[627] The Romans expatriated themselves to such a degree that, when Mithridates began war, and caused all the Roman citizens spread over his states to be massacred in one day, they amounted to 150,000, according to Plutarch (Sylla, xlviii.); 80,000 according to Memnon (in the Bibliotheca of Photius, Codex CCXXIV. 31) and Valerius Maximus (IX. 2, § 3).—The small town of Cirta, in Africa, could only be defended against Jugurtha by Italiotes. (Sallust, Jugurtha, 26.)

[628] Sallust, Jugurtha, 35.

[629] "And Rome refused to admit in the number of her citizens the men by whom she had acquired that greatness of which she was so proud as to despise the peoples of the same blood and of the same origin." (Velleius Paterculus, II. 15).

[630] See the list of Censuses at Note (^4) of page 256.

[631] Mommsen, Geschichte Roms, I., p. 785.

[632] The lands taken from the town of Leontium were of the extent of thirty thousand jugera. They were, in 542, farmed out by the censors; but at the end of some time, there remained only one citizen of the country among the eighty-four farmers who had installed themselves in them; all the others belonged to the Roman nobility. (Mommsen, ii. 75.— Cicero, Second Prosecution of Verres, III. 46 et seq.)

[633] Plutarch, Tiberius Gracchus, 9.

[634] Diodorus Siculus, Fragments, XXXIV. 3.

[635] Diodorus Siculus, Fragments, XXXVI., p. 147, ed. Schweighæuser.

[636] Strabo, XIV. v. 570.

[637] "Our ancestors feared always the spirit of slavery, even in the case where, born in the field and under the roof of his master, the slave learnt to love him from his birth. But since we count ours by nations, each of which has its manners and gods, or perhaps has no gods, no, this vile and confused assemblage will never be kept under but by fear." (Tacitus, Annales, XIV. 44.)

[638] In 442, the censor Appius Claudius Cæcus causes the freedmen to be inscribed in all the tribes, and allows their sons the entrance to the Senate. (Diodorus Siculus, XX. 36.)—In 450 the censor Q. Fabius Rullianus (Maximus) confines them to the four urban tribes (Titus Livius, IX. 46); towards 530, other censors opened again all the tribes to them; in 534, the censors L. Æmilius Papus and C. Flaminius re-established the order of 450 (Titus Livius, Epitome, XX.); an exception is made in favour of those who have a son of the age of more than five years, or who possess lands of the value of more than 30,000 sestertii (XLV. 15); in 585, the censor Tiberius Sempronius Gracchus expels them from the rustic tribes, where they had been again introduced, and unites them in one sole urban tribe, the Esquiline. (Titus Livius, XLV. 15.—Cicero, De Oratore, I. ix. 38.)—(639.) "The Æmilian law permits freedmen to vote in the four urban tribes." (Aurelius Victor, Illustrious Men, 72.)

[639] Valerius Maximus, VI. 2, § 3.—Velleius Paterculus, II. 4.

[640] "I know Romans who have waited for their elevation to the consulship to begin reading the history of our ancestors and the precepts of the Greeks on military art." (Speech of Marius, Sallust, Jugurtha, 85.)

[641] Plutarch, Tiberius Gracchus, 8.

[642] "Tiberius Gracchus genere, forma, eloquentia facile princeps." (Florus, III. 14.)

[643] Velleius Paterculus, II. 2.—Seneca the Philosopher, De Consolatione, ad Marciam, xvi.

[644] Plutarch, Parallel between Agis and Tiberius Gracchus, iv.

[645] "Pure and just in his views." (Velleius Paterculus, II. 2.)—"Animated by the noblest ambition." (Appian, Civil Wars, I. 9.)

[646] Plutarch, Tib. Gracchus, 9.

[647] "It was at the instigation of the rhetorician Diophanes and the philosopher Blossius that he took counsel of the citizens of Rome most distinguished for their reputation and virtues: among others, Crassus, the grand pontiff; Mucius Scævola, the celebrated lawyer, then consul; and Appius Claudius, his father-in-law." (Plutarch, Tib. Gracchus, 9.)

[648] Plutarch, Tib. Gracchus, 9.

[649] Aulus Gellius relates two passages from the speech of C. Gracchus, which we think ought rather to be ascribed to Tib. Sempronius Gracchus. In one, he has stated the case of a young noble who caused a peasant to be murdered because he made a joke upon him as he passed in a litter; in the other, he told the story of a consul who ordered the most considerable men in the town of Teanum to be beaten with rods, because the consul's wife, going to bathe, had found the baths of the town not clean. (Aulus Gellius, X. 3.)

[650] Appian, Civil Wars, I. 12.

[651] Plutarch, Tib. Gracchus, 16.

[652] Appian, Civil Wars, I. 13.

[653] Plutarch, Tib. Gracchus, 12.

[654] Machiavelli, Discourse on Titus Livius, I. 37.

[655] Plutarch, Tib. Gracchus, 16.

[656] Appian, Civil Wars, I. 14.

[657] Plutarch, Tib. Gracchus, 16, 22.

[658] Plutarch, C. Gracchus, 5.

[659] They interdicted to the magistrates deposed by the people the exercise of all functions, and authorised criminal proceedings against the magistrate who had been the author of the illegal banishment of a citizen. The first of these struck openly at Octavius, whom Tiberius had deposed; the second at Popilius, who, in his prætorship, had banished the friends of Tiberius. (Plutarch, C. Gracchus, 8.)

[660] Appian, Civil Wars, I. 21.

[661] "In 556, the curule ediles Fulvius Nobilior and Flaminius distributed to the people a million of modii of Sicilian wheat, at two ases the bushel." (Titus Livius, XXXIII. 42.)

[662] Appian, Civil Wars, I. 21.—Cicero, Tusculan Disputations, III. 20.

[663] Plutarch, C. Gracchus, 7. According to what Polybius says, the period of service was fixed at ten years, for we read in Plutarch: "Caius

Gracchus said to the censors that, obliged only by the law to ten campaigns, he had made twelve." (Plutarch, C. Gracchus, 4.)

[664] Fifth Period.—Roman Colonies.

*Dertona* (630). In Liguria, now *Tortona*.

*Fabrateria* (630). Among the Volsci (*Latium Majus*). Now *Falvaterra*. A colony of the Gracchi.

*Aquæ Sextiæ* (631); *Aix* (Mouths of the Rhone). Cited erroneously as a colony, was only a *castellum*.

*Minervia* (Scylacium) (632). In Calabria, now *Squillace*. A colony of the Gracchi.

*Neptunia* (Tarentum) (632). In Calabria, now *Taranto*. A colony of the Gracchi.

*Carthago* (Junonia). In Africa. A colony of the Gracchi, was only commenced.

*Narbo Martius* (636). In Narbonnese Gaul, now *Narbonne*. Founded under the influence of the Gracchi.

*Eporedia* (654). In Transpadane Gaul, now *Ivrea*.

In this period Rome ceases to found Latin colonies. The allied countries and the towns of the Latin name began to demand the right of city; the assimilation of Italy, in respect to language and manners, is indeed so advanced that it is superfluous, if not dangerous, to found new Latin cities.

The name of *Colonies of the Gracchi* is given to those which were established essentially for the aid of the poor citizens, and no longer, as formerly, with a strategic view.

Carthage and Narbonne are the first two colonies founded beyond the limits of Italy, contrary to the rule previously followed. The only example which could be mentioned as appertaining to the previous period is that of *Italica,* founded in Spain by Scipio in 548, for those of his veterans who wished to remain in the country. They received the right of city, but not the title of colony. The inhabitants of *Aquæ Sextiæ* must have been in much the same situation.

[665] Velleius Paterculus, II. 6, 15.—Plutarch, C. Gracchus, 7, 8.

[666] Appian, Civil Wars, I. 19 et seq.

[667] Plutarch, C. Gracchus, 9.—Appian, Civil Wars, I. 23.

[668] Sallust, Jugurtha, 27.—Cicero, Oration on the Consular Provinces, 2, 15; Oration for Balbus, 27.

[669] Cicero, Oration for Rabirius, 4.

[670] Plutarch, C. Gracchus, 7, 12.—According to Velleius Paterculus (II. 6), "he would have extended this right to all the peoples of Italy as far as the Alps."

[671] Pseudo-Sallust, First Letter to Cæsar, vii.—Titus Livius, XXVI. 22.

[672] "Aut censoria locatio constituta est, ut Asiæ, lege Sempronia." Cicero, Second Prosecution of Verres, III.—See, on this question, Mommsen, Inscriptiones Latinæ Antiquissimæ, pp. 100, 101.

[673] In the province, the domain of the soil belongs to the Roman people; the proprietor is reputed to have only the possession or usufruct. (Gaius, Institutes, II. 7.)

[674] The senators were reproached with the recent examples of prevarication given by Cornelius Cotta, by Salinator, and by Manius Aquilius, the conqueror of Asia.

[675] Yet the Epitome of Titus Livius (LX.) speaks of 600 knights instead of 300. (See Pliny, Natural History, XXXIII. 7.—Appian, Civil Wars, I. 22.—Plutarch, C. Gracchus, 7.)

[676] Plutarch, C. Gracchus, 12.

[677] Appian, Civil Wars, I. 24.

[678] Appian, Civil Wars, I. 17.

[679] "I am not one of those consuls who think that it is a crime to praise in the Gracchi, as magistrates whose counsels, wisdom, and laws carried a salutary reform into many parts of the administration." (Cicero, Second Speech on the Agrarian Law, 5.)

[680] Appian, Civil Wars, I. 27.

[681] Sallust, Jugurtha, 31.

[682] Sallust, Jugurtha, 5.

[683] "Marius had only made his temper more unyielding." (Plutarch, Sylla, 39.)—"Talent, probity, simplicity, profound knowledge of the art of war, Marius joined to the same degree the contempt of riches and pleasures with the love of glory." (Sallust, Jugurtha, 63.)—Marius was born on the territory of Arpinum, at Cereatæ, now Casamari (the house of Marius).

[684] "Obtained the esteem of both parties." (Plutarch, Marius, 4.)

[685] Sallust, Jugurtha, 85.

[686] Plutarch, Marius, 10.

[687] Plutarch, Marius, 19.

[688] Plutarch, Marius, 11.

[689] Plutarch, Marius, 28.

[690] Plutarch, Marius, 29.

[691] Titus Livius, XXIII. 22.

[692] In our opinion, bellum sociale, or sociorum, has been wrongly translated by "social war," an expression which gives a meaning entirely contrary to the nature of this war.

[693] Velleius Paterculus, II. 15.

[694] List of the different Censuses:—

| Year of Rome | Census | |
|---|---|---|
| 187. | 80,000. | The first census under Servius Tullius. (Titus Livius, I. 44. —Dionysius of Halicarnassus, IV. 22.—Eutropius, I. 7.) |
| 245. | 130,000. | (Plutarch, Publicola, 14.) |
| 278. | 110,000. | (Upwards of). (Dionysius of Halicarnassus, IX. 25.)—119,309 according to Eutropius, I. 14; and 120,000 according to G. Syncellus, 452, ed. Bonn. |
| 280. | 190,000. | (Rather more than). (Dionysius of Halicarnassus, IX. 36.) |
| (Towards 286). | 8,714. | (sic.) (Titus Livius, Epitome, III., ed. O. Jahn.) Correct it to 118,714. |
| 295. | 117,319. | (Titus Livius, III. 24.)—117,219 according to the Epitome. |
| 331. | 120,000. | (Canon of Eusebius, Olympiad lxxxix. 2; 115,000 according to another manuscript.) This passage is wanting in the Armenian translation. |
| 365. | 152,573. | (Pliny, Natural History, XXXIII. 16, ed. Sillig.) |
| 415. | 165,000. | (Eusebius, Olymp. cx. 1.) |
| 422 to 435 | 250,000 | (Titus Livius, IX. 19.—G. Syncellus, Chronographia, 525, has 250,000. the number 260,000.) |

| | | |
|---|---|---|
| 460. | 262,321. | (Titus Livius, X. 47; the Epitome, 272,320.— Eusebius, Olymp. cxxi. 4, writes 270,000; the Armenian translator, 220,000.) |
| 465. | 272,000. | (Titus Livius, Epitome, XI.) |
| 474. | 287,222. | (Titus Livius, Epitome, XIII.) |
| 479. | 292,334. | (Eutropius, II. 10.)—271,234 according to Titus Livius (Epitome, XIV.). |
| 489. | 382,234. | (Titus Livius, Epitome, XVI.) Correct it to 282,234. |
| 502. | 297,797. | (Titus Livius, Epitome, XVIII.) |
| 507. | 241,212. | (Titus Livius, Epitome, XIX.) |
| 513. | 260,000. | (Eusebius, Olymp. cxxxiv. 4.) |
| 534. | 270,213. | (Titus Livius, Epitome, XX.) |
| 546. | 137,108. | (Titus Livius, XXII. 36.)—This enormous difference is wrongly ascribed to the losses experienced in the first five years of the Second Punic war, and Titus Livius states but a very small difference, minor aliquanto numerus quam qui ante bellum fuerat, which would give us cause to believe in an error of the copyist in the number of the census, so that we should read 237,108. |
| 550. | 214,000. | (Titus Livius, XXIX. 37; Fasti Capitolini.)— The censors, as is formally stated, had extended their operations to the armies; in addition to which, many allies and Latins had come to take their domicile in Rome, and had been included in the census. |
| 561. | 143,7 04. | (Titus Livius, XXXV. 9.) Here, also, there doubtless exists an error; we must read 243,704. Perhaps, too, the censors did not include in that number of citizens the soldiers in campaign. |
| 566. | 258, 318. | (Titus Livius, XXXVIII. 36); Epitome, 258,310. Many allies of the Latin name had been included in the census. |

| | | |
|---|---|---|
| 576. | 288, 294. | (Titus Livius, Epitome, XLI.) The figures of the census of preceding and following years lead us to adopt this number, though the manuscripts give only 258,294. |
| 581. | 269, 015. | (Titus Livius, XLII. 10); Epitome, 267,231. "The reason of the inferiority of the census of 581 was," according to Titus Livius, "the edict of the Consul Postumius, in virtue of which those who belonged to the class of the Latin allies were to return, to be taken for their censuses, in their respective towns, according to the edict of the Consul C. Claudius, so that there was not a single person of the allies who was taken at Rome." (Titus Livius, XLII. 10.) |
| 586. | 312, 805. | (Titus Livius, Epitome, XLV.) |
| 591. | 337, 022. | (Titus Livius, Epitome, XLVI.) |
| 595. | 328, 316. | (Titus Livius, Epitome, XLVII.) |
| 600. | 324, 000. | (Titus Livius, Epitome, XLVIII.) |
| 608. | 334, 000. | (Eusebius, Olymp. clviii. 3.) |
| 613. | 327, 442. | (Titus Livius, Epitome, LIV.) |
| 618. | 317, 933. | (Titus Livius, Epitome, LVI.) |
| 623. | 318, 823. | (Titus Livius, Epitome, LIX.) |
| 629. | 394, 726. | (Titus Livius, Epitome, LX.) |
| 639. | 394, 336. | (Titus Livius, Epitome, LXIII.) |
| 667. | 463, 000. | (Eusebius, Olymp. clxxiv. 1.) |
| 684. | 900, 000. | (Titus Livius, Epitome, XCVIII.)—Dio Cassius (XLIII. 25) relates that the census ordered by Cæsar after the civil war had presented a frightful diminution of the number of the population (δεινὴ ὀλιγανθρωπία). Appian (II. 102) says that this number had only reached about the half of the previous census. According to Plutarch (Cæsar, 55), upon 320,000 citizens counted before the war, Cæsar had only found 150,000. They confounded the registers of the distribution of wheat with the lists of the census. (See Suetonius, Cæsar, 41.) |

Augustus says expressly that between the years 684 and 726 there was no census taken, post annum alterum et quadragesimum. (Monument of Ancyra, tab. 2.)—The number of citizens whom he found at that epoch, 4,063,000, is about that which Cæsar might have declared. (Photius, Biblioth., cod. xcvii.—Fragm. Histor., ed. Müller, III. 606.)

| | | |
|---|---|---|
| 726. | 4,063,000. | Closing of the lustrum by Augustus on his sixth consulship, with M. Agrippa for his colleague. (Monument of Ancyra.) |
| 746. | 4,233,000. | Second closure of the lustrum by Augustus alone. (Monument of Ancyra.) |
| 767. | 4,037,000. | According to the Monument of Ancyra; 9,300,000 according to the Chronicle of Eusebius; third closure of the lustrum by Augustus and Tiberius Cæsar, his colleague, under the consulate of Sex. Pompeius and Sex. Appuleius. |

[695] These two words are found on the Italiote medals struck during the war. A denarius in the Bibliothèque Impériale presents the legend ITALIA in Latin characters, and, on the reverse, the name of Papius Mutilus in Oscan characters: ⟩⊦ ⊓ ᴎᴎ ⊓ ⟩, Gai, PAAPI + G (ai fili).

[696] This measure satisfied the Etruscans. (Appian, Civil Wars, I. 49.)

[697] Velleius Paterculus, II. 20.—Appian, Civil Wars, I. 49.

[698] See Note (^1) to page 226.

[699] "P. Sulpicius had sought by his rectitude the popular esteem: his eloquence, his activity, his mental superiority, and his fortune, made of him a remarkable man." (Velleius Paterculus, II. 18.)

[700] Plutarch, Marius, 36.

[701] Plutarch, Sylla, 11.

[702] Appian, Civil Wars, I. 57.

[703] Appian, Civil Wars, I. 59. "Populus Romanus, Lucio Sylla dictatore ferente, comitiis centuriatis, municipiis civitatem ademit." (Cicero, Speech for his House, 30.)

[704] "In conferring upon the peoples of Italy the right of Roman city, they had been distributed into eight tribes, in order that the strength and number of these new citizens might not encroach upon the dignity of the old ones, and that men admitted to this favour might not become more powerful than those who had given it to them. But Cinna, following in the steps of Marius and Sulpicius, announced that he should distribute them in all the tribes; and, on this promise, they arrived in crowds from all parts of Italy." (Velleius Paterculus, II. 20.)

[705] Velleius Paterculus, II. 20.

[706] Plutarch, Pompeius, 3.

[707] Plutarch, Sertorius, 5.

[708] "Cinna counted on that great multitude of new Romans, who furnished him with more than three hundred cohorts, divided into thirty legions. To give the necessary credit and authority to his faction, he recalled the two Marii and the other exiles." (Velleius Paterculus, II. 20.)

[709] Quod parcius telum recepisset. This expression appears to be borrowed from the combats of gladiators, which derived their origin from similar human sacrifices performed at the funerals. (See Cicero, Speech for Roscius Amerinus, 12.—Valerius Maximus, IX. xi. 2.)

[710] Plutarch, Sylla, 6.

[711] Appian, Civil Wars, I. 77.

[712] Appian, Civil Wars, I. 79.

[713] Appian, Civil Wars, I. 95.

[714] Velleius Paterculus, II. 27. The Samnites thus designated the Romans, in allusion to the wolf, the nurse of the founder of Rome. A Samnite medal represents the bull, the symbol of Italy, throwing the wolf to the ground. It bears the name of C. Papius Mutilus, with the title Embratur, an Oscan word corresponding to the Latin imperator.

[715] "Thus terminated two most disastrous wars: the Italic, called also the Social War, and the Civil War; they had lasted together ten years; they had mown down more than a hundred and fifty thousand men, of whom twenty-four had been consuls, seven prætors, sixty ediles, and nearly two hundred senators." (Eutropius, V. 6.)

[716] "Sylla fomented these disorders by loading his troops with largesses and profusions without bounds, in order to corrupt and draw to him the soldiers of the opposite parties." (Plutarch, Sylla, 16.)

[717] Dio Cassius (XXXIV. cxxxvi. § 1) gives the number as 8,000; Appian as 3,000. Valerius Maximus speaks of three legions (IX. 2, § 1).

[718] "A great number of allies and Latins were deprived by one man of the right of city, which had been given to them for their numerous and honourable services." (Speech of Lepidus, Sallust, Fragm., I. 5.)—"We have seen the Roman people, at the proposal of the dictator Sylla, take, in the comitia of centuries, the right of city from several municipal towns; we have seen it also depriving them of the lands they possessed.... As to the right of city, the interdiction did not last even so long as the military despotism of the dictator." (Cicero, Speech for his House, 30.)

[719] Appian, Civil Wars, I. 95.—Velleius Paterculus, II. 28.

[720] Appian, Civil Wars, I. 95.

[721] Strabo, V. iv. 207.

[722] Dio Cassius, XXXIV. 137, § 1.

[723] Dio Cassius, XXXIV. 137.

[724] Valerius Maximus, IX. ii. 1.

[725] Plutarch, Cato of Utica, 21.

[726] Appian, Civil Wars, I. 96.—Titus Livius, Epitome, LXXXIX.

[727] Appian, I. 100.—Velleius Paterculus, II. 31.—The auxilium was the protection accorded by the tribune of the people to whoever claimed it.

[728] Appian, Civil Wars, I. 100 et seq.

[729] Appian, Civil Wars, I. (See, on an inscription raised by the freedmen in honour of the dictator, and which has been discovered in Italy, Mommsen, Inscriptiones Latinæ Antiquissimæ, p. 168.)

[730] Titus Livius, Epitome, LXXXIX.

[731] Appian, Civil Wars, I. 100.

[732] Appian, Civil Wars, I. 100.—In 574, the age required for the different magistracies had already been fixed. (Titus Livius, XL. 44.)

[733] Appian, Civil Wars, I. 101.—Titus Livius, Epitome, LXXXIX.

[734] Aulus Gellius, II. 24.

[735] Cicero, Familiar Letters, III. 6, 8, 10.

[736] Titus Livius, Epitome, LXXXIX.—Tacitus, Annals, XI. 22.—Aurelius Victor, Illustrious Men, lxxv.

[737] Cicero, De Oratore, II. 39.—"A law which, among the ancients, embraced different objects: treasons in the army, seditions at Rome, diminution of the majesty of the Roman people by the bad administration of a magistrate." (Tacitus, Annals, I. 72.)

[738] Appian, Civil Wars, I. 104.

[739] He waited the death of the dictator to rob the treasury of a sum which he owed to the State. (Plutarch, Sylla, 46.)

[740] Appian, Civil Wars, I. 106.

[741] Sylla had taken the name of Fortunate (Felix). (Mommsen, Inscriptiones Latinæ Antiquissimæ, p. 168), or of Faustus, according to Velleius Paterculus.

[742] "It cannot be denied that Sylla had then the power of a king, although he had restored the Republic." (Cicero, Speech on the Report of the Aruspices, 25.)

[743] The celebrated German author, Mommsen (Roman History, III. 15), does not admit this date of 654. He proposes, under correction, the date of 652, for the reason that the ages required for the higher offices of State, since Sylla's time, were thirty-seven for the edileship, forty for the prætorship, forty-three for the consulship, and as Cæsar was curule ædile in 689, prætor in 692, consul in 695, he would, had he been born in 654, have filled each of these offices two years before the legal age.

This objection, certainly of some force, is dispelled by other historical testimony. Besides, we know that at Rome they did not always observe the laws when dealing with eminent men. Lucullus was raised to be chief magistrate before the required age, and Pompey was consul at thirty-four. (Appian, *Civil Wars*, I. 14.)—Tacitus speaks on this matter thus: "With our ancestors this magistracy (the questorship) was the prize of merit only, for every citizen of ability had then the right to aim at these honours; *even age was so little regarded, that extreme youth did not exclude from either the consulship or the dictatorship.*" (*Annals*, XI. 22.)—In any case, if the opinion of M. Mommsen be adopted, the birth of Cæsar must be referred to 651, not 652. For, if he was born in the month of July, 652, he could only be forty-three years of age in the month of

July, 695; and as the nomination of the consuls preceded by six months their entering into office, it would be in the month of July, 694, when he would have attained the legal age, which would bring the date of his birth to the year 651. But Plutarch (*Cæsar*, 69), Suetonius (*Cæsar*, 88), and Appian (*Civil Wars*, II. 149) all agree in saying that Cæsar was fifty-six when he was assassinated on the 15th of March, 710, which fixes his birth in the year 654. On the other hand, according to Velleius Paterculus (II. 43), Cæsar was appointed flamen of Jupiter by Marius and Cinna when scarcely out of infancy, and at Rome infancy ended at about fourteen; and the consulship of Marius and Cinna being in 668, Cæsar, according to our calculation, would then, in fact, have entered on his fourteenth year. The same author adds that he was about eighteen in 672, when he left Rome to escape the proscriptions of Sylla, a new reason for retaining the preceding date.

Cæsar made his first campaign in Asia, at the taking of Mitylene, in 674 (Titus Livius, *Epitome*, LXXXIX.), which makes him twenty at the date of his entrance into the service. According to Sallust (*Catilina*, 49), when Cæsar was nominated grand pontiff in competition with Catulus, he was almost a youth (*adolescentulus*); and Dio Cassius says the same, in nearly the same terms. Doubtless they expressed themselves thus because of the great disproportion in the age of the two candidates. The expression of these authors, although unfitting, nevertheless agrees better with our reckoning, which ascribes thirty-seven years of age to Cæsar, than to the other, which gives him thirty-nine. Tacitus also, as we shall see in a note to a subsequent page, when speaking of the accusation against Dolabella, tends to make Cæsar too young rather than too old.

[744] The family of the Julii was very ancient, and we find personages bearing this name from the third century of Rome. The first of whom history makes mention was C. Julius Julus, consul in 265. There were other consuls of the same family in 272, 281, 307, 324; consular tribunes in 330, 351, 362, 367; and a dictator, C. Julius Julus, in 402; but their filiation is little known. The genealogy of Cæsar begins in a direct line only from Sextus Julius Cæsar, prætor in 546. We borrow the genealogy of the family of the Julii from the History of Rome by Families, by the learned professor W. Drumann (Vol. III., page 120; Kœnigsberg, 1837), introducing one variation only, explained in Note (4) of page 290.

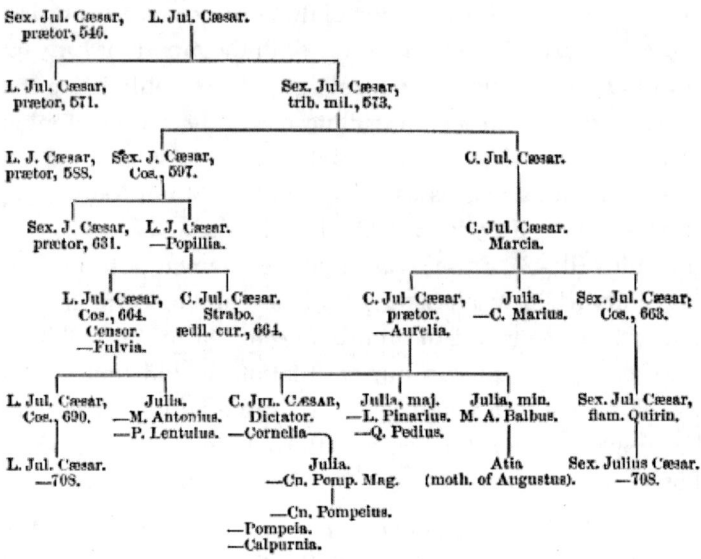

The opinion most accredited with the ancients, on the origin of the name of Cæsar, was that Julius slew an elephant in a fight. In the Punic tongue *cæsar* signifies "an elephant." The medals of Cæsar, as grand pontiff, confirm this hypothesis; on the reverse is an elephant crushing a serpent beneath its feet. (Cohen, *Consular Medals*, plate xx. 10.)—We know that some symbols on the Roman medals are a species of canting heraldry. Pliny gives another etymology of the name of Cæsar: "Primusque Cæsarum a cæso matris utero dictus, qua de causa et *Cæsones* appellati." (*Natural History*, VII. 9.)—Festus (p. 57) thus expresses himself: "*Cæsar a cæsarie* dictus est; qui scilicet cum cæsarie natus est;" and page 45: "*Cæsariati* (comati)."—Finally, Spartianus (*Life of Ælius Verus*, ii.) sums up in these words the greater part of the etymologies: "*Cæsorem* vel ab elephante (qui lingua Mauroram *cæsar* dicitur) in prœlio cæso, cum qui primus sic appellatus est, doctissimi et eruditissimi viri putant dictum; vel quia mortua matre, ventre cæso sit natus; vel quod cum magnis crinibus sit utero parentis effusus; vel quod oculis cæsiis et ultra humanum morem viguerit." (See Isidore, *Origines*, IX. iii. 12.—Servius, *Commentary on the Æneid*, I. 290, and Constantine Manasses, p. 71.)

[745] Pliny, Natural History, VII. 53.—"Cæsar was in his sixteenth year when he lost his father." (Suetonius, I.)

[746] "He sprang from the noble family of the Julii, and, according to an opinion long believed in, he derived his origin from Venus and Anchises." (Velleius Paterculus, II. 41.)

[747] In fact, the gens Marcia, one of the most illustrious patrician families in Rome, reckoned among its ancestors Numa Marcius, who married Pompilia, the daughter of Numa Pompilius, by whom he had Ancus Marcius, who was King of Rome after the death of Tullus Hostilius. (Plutarch, Coriolanus, I; Numa, 26.)

[748] Suetonius, Cæsar, vi. This passage, as generally translated, is unintelligible, because the translators render the words Martii Reges by the Kings Martius, instead of the family of Marcius Rex.

[749] Plutarch, Cæsar, 10.

[750] "So Cornelia, mother of the Gracchi; Aurelia, mother of Cæsar; Atia, mother of Augustus, all presided over the education of their children, we are told, and made them into great men." (Tacitus, Dialogue concerning Orators, 28.)

[751] "Ingenii magni, memoriæ singularis, nec minus Græce quam Latine doctus." (Suetonius, On Illustrious Grammarians, 7.)

[752] "A sermone Græco puerum incipere malo." (Quintilian, Institution of Oratory, I. i.)

[753] Claudius, addressing a foreigner who spoke Greek and Latin, said, "Since thou possessest our two languages." (Suetonius, Claudius, 42.)

[754] Καί σύ, τέκνον! (Suetonius, Cæsar, 82.)

[755] Suetonius, Cæsar, 56.

[756] "Still quite young, he seems to have attached himself to the kind of eloquence adopted by Strabo Cæsar, and he has even given, in his Divination, several passages, word for word, of the discourse of this orator for the Sardinians." (Suetonius, Cæsar, 55.)

[757] Aulus Gellius, IV. 16.

[758] "For Cæsar and Brutus have also made verses, and have placed them in the public libraries. Poets as feeble as Cicero, but happier than he, in that fewer people knew what they had done." (Tacitus, Dialogue concerning Orators, 21.)

[759]

> Tu quoque, tu in summis, o dimidiate Menander,
> Poneris, et merito, puri sermonis amator.
> Lenibus atque utinam scriptis adjuncta foret vis
> Comica, ut æquato virtus polleret honore
> Cum Græcis; neque in hac despectus parte jaceres!
> Unum hoc maceror et doleo tibi deesse, Terenti.
> (Suetonius, *Life of Terence*, 5.)

[760] "Liberal to prodigality, and of a courage above human nature and even imagination." (Velleius Paterculus, II. 41.)

[761] "He held, undeniably, the second rank among the orators of Rome." (Plutarch, Cæsar, 3.)

[762] "Nam cui Hortensio, Lucullove, vel Cæsari, tam parata unquam adfuit recordatio, quam tibi sacra mens tua loco momentoque, quo jusseris, reddit omne depositum?" (Latinus Pacatus, Panegyricus in Theodosium, XVIII. 3.) — (Pliny, Natural History, VII. 25.)

[763] "Quamvis moderate soleret irasci, maluit tamen non posse." (Seneca, De Ira, II. 23.)

[764] Plutarch, Cæsar, 4.

[765] Plutarch, Cæsar, 19.

[766] "To the external advantages which distinguished him from all the other citizens, Cæsar joined an impetuous and powerful soul." (Velleius Paterculus, II. 41.)

[767] Suetonius, Cæsar, 15.

[768] "By his voice, his gesture, the grand and noble air of his person, he had a certain brilliant manner of speech, without the least artifice." (Cicero, Brutus, 75; copied by Suetonius, Cæsar, 55.)

[769] Plutarch, Cæsar, 18.

[770] "From his first youth he was much used to horseback, and had even acquired the facility of riding with dropped reins and his hands joined behind his back." (Plutarch, Cæsar, 18.)

[771] "He ate and slept without enjoying the pleasure of either, and only to obey necessity." (Velleius Paterculus, II. 41.)

[772] Suetonius, Cæsar, 53. — (Plutarch, Cæsar, 18 and 58.)

[773] "And when," says Cicero, "I look at his hair, so artistically arranged; and when I see him scratch his head with one finger, I cannot believe that such a man could conceive so black a design as to overthrow the Roman Republic." (Plutarch, Cæsar, 4.)

[774] Suetonius, Cæsar, 45. — Cicero said likewise, "I suffered myself to be caught by the fashion of his girdle," alluding to his hanging robe, which gave him an effeminate appearance. (Macrobius, Saturnalia, II. 3.)

[775] Dio Cassius, XLIII. 43.

[776] Velleius Paterculus, II. 41.

[777] Suetonius (Cæsar, 1) says that Cæsar was designated (destinatus) flamen. Velleius Paterculus (II. 43), that he was created flamen. In our opinion he was created, but not inaugurated, flamen. Now, as long as this formality was not accomplished, he was only the flamen designate. What proves that he had never been inaugurated is, that Sylla could revoke it; and, on another hand, Tacitus says (Annales, III. 53) that, after the death of Cornelius Merula, the flamenship of Jupiter remained vacant for seventy-two years, without any interruption to the special worship of this god. So that, evidently, they did not count the flamenship of Cæsar as real, since he had never entered on his office.

[778] "Dimissa Cossutia ... quæ pretextato desponsata fuerat." (Suetonius, Cæsar, 1.)—This passage from Suetonius clearly indicates that he was betrothed, and not married, to Cossutia; for Suetonius uses the word dimittere, which means "to free," and not the word repudiare in its true meaning; besides, desponsata signifies betrothed.—Plutarch says that Cornelia was the first wife of Cæsar, though he pretends that he married Pompeia as his third. (Plutarch, Cæsar, 5.)

[779] Plutarch, Cæsar, 5.

[780] Velleius Paterculus, II. 41.

[781] "What an infamy to introduce into his house a pregnant woman, with her husband still living; and to thrust from it, ignominiously and cruelly, Antistia, whose father had just perished for the husband who repudiated her!" (Plutarch, Pompey, 8.)

[782] Suetonius, Cæsar, 1.

[783] Plutarch, Cæsar, 1.—Suetonius, Cæsar, 74.

[784] Suetonius, Cæsar, 74.

[785] Suetonius, Cæsar, 1.

[786] The vestals enjoyed great privileges: if they met by chance a criminal on his way to execution, he was set at liberty. (Plutarch, Numa, 14.)— Valerius Maximus (V. iv. 6) reports the following fact: "The vestal Claudia, seeing that a tribune of the people was about to drag her father, Appius Claudius Pulcher, with violence from his triumphal car, interfered between the tribune and him, by virtue of her right to oppose violence."—Cicero (Oration for Cœlius, 14) likewise alludes to this celebrated anecdote.

[787] Suetonius, Cæsar, 1.

[788] Suetonius, Cæsar, 2.

[789] Suetonius, Cæsar, 2.—Pliny, XVI. 4.—Aulus Gellius, V. 6.

[790] C. Cæsar, grand pontiff, in his discourse for the Bithynians, thus expresses himself in his exordium:—"The hospitality which I have received from King Nicomedes, and the bond of friendship which unites me to those whose cause is under debate, do not permit me, Marcus Juncus, to decline this office (that of being the advocate of the Bithynians); for death ought not to efface from the memory of their kindred the recollection of those who have lived, and we could not, without the last degree of disgrace, abandon our clients, those to whom, after our kindred, we owe our support." (Aulus Gellius, V. xiii. 1.)

[791] "Nothing damaged his reputation for chastity," says Suetonius, "except his sojourn with Nicomedes; but the opprobrium which resulted from it was grave and lasting; it exposed him to the sneers of all. I will say nothing of those well-known verses of Calvus Licinius—

> ... 'Bithynia quidquid
> Et pedicator Cæsaris unquam habuit.'

I will be silent on the speeches of Dolabella and Curio the father, ... neither will I linger over the edicts in which Bibulus publicly exposed his colleague by speaking of him as the *queen of Bithynia*.... M. Brutus informs us that a certain Octavius, whose craziness allowed him to say what he would, being one day in a numerous assembly, called Pompey *king*, then saluted Cæsar by the name of *queen*. C. Memmius also reproaches him for having mixed himself up with other debauchees to present Nicomedes with cups and wine at table, and he quotes the names of several Roman merchants who were among the guests.... Cicero apostrophised him once in full Senate. Cæsar was defending there the cause of Nysa, daughter of Nicomedes; he recalled the obligations which he owed to this king. 'Let us pass by all that, I beg you,' cried Cicero: 'we know only too well what he has given thee, and what he has received from thee.' On his triumph over the Gauls, the soldiers, among other satirical verses which it was their custom to sing as they followed the car of the general, repeated these, which are well known:—

> 'Gallias Cæsar subegit, Nicomedes Cæsarem.
> Ecce Cæsar nunc triumphat, qui subegit Gallias;
> Nicomedes non triumphat, qui subegit Cæsarem.'"
> (Suetonius, *Cæsar*, 40.)

[792] Cicero, Letters to Atticus, II. 19.

[793] These reports, like other calumnies, were propagated by Cæsar's enemies, such as Curio and Bibulus, and repeated in the ridiculous annals of Tanusius Geminus (Suetonius, Cæsar, 9), the authority of which Seneca despised. "Thou knowest that not much account is made of these annals of Tanusius, and how they are designated." (Seneca, Epistle 93.)—Catullus (xxxvi. 1) gives us that term of contempt to which Seneca alludes (cacata charta).

[794] "Marius had in his army a nephew, called Caius Lucius, who, overcome by a shameful passion for one of his subordinates, offered him an act of violence. The man drew his sword and killed him. Cited before the tribunal of Marius, instead of being punished he was loaded with praises by the consul, who gave him one of the crowns which were the usual reward of courage." (Plutarch, Marius, 15.)

[795] "Cæsar was not vexed at being accused of loving Cleopatra; but he could not bear that they should say he had been loved by Nicomedes. He swore it was a calumny." (Xiphilinus, Julius Cæsar, p. 30, Paris edition, 1678.)

[796] Orosius, V. 23.

[797] Suetonius, Cæsar, 3.

[798] Florus, III. 23.

[799] Appian, I. 107.

[800] Suetonius, Cæsar, 3.

[801] Sallust, Fragments, I., p. 363.

[802] Florus, III. 23.

[803] Suetonius, Cæsar, 3.

[804] "The Romans regarded as honourable accusations which had no private enmity as their motive, and they liked to see young men attach themselves to the pursuit of the guilty, as generous dogs attack wild beasts." (Plutarch, Lucullus, 1.)

[805] Plutarch, Cæsar, 4.—Asconius, Discourse for Scaurus, XVI. ii. 245, edit. Schütz.

[806] Valerius Maximus, VIII. ix. § 3.—"Cæsar was twenty-one years of age when he attacked Dolabella, in a speech which we still read to-day with admiration." (Tacitus, Dialogue on the Orators, 34.)—According to the chronological order which we have adopted, Cæsar, instead of twenty-one, would have been twenty-three years old; but as Tacitus, in the same citation, also errs, by two years, in making Crassus, who

had accused Carbo, nineteen instead of twenty-one, we may suppose that he has committed the same mistake with Cæsar. In fact, Crassus tells his own age in Cicero (On the Orators, III. 20, § 74): "Quippe qui omnium maturrime ad publicas causas accesserim, annosque natus unum et viginti nobilissimum hominem in judicium vocarim." — Crassus, the orator, was born in 614; he accused Carbo in 635, the date given by Cicero.

[807] Plutarch, Cæsar, 3.—Asconius, Commentaries on the Oration, "In Toga Candida," pp. 84, 89, edit. Orelli.

[808] Dialogue on the Orators, 21.

[809] Cicero, Oration for Cluentius, 59. The manuscripts of Cicero bear Cn. Decitius.

[810] This island, now called Fermaco, is at the entrance of the Gulf of Assem-Kalessi. Pliny and Stephen of Byzantium are the only geographers who mention it, and the last tells us further, that it was here that Attalus, the famous lieutenant of Philip of Macedon, was slain by Alexander's order.

[811] Polyænus, Stratagems, VII. 23.

[812] Suetonius, Cæsar, 4.

[813] Velleius Paterculus, II. 41.

[814] Plutarch, Cæsar, 2.

[815] Plutarch, Crassus, 8.

[816] Suetonius mentions, as an act of humanity, that their corpses alone were nailed to the cross, Cæsar having had them strangled beforehand to shorten their agony. (Suetonius, Cæsar, 74.—Velleius Paterculus, II. 42.)

[817] Suetonius, Cæsar, 4.

[818] Velleius Paterculus, II. 43.—Asconius, On the Oration of Cicero against Pisa; edit. Orelli.

[819] Velleius Paterculus, II. 53.

[820] Suetonius, Cæsar, 5.—Plutarch, Cæsar, 5.

[821] The tribunes by the nomination of the general were usually called rufuli, because they were established by the law of Rutilius Rufus; the military tribunes elected by the people were called comitati; they were held as veritable magistrates. (Pseudo-Asconius, Commentary on the First Speech of Cicero against Verres, p. 142, edit. Orelli; and Festus under Rufuli, p. 261, edit. Müller.)

[822] Plutarch, Sertorius, 15, 16.

[823] "The enemy was already master of the passes which lead to Italy; from the foot of the Alps, he (Pompey) drove him back to Spain." (Sallust, Letter from Pompey to the Senate.)

[824] Velleius Paterculus, II. 30.—100,000 according to Appian (Civil Wars, I. 117).

[825] Plutarch, Lucullus, 8.

[826] Sallust, Fragments, III. 258.

[827] Appian, Civil Wars, I. xiv. 121.

[828] "The Republic, wounded and sick, so to say, had need of repose, no matter at what price." (Sallust, Fragments, I. 68.)

[829] "We see how far are carried the jealousy and animosity which the virtue and activity of the new men light up in the heart of certain nobles. If we turn away our eyes never so little, what snares do they not lay for us! One would say that they were of another nature, another kind, so much are their feelings and wishes opposed to ours." (Cicero, Second Prosecution of Verres, v. 71.)—"The nobility transmitted from hand to hand this supreme dignity (the consulship), of which they were in exclusive possession. Every new man, whatever his renown and the glory of his deeds, appeared unworthy of this honour; he was as if sullied by the stain of his birth." (Sallust, Jugurtha, 63.)

[830] Sallust, Catilina, 52.

[831] Plutarch, Lucullus, 9.

[832] Cicero, First Prosecution of Verres, 8, 9, 12; Second Prosecution, i. 29.— Pseudo-Asconius, On the first Prosecution of Verres, page 145, edit. Orelli. The orations of Cicero are full of allusions to these agents for the purchase of votes and judges.

[833] "In these later years, the men who make a trade of intriguing in elections have been enabled, by diligence and address, to obtain from the citizens of their tribes all that they chose to demand. Endeavour, by any means you will, to make these men serve you sincerely and with the steadfast will to succeed. You would obtain it if men were as grateful as they ought to be; and you will obtain it, I am afraid, since, for two years, four societies of those most influential in elections— those of Marcus Fundanius, Quintas Gallius, Gaius Cornelius, and Gaius Orcivius—have engaged themselves for you. I was present

when the causes of these men were entrusted to you, and I know what was promised to you, and what guarantees have been given to you by their associates." (On the Petition for the Consulship addressed to Cicero by his brother Quintus, 5.)

[834] Cicero, First Prosecution of Verres, 13.

[835] "Each city of the conquered peoples has a patron at Rome." (Appian, Civil Wars, II. 4.)

[836] Cicero, Second Prosecution of Verres, III. 89. Cicero adds in a letter, "We may judge, by the sufferings of our own fellow-citizens, of what the inhabitants of the provinces have to endure from the public farmers (publicani). When several tolls were suppressed in Italy, remonstrances were made not so much against the principle of taxation as against abuses in levying it, and the cries of the Romans on the soil of the country tell only too plainly what must be the fate of the allies at the extremity of the empire." (Letters to Quintus, I. 1, § 33.)

[837] Dio Cassius, 86; Fragments, CCCI. edit. Gros.

[838] Cicero, On Duties, II. 17; Letters to Quintus, II. 6, § 4.—Plutarch, Brutus, 14.

[839] Florus, III. 21.

[840] "The name of C. Marius—of that great man who we may justly call the father of the country, the regenerator of our liberty, the saviour of the Republic." (Cicero, Speech for Rabirius, 10.)—"I have, as your guarantee, your indignation against Sylla." (Dio Cassius, XXXVI. 17, Oration of Catulus to the Senate.)—"Where can we find a personage (Marius) more serious, more firm, more distinguished by courage, circumspection, conscience?" (Cicero, Speech for Balbus, 25.)—"Not only do we suffer his acts (Sylla's), but to prevent worse disasters, greater ills, we give them the sanction of public authority." (Cicero, Second Prosecution of Verres, III. 35.)

[841] Plutarch, Cæsar, 6.

[842] Plutarch, Pompey, 12.

[843] Pompey slew Carbo, Perpenna, and Brutus, the father of the assassin of Cæsar, who had yielded themselves to him: the first had protected his youth and saved his patrimony. (Valerius Maximus, V. iii. v.)

[844] Count Franz de Champagny, Les Cæsars, I. p. 50.

[845] "It was in his character to show little regard for what he was ambitious to obtain." (Dio Cassius, XXXVI. 7.)—"Pompey, with a heart as depraved as his face was pure." (Sallust, Fragments, II. 176.)

[846] "At last, when Pompey, haranguing the people for the first time at the gates of the city, in his capacity of consul-designate, came to treat of the matter which seemed to have been most ardently expected, and let it be understood that he would re-establish the power of the tribunes, he was received with applause, and a slight murmur of assent; but when he added that the provinces were devastated and oppressed, the tribunals disgraced, the judges without shame, and that he wished to be watchful of these abuses, and to restore good order, then it was not by a simple murmur, but by unanimous acclamations, that the people testified their desires." (Cicero, First Prosecution of Verres, 15.)

[847] Catulus, when asked his opinion on the re-establishment of the tribunary power, began in these authoritative words:—"The conscript fathers administer justice evilly and scandalously; and if, in the tribunals, they had but answered the expectations of the Roman people, the power of the tribunes would not have been so warmly regretted." (Cicero, First Prosecution of Verres, 15.)

[848] "His enemies had nothing else to reproach him with than the preference which he gave to the people over the Senate." (Plutarch, Pompey, 20.)

[849] "He seconded with all his might those who wished to restore the power of the tribunes." (Suetonius, Cæsar, 5.)

[850] 7,100 talents. (Plutarch, Crassus, 1.)

[851] Plutarch, Crassus, 2.—Cicero, On Duties, I. 8.

[852] Plutarch, Crassus, 7.

[853] Plutarch, Crassus, 8.

[854] Plutarch, Crassus, 8.

[855] Plutarch, Crassus, 1, 16.

[856] "Cotta judicandi munus, quod C. Gracchus ereptum Senatui, ad equites, Sylla ab illis ad Senatum transtulerat, æqualiter inter utrumque ordinem partitus est." (Velleius Paterculus, II. 32.)

[857] "Equidem mihi videor pro nostra necessitate, non labore, non opera, non industria defuisse." (Certainly, I believe I have displayed all the zeal, all the endeavour, all the ability which our kinship demands.) Cæsar, quoted by Aulus Gellius, XIII. 3.—Nonius Marcellus, "On the different significations of words," under the word Necessitas.

[858] Sallust, Fragments, I. 68.

[859] Plutarch, Pompey, 21.

[860] Plutarch, Cæsar, 5.—Suetonius, Cæsar, 6.

[861] Plutarch, Cæsar, 5.

[862] The images of Æneas, of Romulus, and of the Kings of Alba Longa also figured in the funeral canopy of the Julia family. (Tacitus, Annales, IV. 9.)

[863] Plutarch, Cæsar, 5.—Velleius Paterculus, II. 43.

[864] Cicero, Oration on the Manilian Law, 12; For Fonteius, 2.

[865] Cæsar, Civil War, I. 37.

[866] "Sextus Pompeius Cordubam tenebat, quod ejus provinciæ caput esse existimabatur." (Cæsar, The War in Spain, III.—Plutarch, Cæsar, 17.)

[867] Cicero, Second Prosecution of Verres, II. 13.—Paulus Diaconus, under the word Conventus.—Müller, p. 41.

[868] Cicero, Second Prosecution of Verres, II. 20, 24, 30; IV. 29.—Familiar Letters, XV. iv.

[869] Pliny, Natural History, III. i., and IV. xxxv. The three conventus of Lusitania were held at Emerita, Pax Julia (Béja), and at Scalabis: the four of Bætica were, Gades, Corduba, Astijo, Hispalis (Cadiz, Cordova, Ecija, and Seville).

[870] Dio Cassius, XLIV. 39, 41.

[871] "From the beginning of my questorship, I have shown a special affection for the province." (Speech of Cæsar to the Spaniards, at Hispalis, Commentaries, The War in Spain, 43.)

[872] Plutarch, Cæsar, 5.

[873] Titus Livius, XXI. 21.—Florus, II. 17.

[874] Plutarch, Parallel between Alexander and Cæsar, 6.—Suetonius, Cæsar, 7.

[875] Suetonius, Cæsar, 8.

[876] Suetonius, Cæsar, 8.

[877] Velleius Paterculus, II. 31.

[878] Daughter of Q. Pompeius Rufus, and Fausta, daughter of Sylla. (Plutarch, Cæsar, 5.—Suetonius, Cæsar, 6.)

[879] The ships of the corsairs amounted to more than a thousand, and the towns which they took to four hundred. (Plutarch, Pompey, 23.)

[880] Plutarch, Pompey, 24.

[881] Cicero, Speech on the Manilian Law, 12.

[882] "Aulus Gabinius was a very bad citizen, in no wise inspired by love of the public good." (Dio Cassius, XXXVI. 6.)

[883] Dio Cassius, XXXVI. 7.

[884] Plutarch, Pompey, 26.

[885] Dio Cassius, XXXVI. 20.—Appian, War of Mithridates, 94.

[886] Plutarch, Pompey, 27.—"The very day on which you placed your naval armies under his orders, the price of corn, until then excessive, fell at once so low that the richest harvest, in the midst of a long peace, would have scarcely produced so happy an abundance." (Cicero, Oration for the Manilian Law, 15.)

[887] Florus and Appian do not quite agree on the division of these commands. (Appian, War of Mithridates, 95.—Florus, III. 6.)

[888] Velleius Paterculus, II. 32.—Plutarch, Pompey, 29.

[889] Dio Cassius, XXXV. 14 and 15.

[890] Plutarch, Pompey, 31.

[891] Cicero, Oration for the Manilian Law, 16.

[892] Plutarch, Pompey, 31.

[893] Cicero, Oration for the Manilian Law, 23.

[894] Dio Cassius, XXXVI. 26.—Plutarch, Lucullus, 50, 52.

[895] "The tribune Manilius, a venal soul, and the debased instrument of the ambition of others." (Velleius Paterculus, II. 33.)

[896] "As to the Valerians, informed that the magistrates at Rome had given them their discharge, they immediately abandoned their flags." (Dio Cassius, XXXV. 15.)

[897] "They called Valerians the soldiers of Valerius Flaccus, who, having passed into the command of Fimbria, had left their general in Asia to join themselves to Sylla." "These same soldiers, under the orders of Pompey (for he enrolled the Valerians anew), did not dream even of revolt, so much does one man carry it over another." (Dio Cassius, XXXV. 16.)

[898] "There was no shame," he said, "in submitting to him whom fortune raised above all the others." (Velleius Paterculus, II. 37.)

[899] Dio Cassius, XXXV. 16.

[900] This is taken from a passage of Cicero compared with another of Sallust. In fact, Cicero, in his Oration for Murena (23), thus expresses

himself Confusionem suffragiorum flagitasti, prorogationem legis Maniliæ, æquationem gratiæ, dignitatis, suffragiorum." It is clear that Cicero could not allude to the Manilian law on the freedmen, but to that of Caius Gracchus, since Sallust employs nearly the same words concerning this law, saying: "Sed de magistratibus creandis haud mihi quidem absurde placet lex, quam C. Gracchus in tribunatu promulgaverat: ut ex confusis quinque classibus sorte centuriæ vocarentur. Ita coæquali dignitate pecunia, virtute anteire alius alium properabit." (Sallust, Letters to Cæsar, vii.)

[901] Dio Cassius, III. 36, 40.

[902] Plutarch, Cæsar, 5.

[903] Suetonius, Cæsar, 10.—Plutarch, Cæsar, 10.

[904] Titus Livius, IX. 40.

[905] Dio Cassius, XXXVII. 8.

[906] "The gladiators whom you have bought are a very fine acquisition. It is said that they are well trained, and if you had wished to let them out on the last occasion, you would have regained what they have cost you." (Cicero, Letters to Atticus, IV. 4.)

[907] Servius, Commentary on Book III. verse 67 of the Æneid.—Tertullian, On the Shows, V.—Titus Livius, XXIII. 30; XXIX. 46.—Valerius Maximus, II. iv. § 7.

[908] "When Cæsar, afterwards dictator, but then ædile, gave funeral games in honour of his father, all that was used in the arena was of silver; silver lances glittered in the hands of the criminals and pierced the wild beasts, an example which even simple municipal towns imitate." (Pliny, Natural History, XXXIII. 3.)

[909] Suetonius, Cæsar, 10.

[910] Suetonius, Cæsar, 11.

[911] Plutarch, Cæsar, 6.

[912] Plutarch, Cæsar, 6.

[913] Plutarch, Cæsar, 6.

[914] Suetonius, Cæsar, 11.—Cicero, First Oration on the Agrarian Law, i. 16.

[915] Justin, xxix. 5, Scholiast of Bobbio, On the Oration of Cicero, "De Rege Alexandrino," p. 350, edit. Orelli.

[916] Cicero, Second Oration on the Agrarian Law, xvi.

[917] "Augustus made it one, among other state maxims, to sequester Egypt, forbidding the Roman knights and senators of the first rank ever to go there without his permission. He feared that Italy might be famished by the first ambitious person who should seize the province, where, holding the keys of both land and sea, he might defend himself with very few soldiers against great armies." (Tacitus, Annals, II. 59.)

[918] Suetonius, Cæsar, 11.

[919] Dio Cassius, XXXVII. 9.

[920] "You name me a foreigner because I have come from a municipal town. If you regard us as foreigners, although our name and rank were formerly well established at Rome, and in public opinion, how much then must these competitors be foreigners in your eyes, this élite of Italy, who come from all parts to dispute with you magistrateships and honours?" (Cicero, Oration for Sylla, 8.)

[921] See Drumann, Julii, 147.

[922] J. Paul, Sentences, V. iv., p 417, edit. Huschke.—Justinian, Institutes, IV. xviii. § 5.—Appian, On the Office of the Proconsul, vii.

[923] "Then, in the instructions directed against the sicarii, and the exceptions proposed by the Cornelian law, he ranked among these malefactors those who, during the proscription, had received money from the public treasury for having brought to Sylla the heads of Roman citizens." (Suetonius, Cæsar, 11.)

[924] Plutarch, Cato, 21.—Dio Cassius, XLVII. 6.

[925] Cicero, Third Speech on the Agrarian Law, 4.

[926] Dio Cassius, XXXVII. 10.—Asconius, Commentary on the Orations of Cicero, "In Toga Candida," pp. 91, 92, edit Orelli.

[927] Asconius, In Toga Candida, p. 91.

[928] Sallust, Catiline, 19.

[929] Plutarch, Cicero, 15.

[930] "I am preparing at this moment to defend Catiline, my competitor. I hope, if I obtain his acquittal, to find him disposed to come to an understanding with me on our next steps. If he is against this, I will [I shall know what to do (?)] take my way." (Cicero, Letters to Atticus, I. ii.)

[931] Cicero, Oration for Sylla, 29.

[932] Plutarch, Cato, 3.

[933] Asconius, Cicero's Oration, "In Toga Candida," p. 82, edit. Orelli.

[934] Plutarch, Cicero, 3.

[935] They called new men those who amongst their ancestors counted none that had held a high magistracy. (Appian, Civil Wars, II. 2.) — Cicero also confirms this fact: "I am the first new man that, for a great number of years, is remembered to have been appointed consul; and this eminent post, in which the nobility were in a manner entrenched, and to which they had closed all the avenues, you have, to place me at your head, forced the barriers; you have desired that merit henceforth find them open." (Cicero, Second Oration on the Agrarian Law, 1.)

[936] Sallust, Catiline, 23.

[937] "Cicero favoured sometimes the one, sometimes the other, to be sought after by both parties." (Dio Cassius, XXXVI. 26.)

[938] Second Oration on the Agrarian Law, 25.

[939] The territories conceded by a treaty being excepted, which freed from this obligation the African territory, which had become, since Scipio, the property of the Republic, and given by Pompey to Hiempsal. In Campania every colonist was obliged to have ten jugera, and, on the territory of Stella, twelve.

[940] Cicero, Second Oration on the Agrarian Law, 26.

[941] Cicero, Letters to Atticus, II. 1. — Plutarch, Cicero, 17. — "When young Romans, full of merit and honour, have found themselves in such a position that their admissibility to magistracies has effected the overthrow of the State, I have dared to brave their enmity, to interdict their access to the comitia and to honours." (Cicero, Oration against L. Piso.)

[942] "They wish to deprive the Republic of all refuge, of every guarantee of safety in difficult conjunctures." (Cicero, Oration for Rabirius, 2.)

[943] "This supreme power which, according to the institutions of Rome, the Senate confers upon the magistrates, consists in raising troops, in making war, in keeping to their duties, by every means, the allies and citizens; in exercising supremely, equally at Rome or abroad, both civil and military authority. In all other cases, without the express order of the people, none of these prerogatives are conferred upon the consuls." (Sallust, Catiline, 29.)

[944] Cicero, Oration for Rabirius, 9.

[945] Suetonius, Cæsar, 12.

[946] Dio Cassius, XXXVII. 26, 27.

[947] Macrobius, Saturnalia, I. 16.—Priscian, vi., p. 710, edit. Putsch.—
Macrobius (l. c.) quotes the 16th book of the treatise of Cæsar on the
Auspices.—Dio Cassius (xxxvii.) expresses himself thus: "Above
all, because he had supported Labienus against Rabirius, and had
not voted for the death of Lentulus." But the Greek author errs: the
nomination of Cæsar to the high pontificate took place before the
conspiracy of Catiline. (See Velleius Paterculus, II. 43.)

[948] Appian, Civil Wars, II. 1, 8, 14.

[949] Plutarch, Cæsar, 7.

[950] Plutarch, Cæsar, 7.

[951] Suetonius, Cæsar, 13.

[952] Suetonius, Cæsar, 46.

[953] "On the 23rd of August, the day of inauguration of Lentulus, flamen
of Mars, the house was decorated, and couches of ivory were set up
in the triclinia. In the two first halls were the pontiffs Q. Catulus, M.
Æmilius Lepidus, D. Silanus, C. Cæsar, king of the sacrifices, and ...
L. Julius Cæsar, augur. The third received the vestals. The repast was
thus composed:—For the first course: sea-urchins, raw oysters in any
quantity, pelorides (a kind of oyster of extraordinary size), spondyli
(shell-fish of the oyster kind), thrushes, asparagus; and, lower down, a
fat hen, a vol-au-vent of large oysters, and sea-acorns black and white
(sea and river shell-fish according to Pliny). Then more spondyli,
glycomarides (another shell-fish mentioned by Pliny), sea-nettles,
beccaficos, filets of venison and wild boar, fatted fowls powdered with
flour, beccaficos, murices and purple fish (shell-fish bristling with
points, which yielded the purple of the ancients). Second course: sows'
udders, wild boar's head, fish-pie, sows' udder-pie, ducks, boiled teal,
hares, roast fowls, starch (flour that is obtained in the same manner as
starch, without grinding—many sorts of creams, amylaria, were made
of it), loaves from Picenum." (Macrobius, Saturnalia, III. 9.)

[954] "It was at the very point when it required no more to upset the
weakly government than a slight impulse from the first bold man who
presented himself." (Plutarch, Cicero, 15.)

[955] Cicero, Oration for M. Cælius, 5. This oration was delivered in the year
698.

[956] Plutarch, Cicero, 19.

[957] Sallust, Catiline, 27, 28.

[958] This is deduced from what Florus (III. 6) says of the command of the fleet which L. Gellius had, and from a passage in Cicero. (First Oration after his Return, 7.)—L. Gellius expresses himself clearly upon the danger the Republic had run, and proposed the awarding of a civic crown to Cicero. (Cicero, Letters to Atticus, XII. 21; Oration against Piso, 3.—Aulus Gellius, V. 6.)

[959] Cicero, First Catiline Oration, 1; Second Catiline Oration, 1.

[960] Sallust, Catiline, 32.

[961] Sallust, Catiline, 30, 31.—Plutarch, Cicero, 17.

[962] Sallust, Catiline, 47.

[963] Sallust, Catiline, 51.—Appian, Civil Wars, II. 6.

[964] Cicero, Fourth Catiline Oration, 1.

[965] Cicero, Fourth Catiline Oration, 2.

[966] Second Catiline Oration, 4.

[967] First Oration against Catiline, 2.

[968] Second Oration on the Agrarian Law, 5.

[969] Suetonius, Cæsar, 14.

[970] Cicero, Fourth Oration against Catiline, 5.

[971] Sallust, Catiline, 52.

[972] Plutarch, Cato, 28.—See the Comparison of Alexander and Cæsar, 7.

[973] Suetonius, Cæsar, 53.

[974] Sallust, Catiline, 52.

[975] Plutarch, Cicero, 28.

[976] Sallust, Catiline, 49.

[977] Suetonius, Cæsar, 8.

[978] Sallust, Catiline, 49.

[979] "They feared his power and the great number of friends by whom he was supported, for everybody was persuaded that the criminals would be involved in the absolution of Cæsar, much more than Cæsar in their punishment." (Plutarch, Cicero, 27.)

[980] "And I have myself since heard Crassus say openly that this cruel affront had been caused him by Cicero." (Sallust, Catiline, 48.)

[981] We may read in the historians of the time the recital of fables invented at will to ruin the conspirators. Thus Catiline, seeking to bind by an oath accomplices in his crime, is represented as causing cups filled with human blood and wine to be passed round. (Sallust, Catiline, 22.) — According to Plutarch, they slaughtered a man, and all ate of his flesh. (Plutarch, Cicero, 14. — Florus, IV. 1.)

[982] Cicero himself acknowledged that these accusations were commonplaces for the necessity of the cause. In a letter to Atticus, he describes a scene which passed in the Senate a short time after the return of Pompey to Rome. He tells us that this general satisfied himself with approving all the acts of the Senate, without imputing anything personal to him (Cicero); "but Crassus," he continues, "rose and spoke with much eloquence.... Brief, he attacked all the commonplace of sword and flame, which I have been accustomed to treat, you know in how many ways, in my orations, of which you are the sovereign critic." (Cicero, Letters to Atticus, I. 14.)

[983] "The populace, who at first, through the love of novelty, had been only too much inclined for this war, changes its sentiments, curses the enterprise of Catiline, and exalts Cicero to the skies." (Sallust, Catiline, 48.)

[984] Sallust, Catiline, 39. — Dio Cassius, XXVII. 36.

[985] "Many young estimable noblemen were attached to this wicked and corrupt man." (Cicero, Oration for M. Cælius, 4.) — "He had drawn around him men perverse and audacious, at the same time that he had attached to himself numbers of virtuous and steady citizens, by the false semblances of an affected virtue." (Cicero, ibid. 6.)

[986] Sallust, Catiline, 17.

[987] "And this silver eagle, to which he had consecrated in his house an altar." (Cicero, Second Oration against Catiline, 6.)

[988] Sallust, Catiline, 20.

[989] Sallust, Catiline, 33. Speech of the envoys sent by Mallius to Marcius Rex.

[990] Sallust, Catiline, 30.

[991] Sallust, Catiline, 36.

[992] "Meanwhile, he kept refusing slaves, who, from the beginning, had never ceased joining him in large bands. Full of confidence in the resources of the conspiracy, he regarded any appearance of confounding the cause of the citizens with that of the slaves as contrary to his policy." (Sallust, Catiline, 56.)

[993] Sallust, Catiline, 44.

[994] "People who will fall at our feet, if I show them, I do not say the points of our swords, but the edict of the prætor." (Cicero, Second Oration against Catiline, 3.)

[995] Sallust, Catiline, 61.

[996] Dio Cassius, XXXVII. 10.

[997] The Emperor Napoleon, in the Mémorial de Sainte-Hélène, also treats as a fable this opinion of the historians that Catiline desired to burn Rome, and give it up to pillage, in order afterwards to govern a ruined city. The Emperor thought, said M. de Las Cases, that it was rather some new faction, after the manner of Marius and Sylla, which, having been unsuccessful, had seen all the unfounded accusations that are brought in such cases heaped upon its leader.

[998] Cicero, Oration for Flaccus, 38.

[999] "He excited public cavil, not by evil actions, but by his habit of self-glorification. He never went to the Senate, to the assemblies of the people, to the courts of law, without having on his lips the names of Catiline and Lentulus." (Plutarch, Cicero, 31.)

[1000] Cicero, Familiar Letters, v. 7.

[1001] See Cæsar's speech, quoted above.

[1002] It may be interesting to reproduce here, from the letters of Cicero, the list of the discourses which he delivered during the year of his consulship. "I wished, I also, after the manner of Demosthenes, to have my political speeches, which may be named consulars. The first and second are on the Agrarian Law; the former before the Senate on the calends of January; the second before the people; the third, about Otho; the fourth, for Rabirius; the fifth, on the children of the proscribed; the sixth, on my relinquishing my province; the seventh is that which put Catiline to flight; the eighth was delivered before the people the day after his flight; the ninth, from the tribune, the day when the Allobroges came to give their evidence; the tenth, before the Senate, on the 5th of December. There are two more, not so long, which may be described as supplementary to the two first on the Agrarian Law." (Cicero, Letters to Atticus, II. 1.)

[1003] Velleius Paterculus, II. 40.—Dio Cassius, XXXVII. 21.

[1004] Suetonius, Cæsar, 46.

[1005] Dio Cassius, XXXVII. 44; XLIII. 14.

[1006] Suetonius, Cæsar, 16.

[1007] Dio Cassius, XXXVIII. 43.—Suetonius, Cæsar, 16.—Cicero, Oration for Sestius, 29.

[1008] Suetonius, Cæsar, 16.

[1009] Cicero, Letters to Atticus, II. 24.

[1010] Plutarch, Cæsar, 9.

[1011] Suetonius, Cæsar, 17.

[1012] Suetonius, Cæsar, 17.

[1013] Suetonius, Cæsar, 50.

[1014] Suetonius, Cæsar, 50.

[1015] Plutarch, Cæsar, 10.

[1016] Suetonius, Cæsar, 1.—Plutarch, Cicero, 27; Plutarch, Cæsar, 10.— "This sacrifice is offered by the vestal virgins, on behalf of the Roman people, in the house of a magistrate who has the right of imperium, with ceremonies that it is not allowable to reveal. The goddess to whom it is offered is one whose very name is a mystery to men, and whom Clodius terms the Good Goddess (Bona Dea), because she forgave him so gross an outrage." (Cicero, Oration on the Report of the Augurs, 17.)—The Good Goddess, like the majority of the divinities of the earth among the ancients, was regarded as a sort of beneficent fairy who presided over the fertility of the fields and the conception of women. The nocturnal sacrifice was celebrated at the beginning of December, in the house of the consul or the prætor, by the wife of that magistrate, or by the vestal virgins. At the commencement of the festival they made a propitiatory sacrifice of a pig, and prayers were offered for the prosperity of the Roman people.

[1017] Cicero, Letters to Atticus, I. 14.

[1018] Cicero, Letters to Atticus, I. 16.

[1019] Cicero, Letters to Atticus, I. 17.

[1020] Appian, Mithridatic War, 101.

[1021] Appian, Mithridatic War, 106.

[1022] Dio Cassius, XXXVII. 20.

[1023] Dio Cassius, XXXVII. 44. In contradiction to other authors, Dio Cassius asserts that the elections were adjourned. (Plutarch, Pompey, 45.)

[1024] "The more men were terrified, the more they were re-assured, on seeing Pompey return to his country as a simple citizen." (Velleius Paterculus, II. 40.)

[1025] Cicero, Letters to Atticus, I. 12.

[1026] Metellus was subjugating Crete, when Pompey sent one of his lieutenants to depose him, under the pretence that that island was included in his own wide jurisdiction by sea.

[1027] Dio Cassius, XXXVII. 49.

[1028] "No rectitude, no candour, not a single honourable motive in his policy; nothing elevated, nothing strong, nothing generous." (Cicero, Letters to Atticus, I. 12.)

[1029] Plutarch, Pompey, 47.

[1030] Pliny, Natural History, XXXVII. 5.

[1031] Vases from Carmania that were highly prized. They reflected the colours of the rainbow, and, according to Pliny, a single one was sold for seventy talents (more than 300,000 francs [£12,000]). (Pliny, Natural History, XXXVII, 7, 8.)

[1032] Pliny, XXXIII. 54.—Strabo, XII. 545.

[1033] Appian, War against Mithridates, 116.

[1034] Pliny, Natural History, XII. 9, 54.

[1035] Dio Cassius, XXXVI. 2.—Velleius Paterculus, II. 34.

[1036] Appian, War against Mithridates, 117.

[1037] Plutarch, Pompey, 47.—Dio Cassius, XXXVII. 21.

[1038] Cicero, Oration for Murena, 14.

[1039] Cicero, Letters to Atticus, I. 18.

[1040] Dio Cassius, XXXVII. 50.

[1041] Cicero, Letters to Atticus, I. 19.

[1042] Cicero, Letters to Atticus, I. 19.

[1043] Cicero, Oration on the Agrarian Law, II. 27.

[1044] "Your ancestors never set you the example of buying lands from individuals in order to send colonies thither. All the laws, up to the present time, have contented themselves with establishing them on the lands belonging to the State." (Cicero, Oration on the Agrarian Law, II. 25.)

[1045] Plutarch, Cato of Utica, 36.

[1046] Dio Cassius, XXXVII. 51.

[1047] Plutarch, Cato, 35.

[1048] "People abuse the Senate; the equestrian order stands aloof from it. Thus this year will have seen the overthrow of the two solid foundations on which I, single-handed, had planted the Republic— the authority of the Senate and the union of the two orders." (Cicero, Letters to Atticus, I. 18.)

[1049] Cicero, Letters to Atticus, II. 1.

[1050] Plutarch, Cæsar, 12.—Appian (Civil Wars, II. 2, § 8) speaks of twenty-five million sestertii—i.e., 4,750,000 francs [£190,000].

[1051] Suetonius, Cæsar, 18.

[1052] Cicero, Letter to Atticus, I. 14, 16.

[1053] "From his youth up he was zealous and true to his clients." (Suetonius, Cæsar, 71.)

[1054] Suetonius, Cæsar, 12.

[1055] Plutarch, Cæsar, 12.

[1056] Plutarch, Cæsar, 12.

[1057] A chain of mountains in Portugal, now called Sierra di Estrella, separating the basin of the Tagus from the valley of Mondego. According to Cellarius (Ancient Geography, I. 60), Mount Herminium is still called Arminno. The principal oppidum belonging to the population of these mountains seems to have been called Medobrega (Membrio). It is mentioned in Cæsar's Commentaries, War of Alexandria, 48.

[1058] Probably in the modern province of Leyria.

[1059] A survey made, in August, 1861, by the Duc de Bellune, leaves no doubt that the peninsula of Peniche was once an island. The local traditions state that in ancient times the ocean advanced as far as the town of Atoguia; but since Dio Cassius speaks of the rising tide which swept away soldiers, we must believe that there were fords at low tide. We give extracts from Portuguese authors who have written on this subject.

Bernard de Brito (*Portuguese Monarchy*, I. p. 429, Lisbon, 1790) says:— "As along the entire coast of Portugal we cannot find, at the present time, a single island that fulfils the conditions of the one where Cæsar sought to disembark better than the peninsula, on which there is a locality which, taking its name from its situation, is called *Peniche*, we shall maintain, with our countryman Resende, that it is to this that all the authors refer. And I do not believe it possible to find one more suitable in every way than this: because, over and above the fact that it is the only one, and situated at but a short distance from the mainland, we see that when the tide is low it is possible to traverse the strait dryshod, and with still greater facility than would have been possible in ancient times, because the sea has silted up sand against a large portion of this coast, and brought it to pass that the sea does not rise to so high a point upon the land. Still, it rises high enough to make it necessary, at high tide, to use a boat to reach the island, and that in a space of about 500 paces in width, which separates the island from the mainland."

The following is the passage of Resende: — "Sed quærendum utrobique quænam insula ista fuerit terræ contigua, ad quam sive pedibus sive natatu profugi transire potuerint, ad quam similiter et milites trajicere tentarint? Non fuisse Londobrin, cujus meminit Ptolomæus (*Berligam* modo dicimus), indicio est distantia a continente non modica. Et quum alia juxta Lusitaniæ totius littus nulla nostra ævo exstet, hæc de qua Dion loquitur, vel incumbenti violentius mari abrasa, vel certe peninsula illa oppidi Peniche juxta Atonguiam, erit intelligenda. Nam etiam nunc alveo quingentis passibus lato a continente sejungitur, qui pedibus æstu cedente transitur, redeunte vero insula plane fit, neque adiri vado potest. Et forte illo sæculo fuerit aliquanto major." (L. André de Resende. *De Antiquitatibus Lusitaniæ cæteraque Historica quæ exstant Opera*, Conimbricæ, 1790, I., p. 77.)

Antonio Carvalho (*Da costa corografia Portuguesa*, II. p. 144, Lisbon, 1712) sets forth the same view.

The preceding information is confirmed by the following letter of an English bishop who accompanied the Crusaders, at the time of the siege of Lisbon, in the reign of Alfonso Henrique, a.d. 1147: — "Die vero quasi decima, impositis sarcinis nostris cum episcopis velificare incepimus iter prosperum agentes. Die vero postera ad insulam Phenicis (vulgo *Peniche*) distantis a continente quasi octingentis passibus feliciter applicuimus. Insula abundat cervis et maxime cuniculis: liquiricium (*lege* glycyrrhizum) habet. Tyrii dicunt eam Erictream. Peni Gaddis, id est septem, ultra quam non est terra: ideo extremus noti orbis terminus dicitur. Juxta hanc sunt duæ insulæ quæ vulgo dicuntur Berlinges, id est Baleares lingua corrupta, in una quarum est palatium admirabilis architecturæ et multa officinarum diversoria regi cuidam, ut aiunt, quondam gratissimum secretale hospicium." (Letter of an English Crusader on the sack of Lisbon, in *Portualliæ Monumenta Historica, a sæculo octavo post Christum usque ad quintum decimum, justa Academiæ Scientiarum Olisiponensis edita.* Volumen I., fasciculus iii. Lisbon, 1861, p. 395.)

[1060] Dio Cassius, XXXVII. 52, 53.—"Cæsar, as soon as he arrived, defeated the Lusitanians and the inhabitants of Galicia, and advanced as far as the outer sea. Thus he caused people who had never yet recognised the authority of the Romans to submit to them, and returned from his government loaded with glory and wealth, of which he gave a part to his soldiers." (Zonaras, Annales, X. 6.)

[1061] Appian, Civil Wars, II. 8.

[1062] Cæsar, Spanish War, 42.

[1063] Plutarch, Cæsar, 12.

[1064] "There come forward a whole army of accusers against those who enriched themselves by usury in contempt of a law passed by Cæsar when he was dictator, regulating the proportion to be observed between the debts and possessions in Italy: a law which had for a long while fallen into desuetude through the interest of individuals." (Tacitus, Annals, vi. 16.—Suetonius, Cæsar, 42.)

[1065] "I will not enumerate all the marks of honour with which Cæsar distinguished the people of this town when he was prætor in Spain; the divisions he found means of healing among the citizens of Gades; the laws which, with their consent, he gave them; the old barbarism of their manners and customs, which he caused to disappear; the eagerness with which, at the request of Balbus, he loaded them with benefits." (Cicero, Oration for Balbus, 19.)

[1066] "From his youth he was acquainted with Cæsar, and that great man was pleased with him. Cæsar, among the crowd of friends he had, marked him out as one of his intimates when he was prætor: when he was consul, he made him overseer of the manufactory of his military engines. He had experience of his prudence; appreciated his devotion; accepted his acts of kindness and his affection. At that time Balbus shared nearly all the labours of Cæsar." (Cicero, Oration for Balbus, 28.)

[1067] "For this man (Cæsar) began by being prætor in Spain, and, distrusting the loyalty of this province, he would not give its inhabitants the chance of being subsequently more dangerous, through a delusive peace. He chose to do what was of importance to the interests of the Republic rather than to pass the days of his magistracy in tranquillity; and as the Spaniards refused to surrender, he compelled them to it by force. So he surpassed in honour those who had preceded him in Spain; for it is a harder task to keep a conquest than to make one." (Dio Cassius, XLIV. 41.)

[1068] Suetonius, Cæsar, 54.

[1069] "Cæsar arrives in two days." (Cicero to Atticus, II. 1, June, 694.)

[1070] Thence the name of candidate.

[1071] "Many candidates for the consulship had been nominated in their absence; as, for instance, Marcellus, in 540." (Titus Livius, XXIV. 9.)

[1072] Plutarch, Cato, 36.

[1073] Florus, III. 23.

[1074] Cicero, Letters to Atticus, I. 18.

[1075] Cicero, Letters to Atticus, I. 18.

[1076] Cicero, Letters to Atticus, II. 1.

[1077] "It even appears that Cicero had lent the accused a million of sestertii to purchase a mansion on the Palatine." (Aulus Gellius, XII. 12.)

[1078] Cicero, Letters to Atticus, I. 12.

[1079] Cicero, Letters to Atticus, I. 19.

[1080] Cicero, Letters to Atticus, II. 1.

[1081] Cicero, Letters to Atticus, I. 19.

[1082] Suetonius, Cæsar, 50.

[1083] Cicero, Letters to Quintus, I. 1, 11.

[1084] Cæsar, when consul and dictator, declared many foreign cities free.

[1085] It will be seen in the next chapter that Cæsar recognized as friends to the Roman people Auletes, king of Egypt, and Ariovistus, king of the Germans.

[1086] Duumvirs, decemvirs, vigintivirs were the names given to magistrates who shared the same duties in boards of two, ten, or twenty. In the present case, however, the object was only to bind together the men of the greatest importance by a secret bond. Therefore the word triumvirate would be a misnomer.

[1087] "He wished me to join these three intimate consular men." (Cicero, Oration on the Consular Provinces, 17.)

[1088] Dio Cassius, XXXVII. 57.

[1089] Cicero, Familiar Letters, V. 12.

[1090] Suetonius, Cæsar, 19.—Eutropius, VI. 14.—Plutarch, Cæsar, 13.

[1091] Suetonius, Cæsar, 19.

[1092] Plutarch, Cato, 26.—Suetonius, 19.

[1093] "But will you say that we can only have the knights on our side by paying for them? What are we to do? Have we a choice of means?" (Cicero, Letters to Atticus, II. 1.)

[1094]

> "Inde domum repetes toto comitante senatu,
> Officium populi vix capiente domo."
> Ovid, *Ex Ponto*, IV. Epist. 4.

[1095] Suetonius, Cæsar, 19.

[1096] Dio Cassius, XXXVIII. 1.

[1097] Appian, Civil Wars, II. 10.

[1098] Cicero, Epistle to Atticus, II. 3.—"When consul, he wished me to take part in the operations of his consulship. Without approving them, I felt nevertheless grateful to him for his deference." (Oration on the Consular Provinces, 17.)

[1099] Plutarch, Cæsar, 14.—Suetonius, Cæsar, 21.

[1100] Plutarch, Cæsar, 14.

[1101] Plutarch, Cato, 24.

[1102] Plutarch, Cato, 59.

[1103] Suetonius, Cæsar, 20.

[1104] Titus Livius, IX. 8.

[1105] Appian, Civil Wars, II. 7.

[1106] Cicero, Familiar Letters, XIII. 4.

[1107] Dio Cassius, XXXVIII. 1.

[1108] Epistles to Atticus, I. 18.—In allusion to a former law, we read as follows: "The senators who have discussed the present law shall be held, within ten days following the plebiscitum, to swear to maintain it before the questor, in the treasury, in open day, and taking for witnesses Jupiter and the gods Penates." (Table of Bantia, Klenze, Philologische Abhandlungen, IV. 16-24.)

[1109] Dio Cassius, XXXVIII. 1.

[1110] Dio Cassius, XXXVIII. 2.

[1111] Ateius Capito, Treatise on the Duties of the Senator, quoted by Aulus Gellius, IV. 10.—Valerius Maximus, II. 10, § 7.

[1112] Dio Cassius, XXXVIII. 4.

[1113] Suetonius, Cæsar, 21.

[1114] Appian, Civil Wars, II. 11.

[1115] Dio Cassius, XXXVIII. 6.

[1116] The consuls, prætors, and generally all those who presided at an assembly of the people, or even who attended in quality of magistrates, had a right of veto, founded on popular superstition. This right was exercised by declaring that a celestial phenomenon had been observed by them, and that it was no longer permitted to deliberate. Jupiter darting thunder or rain, all treating on affairs with the people must be stopped; such was the text of the law, religious or political, published in 597. It was not necessary that it should thunder or rain, in fact; the affirmation of a magistrate qualified to observe the sky being enough. (Cicero, Oration for Sextius, 15.—Oration on the Consular Provinces, 19.)—(Asconius, In Piso, p. 9, ed. Orelli.)—(Orelli, Indices to his edition of Cicero, VIII. 126.)—(Index Legum, articles Laws Ælia and Fusia.)

[1117] Valerius Maximus, III. vii. 6.

[1118] Plutarch, Cato, 37.

[1119] Dio Cassius, XXXVIII. 7.—"The Campanian law contains a provision which compels the candidates to swear, in the assembly of the people, that they will never propose anything contrary to the Italian legislation upon property. All have sworn, except Laterensis, who preferred desisting from the candidature for the tribuneship to taking the oath, and much gratitude has been shown to him for it." (Cicero, Epistles to Atticus, II. 18.)

[1120] This appears from the words of Dio Cassius (XXXVIII. 1). Several scholars are unwilling to admit the existence of two agrarian laws; yet Cicero, in his letter to Atticus (II. 7), written in April, announces that the twenty commissioners are named. In this first law (Familiar Letters, XIII. 4), he mentions the ager of Volaterra, which was certainly not in Campania. In another letter of the beginning of May (Letters to Atticus, II. 16), he speaks of Campania for the first time, and says that Pompey had approved the first agrarian law. Finally, in that written in the month of June (Letters to Atticus, II. 18), he speaks of the oath taken to the agrarian laws. Suetonius (Cæsar, 20) and Appian (Civil Wars, II. 10) mention the Julian agrarian laws in the plural. Titus Livius (Epitome of Book CIII.) speaks of the leges agrariæ of Cæsar; and Plutarch (Cato,

38) says positively: "Elated with this victory, Cæsar proposed a new law, to share among the poor and indigent citizens nearly all the lands of Campania;" and previously, in chapter 36, the same author had said of Cæsar, that he proposed laws for the distribution of the lands to the poor citizens. Thus there were positively two laws published at an interval of some months; and if the object of the second was the distribution of the ager Campanus, the first had without doubt a more general character. Dio Cassius, after having related the proposal of the first agrarian law, in which Campania was excepted, says similarly: "Besides, the territory of Campania was given to those who had three children or more" (XXXVIII. 7).

[1121] Cicero, Second Philippic, 15.

[1122] Liber Coloniarum, edit. Lachmann, pp. 220, 235, 239, 259, 260.— Several of these colonies probably dated no farther back than the dictatorship of Cæsar.

[1123] Suetonius, Cæsar, 20.—Velleius Paterculus, II. 44.—Appian, Civil Wars, II. 10.—"Capua mura ducta colonia Julia Felix, jussu imperatoris Cæsaris a xx. viris deducta." (Liber Coloniarum, I. p. 231, edit. Lachmann.)

[1124] Cicero, Second Philippic, 39.

[1125] Dio Cassius, XXXVIII. 1.—Cicero, Epistles to Atticus, II. 19.

[1126] Cicero, Epistles to Atticus, II. 7.

[1127] Cicero, Oration on the Consular Provinces, 17.

[1128] Cicero, Familiar Letters, VIII. 10.

[1129] Appian, Civil Wars, II. 13.—Scholiast of Bobbio on Cicero.—Cicero, Oration for Plancus, p. 261, edit. Orelli.

[1130] Cicero, Oration for Plancus, 14.

[1131] Cicero, Letters to Atticus, II. 1.—Suetonius, Cæsar, 20.

[1132] Suetonius, Cæsar, 20.—Dio Cassius, XXXVIII. 7.—Appian, II. 13.

[1133] Suetonius, Cæsar, 20.

[1134] Cicero, Second Oration on the Agrarian Law, 16.—Scholiast of Bobbio on Cicero's Oration In Rege Alexandrino, p. 350, edit. Orelli. This Ptolemy Alexas, or Alexander, appears to have been a natural son of Alexander I., younger brother of Ptolemy Lathyrus, who is also called Ptolemy Soter II.; in this case he would be, though illegitimate, cousin of Ptolemy Auletes. He had succeeded Alexander II., legitimate son of Alexander I., who married his step-mother, Berenice, only legitimate daughter of Ptolemy Soter II.

[1135] Cicero, Letters to Atticus, II. 16.—The King of Egypt gave nearly 6,000 talents (35 millions of francs) to Cæsar and Pompey. (Suetonius, Cæsar, 14.)

[1136] Suetonius, Cæsar, 54.—Dio Cassius, XXXIX. 12.—Cæsar's expressions (War of Alexandria, 33, and Civil Wars, III. 107) show the friendship of Ptolemy Auletes for the Romans.

[1137] Cæsar, War in Gaul, I. 35.—Plutarch, Cæsar, 35.—Dio Cassius, XXXVIII. 34.

[1138] Suetonius, Cæsar, 20.

[1139] Plutarch, Cato, 38.—"It was about the sixth hour, when, in the course of my speech in court for C. Antonius, my colleague, I deplored certain abuses which prevailed in the State, and which seemed to me to be closely allied to the case of my unfortunate client. Some ill-disposed persons reported my words to certain men of high position in different terms to those I had used; and on the same day, at the ninth hour, the adoption of Clodius was carried." (Cicero, Oration for his House, 16.)

[1140] Appian, Civil Wars, II. 14.—Dio Cassius, XXXVIII. 12.—Plutarch, Pompey, 50.—Cicero, 39.

[1141] Cicero, Oration for Sestius, loc. cit.

[1142] Cicero, writing to Atticus about Cæsar's first consulship, says: "Weak as he was then, Cæsar was stronger than the entire State." (Letters to Atticus, VII. 9.)

[1143] "Bibulus thought to render Cæsar an object of suspicion. He made him more powerful than before." (Velleius Paterculus, II. 44.)

[1144] Suetonius, Cæsar, 20.

[1145] Cæsar rode an extraordinary horse, whose feet were shaped almost like those of man, the hoof being divided in such a way as to present the appearance of fingers. He had reared this horse, which had been foaled in his house, with great care, for the soothsayers had predicted the empire of the world to its master. Cæsar was the first who tamed it: before that time the animal had allowed no one to mount it. Finally, he erected a statue to its honour in front of the Temple of Venus Genetrix." (Suetonius, Cæsar, 61.)

[1146] "I am quite of opinion that the right of absent candidates to solicit the offices of the priesthood may be examined by the comitia, for there is a precedent for that. C. Marius, whilst in Cappadocia, was elected augur by the law Domitia, and no subsequent law has forbidden the course; for the Julian Law, the last on the subject of the priesthood, states: 'He who is a candidate, or he whose right to become one has been examined.'" (Cicero, Letters to Brutus, I. 5.)

[1147] Cicero, Oration against Piso, 37.

[1148] Cicero, Oration on the Consular Provinces, 4.—Oration against Piso, 21.

[1149] Cicero, Oration against Piso, 16; Letters to Atticus, V. 10, 16, 21.— First Philippic, 8.

[1150] "You have obtained," says he, addressing Piso, "a consular province with no other limits than those of your cupidity, in contravention of the law of your son-in-law. In fact, by a law of Cæsar's, as just as it is salutary, free nations used to enjoy a full and entire liberty." (Cicero, Oration against Piso, 16.)

[1151] Cicero, Oration against Piso, 25; Familiar Letters, II. 17; Letters to Atticus, VI. 7.—"I will add, that if the ancient right and antique usage were still in force, I should not have had to send in my accounts till after I had discoursed about them, and had them audited with good humour, and the formalities that our intimacy justifies. What I would have done in Rome according to the old fashion, I ought, according to the Julian law, to have done in my province: send in my accounts on the spot, and only deposit in the treasury an exact copy of them. I was obliged to follow the provisions of the law. The accounts, duly audited and compared, were to be deposited in two towns, and I chose, in the terms of the law, the two most important—Laodicea and Apamea.... I come to the point of the customary presents. You must know that I had only included in my list the military tribunes, the prefects, and the officers of my house (contubernales). I even made a blunder. I thought I was allowed any latitude in point of time. Subsequently I learnt that the request ought to be sent in during the thirty days allowed for the settling the accounts. Happily, all is safe as far as the centurions are concerned, and the officers of the household of the military tribunes— for the law is silent in regard to the latter. (Cicero, Familiar Letters, V. 20.)

[1152] Dio Cassius, XLIII. 25.

[1153] "I say nothing about the golden crown that has been so long a torture to you, in your uncertainty as to whether you ought to demand it or not. In fact, the law of your son-in-law forbad them to give it or you to receive it, unless your triumph had been granted you." (Cicero, Oration against Piso, 37.)

[1154] Cicero, Oration against Piso, 37; Letters to Atticus, V. 10, 16.

[1155] "Take notice, I beg you, that I paid into the hands of the farmers of the revenues at Ephesus twenty-two millions of sestertii, a sum to which I have a perfect right, and that Pompey laid hands on the whole. I have made up my mind on the subject—whether wisely or unwisely matters not." (Cicero, Oration against Piso, xxxvii. 16.)

[1156] Cicero, Oration against Piso, 21.

[1157] Cicero, Oration on the Consular Provinces, 2, 3, 4.

[1158] "Is there any position more disgraceful than that of a senator, who goes on a mission without the slightest authorisation on the part of the State? It was this kind of mission that I should have abolished during my consulship, even with the consent of the Senate, notwithstanding the apparent advantages it held out, had it not been for the senseless opposition of a tribune. At any rate I caused its duration to be shortened: formerly it had no limit; now I have reduced it to a year." (Cicero, On Laws, III. 8.)

[1159] "Moreover, I think that the Julian law has defined the duration of free embassies: nor will it be easy to extend it." (Cicero, Letters to Atticus, XV. 11.—Orelli, Index Legum, p. 192.)

[1160] Cicero, Oration for Sestius, 64. "Liberty torn from nations and individuals on whom it had been conferred, and whose right had been, by virtue of the Julian law, so precisely ensured against all hostile attacks." (Oration against Piso, xxxvii. 16.)

[1161] Cicero, Familiar Letters, VIII. 8.—Several of its chapters have been preserved in the Digest, XLVIII. tit. XI. It is generally supposed that the fragments inscribed on a tablet of brass in the Museum of Florence belong to the same law. They have been published by Maffei, Museum Veronese, p. 365, No. 4, and commented on by the celebrated Marini, in his work on the Monuments of the Fratres Arvales, I. pp. 39, 40, note 44.

[1162] Suetonius, Cæsar, 42.

[1163] Cicero, Oration for Rabirimus Postumus, 4, 5.

[1164] Fragments of the Julian law, De Repetundis, preserved in the Digest, XLVIII. tit. XI.

The law is directed against those who, holding a magistracy, an embassy, or any other office, or forming part of the attendants of these functionaries, receive money.

They may receive money to any amount from their cousins, their still nearer relatives, or their wives.

The law includes those who have received money: For speaking in the Senate or any public assembly; for doing their duty or absenting themselves from it; for refusing to obey a public order or for exceeding it; for pronouncing judgment in a criminal or a civil case, or for not pronouncing it; for condemning or acquitting; for awarding or withdrawing the subject of a suit; for adjudging or taking an object in litigation; for appointing a judge or arbitrator, changing him, ordering him to judge, or for not appointing him or changing him, and not ordering him to judge; for causing a man to be imprisoned, put in irons, or set at liberty; for accusing or not accusing; for producing or suppressing a witness; for recognising as complete an unfinished public work; for accepting wheat for the use of the State without testing its good quality; for taking upon himself the maintenance of the public buildings without a certificate of their good condition; for enlisting a soldier or discharging him.

All that has been given to the proconsul or prætor contrary to the provisions of the present law, cannot become his by right of possession.

Sales and leases are declared null and void which have been made, for a high or a low price, with a view to right of possession by a third.

The magistrates are to abstain from all extortion, and receive as salary but 100 pieces of gold each year.

The action will lie equally against the heirs of the accused, but only during the year succeeding his death.

No one who has been condemned under this law can be either judge, accuser, or witness.

The penalties are exile, banishment to an island, or death, according to the gravity of the offence.

[1165] Dio Cassius, XXXVIII. 8.

[1166] De alternis consiliis rejiciendis. (Cicero, Oration against Vatinius, 11.—Scholiast of Bobbio, pp. 321, 323, edit. Orelli.)

[1167] "The citizens who, not being of your order, cannot, thanks to the Cornelian laws, challenge more than three judges." (Cicero, Second Prosecution of Verres, II. 31.)

[1168] Suetonius, Cæsar, 28.

[1169] Cicero, Familiar Letters, XIII. 35. "Pompeius Strabo, father of Pompey the Great, re-peopled Comum. Some time after, Scipio established 3,000 inhabitants there; and, finally, Cæsar sent 5,000 colonists, the most distinguished of whom were 500 Greeks." (Strabo, cxix.)

[1170] Cicero, Letters to Atticus, II. 18.—Dio Cassius, XXVIII. 8.

[1171] Dio Cassius, XXVIII. 8.—Orelli, Index Legum, 178.

[1172] Cicero, in his speech against Vatinius, chap. 6, while reproaching him for having disregarded the auspices, exclaims, "I ask you first, Did you refer the matter to the Senate, as Cæsar did?"

"It is true that Cæsar's acts were, for the benefit of peace, confirmed by the Senate." (Cicero, Second Philippic, 39.)

[1173] Dio Cassius, XXXVIII. 7.

[1174] Cæsar conducted himself with discretion in his consulship." (Plutarch, Crassus, 17.)

[1175] "Cæsar published laws that were worthy, I will not say of a consul, but of the most reckless of tribunes." (Plutarch, Cæsar, 14.)

[1176] Cicero, Letters to Atticus, VI. 1.—Appian, Civil Wars, II. 13.

[1177] Pliny, Natural History, XXXIII. 5. Drumann and Mommsen, like ourselves, refuse their belief to the assertion of Suetonius.

[1178] Plutarch, Lucullus, 9.

[1179] Suetonius, Cæsar, 22.—Plutarch, Cæsar, 14.

[1180] Appian, Civil Wars, II. 14.

[1181] Plutarch, Crassus, 17.

[1182] Dio Cassius, XXXVIII. 8.—Suetonius, Cæsar, 22.

[1183] Suetonius, Cæsar, 22.

[1184] Dio Cassius, XL. 34.

[1185] "At the gladiatorial exhibition, the giver of the show and all his attendants were received with hisses. At the games in honour of Apollo, the tragedian Diphilus made a pointed allusion to our friend Pompey in the lines—

"'Tis through our woes that thou art great,'

and was called upon to repeat the words a thousand times. Further on, the whole assembly cheered him when he said,

'A time shall come, when thou thyself shall weep
That power of thine so deadly'—

for they are lines that one might have said were written on purpose by an enemy of Pompey. The words

'If nought, nor law, nor virtue, hold thee back,'

were received with a tempest of acclamation. When Cæsar arrived, he met with a cold reception. Curio, on the other hand, who followed him, was saluted with a thousand cheers, as Pompey used to be in the prosperous times of the Republic. Cæsar was annoyed, and sent off a courier post haste to Pompey, who is, they say, at Capua." (Cicero, *Letters to Atticus*, II. 19.)

[1186] Suetonius, Cæsar, 9.

[1187] Cicero, Letters to Atticus, II. 19.

[1188] "Bibulus is being praised to the skies, I know not why; but he is being extolled as the one only man who, by temporising, has restored the State. Pompey, my idol Pompey, has been his own ruin, as I own with tears to-day; he has no one left who takes his side from affection. I am afraid that they will find it necessary to resort to intimidation. For my own part, I forbear, on the one hand, to combat their views on account of my ancient friendship with them, and, on the other, my antecedents prevent my approving of what they are about; I preserve a middle course. The humour of the people is best seen in the theatres." (Cicero, Letters to Atticus, II. 19, 20, 21.)

[1189] "He keeps prudently in the background, but hopes at a safe distance to witness their shipwreck." (Cicero, Letters to Atticus, II. 7.)

[1190] Cicero, Letters to Atticus, II. 13.

[1191] Cicero, Letters to Atticus, II. 17.

[1192] Cicero, Letters to Atticus, II. 20, 21.

[1193] Dio Cassius, XXXVIII. 11.

[1194] Cicero, Letters to Atticus, II. 24.

[1195] Cicero, Oration against Vatinius, II.—Dio Cassius, XXXVIII. 9.

[1196] Scholiast of Bobbio, On Cicero's Oration against Vatinius, p. 330, edit. Orelli.—Appian, Civil Wars, II. 2 and 12.

[1197] Appian, Civil Wars, II. 12.

[1198] Suetonius, Cæsar, 20.

[1199] "He (Ariovistus) knows, by his messengers, that in causing Cæsar's death he would gratify a number of great persons at Rome; his death would win to him their favour and friendship." (Cæsar, War in Gaul, I. 44.)

[1200] Dio Cassius, XXXVIII. 12.

[1201] Cicero, Letters to Quintus, I. 2.

[1202] Suetonius, Cæsar, 23; Nero, 2.

[1203] Suetonius, Cæsar, 23.—Valerius Maximus, III. 7, 9.

[1204] "At the gates of Rome there was a general invested with authority for many years, and at the head of a great army (cum magno exercitu). Was he my enemy? I do not say he was; but I knew that when people said so, he was silent." (Cicero, Oration after his return in the Senate, 13.)—"Oppressos, vos, inquit, tenebo exercitu Cæsaris." (Cicero, Letters to Atticus, II. 16.)—"Clodius said he would invade the curia at the head of Cæsar's army." (Cicero, Oration on the Report of the Augurs, 22.)—"Cæsar had already gone out of Rome with his army." (Dio Cassius, XXXVIII. 17.)

[1205] In several passages of Cicero's letters, Cæsar is represented as being at the gates of Rome at the head of his army; and yet we know from his Commentaries that at the beginning of the war in Gaul he had only four legions, of which one was stationed on the banks of the Rhine, and the three others at Aquileia, in Illyria. It is, therefore, difficult to understand how he could have had troops at the gates of Rome, of which no further mention is made in the course of his campaign. The only way to reconcile the letters of Cicero with the Commentaries is to allow that Cæsar, independently of the legions which he found beyond the frontiers of Italy, summoned to his standard the volunteers and Roman veterans who were desirous of following him. Mustering at the gate of Rome, they joined him subsequently in Gaul, and were merged in the legions. This supposition is the more probable, as in 700, when the question of re-electing Pompey and Crassus to the consulship was brought forward, Cæsar sent to Rome a great number of soldiers to vote in the comitia. Hence, as all the legions had been recruited in Cisalpine Gaul, the inhabitants of which did not possess the right of Roman city, he must have had other Roman citizens in his army. Besides, if Cæsar appealed to the veterans, he only followed the example of nearly all the Roman generals, and among others of Scipio, Flamininus, and Marius. In fact, when Cornelius Scipio departed for the war against Antiochus, there were five thousand volunteers at the gates of Rome—citizens as well as allies—who had served in all the campaigns of his brother, Scipio Africanus. (Titus Livius, XXXVII. 4.)—"When Flamininus left to join the legions in Macedonia, he took with him three thousand veterans who had fought against Hannibal and Hasdrubal." (Plutarch, Flamininus, III.)—"Marius, before leaving for the war against Jugurtha, appealed to all the bravest soldiers of Latium. He knew most of them for having served under his eyes, and the rest by reputation. By force of solicitation, he obliged even the veterans to go with him." (Sallust, War of Jugurtha, LXXXIV.)

[1206] "At the present moment he (Clodius) is agitating and raging; he knows not what he wants; he makes hostile demonstrations on this side and on that, and seems to intend to leave to chance where he shall strike. When he gives a thought to the unpopularity of the present state of things, you would say he was going to fly at the authors of it; but when he sees on which side are the means of action and the armed force, he turns round against us." (Cicero, Letters to Atticus, II. 22.)

[1207] These clubs (collegia compitalitia) had an organisation which was almost military, divided into districts, and composed exclusively of the proletaries. (See Mommsen, Roman History, III. 290.)—"The slaves enrolled under pretence of forming corporations." (Cicero, Oration after his return in the Senate, 13.)

[1208] An exception, however, was made in 690, in favour of the corporations of artisans. (Asconius, In Pisone, IV. p. 7; In Corneliana, p. 75, edit. Orelli.)

[1209] Cicero, Oration against Piso, 4.—Asconius, On the Oration of Cicero against Piso, pp. 7, 8, edit. Orelli.—Dio Cassius, XXXVIII. 13.

[1210] Dio Cassius, XXXVIII. 13.

[1211] Dio Cassius, XXXVIII. 17.

[1212] "I receive from Cæsar the most flattering invitations, asking me to join him as lieutenant." (Cicero, Letters to Atticus, II. 17.)—"He has got my enemy (Clodius) transferred to the plebeian order: either because he was irritated to see that even his kindness could not persuade me to join his side, or because he yielded to the urgency of others. My refusal could not have been regarded as an insult, for subsequently to it he advised me, nay, even entreated me, to serve him as lieutenant. I did not accept this office, not because I thought it beneath me, but because I was far from suspecting that the State could possibly have, after Cæsar, any consuls so infamous as these (Piso and Gabinius)." (Cicero, Oration about the Consular Provinces, 17.)

[1213] "Thanks to the pains I take, my popularity and my strength increase daily. I do not meddle with politics in any way—not the least. My house is crowded; my friends gather round me when I go abroad; my consulate seems to be beginning afresh. It rains protestations of attachment; and my confidence is such that at times I long for the strife, which I ought always to dread." (Cicero, Letters to Atticus, II. 22.)—"Let Clodius bring his accusation. Italy will rise as one man." (Cicero, Letters to Quintus, I. 2.)

[1214] Cicero, Oration against Vatinius, 16.

[1215] Plutarch, Pompey, 48.

[1216] Plutarch, Cicero, 41.

[1217] Velleius Paterculus, II. 45.

[1218] Suetonius, XXIII.

[1219] "The rumours which preceded Pompey had caused great consternation there, because it had been said that he meant to enter the city with his army." (Plutarch, Pompey, 45.)—"However, every one dreaded Pompey in the greatest degree; no one knew whether he would disband his army or not." (Dio Cassius, XXXVII. 44.)